# The Indian Way

Series: Asian Perspectives

General Editor: Charles Wei-hsun Fu

# The Indian Way

**John M. Koller**

Macmillan Publishing Co., Inc.
*New York*

Collier Macmillan Publishers
*London*

# For Patricia

ACKNOWLEDGEMENTS

The author gratefully acknowledges permission to quote from the following:

*Buddhist Texts Through the Ages*, by Edward Conze. (New York: Harper & Row Torchbooks, 1964.)
*Guru Nanak and the Sikh Religion*, by W. H. McLeod. (New York: Oxford University Press, 1968.)
*The Sword and the Flute*, by David R. Kinsley. (Berkeley: University of California Press, 1977.)
"Values and Development in India," *Asian Thought and Society: An International Review*, Vol. 1, No. 2, September 1976, pp. 111-129.



Printed in the United States of America.



Macmillan Publishing Co., Inc.
866 Third Avenue, New York, New York 10022

Collier Macmillan Canada, Inc.

Library of Congress Cataloging in Publication Data

Koller, John M.
The Indian Way

Includes index.
1. India—Religion. 2. Philosophy, Indic.
I. Title.
BL2001.2.K64 294 81-8398
ISBN 0-02-365800-2 AACR2

Printing: 7 8 Year: 9

# Preface

For more than 4000 years, the peoples of the Indian subcontinent have been seeking the deepest truths about the nature of reality and the self, exploring the depths of human consciousness. India's most brilliant thinkers and sincerest religious seekers have been preoccupied with the quest for perfection, for a way to transform this ordinary, limited and imperfect existence into its potential greatness and perfection. Their insights and discoveries have shaped one of the world's richest and longest-lived cultures.

Today, as we seek a wisdom that will enable the peoples of the world to live together securely and well as members of an interdependent global community and that will, at the same time, enable each of us to achieve our fullest personal growth, our need to explore and understand the profound insights of the Indian way is greater than ever.

"What am I, in the deepest recesses of my being?" "How can I realize my human and spiritual potential?" These are the fundamental questions of life for all of us. Because they are also the questions that India's sages have been pondering for the last four thousand years, an understanding of the Indian way is directly relevant to our attempts to improve our self-understanding and the quality of our lives.

Exploring the great ideas of the Indian tradition is a truly exciting intellectual adventure. But it is also an extremely practical adventure, for it will enable us to understand the basis for thinking and acting of nearly one-sixth of the world's people. Even more importantly, it is a way of holding up a cultural mirror, enabling us to see ourselves, our ideas and values, from a new perspective, thereby providing new insight into our own existence.

Writing this book has been simultaneously a way of expressing my gratitude for what I have received from the Indian tradition and a way of exploring this tradition further. The voices of India's great thinkers, speaking through her rich philosophical and religious traditions, have revealed many wonderful secrets of the human heart and mind, enriching my personal existence and illuminating my own culture. This book is a way of sharing what I have received and inviting you to join in the exploration of the Indian way and the process of self-discovery. Throughout, I have attempted to let the Indian way speak for itself, to be its voice, rather than to express my own opinions.

## Acknowledgments

It is impossible to mention everyone who has contributed to *The Indian Way*, but I would be sorely remiss if I did not express my gratitude to the following people. My wife, Patricia, has been my partner on this journey along the Indian way. Since our first visit to India together, almost twenty years ago, she has contributed many insights, ideas, and criticisms, sharing in my scholarly work. Without her love, friendship, and help, my life would be immeasurably poorer, and this book could not have been written. Our son, John Thomas, and our daughter, Christine Ann, not only gave added purpose and meaning to our lives, but helped with the proofreading and index as well.

Among my teachers, Professors S. K. Saksena of the universities of Lucknow and Hawaii and Charles A. Moore of the University of Hawaii initiated me into Indian studies, sharing freely their knowledge and wisdom while insisting on the highest levels of scholarship and philosophical rigour. Professor Kenneth Inada introduced me to the philosopical study of Buddhism, resisting all of my initial attempts to reduce Buddhism to an Asian version of Western thought. Professor T. R. V. Murti of Banaras Hindu University and Professor Kalidas Bhattacharya of Vishva Bharati University helped me more than they probably realized, both during the six weeks of the 1964 East-West Philosphers' Conference and, later, when I came to their universities in India. To Professor George Artola I owe my initiation into Sanskrit—without which much of the Indian tradition would remain closed to me.

John Schumacher, friend, colleague, and former student, has shared in many of the discoveries and much of the excitement that made this book possible. His friendly criticisms—and comments on nearly every page of an earlier draft—have improved the text considerably. Ashok Malhotra, good friend since our student days at the East-West Center, has shared many insights into the Indian way. His reading of the manuscript and suggestions for improvements were very helpful. Isadore Traschen, a colleague in the English Department, made very helpful suggestions concerning both style and substance. David Wieck, Charles Sanford, Dewitt Ellinwood, Theodore Wright, Alok Chakrabarti, J. Uppal, and David Applebaum each shared their reaction to one or more chapters.

At R. P. I., the support of my colleagues in the Philosophy Department and the School of Humanities and Social Science has meant a lot. Dean Thomas Phelan has been encouraging since the beginning. Many students have accompanied me on this journey of self-discovery and pilgrimmage along the Indian way. They have been my teachers as well as my students, and this book is an expression of my gratitude to them. Frances Anderson patiently and carefully typed successive drafts of the manuscript—in addition to doing all of the usual secretarial work for me and eight colleagues in the Philosophy Department.

Thanks also to Kenneth Scott, senior editor at Macmillan for being supportive all the way. Finally, thanks to Charles Wei-hsun Fu, series editor, for inviting me to contribute to the series and for encouragement and helpful suggestions along the way.

*Troy, N.Y.* J.M.K.

# Contents

# 1

# Introduction: Diversity, Change, and Continuity

Images of India are diverse and contrasting. On the one hand India is seen in terms of wise and compassionate world leaders, helping to devise the U.N. charter, holding Oxford appointments, winning Nobel prizes in science or literature, or directing multinational companies. The names of Nehru, Gandhi, Radhakrishnan, Tagore, Bose, and Birla come readily to mind. Others think of India in terms of yogins and fakirs, half-starved ascetics and naked sādhus. In medieval times the prevailing image was that of an exotic land of fabulous wealth. Today many people think of India as the home of 700 million people crushed together in helpless poverty. But others see thrifty, hard-working people successfully engaged in agriculture and commerce. Still, the image of a dreamy people, denying the reality of this world, longing only for relief from life itself, persists. And while some think of India's great humanistic creations in religion and philosophy—the systems of Jainism and Buddhism, for example—others see only a plurality of deities worshipped in every conceivable way. Those who know something about Indian history point proudly to her wonderful accomplishments in astronomy, chemistry, medicine, and mathematics, noting that the base ten number system and the zero, which made possible a revolution in mathematics, are India's gift to the world.

Which is the real India? Actually, all these images—plus many other contrasting ones—capture something of the real India. Despite a common, but mistaken, impression that change has bypassed India, that she has remained committed to the same ancient and unchanging ideas and practices for thousands of years, the truth is that her history is one of amazing diversity and continuous change.

## Diversity

India's diversity begins with her geography, for it is undeniable that diverse geographical conditions contribute to cultural diversity. As every traveler quickly realizes, India—by which we mean the entire subcontinent, including the modern nations of Pakistan, Sri Lanka, Bangladesh, and India—is a land of many different climates and land types. In the North stretches the great Himalayan mountain chain, interrupting the cloud movements and causing the monsoon rain to fall on the hot and parched lands extending from the foothills all the way down into central and southern India. Except for the coastal regions, all of India depends upon these monsoon rains for the water of life. In Bengal, north to Assam, rainfall may measure between 60 and 200 inches a year, bringing annual threats of floods as well as the promise of lush growth. But in the West, rainfall may be less than 10 inches per year, creating large tracts of desert. The South is tropical with very modest seasonal changes, but in the North the winters are bitterly cold and the summer temperatures frequently exceed 110° F. The Indus and Ganges valleys are rich, relatively flat, usually well-watered, agricultural lands, but the central plateau is hilly and rocky, land from which it is difficult to wrest a living even when the climate is favorable. It may well be that no one cultural region in the world has greater diversity of land and climate than does the subcontinent.

A second important source of diversity is linguistic, for India is the home of more than a hundred different languages, with fourteen major languages and four basic language families that are totally unrelated to each other. The ten major languages of the North are all Indo-Āryan, rooted in a Sanskritic base. They have practically nothing in common with the four major languages of the South that belong to the Dravidic family and that predate the Indo-Āryan languages. There are also ancient Sino-Tibetan languages, the Munda languages, and a number of unwritten tribal languages that are probably older than the Indo-Āryan languages and that continue to be used to this day. Because language and culture are so closely related, it is not surprising that North and South India continue to exhibit great cultural differences, contributing to a rich diversity of Indian ways of thought and practice.

Foreign influences through migrations, conquests, and trade are a third source of change and diversity. Even before the Āryans came and imposed their language and many of their ideas on the peoples of India, more than three thousand years ago, Mesopotamian influence had been felt in the "Land of the Indus." And evidence from Indus sites reveals that four thousand years ago India was already a meeting place of races—a fact revealed to every traveler by the racial intermixture of today's population. Negroid, Mongolian, Mediterranean, Proto-Australoid, Alpine, and Armenoid racial types were all living in the Indus region four thousand years ago. It is only natural that these different races would also represent cultural differences and that different ideas and ways of living would have come into contact with and influenced each other, making ancient India a dynamic and vibrant society of great diversity.

But India's diversity goes back to a much more remote past. Archaeological evidence reveals human settlements on the subcontinent more than 200,000 years ago, and the tools these early inhabitants of India left behind reveal at least two quite distinct cultures. The people of the North used the stone flakes they chipped for their tools and weapons and threw away the cores. In the South the stones cores prepared by chipping away the unwanted exterior portions were saved as tools and weapons and the flakes were discarded. This great cultural difference between North and South is also attested to by the totally different linguistical families that survive to this day and by significant cultural differences between them.

Pygmy tools, resembling those found in France, England, and East Africa, dating from around 30,000 B.C., suggest postglacial migration from Europe to the central portions of the subcontinent around this time, adding to the existing diversity and stimulating further change.

Stimulation from interaction with foreign cultures has continued right up to modern times. We are all aware of the Western—especially British—influence of the last two hundred years. However, for seven hundred years before the Europeans made their presence felt in India, the Muslims ruled most of the subcontinent, bringing one of the world's great medieval civilizations into the mainstream of Indian life. But these are only two chapters in a long history of foreign influence.

More than two thousand years before the British came to India, sometime toward the end of the sixth century B.C., Darius I conquered the Indus Valley, bringing Persian civilization to the northwestern portion of India. When Alexander the Great defeated the Persians, just two centuries later, the Greeks moved into this area. Although they were "Indianized" to a greater extent than were the Indians Hellenized, their influence is clearly seen in the Gandhāra art style and in coinage.

Later, during the Roman unification, Greco-Roman influence was felt along the coastal areas, for there was extensive trade with South India. One source tells us that more than 120 ships sailed to India's southern coast every year from Egypt alone, and Tamil poets refer to the endless prosperity of the foreigners bringing their wealth and wine to trade for Indian spices, gems, silks, cottons, and perfumed wood. Indeed, the present-day Christians and Jews of South India trace their beginnings in India to the early days of this trade.

That Indian silks were available for export to Rome is due to earlier contact between China and India, for the silk industry was imported from China. Two thousand years ago trade with China was extensive, a source of contact and interaction frequently overlooked. Also frequently overlooked is the extensive influence that India wielded in the East Indies and Southeast Asia—which for a long period resembled economic and cultural colonies of India more than anything else.

Central Asia also played a significant role in Indian history, as the Parthians (called Pahlavas in India) gained control of Persia early in the second century B.C. and took control of northwestern India within a few years of King Menander's death in about 130 B.C. Parthians were followed by Scythians, better known in India as Śakas, who ruled a large part of India for about a hundred years, only to be replaced by the Yueh-chi tribes known as Kushans. The best known Kushan ruler was Kaniṣka, a generous patron of Buddhism, who was won over by Indian culture in general, and by Buddhism in particular. The Śakas, pushed South and West by the Kushans, eventually found a home in Western India, becoming the primary stock of the present-day Marathas, adopting a majority of Indian ideas and practices, including their places within the caste system.

This pattern of contact through trade in the South and contact through conquest in the Northwest continued over the centuries, with the rule of great kingdoms lasting less than a hundred years on average and sometimes changing hands three or four times within a century. When Islam came in the eighth century it followed the age-old pattern, arriving via trading ships in the South and with the conqueror's sword in the North.

Granted such extensive political change, significant intercultural contacts and great racial, linguistic, and geographical diversities, what is surprising is not that Indian culture was constantly changing, but that it was able to maintain its continuity at all through these changes and in spite of this amazing diversity. This continuity is a testament to the power of the great ideas in cultural life that constitute the basis of the Indian way.

But these ideas do not fit into a monolithic and unchanging pattern by any means. India's political, linguistic, geographical, and racial diversities are matched by the diversity of her thought. Some Indian philosophers are materialists, others idealists; some are monists, others dualists or pluralists; some emphasize empirical knowledge, others meditational insight. While Ājīvikas denied human freedom completely, emphasizing the totally determined nature of the universe, advocates of yoga emphasized the possibility of liberating oneself from nature's determining influences. And while great sages saw knowledge as the vehicle of self-realization, skeptics were rejecting the ways of knowing postulated by other philosophers and questioning the possibility of any knowledge whatever.

Some philosophers maintained that reality consists of discrete things, each complete in itself and not dependent on other things for its existence. But others regarded reality as a seamless web in which all aspects and moments of existence are interconnected with every other aspect or moment, denying independence to individual things or processes—whether mental or material. The materialists emphasized the material world, admitting as real only what could be sensed, with many advocating living for the moment in such a way as to derive the greatest amount of pleasure from each moment of life. At the same time ascetics, convinced that material reality was a form of bondage, were avoiding pleasure and contact with the world to achieve a higher, nonmaterial mode of life.

Religious thought is equally diverse. Some religions are even atheistic, but Vishnuism and Shivaism are theistic. Some Hindus worship one Supreme God while other Hindus worship many deities. Jainas believe in a spiritual self separate from the body, a self that can be liberated at death, but Buddhists reject such an idea. For some Hindus devotion is the way to salvation, while for others knowledge or action are the essential means. And the list of differences—seemingly endless when details are considered—goes on. There is probably no more diverse and pluralistic culture in the world than the Indian. Certainly no one image or description could possibly capture the rich diversity of four thousand years of Indian thought.

## Central Ideas

Yet there are certain important ideas and attitudes that have had a continuing influence on Indian thought and culture and that might be regarded as constituting a central Indian way. It is essentially a way of freedom, of liberation from bondage to suffering and fragmented existence.

Seeking to understand the deepest level of reality and to satisfy the deep human longing for spiritual fulfillment, India's great sages and philosophers devoted themselves to exploring and studying the range and depth of human experience. Impressed with the human capacity for thought, feeling, imagination, and action and with the ability to enter creatively into the shaping of our own humanness, they sought a link between the dynamic energy of reality in its deepest levels and the ground of human existence. Although the wisdom generated by this quest cannot be condensed into a simple formula, the insight of the sages of the Upaniṣads that the fundamental energizing power of the cosmos and the spiritual energy of human beings are one and the same is basic to Indian thought.

At the deepest levels of our existence we share in the very energies and powers that create and structure the universe itself, according to India's greatest sages. And because of our participation in the ultimate energy and power of reality, it is possible to transform our superficial, suffering, and limited existence into a free and boundless existence in which life is experienced at its deepest and most profound level, entirely free from suffering. This spiritual transformation has constituted the ultimate aim in life for most of the Indian people over the ages.

This underlying vision of participation in the ultimate reality and the aim of spiritual transformation of human existence have guided most Indian philosophy and religious thought, giving shape to the Indian way. We need to explore the origins and development of this way and examine its presuppositions and implications if we are to understand the Indian mind. Although this exploration and examination will occupy us the entire length of this book, it will be helpful to identify and briefly describe the key features of the Indian way at the outset.

The underlying visions, as we have already noted, are those of the fundamental unity of existence and of the possibility of complete freedom from the limitations and suffering that characterize ordinary human existence. But these two visions are like brightly shining galaxies, illumined by many associated ideas. We will identify and explain briefly the more important of these ideas now, before going on to a deeper exploration of them in the succeeding chapters.

## REALITY IDEAS

The vision of the ultimate unity of existence includes the ideas of (1) undivided wholeness, (2) levels of reality, (3) the normative dimension of existence, (4) the boundlessness of ultimate reality, (5) the profundity of existence, (6) Gods and Goddesses as limited symbols of the ultimate reality, and (7) the limitations of ordinary means of knowledge.

**Undivided Wholeness.** The world of distinct and separate things and processes is seen to be a manifestation of a more fundamental level of reality that is undivided and unconditioned. Sometimes referred to as the unconditioned (asaṁskṛta) or nondual (advaita) reality, this undivided wholeness constituting the ultimate level of reality is called by various names: Brahman, Ātman, Buddha nature, Thusness, Puruṣa, Jīva, Lord, and so on. What is especially important about this vision is that the ultimate reality is not seen as a separate reality, something apart from ordinary events and things, but as the inner being and ground of ordinary existence. Developed initially in the Vedas and Upaniṣads, this vision of undivided wholeness came to inspire the entire tradition—Buddhist, Jaina, and Yoga systems as well as Hinduism. Each of the succeeding chapters will contribute something to our understanding of this unfolding vision.

**Levels of Reality.** Within the totality of existence there are various levels of reality or orders of being, ranging from non-existence to empirical existence limited by space and time, to consciousness that is limited only by the conditions of awareness, to an indescribable level that is beyond all conditions and limits whatever. The deeper the level of reality, the more fully it participates in the truth of being and the greater its value. Our examination of the teachings of the Upaniṣads

(Chapter 5) will reveal how these levels were conceived initially and how this idea relates to the quest for liberation.

**The Normative Dimension of Existence.** The deepest level of reality, which grounds all the other levels, is normative. It poses an "ought" for life that stems from the heart of existence. Norms for right living are not derived from human reason and imposed on life from the outside, but are an integral part of the fabric of existence. It is true that human reason interprets and applies the norms of true or right living, but the foundation of these norms is much deeper than reason, emanating from the very nature and expression of reality at its deepest level. This is why in India it is generally recognized that a person who is true to the inner norms of existence has incredible power; if Sītā has been true to Rāma, then that act of truth will give her power over fire and permit her to walk from the raging flames unscathed. In Chapter 3 we will explore the source of this idea of the normative nature of reality in the concept of *ṛta*, and in Chapter 4 we will see how the normative dimension of reality grounds *dharma*, the rules for right living.

**Boundlessness of Ultimate Reality.** At the deepest level existence is boundless; there are no limits and all possibilities may co-exist without excluding or compromising each other. At this level opposites do not exclude each other, but co-exist in complementarity, enriching each other. This should not be thought of as some kind of grand synthesis, Hegelian or otherwise, for synthesis is seen as a process of enclosing and restricting possibilities. Time is endless, space is endless, the number of Gods and Goddesses is endless, and so on. Indian mythology especially celebrates the idea that opposites exist together with all of their differences arising and co-existing simultaneously in a totally unrestricted universe of infinite freedom and richness. We will encounter this idea of the boundlessness of existence in many places, ranging from Jaina logic to the Buddhist ideal of universal compassion. But it becomes the special focus of Chapters 10 and 11, which explore devotional religion.

**Profundity of Existence.** The depth and profundity of reality at the ultimate level are such that reason is incapable of apprehending them. Human reason is a wonderful faculty for guiding our investigations of the empirical world and proves extremely useful for understanding the rules of our practical and theoretical activities. But as fond of rational analysis and argument as most Indians are, they generally agree that, because reason operates by differentiating and comparing, it is incapable of comprehending the deepest dimensions of reality that are beyond all divisions and differences. This sense of the profundity of reality underlies Indian mysticism and encourages the emphasis upon meditation and direct insight that we will encounter in one form or another in nearly every system. Chapter 8, on yoga, explores the philosophy of disciplined meditation as a means of removing the obstacles to direct insight into the true nature of reality.

**Gods and Goddesses as Symbols of Power.** Because the ultimate level of reality is undivided, Indian Gods and Goddesses, from Vedic times to the present, are usually understood to be symbols of the ultimate reality rather than the ultimate reality itself. The ultimate has no form and no name; what can be given a name and identifiable characteristics is not the ultimate. As symbols, Gods and Goddesses both participate partially in the higher reality that they symbolize and point beyond themselves to the fullness of that reality. No number of symbols can exhaust the fullness of the ultimate, so there is no limit to the number of Gods. This is why a Hindu can say in the same breath that there are millions of Gods, only one God, and no Gods, for the last two statements mean, respectively, that all Gods symbolize the one ultimate reality and that this reality cannot be captured entirely by a symbol. But that a deity is not the ultimate reality does not mean that it is unreal. On the contrary, because the deity as symbol participates in the deeper levels of reality, its reality is greater than that of our ordinary existence, and by identifying with the deity in love and through ritual action, the power of this deeper level of reality becomes available to help effect a spiritual transformation of life. It is this understanding of deity that underlies Hindu theism and devotionalism. Chapters 10 and 11 examine the functions of the Gods and Goddesses in Hinduism.

**Limits of Ordinary Means of Knowledge.** Because ordinary means of knowledge cannot penetrate the profound and undivided ultimate level of reality, there has been great emphasis on developing extraordinary means of knowledge. Through concentration and meditation direct insight into the true nature of reality at its most profound level becomes possible. The limitations of knowledge mediated through sensory and conceptual filters are overcome in this direct and immediate knowledge through transempirical and transrational insight. Jainism, Buddhism, and the Upaniṣads all emphasize the limitations of ordinary knowledge.

## SYNCRETISM AND TOLERANCE

The influence of this galaxy of seven fundamental reality ideas is at least partially revealed in the syncretic and tolerant attitudes that have characterized Indian thought over the ages.

**Syncretic Tendencies.** Because of the depth and profundity of primordial wholeness of existence, it is accepted that no description, formula, or symbol can adequately convey the entire truth about anything. Each perspective provides a partial glimpse of reality, but none provides a complete view. Different partial—even opposing—visions are regarded as complementing each other, each contributing something to a fuller understanding of reality. Accordingly, every means to penetrate to the ultimate level of reality and to experience one's identity with this reality must be utilized, and Indian thinkers exhibit a ready willingness to adopt new perspectives and new positions. Old positions and perspectives are not abandoned, however. The new is simply added on to the old, providing another dimension to one's knowledge. The new dimension may render the old less dominant or important, but it does not require the latter's rejection. A friend once likened the traditional storehouse of Indian ideas to a four-thousand-year-old attic to which things were added every year but which was never once cleaned out!

**Tolerance.** The conviction that the highest truth is too profound to allow anyone to get an exclusive grasp on it underlies not only the syncretic attitude, but also a general spirit of tolerance in the realm of beliefs. Heresy is practically impossible, because, when no beliefs can be said to be absolutely true, no beliefs can be declared absolutely false. In one family a grandfather may worship Gaṇapati, an uncle worship Vishnu, the mother worship Krishna, and the son be an atheist—all without upsetting the father who is a priest connected with the Devī temple. Perhaps no other culture has permitted—indeed, encouraged—so much religious tolerance; fanaticism has been a rare phenomenon over the centuries. It should be pointed out, however, that this extreme tolerance with respect to beliefs was nearly matched by an intolerance of action. Nonconformity to codes of action were not tolerated by family, caste, or village.

## FREEDOM IDEAS

When we turn to the vision of spiritual transformation and freedom, we discover another constellation of ideas basic to the Indian way. These include the ideas of (1) karmic bondage and liberation from this bondage through (2) asceticism, (3) yoga, (4) ritual, (5) devotion, (6) truthful action (dharma), and (7) the suprarationalism of transforming techniques.

The aim of freedom arises from an understanding of the nature of the undivided wholeness of existence. Because human existence is rooted in, and ultimately identical with, the ultimate reality, there is a deep sense of the wonderful perfection of the human self, a sense that regards ordinary existence, imperfect and limited as it is, as a form of bondage from which liberation should be sought as the most fundamental aim of life.

**Karmic Bondage.** Life is ordinarily lived at a relatively superficial level, a level at which the ultimate reality is experienced only in fragmented and limited forms. These fragmented and partial forms of existence are actually forms of bondage, restricting access to the full power or energy of life flowing from the deepest level of reality. In bondage, the power of ultimate reality is experienced as karma, patterns of energy generated and released through actions that connect processes and events to each other. It is these connections that make possible suffering and happiness and repeated births and deaths. Only by getting rid of the karmic connectors and conditions can one get free of the limitations of existence—limitations experienced most vividly in the cycles of repeated suffering and deaths. Karma can be overcome, however, only by shifting existence to a deeper level, where the ultimate energy is experienced not as fragmented and limited, but as the whole and perfect expression of undivided reality at its deepest level. But how can this be done? How can the bonds of karma be removed?

This question has been addressed by almost all of India's religious and philosophical thinkers. Nearly every chapter will reveal something about the various responses to this question—from the Jaina answer that only knowledge can overcome karma and that all action whatever must cease to the Gītā's answer that only by acting without any attachment to the results can karma be overcome. In Chapters 12 and 13 we will see how the problem of bondage is central to systematic philosophy.

**Asceticism.** In every society cultural ideals are embodied in hero types who provide inspiration for living. In India one of the most influential hero types, from Vedic times to the present, has been the ascetic who has renounced the world in favor of spiritual fulfillment. The ascetic program is to "burn off" the physical and mental bonds of existence through ascetic practices. Developing the psychic and spiritual powers through a combination of ascetic and meditational techniques, the ascetic is able to enter directly into the mysterious depths of the most profound levels of reality, beyond heavens and hells and Gods and Goddesses. In the experienced identity with the ultimate reality, the ascetic hero discovers a full and perfect truth and bliss. Birth and death, sorrows and joys, good and evil—all are left behind, seen finally as only the limited forms of an incomplete existence lived at a shallow level. Experiencing identity with the deepest level of reality, the ascetic discovers perfect freedom; there is nothing in the universe with power to bind and limit. This is the hero of heroes, the conqueror of conquerors, for no other conquest can compare with the conquest of suffering and bondage. These conquerors—Mahāvīra, the Buddha, Mahatma Gandhi, and the countless other "renounced ones"—are the great heroes who from time immemorial have captured the imagination of the Indian people and have shown the way of spiritual progress. In Jainism, as we shall see in Chapter 6, the ascetic ideal is carried to its logical extreme; the ascetic hero engages in a holy fast unto death to achieve perfect purity and total liberation.

**Yoga.** The ascetic ideal, although inherently different, came to be associated with the ideal of the yogin already prior to the sixth century B.C.. The idea of yoga is essentially to use and develop the energies and powers experienced at a lower level of existence in such a way that they become the vehicles for crossing over to a higher level. The two underlying assumptions are that (1) the energies experienced at the lower levels are not different from the energies constituting the core of the highest level; it is just that they are received and experienced in a very limited and fragmented way; and (2) through self-discipline and control, these energies and powers can become self-illumining, revealing the fullness of ultimate reality, the ground of all existence. In Chapter 8 these assumptions are discussed both in terms of the eight sets of yogic techniques designed to achieve the control and illumination needed to reach the highest level of reality and in relation to the philosophy of yoga.

**Devotion.** The other hero type of great influence in religious thought has been that of the *saint* (sādhu), who through personal holiness and fervent love of God gains access to the inner secrets and powers of reality. The development and spread of Hinduism and the attractiveness of Sufic Islam in medieval India were due in large measure to the influence of these God-intoxicated persons who, through their ecstatic poems, songs, and devotional practices, showed the way to the ultimate level of reality through the rapture of loving devotion. The chapters on the Gītā, Devotional Hinduism, and Islam all reveal something of the nature of the devotional way.

**Ritual.** Ritual action has been seen as an important way of entering into the creative process and returning to the source of the creative energy of ultimate reality since the time of the Ṛg Veda more than three thousand years ago. The ritual becomes the means of crossing over from the limitations and fragmentariness of a life lived in separation from its ultimate source to the fullness found in the creative center of reality. The forms of ritual action and their relative importance within the culture have changed over the centuries, but the essential idea of returning one's existence to its source through rituals as a way of restoring wholeness and facilitating participation in the most profound level of reality has been continuous. Chapters 2 and 3 examine the Vedic way of sustaining and renewing life through ritual action.

**Truthful Action or Dharma.** As we have noted, reality is conceived to be essentially normative; each being or event is given both its existence and a rule of action for expressing that existence. In the Vedas this truth of action that is part of a being's very existence is seen in terms of ṛta, a kind of rhythmic ordering that keeps all things in their place and functioning in accord with their inner natures. After the Vedic period this normative dimension of existence came to be seen as dharma, the rule of inner nature that supports and sustains both individual beings and the entire cosmos. By being true to this inner rule a person realizes the deeper foundations of existence and experiences a richness and power of existence that facilitates the transformation to a more profound mode of existence. Although the idea of the power of truth and truthful living was brought to the forefront of modern consciousness and made a basis of reform through the efforts of persons like Dayananda and Gandhi, it has been an important idea for millennia, undergirding Indian morality. Chapter 4 focuses on the concept of dharma.

**Suprarationalism of Transforming Techniques.** As means of spiritual transformation all these techniques go beyond merely rational comprehension. They employ all available human powers, integrating them into a concerted stream of activity that, like a powerful laser, goes straight to its target. Taking the self to be the ultimate ground of being, these techniques enable the self to return to its source in the undivided wholeness of ultimate reality. It may be called Nirvāṇa, Mokṣa, Kaivalya, or Union, but at bottom it is the bliss and freedom of life lived whole, at its most fundamental level.

## Patterns and Processes

In what sense do these fifteen interrelated ideas and two accompanying attitudes constitute the basis of the Indian way of religious and philosophical thought? Certainly not in the sense that they have been the unchanging substratum of a constant Indian vision over the ages, for there has been no unchanging vision, and these ideas have themselves been undergoing continuous modification over the centuries. Not a single important idea can be pointed to that has endured without change through the last three thousand years. And certainly not in the sense that these ideas and attitudes, even in their continuously changing forms and expressions, have anchored the guiding vision of life for everyone at all times. Indian thought has always been pluralistic. There have always been materialists, fatalists, and skeptics. And despite a widespread tendency to see reality at its most basic level as an undivided wholeness, for some thinkers reality was radically plural to the core, while for others undivided wholeness belonged only to spiritual reality, which was regarded as distinct from the reality of matter and mind. There is certainly no unanimity about the nature of reality or the preferred means of spiritual transformation among the classical philosophical visions.

Indeed, we began by pointing out the great diversity and continuous change that have characterized Indian culture since its beginnings. In light of this continuous pattern of change and diversity, it would be exceedingly rash and unwise to claim that there is one unchanging way of thinking and acting that is exclusively and uniquely Indian. Such a claim would represent an implicit attempt to reduce the rich and changing diversity that is India to a single simple formula that would reveal next to nothing of the wide range of changing living ideas that constitute the great traditions of Indian thought. Vedic thought, Jainism, Buddhism, and Hinduism are clearly different ways of thought and must be understood in terms of their differences as well as their similarities. By examining the full diversity and complexity of Indian thought in its various expressions it becomes possible to detect certain underlying ideas and attitudes that, despite important differences between the various visions and ways that have developed over thousands of years, come together to form a larger pattern of continuity that we can meaningfully call the Indian way.

Does it make sense to talk of continuities where there are no constants? No one who knows anything of Indian history thinks that any way of thought or practice has remained constant or changeless. Human history everywhere is the story of process and events. It is not as though there were some constant or continuous string on which the events of history are strung—like beads. There is no such thread, remaining identical with itself over time; there are only the events and processes, linked together in an organic, living way, the way moments and events in the life of an individual person are linked together.

The fact that there are continuities without constants is baffling only from a perspective insisting that separate substances are the fundamental reality of the universe and that takes the logical principles of excluded middle and noncontradiction to be not merely principles of rational organization, but fundamental ontological realities.

More than two thousand years ago a Buddhist sage by the name of Nagasena instructed the Greek king Menander on how continuity itself is part of the flux of process, not requiring any underlying identity or constancy. Nagasena pointed out that the reality of a chariot, like the reality of the self, is not some mysterious substance with a variety of identifiable characteristics adhering to it, but simply an integrated set of parts and processes all functioning together. So here the reality of the Indian way is viewed as a process of changing ideas and practices that function together to constitute a recognizable patterned reality—despite the fact that no underlying unchanging identity can be found.

It should also be pointed out that no claim is being made for the exclusiveness of the Indian way. Even if the basic features of religious and philosophical thought that constitute the Indian way are seen to be similar to the Greek or Chinese ways in important respects, the claim that they constitute the Indian way will still stand, for it is not claimed that this way is unique to India, but only that it is basic to India.

Nor is it being claimed that these basic ideas are to be found in every thinker or in every period. Some of these ideas were extremely important at a particular time, but having given shape to the developing way, then passed more or less unnoticed. The idea of ṛta, the normative nature of reality, was a powerful Vedic idea that came to be taken for granted to such an extent that though the idea survived in the twin concepts of dharma and karma, the very word "ṛta" disappeared from the philosophical and religious vocabulary. Any idea that contributed to the dominant modes of thinking, feeling, and acting in any one period thereby influenced and shaped the thought of the succeeding period and deserves to be noted. Sometimes the influence of ideas extends far beyond the particular religious-philosophical system in which it developed. The actual number of Jainas, for example, has always been relatively small compared with the total population, but their idea of nonhurting (ahiṁsā) quickly became a basic principle of morality in most of the other systems of thought, and their emphasis on asceticism highlights a technique of liberation that has been influential in all of the Indian religions.

To do justice to both the underlying unity and the clearly exhibited diversity of Indian thought, we shall explore the major developments in Indian thought in chronological order yet at the same time not create artificial temporal categories. For example, even though Jainism has a continuous twenty-five-hundred-year history, the various developments within that history are all considered in a single chapter devoted to exploring fundamental Jaina ideas.

It is hoped that this approach will enable the reader to understand each major system or development in its own terms and at the same time exhibit the larger pattern that has given the Indian way its color, flavor, and feeling. Both the basic and the major characteristics of Indian values and thought should be illuminated in the process.

## Suggestions for Further Reading

There are so many books on India that it is difficult to single out only a few. The suggestions at the end of each chapter are made on the criteria of importance, readability, and availability. Most of the suggested books are available in paperback editions published in the United States. Books intended for experts in the field have not been included on the assumption that advanced students of the subject already know the important literature in their field.

Although the bibliography for this first chapter could easily include more than a hundred items, the following are recommended as being especially helpful introductions to Indian thought.

**Histories.** The single best general one-volume history of India is Stanley Wolpert's *A New History of India* (New York: Oxford University Press, 1978). Romila Thaper's *A History of India,* Vol. 1 (Baltimore, Md.: Penguin Books, 1966), is very good on pre-Muslim India, and Percival Spear's *India: A Modern History* (Ann Arbor: University of Michigan Press, 1961) is excellent for the Muslim and British periods.

**Indian Culture.** A. L. Bashman's *The Wonder That Was India* (New York: Taplinger Publishing Co., 1968) is perhaps the finest introduction to Indian culture. The many fine plates are integral to the text and greatly enhance the book. Although it is unfortunately out of print now, most libraries have copies and it is worth looking for. It has been partially replaced by another book edited by the same author, *A Cultural History of India* (Oxford: Clarendon Press, 1975). Norman Brown's 1965 Tagore Memorial Lectures, published as *Man in the Universe: Some Cultural Continuities in Indian Thought* (Berkeley: University of California Press, 1970), are a rewarding study of the major ideas that have shaped the Indian mind over the ages.

**Source Books.** The single best collection of source material is William Theodore DeBary, ed., *Sources of Indian Tradition*, 2 vols. (New York: Columbia University Press, 1967). The introductions are excellent. *The Hindu Tradition,* ed. Ainslie T. Embree (New York: Random House, Inc., 1966), is also an excellent anthology with good introduction but, as the title indicates, is limited to Hinduism. For readers interested in the more technical philosophical sources, *A Source Book in Indian Philosophy*, eds. C. A. Moore and S. Radhakrishnan (Princeton, N.J.: Princeton University Press, 1967), is a good choice, even though the translations used frequently employ nineteenth-century English.

**Art.** Among the many good books on Indian art are those by A. Coomaraswamy, H. Zimmer, S. Kramrisch, and W. Spink. But perhaps the best place to start is with Susan L. Huntington (with John P. Huntington), *The Art of Ancient India*, scheduled for publication later this year by John Weatherhill (Tokyo and New York).

# 2

# Roots of the Indian Way: Indus and Vedic Beginnings

Long before Homer—and probably before the reign of Tutankhamen in Egypt—Āryan poets and seers in India were composing and singing joyous songs to proclaim the wonders of existence and to probe its mysteries. The collection of more than ten thousand of these "wisdom verses" known as the Ṛg Veda is the oldest and most important literary source of subsequent Indian thought and practice. Revealing sophisticated understanding of human nature and penetrating insights into the powers whereby life is transformed, these song-poems are a remarkable testament of human wisdom.

But the Vedic bards who composed and sang these wonderful verses were relative latecomers to the subcontinent. Already a thousand years earlier, around 2000 B.C., the Indus, or Harappan, civilization was flourishing in the valleys and on the plains of the Indus river system. Although much of our knowledge of this great civilization, the remains of which were discovered only in this century, is conjectural, it appears that it was comparable in cultural and technological sophistication to the early civilizations in Egypt and Mesopotamia, and somewhat larger in size. Unfortunately, the only writings to have survived are the still undeciphered glyphics on seals. Lacking written documents, our knowledge of Indus civilization must be constructed solely on the basis of its material remains. But the archaeological reconstruction strongly suggests that the cultural traditions of Indus civilization contributed much to the later development of Indian tradition. Indeed, the picture we have suggests that the twin sources of the mighty stream of Indian civilization and culture are the earlier Indus and Vedic traditions.

In this chapter we will briefly examine the main features of Indus civilization to get a sense of Indian thought and culture before the Vedic views came to prevail. Then we will focus on the Vedas, attempting to identify the central features of the Vedic vision of life. What are the Vedas? What is the nature and function of the deities they honor? What lies beyond the Gods and Goddesses? How is human life related to the reality beyond the Gods? These questions will guide our efforts to understand Vedic thought through an analysis of key texts as we attempt to penetrate the Vedic vision and comprehend how these people understood themselves and their world.

## Indus Civilization

Indus civilization probably began in the Indus River Valley shortly after 3000 B.C. It spread rapidly, moving east almost as far as Delhi, north to the Himalayas, and south almost as far as Bombay, occupying an area greater than one third the size of present-day India by 2000 B.C. It was thus somewhat later, but also considerably larger, than the great early civilizations of Egypt and Mesopotamia, with which there was extensive trade.

By about 1600 B.C. Indus civilization appears to have suffered a serious decline. Although the causes of this decline are unknown, current speculation suggests that earthquakes, flooding, and environmental degradation—resulting in deforestation and overgrazing—may have combined to drive the Indus people out of their homeland. As they spread east and south, they presumably merged with other cultures and lost much of their distinctness.

Scholars used to think that the Āryans had destroyed Indus civilization, but recent archaeological evidence suggests that the civilization was in serious decline before the Āryans became dominant in this area. We are not sure where these people calling themselves "Āryans" (Noble People) came from. Their language resembles Greek, Latin, Old Lithuanian, and various other old European languages, suggesting an ancient kinship with these people, a kinship going back more than four thousand years. What drove these families from their ancient homeland—which scholars speculate was somewhere in the Baltic region of the Soviet Union—and separated them into distinct people calling themselves Greeks, Romans, and Āryans is unknown. But by about 1500 B.C. it appears that the Āryans had migrated through Iran and into India. Their principal religious text, the Ṛg Veda, contains descriptions of great forts and walled cities of Āryan enemies defeated in battle that match archaeologist's descriptions of Indus cities and fortifications, strongly suggesting that increasing Āryan dominance in the Indus region may have hastened the disappearance of an already declining civilization.

Details of encounters and relationships between the Indus people and

Āryans are not known, but granted the extent and accomplishments of Indus civilization, it is probably safe to assume that these people influenced the developing Āryan culture considerably. This assumption is strongly re-enforced by transformations within the Vedic tradition itself from the tenth to the sixth centuries B.C. (see Chapter 5).

On the other hand, we know that by 1000 B.C. the Āryan tradition was well established in India, and it is safe to assume that the Indus people, along with other cultural groups, were significantly affected by the Āryan way of life and absorbed into it, for by the fourth century B.C. practically the entire subcontinent was under the rule of Āryan kings of the Mauryan dynasty.

Two urban centers—Harappa and Mohenjo Daro—reveal some of the accomplishments and complexities of Indus civilization. Mohenjo Daro was a major city, of between 40,000 and 100,000 people. Its streets were laid out in a well-planned rectangular grid pattern. Drains were covered and ceramic tiles were used to line the elaborate water and disposal systems. When we consider also the huge granaries and elaborate bathing facilities—along with the overall organization of these cities—we have reason to believe that the people of the Indus had a sophisticated political system, efficient departments of planning and administration, and complex social organization.

Artifacts reveal an accurate system of weights and measures, utilizing efficient binary and decimal systems of mathematical combination. A variety of toys and games, and what is probably the world's oldest chess set, suggest a culture that delighted in children and had time for play. There is also evidence of trade with other civilizations, as Indus seals have been found in Mesopotamia. Indeed, it has been suggested that the paradisical land called Dilmun in the Gilgamesh epic is none other than the India of Indus civilization.

When we ask about Indus conceptions of human nature, religious practice, their philosophical visions, and the norms that guided their actions, our inability to find answers is disappointing. Archaeological findings suggest an advanced material culture that most likely was associated with equally advanced social and religious thought and practice. But we are probably doomed to ignorance about Indus philosophical and religious thought, for the only surviving writings are the glyphics on the hundreds of seals that have been found. None of the several attempts to decode this language so far has been definitive. But even if a decoding attempt succeeds, we will learn very little, for there are no surviving texts of any kind to translate and interpret. Thus we must reconstruct the nature of this clearly remarkable civilization from the archaeological record.

Fortunately, in the sixty years since Sir John Marshall first discovered the existence of Indus civilization, a great many clues have been found in and around the some three hundred sites identified thus far—even though many of these have not yet been carefully explored. Elaborate ceremonial buildings—even in the smaller towns and villages—indicate that religion played a central role in this civilization. A priesthood is suggested by the masks and horned headdresses that have been discovered. Burials were apparently conducted with great care, suggesting belief in an afterlife, for which careful ceremonial preparations were necessary. Female figurines emphasizing pregnancy and nourishment point to Mother Goddess worship. Concern with religious purification is indicated by the remarkable bathing facilities. The powers of life and virility, particularly as exemplified in male animals, are emphasized. Indeed, the prevalence of bulls and other male animals—along with the apparent importance of the Mother Goddess—suggest a religious preoccupation with fertility.

Indus influence on later developments is suggested by a number of similarities. For example, yoga may have been practiced by the Indus people, for several seals show a figure in a familiar yoga posture. Later Hindu emphasis on the Goddesses as feminine forms of cosmic creative energy may have its source in this early civilization for figurines of the Mother Goddess have been found. Some of the Gods, such as Shiva and Paśupati—"Lords of the beasts" in Hinduism—may also have their origins in Indus culture, for a number of seals show a lordly figure surrounded by animals.

Despite the presumed grandeur of Indus thought and culture, and granted its considerable influence on the Āryan peoples, the fact remains that gradually all the subcontinent came to the "Āryanized" as the Āryan influence spread. By the time of the Mauryan dynasty (fourth century B.C.), Āryan influence had established a huge political kingdom covering practically the entire subcontinent. The religious and philosophical foundation of this increasingly sophisticated and subtle Indian culture was the Veda. Or, to use a Vedic image, the cow that provided spiritual nourishment was the Veda. Accepting the later tradition's tribute to the Vedas as the principal source of thought and culture, we must now turn our attention to the Vedic images, concepts, and symbols.

## The Vedas

According to traditional understanding, the Vedas are verses of wisdom. When they are recited, chanted, and sung as sacred liturgy, they enable the human community to share in the creative wisdom by which a person can be renewed and fulfilled through participation in the energy of the Divine Reality. Without this participation, life is experienced as shallow and fragmented; a person feels confused and alienated. But when one comes to participate in this energy, through sharing in the sacred sounds of wisdom, life is fulfilled and made whole. Dīrghatamas, one of the great seer-poets of the Ṛg Veda expresses this idea beautifully:

I know not what I am:
I wander alone, with troubled mind.
Then comes Speech-awareness,
First-born of the Divine Norm
Of that I receive a share!
(1.164.37)[1]

Although Dīrghatamas is regarded as having "seen" the truth expressed in the vibrant vitality of his verse, neither he nor the other Vedic seer-poets are considered to be authors of the Veda. Indeed, the Indian tradition answers the questions What are the Vedas? and Who are their authors? by proclaiming that they are nothing less than the sacred wisdom of existence and that this wisdom is authorless.

In declaring the Vedas authorless, the tradition does not deny that these verses were shaped by the craft of the Vedic poets. Rather, the tradition is thereby insisting that the wisdom they express springs eternally from the depths of true existence. These eternal sounds of wisdom are heard in the heart of every person open to the sacredness of existence. They are neither the creation of human beings nor the exclusive possession of any person; they are the sounds of wisdom issuing from the very heart of existence itself.

As the wisdom of life, the Veda is that knowledge of the sacred that fulfills human existence. This wisdom is found in the hearts of great persons—the *ṛṣis* or seers—whose experience has taken them to the inner core of existence and nourished their spiritual life. Since this wisdom is achieved through the deepest and most profound possible human experience, it extends as far as humanity itself; it was heard by the very first human beings even as it is heard by us today when we reach into the depths of our humanity. It is in this respect that the Veda is timeless, being simultaneously eternal and contemporary.

Although in principle the Vedas are timeless and authorless, tradition accords a special place to the four collections of texts known as Ṛg Veda, Sāma Veda, Yajur Veda, and Atharva Veda. The first collection contains expressions of profound spiritual experiences of seers and saints in poetic form. These verses were incorporated into the belief and feeling systems of the people as sacred liturgy. Eventually, perhaps by about 1200 B.C., they were gathered together into a single collection of texts known as the Ṛg Veda (wisdom verses). Subsequently, the Sāma Veda, a collection of songs incorporating mostly Ṛg Vedic verses, was established for use in the sacred rites. The Yajur Veda is a collection of liturgical formulas and chants, many incorporating verses from the Ṛg Veda. Still later, another collection of wisdom texts, rather different in character and not based primarily on the Ṛg Veda, was brought together to form the Atharva Veda.

These "wisdom collections" or Vedas have four integral parts: (1) the hymns themselves (*Mantra saṁhitā*); (2) ritually oriented commentaries

[1]All references in this chapter are to the Ṛg Veda unless noted otherwise.

(*Brāhmaṇas*), which provide explanations for the ritual use and meaning of the hymns; (3) ritual and theological speculation (*Āraṇyakas*), which explain the deeper truth of the symbols and images of the rituals; and (4) the *Upaniṣads*, which approach the great mysteries of spiritual existence through concentrated mental effort, meditation, and philosophical reflection. All four parts—Mantras, Brāhmaṇas, Āraṇyakas, and Upaniṣads—are Veda in the sense of sacred wisdom. They are all *śruti* (that which is "heard"), both in the heart of the seer and in the heart of the hearer listening to the seer speak from the heart. But we will follow the common practice of referring only to the first portion, the mantra collection, as Veda, treating the other parts as distinct texts. Where helpful, explanations from the Brāhmaṇas and Āraṇyakas will be referred to in this attempt to understand the Vedic hymns. The Upaniṣads will be considered separately, in Chapter 5.

The verses of the Ṛg Veda, the primary wisdom collection, vibrate with the energies of creation. Like all melodies, they convey and create far more than any associated conceptual meaning can suggest. Their melodious and rhythmic vibrations resonate with the reverberations of cosmos-creating energies. Participating in this creation, the seers found words, rhythms, and melodies with the power to open the human heart, mind, and feelings to these same vibrant world-creating energies. Through the liturgy of sacrificial celebration, these mantric sounds, melodies, and rhythms allowed the Vedic people to join in the process of cosmic creation—particularly self-creation and the creation of community.

Liturgy combines the joyous melodies of song and chant with the symbolic actions of ritual re-creation and sanctification. Vision of reality, vibrant sound of creation, and rhythm of human participation are all combined in the liturgical act. The liturgical nature of the Vedas cannot be overemphasized. These verses are intended to be recited, sung, and chanted, not read. We all know that a verse recited affects us more profoundly than does the same verse read and that a lyric sung has beauty and power that the same lyric read or recited cannot approach. Similarly, the liturgical combination of thought and action that unites feeling and understanding in the ritual re-enactment of primordial creation and sanctification has the power to transform our existence through participation in our own creation far beyond that of ordinary actions and words.

The fact that the verses of the Vedas are poetic in form and liturgical in function warns us against trying to reduce them to strictly rational forms or literal meanings. This sacred wisdom goes far beyond mere intellectual knowledge; it is wisdom heard and felt in the hearts of the great seers and expressed by them in poem and song so that it might resound in the hearts of all people, awakening them to the tremendousness, mysteriousness, and joy of their own being as they participate in cosmic creation.

The language that the poet-seers had to express what they heard in their hearts was ordinary language—language evolved to deal with the ordinary visible world. But they used this language in new ways that were poetic, musical, metaphorical, and highly symbolic, creating vehicles of sound that could carry the hearer into the heart of the creative process of human becoming.

It is very difficult for us, sharing fully in neither the ordinary Vedic world-view nor the extraordinary vision of the seers, to understand this language and to feel its power. We must constantly remind ourselves that the Vedic myths and symbols have their own logic. When we approach them with the logic of linear rational thinking and attempt to force them into conceptual equivalents, we gain clarity and precision at an exorbitant price. The original integrity and richness is lost, and with that is lost also the power of these verses to transform life.

This does not mean that the Vedas are irrational or that they should be approached irrationally. Far from it. These verses are filled with meaning that we must seek to understand in various ways at different levels. But after discovering the conceptual meanings of the central symbols and myths, we must attempt to enter sympathetically into the spirit of the text and to hear its voice. Difficult as it may be, we must try to enter into the inner experiences and imaginings that are expressed with such beauty and power in the Vedas, for these sacred verses have given enduring shape to the Indian way.

## CONTEMPORARY QUALITY

Fortunately, not all the Vedic verses are remote from us. Some appear directly relevant to the contemporary worldwide quest to enter more fully and creatively into life. Indeed, one of the reasons why the Vedas are still relevant to the Indian way today is that the ancient seers were responding to basic questions that all human beings seek to answer—regardless of time or place. This gives the Vedas a kind of timelessness that makes some of the verses seem almost contemporary. The following verses suggest this timelessness.

Do we not all yearn for intelligence and love, for health and wealth, for persuasive speech and happy days? Except that the following verse of Gṛtsamada is addressed to Indra, it might stand as a timeless and universal human petition:

> Grant us, O Indra, the greatest of treasures:
> A good mind and happy love,
> Increased wealth and a healthy body,
> Persuasive speech and happy days.
>
> (2.21.6.6)

The profundity and tenderness of human love expressed so beautifully by the groom to his bride in the following verse is as appropriate to a marriage ceremony today as it was three thousand years ago:

> I am song, you are verse.
> I am Heaven, you are Earth.
> We two shall live here together
> Becoming the parents of children.
> (Atharva Veda, 14.2.71)

The emphasis on friendship in the community of all existence expressed by the poet in the following verse could well serve as an inspiration for a contemporary ecological awareness and as a basic principle for a new eco-moral system:

> O Great One, make me great.
> May all beings see me as a friend;
> May I see all beings as friends;
> May we all see one another as friends.
> (Yajur Veda, 36.18)

The following verse, inquiring into the origins of existence, speaks to us in our present concern to discover the ontological roots of our being:

> Neither existence nor non-existence was there then;
> Neither air-filled space nor sky beyond was there.
> What enveloped all? Where? Under whose protection?
> (10.129)

The insight that the plurality of existence is an expression of a deeper unity, that all things are united in their source, an insight found in the thinking of many great philosophers—and that, as a basic intuition, guides much work in the contemporary sciences—is poetically expressed in the following Ṛg Vedic verses:

> That which is One the sages call by many names;
> They call it Indra, Mitra, Varuṇa,
> Agni or the heavenly Sun-bird.
> (1.164.46)

> With their words the wise poets shape the One
> Into many forms: Agni, Yama, or Mātariśvan.
> (10.114.5)

Yet another Ṛg Vedic hymn reveals that for all their concern with profound and spiritual matters, the poet-seers also had a keen appreciation of the ordinary ways of human beings as they strive for their own wealth, success, and power:

> Many are the ways of human beings;
> Our thoughts go off in many ways.
> The wheel-maker hopes for accidents,
> The doctor for an injured person,
> The priest for a rich benefactor.
> Flow Indu, flow for the sake of Indra.

Day after day the blacksmith seeks
customers with plenty of gold.

. . .

I'm a singer, Dad's a doctor,
Mama grinds flour with a grindstone.
Our thoughts are all for profit,
As we plod along like cows.
Flow Indu, flow for the sake of Indra.

The horse wants a swift chariot,
The entertainer a good laugh,
The penis a hairy slot,
And the frog a stagnant pond.
Flow Indu, flow for the sake of Indra.
(9.112.1–4)

## Gods and Goddesses

Although the foregoing verses suggest areas of shared concerns and perspectives, much of the Ṛg Veda seems more remote to us. For example, one of the first things we notice when turning to the text is that most of the hymns are addressed to Gods or Goddesses. This fact has led many interpreters to think that the Vedas are essentially texts for worship or sacrifice in which the deities are invoked to gain their help and protection. The Gods and Goddesses are mistakenly assumed to be nothing more than anthropomorphized beings, projected into a heavenly realm from which, by some kind of ritual magic, they can intercede on human behalf. Although containing an important element of truth, this interpretation fails to reveal the deeper significance of the Gods and Goddesses as symbols of the fundamental powers of existence.

Indra, Agni, and Soma; Sūrya, Uṣas, and Savitṛ; Varuṇa, Vishnu, and Vāc—the names of the many Vedic deities roll off the tongue creating mysterious feelings of power and awe. Who are these deities? What is their function? Why are they so important to the Vedic people?

The word for God offers an important clue. *Deva* means "shining" or "auspicious." This is precisely what the Gods are; they are the auspicious powers that create and destroy life, controlling the flow and ebb of existence. Speech, consciousness, life, wind, fire, and water—these are among the great powers controlling the pulse of existence that are personified, symbolized, and celebrated as Gods in the Vedas. The range of deities recognized and celebrated by the seers reveals the range of auspicious powers they felt and recognized. The significance and importance of the various Devas tells us a great deal about the perceived significance and importance of these various powers in Vedic life.

Because it is the power symbolized by a God or Goddess that is emphasized, personal characteristics of the deities are usually ignored. For most deities, no important biographical data are given; nothing about their origins, and next to nothing about their personalities, are indicated. There is no sense of a divine family or of a hierarchy of power among the deities. Despite their lack of personality, however, the Vedic deities are not abstract, for the powers they symbolize are directly experienced by every person, and the God or Goddess lives in the immediate experience.

A brief examination of a few major deities will help us to understand the Vedic conception of the Gods and Goddesses better. Agni, for example, is the God of Fire and Lord of the great fire rituals central to Vedic religion. The word *agni* means "fire," suggesting that the Vedic people saw fire as a wonderful and awesome power. As lightning it pierces both heaven and earth, joining them into a cosmic unity. Out of control, it destroys dwellings and consumes forests, animals and humans. But in the hearth, fire transforms raw flesh and vegetation into food for human beings, providing energy for life. It is this inherent power of fire that Agni symbolizes.

Nowhere is the power of fire so awesome and mysterious as in the rituals of sacrificial celebration through which the offerings are transformed from fruit and flesh into the energies and life of renewed existence. In the Ṛg Veda this wondrous power of fire is symbolized in consciousness and is given expression in speech and action as Agni, Lord of the Fire. Agni is addressed in nearly one third of the Ṛg Vedic hymns—such is the perceived importance of the power of fire as a transforming agency.

Soma is the symbol of ecstasy and illumination, the supreme expression of conscious life. Symbolizing both the golden juice of the soma plant and the special luminosity of consciousness achieved through drinking this juice, Soma is honored by having an entire book of the Ṛg Veda devoted to Him. Personified symbol of the highest states of conscious life, He is a mighty Lord of the universe, giving rise to the light of dawn, making the brilliant sun shine as well as stirring the winds into motion and making the rivers flow. But as symbol of the drop of life magnified into the fullness of existence, Soma is the God of pure joyous existence that never ends. "We have drunk the Soma and become immortal. We have attained the light and have found the Gods," sings the poet (8.48.3), celebrating the depth, range, immensity, and power of consciousness experienced through the divine presence of Soma.

Indra, mighty Lord of the Universe, is in many respects the easiest of the Vedic deities to understand, for He is most humanlike. He protects people from harm and gives them strength to overcome their enemies. Lord of the Thunderbolt, this mighty hero strikes the enemy, conquers foes, releases the waters of life, and opens the way for the emergence of existence, overcoming the forces of chaos and non-existence. Human strength and courage—especially the courage and strength required to resist the enemy and protect the family and community—are recognized as great and auspicious powers in the universe. Indra, symbol of these powers, is the most frequently mentioned God in the Ṛg Veda.

Vāc, Goddess of Consciousness and Speech, is to be understood in a similar way. The power of human speech is awesome; by it worlds are transformed and people live and die. It is a power that when encountered in the depth of human experience and imagination requires symbolic expression. The response of the seers is to symbolize this great power as Vāc, Goddess of Speech and Consciousness.

The hymns to Uṣas—Dawn, Daughter of Heaven, Lady of Light, and Bride of the Sun—bespeak the anticipation and joy of the emerging of light out of the darkness. Darkness symbolizes the long night of unmanifest existence, and Uṣas symbolizes the emergence of existence out of the deep darkness of unmanifest possibilities. Dawn represents hope—the hope of humankind to find itself reunited with Sūrya, the sun of its origin, for the light of dawn is associated with the coming of the sun, which as Savitṛ is the generator of all life. When this symbol of dawn and hope is personified, it becomes a Goddess rather than merely a cosmic event and human attitude, and the poet can sing, "O Lady of Noble Birth, Daughter of Heaven, worshipped by all the illustrious, grant us your riches and blessings; Protect us now and forever" (7.77.6).

The powers of heaven and earth—symbolized as Father Sky (Dyaus Pitṛ) and Mother Earth (Pṛthivi)—enclose all the energies and forces of existence and therefore enjoy a special place at the head of the pantheon. But the divine ordering that imparts a rhythm to the cosmic energies, bringing order out of chaos and effecting creation out of disorder and destruction, thereby regulating the powers of heaven and earth, is an even more important and auspicious power. This ordering and rhythm of existence, the divine ṛta, is guarded and protected by Varuna, Lord of the realm mediating between Heaven and Earth at the one extreme and concretely manifested existence and life—the world of humans, plants, and animals—at the other.

Other deities—Rudra, Mitra, Sarasvatī, the twin Aśvins, the group called Maruts, etc.—are also symbolized and personified powers of existence of particular importance within the Vedic experience. Viśvakarman, the All-Maker, and Brahmaṇaspati, Lord of the Holy Power, although addressed as Gods in the hymns, are different. They appear to be conceptual and speculative rather than symbolic and personal. Appearing in later portions of the Ṛg Veda, they are probably the result of speculative effort to identify the power behind the powers represented by the Gods and Goddesses. This would account for their abstract and impersonal character.

This brief glimpse of some of the important Ṛg Veda deities should enable us to see that they represent possibilities of intimate human relationships with the most fundamental cosmic and human powers of existence experienced. By symbolizing the deeper cosmic and human powers as personal, the Vedic people were able to enter into relationship with them, thereby bringing profound human and cosmic dimensions into their ordinary life.

Understanding the Gods and Goddesses to be symbols of the most fundamental powers of existence and life, we can, instead of seeing them merely as anthropomorphic beings, see *through* them, to the humanly encountered powers they symbolize. Indeed, speech and consciousness, or fire and light, are no less wonderful, mysterious, or awesome now than they were to the Vedic people—except that we have lost our sense of wonder and mystery and some of our ability to rejoice in and symbolize the wonderful powers that shape our existence.

## Beyond Gods and Goddesses

Symbolizing the various powers present in existence, the Gods and Goddesses of the Vedas are never regarded as creators of the universe. They shape, form, and order the various processes of existence, functioning as lords, overseers, artisans, engineers, architects, and so on. But unlike the God of Genesis, they are never thought of as creating existence out of nothing. Indeed, the notion of a creator, external to the universe, is not to be found in the Ṛg Veda. Both the material stuff and the intelligence of the universe are eternally contained within it, although at a deeper level than the manifest forms through which they are usually experienced. At the deepest level, intelligence and the material stuff of the universe are not separate or distinct but, rather, constitute the unified primordial ground of all existence.

To the seers it was clear that there is a central intelligent order guiding the universe. This order is present in physical regularities, but goes much deeper, for it proceeds from the very heart of the universe, providing norms for aesthetic, moral, psychic, and religious activities as well. It is this central normative rhythm that is known as *ṛta*, and which the Gods, Varuṇa in particular, must guard and protect.

Ṛta, as the rhythm and structuring of the fundamental energies of the universe, is more fundamental than the Gods and Goddesses. They are quite as subject to the fundamental norm and rhythm of existence as are human beings and other forms of existence. The seers clearly recognized this, claiming that, when the ritual actions succeed in the attempted correspondence with the actions of the Divine Norm (ṛta), then the Gods can neither help nor hinder the process, and the desired results are ensured.

While recognizing ṛta as the fundamental norm and rhythm of the dynamic aspects of existence, the seers also sought an originating principle of existence beyond the Gods. In the tenth book, clearly later than most of the rest of the Ṛg Veda, in the next to last verse of the Hymn of Origins, the Gods are explicitly stated to be later developments, not standing at the very beginning or constituting the ultimate ground of existence: "Who really knows? Who can say / When it was born and from where it came—this creation? / The Gods are later than this world's creation . . . " (10.129.6).

The vision of Dīrghatamas in Book One sees a unity underlying the many powers and aspects of existence. We find him affirming that "That which is One the sages call by many names . . ." (1.64.46). But this unity is expressed through the multiplicity of forms and powers of existence and hence "With their words the wise poets shape the One into many forms: Agni, Yama or Mātariṣvan" (10.114.5).

Examples of speculative thought reaching out to find a single source of existence, a primordial principle lying beyond the realm of Gods, are found in earlier portions of the Ṛg Veda as well. The poet of 8.58.2 sings:

> One only is the fire, burning in many forms.
> One only is the sun, illuminating the whole universe.
> One only is the dawn lighting up all things.
> Truly, the One has become this whole world.

The refrain occurring at the end of each of the twenty-two verses of 3.55 celebrating the accomplishments of various deities affirms the underlying unity of the Gods: "Great is the one Godhead of the Gods."

Recognizing the various deities as different aspects or dimensions of the same underlying ultimate reality enabled the Vedic seers to identify the Gods with each other—on the principle that they were identical in their ground. This identification of one God with another—and all the Gods with each other (the Viśvedevāḥ)—underlies both the multiplicity of Gods and the attitudes of tolerance to deities other than one's favorite from Vedic times to the present.

The recognition that the Gods are not ultimate sometimes leads to a kind of religious atheism, where the Gods are abandoned, ignored, or even repudiated (as in Buddhism and Jainism) in favor of a nonpersonal, but still spiritual, ultimate reality. Vedānta and some forms of Yoga are good examples of this tendency. But even among the devotees of Kālī, Shiva, or Vishnu, these deities are recognized not as the ultimate reality but as personified *symbols* of the ultimate. This would be like a Jew, Christian, or Muslim declaring that God is not the ultimate reality but, rather, a symbol of the ultimate. To the extent that the symbol participates in the reality that it symbolizes, Vishnu (or God) is the ultimate. But to the extent that the reality symbolized goes beyond the symbol, Vishnu (or God) is less than ultimate.

## Existence

Since the Gods and Goddesses are not the ultimate forms of existence, we must explore the Vedic effort to locate the ground of existence beyond the Gods. What is the source of existence? How did existence emerge from this source? These two questions are of great concern to the poets and seers of the Ṛg Veda. In the famous hymn on the origins of existence the poet begins by declaring that he is seeking the primordial: "At first," he says, "there was neither existence [*sat*] nor non-existence [*asat*]" (10.129). In the fourth verse he observes that "The seers, searching in their hearts with wisdom, discovered the connection between existence and non-existence." That they were searching "in their hearts with wisdom" shows that they understood that this was no ordinary rational knowledge, but a deeper intuitive wisdom—a wisdom that arises from the most profound experience of existence.

## INDRA CONQUERS VṚTRA

This concern to understand the source of existence lies behind many of the Vedic hymns. In earlier and less self-conscious portions of the text we find "explanations" of the origins of existence in mythic accounts of existence originating from non-existence. One myth, that of Indra's conquest of Vṛtra, accounts for the emergence of existence out of non-existence by reference to a war between the forces of light and freedom and the forces of darkness and bondage. This is obviously not intended as a scientific explanation, and, if we wish to understand the significance of the mythic account, we must understand the images and symbols of the story in which the "explanation" is given.

The "plot" of the myth is simple. Before the birth of this world there occurred a colossal struggle between the Ādityas—forces of light and freedom—and the Dānavas—forces of bondage and darkness. Initially, the Dānavas were winning, successfully enclosing and holding back the life-giving waters. But then the Ādityas, led by Varuṇa and the other Gods, requested help from Heaven and Earth. Hearing their request, this primordial pair joined together to produce a powerful new God; thus was born a mighty hero—the soma-drinking, thunderbolt-wielding Indra. Fortified with the power of all the Gods and filled with the mighty Soma, he led the Ādityas to victory by slaying the gigantic Vṛtra, dragon leader of the forces of darkness and non-existence. Slicing open the dragon's belly, Indra released the seven pregnant cosmic streams of water that then gave birth to the sun and to all the myriad life-forms that fill the earth.

This, in brief, is the oldest Vedic account of creation, an event that figures prominently in the Ṛg Veda and a story frequently retold in various forms throughout the succeeding ages. The Indra-Vṛtra myth provides us with a point of entry into fundamental features of early Indian thought, for it sounds three important Vedic themes that have a continuing importance in the developing tradition. First, life is revealed to be the victorious fruit of a continuing struggle between the interrelated forces of existence (the Ādityas) and non-existence (the Dānavas). Second, it emphasizes the role of the Gods in securing the conditions of life, for they symbolize the deeper powers inherent in existence. Third, it dramatizes the power of ritual action in achieving victory over non-existence and establishing order in the universe, for Indra's conquering activity was essentially a sacrificial celebration.

Vṛtra, leader of the forces of darkness and bondage, symbolizes non-existence (asat). Indra symbolizes the powers of existence (sat) and creative action. That Indra can overcome Vṛtra and release the waters of life trapped in his belly shows the creative efficacy of action, for this is the creative act by which the sun and all the life forms were created. Clearly, this is not creation out of nothing, for the source of life is already there, enclosed in the cavernous recesses of the dragon. Furthermore, the story tells us that existence (the Ādityas) and non-existence (the Dānavas) engaged in a struggle—indeed, a struggle it appears that the forces of non-existence were going to win until Indra appeared on the scene. Thus, while it is clear that existence and non-existence are opposed to each other, they obviously are not opposed as being and non-being. What, then, is the relation between existence and non-existence symbolized by Indra and Vṛtra?

Vṛtra encloses the waters of life—that is his chief function and the main reason why he must be overcome. What this tells us is that, rather than being the total negation of existence, non-existence is its ground state. Existence refers to what is structured, determined, and moving. By contrast, non-existence is the unstructured, the undetermined, and the unmoving. The waters of life flow from Vṛtra when freed by Indra's action, just as water wells up and flows from the ground when a hole is sunk into the earth. Indeed, what Vṛtra symbolizes is the ground and potency of existence, for he contains the possibilities of all life. When the text says that existence comes from non-existence, it is non-existence in the sense of ground and potency of things—not as the negation of being that is referred to. Vṛtra, enclosing the possibilities of existence in the dark cave of the not-yet-become, is conquered by Indra's heroic creative energy as he unleashes the energies of life pent up in Vṛtra.

Seen in this way, the battle between the Ādityas and Dānavas is the struggle between the inertial potential of existence and the dynamic activity of transformation whereby this potential is actualized and structured. Existence emerges from non-existence as its ground and potency. Just as Lao Tzu, the ancient Chinese sage, says that non-being is the mother of being and being is the source of the ten thousand things, so the Ṛg Veda tells us that non-existence (asat) is the ground of existence (sat) and existence is the source of what is structured, differentiated, and active.

## CREATIVE ACTION

Having seen how non-existence—not in the sense of the absence of existence but in the sense of the "being-able-to-exist" prior to actual structure and differentiation—is the source of actual things, we need to move on to the question of *how* existence emerges from non-existence. In the story we are following, it is clear that Indra's creative action consists in piercing Vṛtra to release the pent-up energies of existence enclosed in the dark caverns of non-existence. But of course, Indra's action is not simply that of taking up a sword and slaying an animal—mythic or real. It is a knowing-acting that pierces the skin of enclosed possibilities of existence, releasing them into the realm of actual existence.

The story makes this point in its own way. Careful preparation is required for this wonderful life-giving act. First, a weapon must be carefully constructed that will effectively reach into the heart of the enclosed possibilities, releasing them. The clever and powerful Tavaṣṭṛ, chief architect and engineer of the Gods, shapes the lightning energy of the thunderbolt for Indra. The thunderbolt is an appropriate instrument, for it emanates in the higher world, but crosses over into this ordinary world, piercing it with the lightning energy.

Even with this wonderful weapon, the outcome is not assured. The text tells us that Indra received the powers of all the Gods before going into battle, so that the strength of Indra was the strength of all the Gods. But this is still not enough, and Indra fortifies himself further by drinking huge beakers of soma, the juice of life itself. The seer is expressing his awareness of the difficulties people face in attempting to continuously re-create themselves out of the possibilities that lie enclosed within the bonds of non-existence. That is, we should not think that the seers are simply retelling an old cosmic myth. Their obvious concern with questions about how human existence is created and maintained through thought and action suggests that the battle between Indra and Vṛtra is allegorical and that the thunderbolt successfully wielded by Indra symbolizes a certain kind of creative human action. Indeed, we shall see when we consider the nature and function of *yajña*—the sacrificial celebration ritual—that the creation and maintenance of existence through human thought and action is the central concern of the Ṛg Veda. For now, let us note that a Ṛg Vedic person finds existence to be radically contingent; there is no God or metaphysical principle guaranteeing the continued existence of the self-in-the-world. Without a continuous re-energizing and re-creating, the present moment of existence will not be renewed in the next, but will disappear into the dark cave of the non-existent.

What the seers saw was the emergence of actual existence—of structured events and things—out of deep darkness. What these dark depths are is not known; that is why they are regarded as dark depths. But out of them come thoughts, actions, objects, and events—a whole world. For any person, Vedic or contemporary, precisely how our experienced self-world comes into existence is a wonderful mystery, although we seem to have lost something of the awe and joy experienced by the Vedic people in confronting their own coming-to-be from season to season, day to day, and moment to moment. But when we attend to our coming-to-be and the coming-into-being of our world, we become aware, as the Vedic seers were, that willing, acting, feeling, and thinking are somehow creatively involved in this coming-to-be. Through these activities there somehow comes into existence our world and our self-in-this-world. This is how humans pierce the dark cavernous depths to release the energy and life-forms that structure and animate our world.

We can now see that the story of the Ādityas and the Dānavas is a creation myth not merely in the sense of describing and explaining the beginnings of the external world, but in the deeper sense of symbolizing the creative actions that all human beings need to engage in as part of the effort to bring about and maintain their existence from moment to moment. This may be a difficult point for many of us to understand, for we tend to assume the *objective givenness* of both our own existence and the existence of the external world. Most of us assume that there exists an external world—a world of objects and events in space and time—quite independent of our existence and experience. Our own existence, too, seems to be given—ready made—and also independent of the external world. But these assumptions—so obviously true for us that we usually do not notice them at all—were not made by the Vedic people. For them the seeings, hearings, feelings, thoughts, and actions that constitute the basis of human experience were ways that self and world came into existence. But self and world are not given in experience as separate realities, but as a unity, a self-world.

There are two ways to get a sense of the Vedic view of self-world creation. The first, and more difficult, is to allow all our concepts and theories to drop away, leaving us with the immediacy of experience. In the immediacy of experience, there is no independent self or world, but a continuously changing richness of events. This world, the world of immediate experience, is continuously being created and left behind (destroyed). This world is simultaneously the self—also continuously being created and destroyed. From the perspective of immediate experience, the continuing creation of a self-world and the ability to direct this creation through thinking, acting, feeling, and willing is both wonderful and awesome.

The second, and easier, approach to the Vedic view—for dropping the constructions of theories and concepts through which we usually view and experience our lives and our world is incredibly difficult—is to emphasize the role of experience in forming our world by imagining cessations of experience. If we were placed in an environment—from birth—in which no sensory inputs were possible, an environment in which nothing could be touched, heard, felt, smelled, or tasted (remove also all our inner senses such as kinesthetic, etc.), there would be no images, thoughts, or feelings. Indeed, there would be no world of any kind for us. But in what sense would there be a self? Without experiences of any kind it would make no sense to say there was a self in that environment. But if, slowly and gradually, a capacity for experience were stimulated by bits of light or sound, a self-world would come into being, at first not separated into self and world. As experience became more abstract and reflective, mental constructions of self and world could be distinguished and separated from each other, and with time we could even learn to arrange these constructions in the familiar way of our ordinary assumptions about the world.

This thought experiment should enable us to see that our awareness of self and world is generated through experience. From a perspective internal to the experience, the experience is *creative* of the self-world. Since the only self and world any of us can have is that of which we are aware, and since that awareness comes through experience, it becomes possible for us to appreciate the Vedic perspective that regards the creation of the self-world as the most wonderful and important activity there is.

What Indra's victory over Vṛtra reveals is that existence can be created out of the possibilities enclosed in non-existence. Human existence is not given once and for all, but is continuously being created and destroyed. The movement from non-existence is never ending so long as there is life, as is the reciprocal movement from existence to non-existence. The supreme challenge to human beings is to create and employ the instrumentalities that will effectively create a continuing self-world that participates most fully in the powers and glories of existence. Meeting this challenge is the central concern of Vedic seers, and the central symbol of this instrumentality is the *yajña*—the sacrificial celebration ritual.

## Summary

We began this chapter with a brief description of the Indus civilization preceding the Vedic age in India to make the point that, although Vedic thought and practice developed in India more than three thousand years ago, it should not be regarded as primitive. We know that the Indus civilization preceding it was complex and sophisticated, with well-planned cities in excess of thirty thousand people, a wide range of industries, foreign trade, and apparently a well-managed, efficient central administration. While very little is known about the religion and philosophy of the Indus, art objects and artifacts suggest a highly developed culture, which most likely influenced the development of Vedic thought and practice that succeeded it, leaving its mark on all subsequent Indian culture. The origins of yoga, ascetic discipline, and many of the Gods and Goddesses of later Hinduism are probably to be found in Indus thought and practice.

Our knowledge of the Vedic age is gleaned from the Vedas, collections of hymns and formulas composed by seers and poets and used in the sacrifical celebrations that dominated Vedic life. The tradition regards these verses as the expression of the wisdom heard in their hearts by the great seers whose spiritual experience took them to the inner core of reality. When recited, chanted, and sung as sacred liturgy, they enable the whole community to share in the creative wisdom by which each person can be renewed and fulfilled through participation in the energy of ultimate reality.

The majority of Vedic verses are addressed to one or another of the Gods and Goddesses who symbolize the great powers of existence: fire, speech, consciousness, sun, wind. But these deities are not the ultimate creators or controllers of the universe; creation and control issue from a more fundamental power lying beyond the limits of existence and non-existence. In the Hymn of Origins the seer begins by noting that existence and non-existence have their origin in some prior reality—a reality that lies beyond all language and thought and is called simply THAT, or THAT ONE.

The account of Indra's victory over Vṛtra suggests that life is the victorious fruit of a continuous struggle between the forces of existence and non-existence, a struggle that allows the underlying ground of reality to be shaped and energized into actual existence. This is not, however, a victory that is won once and forever; existence is radically contingent, in constant danger of collapsing into non-existence unless sustained by a continuing effort to renew it. Seeing the implication of this vision for human life, the seers of the Veda understood that the supreme challenge to human beings is to find the instrumentalities needed to sustain and renew their own humanness from moment to moment, that will be effective in the continuous effort to re-create the self-world constantly in danger of being swallowed up by non-existence. In the next chapter we will see how, when incorporated ritually into sacrificial celebration (yajña), thinking, willing, feeling, and acting were seen as accomplishing this wonderful feat.

## Suggestions for Further Reading

*The Roots of Ancient India: The Archaeology of Early Indian Civilization,* by Walter A. Fairservis, Jr., 2nd rev. ed. (Chicago: University of Chicago Press, 1975), is a well-rounded account of the beginnings of Indian civilization taking into account the contributions made by leading scholars in a variety of disciplines. Chapters VI–VIII (pp. 217–311) are especially helpful for understanding Indus civilization; an excellent bibliography cites literature on early Indian civilization published before 1975.

*The Indus Civilization,* by Sir Mortimer Wheeler, 3rd ed. (Cambridge: Cambridge University Press, 1968), is a classic account. Although not as up to date or as full or well balanced as the Fairservis work, this small well-written volume is an excellent place to begin the exciting exploration of Indus civilization.

*Hymns from the Ṛg Veda,* trans. Jean Le Mée, with photographs by Ingbert Gruttner (New York: Alfred A. Knopf, Inc., 1975), is a wonderful book with which to begin. While it contains only a small fraction of the Ṛg Veda, the selections are judicious, the translations excellent, and the format a visual delight, giving the reader a feel for the wisdom of the verses translated. The beautiful photographs on every page are an integral part of the book.

# 3

# Creation and Celebration in the Vedas

## Source of Existence

In the Hymn of Origins, the seer, looking for that which is prior to existence and non-existence, concludes with the remark that only He in the highest heaven could know that reality—and perhaps even He could not! In other hymns, what is beyond the distinction between existence and non-existence is simply called THAT or THAT ONE. The emergence of existence out of non-existence is seen as possible only because the opposition between them is not total. Their very opposition suggests that they are the results of a division of a prior reality. Just as a fruit might be split into two halves, so too might the primary reality be split into the two opposing parts of existence and non-existence. The very opposition between them points to their prior unity, even as the two halves of the fruit suggest their prior wholeness. It is this undivided wholeness that is sought as THAT ONE, for it is the ground of all existence and non-existence.

The problem is that, because the differentiation between existence and non-existence marks the boundaries of conceptual thought and language, this prior reality cannot be thought or talked about in conceptual terms. Conceptual thought is rooted in the absolute difference between what is, and what is not. But the absoluteness of this difference is precisely what the vision of a prior undivided wholeness of reality repudiates. Consequently, the quest for the undivided reality cannot be purely conceptual, for conceptual thought cannot go beyond the limits of existence and non-existence, and THAT lies beyond those limits.

The Hymn of Origins, translated here in its entirety, reveals the seer's efforts to go beyond existence and non-existence to a prior reality that is their unifying ground. Throughout he is forced to struggle within the confining limits of the *is* and the *is not*. And although he cannot say anything beyond these limits, his words clearly point beyond them, suggesting both the limitations of language and the profundity of what lies beyond what can be said.

HYMN OF ORIGINS

1. In the beginning there was neither existence nor non-existence;
   Neither the world nor the sky beyond.
   What was covered over? Where? Who gave it protection?
   Was there water, deep and unfathomable?
2. Then was neither death nor immortality,
   Nor any sign of night or day.
   THAT ONE breathed, without breath, by its own impulse;
   Other than that was nothing at all.
3. There was darkness, concealed in darkness,
   And all this was undifferentiated energy.
   THAT ONE, which had been concealed by the void,
   Through the power of heat-energy was manifested.
4. In the beginning was love,
   Which was the primal germ of the mind.
   The seers, searching in their hearts with wisdom,
   Discovered the connection between existence and non-existence.
5. They were divided by a crosswise line.
   What was below and what was above?
   There were bearers of seed and mighty forces,
   Impulse from below and forward movement from above.
6. Who really knows? Who here can say?
   When it was born and from where it came—this creation?
   The Gods are later than this world's creation—
   Therefore who knows from where it came?
7. That out of which creation came,
   Whether it held it together or did not,
   He who sees it in the highest heaven,
   Only He knows—or perhaps even He does not know!

(10.129)[1]

This hymn is considerably later than the hymns dealing with the Indra-Vṛtra myth. It expresses familiarity with attempts to explain the origins of existence in non-existence, but it pushes beyond this concern in an attempt to reach that which is absolutely primordial. If existence and non-existence are opposed to each other there must be a prior reality that is the source and basis for this opposed pair. As though

[1]All quotations in this chapter are from the Ṛg Veda unless noted otherwise.

recognizing that concepts and theories are inadequate here, the seer proceeds by questioning various possibilities. Wishing to probe beyond existence and non-existence, to go beyond heaven and earth, questions about how existence was covered over with water and about how it was protected by some greater power do not go far enough. Going beyond the dualities that separate death from deathlessness, night from day, and breath from the breather, it is discovered that no assertions—or denials—can be made. Indeed, then all is darkness, concealed in darkness. If that primordial reality is to be recognized, it must first be manifested—in terms of the dualities of existence and non-existence. The undivided reality is not to be found outside of, or separate from, existing things.

But if the mind cannot fathom the primordial reality, then perhaps something prior to the mind—which divides and separates reality—can reach there. In love, the act of gathering and making whole, say the seers, is to be discovered the roots of existence in non-existence. Using the imagery of love—"bearers of seed and mighty forces," "impulse from below and forward movement above"—the seer suggests, in verse 4, that existence and non-existence join together to give birth to the things of the world. But even love does not go beyond this creating of manifest existence. Here is the mystery of life that cannot be penetrated, not even by "the one who sees in the highest heaven." The implicit suggestion is that we must remain open to this mystery and participate in it as we engage in the project of continuously re-creating our self-world.

How can humans open themselves to this creative mystery and through its power create, transform, and maintain their existence? That which is prior to existence and non-existence is the primordial source: how can we return to this source to receive its life-creating energy? The Vedic response to this central concern can be summed up in one word: *yajña*, sacrificial celebration.

## Sacrificial Celebration

The pervasive importance of yajña is obvious to anyone who has even glanced through the verses of the Vedas or looked at the Brāhmaṇa texts. Unquestionably, it is the ruling image of the Vedic texts and Vedic life. By "ruling image" is meant the embodiment of those underlying attitudes, ideas, and norms that shape human experience, giving it a particular structure and meaning, thereby providing a basis for human knowledge and action. By analogy, we could say that the ruling image of modern science is measurement. All observations and explanations must be grounded in, and refer to, measurement. Within the Vedic world-view, all events and actions are grounded in and refer to yajña.

## YAJÑA AS CELEBRATION

Yajña has usually been interpreted as sacrifice. This is most unfortunate, because sacrifice connotes the wrong images and associations from the beginning. A yajña is clearly a celebration, something easily overlooked when focusing on it as sacrifice. Perhaps it would be better to translate this word as "sacrificial celebration," an expression that points to both the sacrificial and the celebrative dimensions of yajña. The reason for insisting on the celebrative dimension is that the whole of the Ṛg Veda is essentially a collection of songs of celebration. What is being celebrated is existence itself—in its various powers, transformations, and mysteries. Most of the hymns are addressed to Gods or Goddesses, the symbols of the powers of existence. Celebrating the powers symbolized by the Gods, the hymns open the way to human sharing in these powers.

The spirit of celebration and a sense of the joy of participating in the divine powers of existence shines through numerous verses. Agni, the center of yajña, is described as the "priest of joy," "blessed with the joy of youth," and "Lord of all treasure":

> At yajña the prayerful community worships Agni,
> Priest of all joy, blessed with youth.
> He, untiring envoy to the Gods at the hour of offering,
> He is the Lord of all treasure.
>
> (7.10.5)

Since it is to Agni (Lord of the Fire) that the offering is made and by Agni is consumed and transformed, it is fitting that he should be thought of as "Lord of all treasure" and the offering be seen as a celebration.

In the Yajur Veda, Agni, Lord of the Yajña, is addressed in the following words:

> You are sacred drink, may I enjoy your sacred drink!
> You are greatness, may I share in your greatness!
> You are power, may I share in your power!
> You are treasures, may I share in your treasures!
>
> (3.9.20)

In the Śatapatha Brāhmaṇa, devoted to explaining the performance of yajña, we find the Lord of the Yajña addressed as the source of joy and grace:

> You, O Agni, are the righteous, the truthful, the mighty, and most wonderful. You are indeed manifest to all; you, O Agni, are present everywhere. People rank Agni highest for grace and joy, for grace and joy undoubtedly reside in yajña. You, heaven, ruler, and divine one, we humans invoke with song."
>
> (8.3.1.34)

One of the fascinating features of the Ṛg Veda is the self-consciousness that illuminates many of its verses. Not only is joy expressed, but the seer-poet is aware of this. For example, in 10.100.6 we find, "May our yajña be ready and pleasing to all the people gathered here. For freedom and perfect joy we pray."

The first stanza of 10.68 expresses in a particularly beautiful way the idea that the yajña is a celebration and expression of gladness of heart and joy:

> Like birds, splashing in water, that keep watch,
> Like the loud voice of the thundering clouds,
> Like the joyous streams bursting from the mountains,
> Have our [yajña] recitals sounded to the Lord of Wisdom!

## EXPERIENTIAL ROOTS OF YAJÑA

As celebration of the powers of existence, yajña is deeply rooted in primordial human experience. When a person is able to go beyond the objects of ordinary experience and enter directly into the experiencing activity itself—an activity that unifies subject and object rather than separates them—then it becomes possible to glimpse and feel the wondrous powers that create human existence-in-the-world. Here the creative powers are experienced in the context of an awareness of the beauty and joy—indeed, the blessedness—of the life that comes as a wonderful gift, totally unearned. Although it might be said that such experience is worthy of celebration, the truth is that such experience is, *in itself*, celebration. To live in this awareness is the ultimate celebration of life.

But this rejoicing in the gift of existence in all its richness and mystery is a celebrative act that simultaneously reveals profound limitations of ordinary human existence. Experienced by a self separated from the ground of its own being, human agency is incapable of creating existence; human wisdom cannot plumb its mysteries; human goodness cannot create the community required for individual existence; and human speech can neither grasp nor express the profundity of this existence. Fortunately, the experienced fullness and power of existence furnishes a ground and energy for the human attempt to burst the bonds of the simultaneously experienced finitude of existence.

Yajña can be seen as the response to this primordial human experience of the profound depths and fullness and the simultaneous recognition of the limitations of existence. Responding to the experienced power and joy it is celebrative; responding to the felt need to transcend finitude it is sacrificial; but it is never one to the exclusion of the other. In the experienced limitations of human existence is the discovery that human beings are different; that we are distinct from other features of reality and not identical with the power of existence itself. Becoming aware of ourselves coming into being, we sense a loss of the fullness of the ground from which we have emerged. It is this sense of separation from the origins of our being that underlies the urge to return to the source, to become whole again, that seeks, through the celebrative rituals, to create relationships and communion with the Gods, the higher powers of existence.

## BECOMING WHOLE

Participating in yajña is a way of returning to the source, of making whole what has been ruptured. As such it joins together the reality of the Gods, the cosmos, and human existence into a relationship resembling the original unity of being. This returning to the ground of becoming recovers the fullness of human existence by sharing in the powers of existence manifested in the cosmic and divine realms. Thus, yajña is a returning of existence to the original source, and through this returning there is a renewing and recreating of the energies of existence and an experienced fullness of being; yajña is a rejoicing in the communion of human with divine and natural existence and the creating of a new existence out of this communion. Through this sacrificial celebration a new relationship of communion is established, allowing the divine power that flows through nature, humankind, and the Gods to unite these three expressions of existence. Achieving this communion and this power of existence is regarded by the Vedic seers as the necessary condition of maintaining and renewing life.

The Śatapatha Brāhmaṇa is emphatic about the necessity of yajña for existence: "Creatures who are not allowed to take part in yajña are reduced to nothingness." The author goes on to explain that for this reason the human yajña should be extended to all beings: "Therefore the celebrant admits all those not annihilated into the yajña—humans and beasts, Gods and birds, trees and plants, and everything that exists. Thus, the entire universe takes part in sacrificial celebration [yajña]." The author then proceeds to explain that originally this was a shared communion feast, through which existence was created and renewed, and points out that this is still the case, even though Gods and ancestors are not visible these days as they were long ago.

Drawing together the different aspects of yajña that we have been examining, we can say that it is simultaneously (1) the celebration of the achieved powers of existence, (2) the renewal of existence by returning to the ground of becoming, and (3) the creation of new existence out of the offering of the fullness of present existence. Clearly, yajña is not merely a matter of making sacrificial offerings to the Gods in exchange for their benefits and blessings. Rather, it is the participatory act through which human beings create and maintain their existence in the world.

No wonder that the great seer Dīrghatamas says that "yajña is the center of the world," for the world turns on yajña just as the wheel of the cart turns on its axle. The seer's increasing insight into the fundamental processes of existence recognized a pattern of creating and energizing of existence through celebrative participation and offering. This pattern is the prototypical yajña, a pattern that when symbolically re-created through the rituals of sacrificial celebration would allow human beings to renew and recreate their own existence through participation in the primordial yajña creative of this entire existence.

Everything that exists has its origins in yajña. In the imagery of 10.130, the creation of the universe is likened to the making of cloth. The rituals are the threads, the chants are the shuttles, and the celebrants are the weavers. Yajña is the loom on which the fabric of the universe is woven. Another text likens yajña to a tree, the top of which reaches the highest heavens, the middle of which fills the atmosphere, and the roots of which are the foundations of the earth, thereby bringing together the three worlds in the creative act of sacrificial celebration (Śatapatha Brāhmaṇa, 3.7.1.4).

In an early Ṛg Vedic text (1.91.20) we find a list of especially prized things that are said to come from making the offering: a milk cow; a fast horse; and a son fit for home, work, the assembly, and the council—a son who is a glory to his father. In another early verse, the seer declares that immortality is achieved through the power of yajña:

> By the power of Yajña, rooted in the highest heaven,
> Established in the cosmic rhythm [ṛta] by the Divine Norm [ṛta]
> Our mortal ancestors achieved immortal seats
> In those higher spheres which firmly support the heavens.
> (5.15.2)

A fairly late Śatapatha Brāhmaṇa text describes Brahmā, the creative urge of the universe as saying, "Come let me offer myself in living things, and all living things in myself. Then, having offered himself in all living things and all living things in himself, he acquired greatness, self-radiance, and sovereignty" (13.7.1.1.1). What a wonderful way of saying that yajña is the way of renewing existence through contact with the fundamental source of existence! Not only things, but the creative urge of existence itself, comes from yajña.

## Sacrificial Celebration of the Cosmic Person

Although the Hymn to the Cosmic Person (10.90) is suspected of being a relatively late addition to the Ṛg Veda, it summarizes a good deal of earlier thought and is extremely helpful to our attempt to understand the nature and function of sacrificial celebration.

This hymn, which refers to a primordial world-creating yajña, the symbolic prototype of the yajña that ordinary beings participate in, affirms that yajña is the supreme power; all of existence comes into being through this power. It also affirms the underlying unity of the human, cosmic, and divine realities, for all are seen as emerging out of the same original reality, a reality symbolized in this hymn by the cosmic Person. Humanness is rooted in the most basic level of reality, and through our participation in yajña we participate in the underlying unity of all existence, thereby renewing our link with the ultimate and with the elements of the cosmic world around us.

In this hymn, reality is conceived of as a gigantic person; everything that exists is part of this cosmic person. The greatness of this person is emphasized by noting that he has a thousand heads, eyes, and feet—a person, yes, but obviously a most extraordinary person. Indeed, the next line says that, although he envelops the whole world, he is greater than this earth, going beyond in all possible ways ("ten fingers beyond").

In seeing the universe as a person, the seers reveal that (1) they were concerned primarily with human becoming and with the relationship between cosmic and human becoming and (2) they regarded human existence as the most basic and profound mode of existence.

1. A thousand headed is the cosmic Person.
   With a thousand eyes and feet,
   Enveloping the earth on all sides,
   And going ten fingers beyond.
2. The cosmic Person, indeed, is everything,
   All that has been and all that will be;
   Lord of the immortal spheres,
   Transcending what is nourished by food.

The next two verses tell us that the wondrous powers and greatness of all this existence that we are able to experience do not exhaust this great Person; indeed, they constitute only a small part of his being. Three fourths of the Person transcends this ordinary world, whereas one fourth of him constitutes this entire existence.

3. Such is its greatness and power,
   And greater yet than this is the cosmic Person;
   All beings are only one-fourth of him,
   Three-fourths are immortal in heaven.
4. Three-fourths of the cosmic Person rose on high,
   One-fourth was born again here,
   Moving in all directions, into
   The living and non-living alike.

Here the seers are telling us emphatically that there are different levels of reality and that the empirical and manifest forms of existence are only the first level—superficial and shallow in comparison with the other levels ("immortal in heaven"). But these levels are not totally separated or divorced from each other; they have the continuity of the organic Person, of whom they are parts. The one fourth constituted by all of the manifest forms of existence on earth is truly a part of this great Person, even though not the greatest part.

The fifth verse is transitional, moving from the image of this great cosmic Person as the ground of all existence to the image of this Person as offering the fullness of his existence in the sacrificial celebration. Here the seers reveal their conviction that only through yajña can existence be created or renewed. Even the cosmic Person can only create this world out of himself through offering himself in the yajña.

> 5. From the cosmic Person was born Virāj—the shining one,
> And from Virāj was born the cosmic Person,
> Who from the moment of birth was extended
> Over the earth, both in front and behind.

As verses 6 and 7 reveal, the Gods, symbolizing the deeper powers of existence, perform the world-creating yajña using the Person as their offering. The seasons constitute the various elements, for this is a cosmic celebration in which all the elements participate. Sprinkling the juices of life on the sacred grass makes the Person's life-powers available to all the various potential forms of existence, giving them the energy needed to break the bonds of non-existence and emerge as actual structured existence.

> 6. With the cosmic Person as their offering
> The Gods performed the sacrificial celebration.
> Spring was taken as the clarified butter,
> Summer was the fuel and Autumn the oblation.
> 7. This sacrificial Person, the First-born,
> They sprinkled on the sacred grass.
> With him the Gods performed the sacrificial celebration,
> As did the Seers and the Heavenly Beings.

The seer does not want us to think that yajña was a world-making ritual that only occurred once, long ago—at the beginning of this cosmic existence. He points out that not only did the Gods participate in this wonderful yajña, but so did the heavenly beings and great human beings—the seers. By implication, all humans must participate in the yajña whereby existence and life are energized or else lose their humanness.

All forms of existence are grounded in, and originate from, the primordial sacrificial celebration. The eighth verse proclaims the origin of the insects and birds and the tame and wild animals in the life energy ("milk mixed with butter") created by the yajña:

> 8. From the sacrificial celebration, fully accomplished,
> Was gathered milk mixed with butter.
> From that came the winged creatures
> And the animals of the forest and village.

Signs and symbols of human consciousness are grounded in and energized by yajña just as surely as are other forms of existence.

Through yajña, human consciousness enters into the consciousness of the primordial reality, creating a structure of chants, songs, formulas, and actions whereby the energy of this reality becomes available for the renewal of existence. The ninth verse tells us that the songs, meters, and formulas of the yajña were themselves born from yajña. In other words, sacrificial celebration is the original energy of existence; there is nothing prior to it, and thus the origin of yajña cannot be anything other than yajña itself.

9. From that original sacrificial celebration
   Were born the chants and songs.
   From it were born the various meters and
   From it were born the formulas of sacrificial celebration.

The seer assures us, in verse 9, that the yajñas in which people participate today are symbolically identical to that original yajña of the cosmic Person and employ the same rituals.

Verses 11–14 present us with a number of correspondences between the cosmic Person and human society and between the Person and the natural world. These correspondences establish the interconnectedness of the social classes, features of the natural world, and even the Gods. Both the order and relationships within these spheres are seen as established in the originating source of all existence—the primordial Person. These verses reveal a strong feeling for the unity of all existence.

11. When they divided the cosmic Person,
    Into how many parts did they divide him?
    What did they call his mouth? What his arms?
    What did they call his legs? What his feet?
12. His mouth was the priestly class,
    His arms the warrior-princes.
    His legs were the producers,
    His feet the servant class.
13. From his mind was born the moon,
    From his eye was born the sun.
    Indra and Agni came from his mouth,
    And the wind was born of his breath.
14. From his navel came the atmosphere,
    The sky came from his head.
    From his feet came earth, from ears the four directions.
    Thus they formed the worlds.

Verse 15 is concerned with the internal structure of the yajña. The structure of the ritual is "enclosed" or framed by the sounds of seven musical notes. If we interpret the seven sticks of the enclosure to be the sounds of the seven musical notes and the "thrice seven pieces of firewood" to be different arrangements of the seven-note musical scale, the fifteenth verse can be seen as revealing the symbolic significance of musical sounds for the creative activity of yajña.

15. Seven were the sticks of the enclosure,
Thrice seven the pieces of firewood,
When the Gods, celebrating the sacrifice,
Bound the cosmic Person as the offering.

The sixteenth and final verse emphasizes that since yajña is the primordial energy ground of all existence there can be nothing prior to it. The Gods, representing the ultimate powers of existence, offer yajña itself to yajña, for originally there is nothing other than yajña. Sacrificial celebration is the ground and energy of all existence.

16. With sacrificial celebration the Gods offered to sacrificial celebration;
These were the original holy rituals.
These powers reach up to heaven,
Where dwell the Gods of old and Heavenly Beings.

## Intentionality of Yajña

Sacrificial celebration is by no means a kind of blind and mechanical ritual action. On the contrary, it is simultaneously both a knowing and an acting that is capable of sustaining, transforming, and creating human existence through joining the deepest modes of personal life with the primordial energy and ground of existence itself. It is a form of knowing that unites the heart and the mind, that informs the intelligence of human beings through the powers of feeling, willing, and acting. Knowing and acting are not separated for the Vedic people. The Vedic urgency is that we must act to know and know to act and that without knowing-acting there is no way to keep ourselves or our world going. The knowing-acting symbolized by yajña is regarded as necessary for life and world.

Sacrificial celebration is the Vedic acting-knowing par excellence, for it reaches from the Gods to humans, channeling life and energy from the primordial sources of existence to the manifest forms found in this ordinary world. Without the bonds created by yajña, this energizing power of existence would be unavailable to us and our world, and we would be swallowed up by Vṛtra, the dragon of non-existence. The bond is established by offering the manifested, actualized forms of existence so they can be re-established in the next moment through the primordial energy in which existence is grounded. The old—the culmination of all that has existed to this point—must be sacrificed, that is, returned to the source for renewal. But this returning is at the same time the beginning of a new existence that is established or created on the basis of the offering. The celebrative dimension of yajña is rooted in this new existence, for it expresses the energy and joy of existence.

Human intentionality is the key to effective sacrificial celebration. The first point to note is so obvious that it is easily overlooked; yajña is impossible without the hymns. But the hymns represent the human creative act; they are a celebration and offering of human consciousness and intentionality. Indeed, the yajña hymns can be seen as an intentional creation of existence, reaching into the fundamental recesses of the primordial energies of existence through the instrumentalities of liturgical knowing-acting. It is similar to the intentional creation of existence that we engage in when we reach out into the world through our knowledge and action, creating and maintaining ourselves in this environment of knowing-acting through play, study, teaching, or meditation on a Vedic verse.

Although our biological existence may continue without this continual self-offering, our uniquely human life cannot. When we play tennis, for example, we must give the best we have; to hold back and fail to offer the best and fullest expression of our tennis-playing existence is to surrender that existence and allow it to die. On the other hand, to offer our best—to play with all our energies and resources—not only effectively celebrates these powers and abilities (and every athlete knows the joy of "having given my best"), but this offering of the best and fullest of existence is experienced as an effective way of renewing and increasing these powers and abilities.

For humans to hold back the fullness of existence is to lose their existence, to die just as surely as one dies when eaten slowly by cancerous growth in the body. On the other hand, to offer and celebrate the fullness of our existence in each moment is at the same time to create our existence in the next moment. Only to the extent that we give of ourselves to others in love, for example, do we grow in love. When we hold ourselves back, love dies. And without love, we die in our unique humanness.

## SPEECH-CONSCIOUSNESS

To appreciate the intentionality of yajña, we must explore the nature and status of speech and the consciousness in which it is grounded. *Vāc* is the Vedic word for speech that refers both to speech sounds and to the consciousness in which speech sounds are grounded. Not simply speech as we would ordinarily think of it, vāc goes beyond mere words to the consciousness that makes possible speaking and hearing, designating the underlying speech-consciousness. This speech-consciousness makes possible discovery and revelation, for it is through speech that consciousness uncovers and reveals reality. Because of this profound and wonderful power, speech-consciousness is elevated to the status of a deity, symbolized by the great Goddess Vāc.

Vāc has two distinct but inseparable dimensions. First, it is the luminosity or consciousness that constitutes the inner being of all that exists, providing the power through which the non-existent is transformed into existence. Second, as speech, it is heard and uttered, creating the reality of sounds and shapes that are taken to be the events and objects making up the world around us.

All existence is grounded in vāc as the underlying consciousness. The hymns constitute a passage to this underlying consciousness, thereby empowering the yajña as an effective instrument for ritual participation in the fundamental creative movements of existence.

The seers were aware of their own self-world's constantly changing, aware of continuously coming into existence and passing out of existence. This awareness reveals, indirectly, a ground out of which self and world emerge, as they come into existence, and into which they return as they pass out of existence. Furthermore, this existence-awareness is experienced as contingent and vulnerable. Nothing guarantees the continuity of existence; experience reveals only a coming and going, a continuously changing self-world. Only the activities of consciousness prevent the experienced self-world from returning to the darkness of non-existence.

As it became clearer to the seers that, indeed, it is human activity that keeps the self-world in existence and that within human activity it is particularly the activities of speech-consciousness that bring about continued existence of the self-world, they came to emphasize the powers of consciousness expressed in speech sounds. The most powerful—and beautiful—speech sounds are those of the seer-poets who create new self-worlds through their intentional use of symbols and sounds. This power is regarded as a power that is shared with the Gods, and thus the hymns when recited, chanted, and sung are ways to the Gods, ways of sharing with them in the divine powers of existence.

Speech, like consciousness, its source, participates in both the physical and spiritual realms. Indeed, in its mode as prayer, which is the most fundamental mode of speech-consciousness, it functions to mediate between body and spirit, thereby returning them to their original unity.

Dīrghatamas inquires into the origins of speech consciousness with the question, "What is the highest heaven of speech [vāc]?" In the next verse he identifies prayer as the origin, saying "Prayer is the highest heaven in which speech [vāc] dwells" (1.164.35). He is here acknowledging that consciousness originates in the communion of the various powers of the universe, for in the Ṛg Veda the primary function of prayer is to establish communion and community. This clue helps us to see that the wondrous power of speech-consciousness lies in its ability to unite us with other persons and other realities, to reach into the interior structure of reality renewing the vitality of our existence through this communion. It is through speech-consciousness that we can reach into our own heart, the hearts of other persons, and the heart of reality.

It appears that in Vedic times speech was regarded as the voice of consciousness, not to be separated sharply from the consciousness in which it is grounded. It also appears that the importance of speech-consciousness is due to a recognized parallel between how things come into awareness in human consciousness and how things come into existence. The world is present only insofar as it is known. Its becoming present to us or coming into being in our awareness is made possible by consciousness. But just as the world comes into being in our knowledge through consciousness, so does the world come into its own being through some kind of primordial intelligence or consciousness. It is possible to know the world through consciousness because the world has its origin in—is grounded in—consciousness. As Dīrghatamas says, "From her [Vāc] flow the oceans; through her exist the four regions [of space]; from her flows the ground [*akṣara*] of the Veda; on her the entire universe stands" (1.164.42).

But three verses later, he reminds us that only the manifested forms of speech-consciousness are known by ordinary persons; the deepest levels are hidden from all but the wise and immortal seers: "Vāc was divided into four parts. The wise (and immortal) brāhmaṇas know them all. The three parts which are hidden are not attained by ordinary mortals; they speak only the fourth part." Clearly, although existence is knowable because it is grounded in consciousness, this is no ordinary consciousness, and it cannot be known through ordinary consciousness. Somehow or other, the deepest levels of consciousness must be plumbed in order to share in the primordial consciousness in which all existence is grounded.

Human participation in this primordial consciousness reveals that the various forms of existence are all rooted in this same consciousness. Speech-consciousness, in its deepest aspects, is therefore identified with the source and center of existence itself. The hymn to the Devī—the Goddess of Speech-Consciousness—in which speech-consciousness is allowed to speak for herself illustrates this view in a revealing and charming way.

## DEVĪ SŪKTA

(Hymn to the Goddess of Consciousness and Speech)

1. I move with the Rudras and Vasus,
   the Ādityas and all the Gods.
   I support Mitra and Varuṇa,
   Indra, Agni and the two Aśvins.
2. I support the growing Soma,
   Also Tvaṣṭṛ, Puṣan and Bhaga.
   I shower gifts on the faithful patron of the sacrifices,
   Who offers oblation and presses Soma.
3. I am the ruling queen, the gatherer of treasures,
   Full of wisdom, foremost of those worthy of sacrifice.
   To all places have the Gods distributed me;
   I enter many homes and take numerous forms.

4. The person who sees, who breathes, who hears words spoken,
He obtains his nourishment from me alone.
Even though they do not recognize me, yet they dwell in me.
Listen, you who know! I speak in truth.
5. It is I who utters the word that brings joy to Gods and humans.
To the person I favor I give my power;
I make him a God,
A perfect sacrificer, a Seer.
6. It is I who draw the mighty bow of Rudra,
That an arrow may pierce the enemy of wisdom.
Among the people, I arouse the fury of battle,
I have pierced both Heaven and Earth.
7. At the summit of the world, I give birth to the Father.
My origin is in the Waters, in the deep ocean.
From there I spread through all existing worlds,
And with my forehead, touch the heaven above.
8. I breathe powerfully, like the wind,
While holding all the worlds.
So mighty and splendid is my power,
I go beyond the heavens and beyond the earth.

(10.125)

As personified speech-consciousness speaks, she reveals that she moves with the Gods, empowering them and supporting them. The wondrous and mysterious powers of existence, personified as deities, are grounded in, and supported by, speech-consciousness. Describing herself as the "queen of existence" and "full of wisdom and treasures," she notes that she is present everywhere. "Entering many homes and taking many forms" may be taken to say that consciousness resides in all things, taking the form of the different things in which it resides.

The fourth verse explicitly affirms that human existence is grounded in primordial speech-consciousness. It is the energy of this primordial consciousness that supports and nourishes human life. The remaining verses make clear that this consciousness is not limited or restricted to humans. All things, powers, and actions are grounded in this primordial consciousness. Prior even to the father of the universe, this primordial speech-consciousness energy is the original energy-stuff out of which all existence originates and in which it is all grounded. But this primordial energy of speech-consciousness is not limited to existing things, for as the Goddess says, "I go beyond the heavens and the earth."

Granted this vision of the fundamental nature and power of speech-consciousness, it is not surprising that the Vedic seers should think that they could create a passage to these primordial and ultimate depths of existence. Liturgical speech and actions, though expressed through human consciousness, ultimately are grounded in the primordial consciousness in which all existence shares.

It is important for us to recognize that, within this Vedic vision, things and processes have a natural luminosity. They are not dark and dumb, waiting to be lit up by human intelligence through the knowing processes. Rather, all existence is grounded in primordial consciousness and naturally illuminated, just as our own human existence is naturally illuminated by consciousness. As so much later Indian thought stresses, the task of knowing is to uncover this inherent luminosity of existence. Truth is inherent in existence; knowing is merely a matter of removing our own blinders, of allowing this truth and luminosity to shine through our own consciousness.

Knowing as an uncovering of the inherent consciousness and luminous nature of things requires an uncovering of the consciousness and luminous nature of our own existence as a necessary first condition. This uncovering is a matter of acting-feeling-willing-knowing that involves every aspect of human existence. Yajña represents an instrumentality of this kind of total "knowing" whereby every feature and power of existence is engaged in the liturgical act. Through the liturgical knowing-acting of sacrificial celebration, the limitations of ordinary existence are revealed and the grounding of human existence in those more fundamental powers of existence wherein all things are grounded is experienced. As the texts say, yajña enables humans to enter into the realms of the Gods.

Although human existence is grounded in the same primordial consciousness-existence in which all things are rooted, experiencing this ground does not transform us into beings other than human. We remain human, although now our humanness is recognized as the wonderful thing that it really is, and through this experience we are able to live more completely and fully. As the celebrant says, upon completion of the ritual action, "O Agni, I have made my vow, I have made good my vow, I become a man again . . . I descend again from the world of the Gods into the worlds of humans" (Śatapatha Brāhmaṇa, 1.1.1.4–7).

## Ṛta, Fundamental Norm of Existence

We have seen how yajña constitutes the primary effective means for sustaining and renewing human existence by opening it to the deeper powers in which all existence is grounded, establishing thereby a communion with nature and the Gods. The question to be raised at this point is, What makes yajña work? How can this ritual unlock the deeper creative energies required for maintaining and renewing manifest existence?

The answer is that yajña works because of ṛta. Yajña is the ritual correspondence to ṛta, the original rhythm of existence by which the manifest world emerges from the primordial ground of existence and is established in orderliness.

There is no exact English equivalent for ṛta; it combines aspects of our ideas of rhythm, norm, order, energy, and the well formed. It is regarded as guiding all forms of existence, giving them energy and existence. According to the Ṛg Veda, the rhythm of day and night, the succession of the seasons, and the cycles of birth, growth, decay, and regeneration proceed from ṛta. By it rains fall, winds blow, plants grow, and animals reproduce. From her ("the lovely Ṛta"), as the dynamic principle of all movement and change, flow the various rhythms of existence. It is ṛta that directs the emergence, dissolution, and re-emergence of existence at the cosmic level and that gives to each thing and event its own structure and nature. Ṛta is both the basic ordering principle of the universe and the ground of whatever is well ordered. Without it there would be only chaos instead of existence. Or, from a social perspective, there would be immorality and disorder instead of human community.

Ṛta is regarded as fully present and operative at the deepest levels of reality, but only partially present and operative at the shallower and manifest levels. As indicated in the hymns to the cosmic Person and to the Goddess of Speech-Consciousness, reality is seen as divided into different portions or levels. The deepest level, the three fourths, is hidden or unmanifested. The manifested level, the portion that can be experienced and described in ordinary ways, is only a small fraction—one fourth—of reality. This vision of a dual reality permeates the Vedic view of existence. "This world" (*aihika*) is frequently contrasted with "that world" (*āmuṣmika*), with the latter regarded as the source and the deeper reality of the former. Things and events in this ordinary empirical world exist and function only to the extent that they embody ṛta. And precisely to that extent do they possess reality or being (sat). What belongs to "this world" embodies ṛta only partially; "that world" possesses it fully. Ultimately, ṛta provides the basis for the being and function of all existence, and this world can continue to exist only to the extent that it is supported by ṛta, which functions *fully* only at the deeper level of unmanifested reality.

It should not be thought that "this world" and "that world" are two different realities. They are simply different levels of the same reality, just as waves and foam on the surface of the water are part of the same reality that is the deeper, underlying stillness. To use an analogy from later Indian thought, it is like the oceans and lakes that through evaporation provide the moisture needed for the rains to fall. The oceans, lakes, and streams are not the same as the rain, yet they are not different; and without them as a source, the rains would not fall. Similarly, this ordinary manifest existence is rooted in that deeper unmanifested existence through the functioning of ṛta.

Yajña is the ritual correspondent to ṛta, the fundamental norm of existence. It provides a way for humans to open their ordinary, manifested existence to the deeper powers of the unmanifested ultimate reality, thereby transforming ordinary existence into something profound and extraordinary. This explains why sacrificial celebration constitutes the central Vedic mode of knowing-acting and why the Vedic seers were so preoccupied with finding correspondences between this ordinary world and that extraordinary world of sacred reality. Each correspondence found added to the ritual power to penetrate and embody more fully the fundamental norm of existence. It also explains why the Gods were not ultimately important, for it is the acting-knowing of the ritual that achieves the correspondence to ṛta, thereby tapping its energy and order. The Gods merely symbolize that deeper energy and order; they do not create or control it. Thus, it is not surprising that, as the seers sought the most fundamental level of reality, they eventually went beyond the Gods, focusing on that Great-Making Power (Brahman) from which all other powers derive. This development, central to the Upaniṣads, will be explored in Chapter 5.

## Summary

The Vedic seers were convinced that beneath the obvious forms of existence, and beyond the logic of *is* and *is not*, lies an undivided wholeness that is the ultimate ground of the being and energy of life. The Hymn of Origins shows the seer seeking this ultimate reality, an unnamable THAT, beyond the grasp of logic and language. But as the ground and energy of existence, this unnamable, undivided wholeness holds the key to the creation and renewal of all existence. How can human beings make available to themselves the sacred power of this reality to maintain and renew their existence? This is the central question of the Vedic seers. Their answer, in a word, was, through yajña.

Yajña is simultaneously a celebration of the mysterious power and joy of existence and a sacrificial offering of the fullness of this existence to its original source for renewal. Penetrating the fundamental processes of existence, the seers recognized a pattern of creating and energizing of existence through celebrative participation in these processes. This whole universe was seen to result from the yajña of the primordial Person as He celebrated His existence and offered it to Himself for renewal.

The Hymn to the Cosmic Person reveals how the universe emerged from this primordial yajña, which is the prototype of the yajña that humans must also participate in to re-create and maintain their existence. Each person must also open his or her existence to the deeper powers in which it is grounded through the yajña of personal offering and celebration. This is the effective means of establishing communion with nature and the Gods, and of renewing one's life from moment to moment.

The effectiveness of yajña is seen to follow from the fact that it participates in ṛta, the original rhythm of existence by which the manifest world emerges from the primordial ground of existence and is established in its orderliness. Because yajña is the ritual correspondent to ṛta, it provides a way for humans to participate in the power and being of the ultimate reality, thereby sharing in their own continuous renewal.

## Suggestions for Further Reading

*The Vedic Experience: Mantramañjarī,* by Raimundo Panikkar (Los Angeles: University of California Press, 1977), is a wonderful collection of teachings from the Vedas, Brāhmaṇas, and Upaniṣads. The introductions preceding the translations in each section give the reader a sense of the life and vigor of the Vedic experience. No other anthology comes close to matching choice of material, quality of translation, and helpfulness of commentaries found in this treasury of Vedic thought.

*Meditations Through the Ṛg Veda,* by Antonio T. de Nicolas (Stony Brook, N.Y.: Nicolas Hays, 1976), explores the intentional life of the Vedic seers. Although not always agreeing with de Nicolas, I found this book helpful and rewarding and have been influenced by it—perhaps more than I realize. The chief merit of this rather sophisticated work is that it forces the reader to confront himself or herself through the Vedic visions.

*Hymns of the Ṛg Veda,* trans. Ralph T. H. Griffith and ed. J. L. Shastri, new rev. ed. (Delhi: Motilal Banarsidass, 1973), is the only readily available English translation of the entire Ṛg Veda. The translation is sometimes inaccurate and the language frequently archaic, but it contains every verse.

*Poetry and Speculation of the Ṛg Veda,* by Willard Johnson (Berkeley: University of California Press, 1980), explores Vedic consciousness through an analysis of the function of enigmatic riddles within Ṛg Vedic poetry. A very provocative little book, especially for anyone interested in the philosophical dimensions of poetry.

# 4

# Self and Society: Norms of Life

A major change in values and attitudes occurred in Indian society between the time that the Ṛg Veda was compiled (1200 B.C.?) and the time that the classical treatises on law and society were formulated (400 B.C.?). The chief agent of this change was the idea of re-death and the emerging preoccupation with discovering and practicing ways of stopping the unending round of births and deaths that afflicted every person. In this chapter we will examine the Vedic values and follow the changes in the conception of the "good life" that led to the classical attitudes and values of Indian society. The following questions are particularly important: What were the fundamental aims in life? What determined the rightness of actions? How was society organized? What was the ideal organization of life for the individual? What place did religious ritual and sacramental activity hold? What sort of political rule dominated?

## Vedic Values

In the previous chapter we saw how the rituals of sacrificial celebration dominated Vedic life. Existence itself was seen as dependent upon yajña, and therefore nothing was more valuable or sacred than the holy rituals. But the Vedic people were extremely practical and did not view existence in the abstract. The petitions to the Gods and the prayers accompanying the ritual offerings show clearly that existence was viewed in terms of its concrete, detailed components. What was requested and sought through the prayers and offerings were health, longevity, fame, wealth, strength, courage in battle, intelligence, virtue, persuasive speech, love-filled homes, good harvests, and increase in herds, along with obedient and exemplary children who would bring honor to the family.

Although the Vedic people were deeply religious, regarding both domestic rituals and the public rituals of sacrificial celebrations as necessary for the renewal of life and the achievement of their aims in life, their concerns were very much this-worldly. Their attitude toward life was positive; life is to be lived to the fullest and joyously celebrated with festive music and dancing. Wealth and enjoyment are to be pursued wholeheartedly—although always in accord with the demands of morality.

It is important to note that immortality or release from the body were not sought. Instead we find a petition asking, "May we live for a hundred years!" (Ṛg Veda, 7.66.16). Although it was commonly assumed that upon death the departing person will journey on to a heavenly reward, there was little speculation about or emphasis on the afterlife. The Vedic people did not divide life into opposing material and spiritual modes. Every aspect of life was sacred, and so long as activities were governed by moral norms, they were legitimate, whether aiming at securing wealth, sexual enjoyment, or honoring the Gods. The later attitude that devalued the body and this world in favor of a spiritual self and a spiritual world is entirely absent in the Ṛg Veda.

Nor are monasticism or asceticism praised as superior ways of life. Participation in social life and public affairs was expected of everyone; parents prayed for a child who would become a leader of the assembly. The individual and society were not seen as opposed to each other. The family, in which the individual and social dimensions of existence are integrated, was regarded as the fundamental unit of human existence. Community was highly valued among the Vedic people, and the mutual interdependence of all beings was seen as a basis for sharing life's blessings with others. Offering ritual food to the departed ancestors, the Gods, spirits, and animals was common practice, and eating without sharing was condemned as sinful. The very last verse of the Ṛg Veda is a beautiful expression of the aim of human community:

> Let your aims be one and the same;
> Let your hearts be joined together.
> May your minds be in accord, and
> At peace with all, so may you be.
> (10.191.4)

Vedic morality was rooted in ṛta, the norm that regulates all existence. Living in accord with this norm was recognized as the way to a full and prosperous life: "Sweetly blows the breeze for one who lives according to ṛta; rivers flow with sweetness for him" (Ṛg Veda, 1.90.6). Those actions in accord with ṛta are right; those opposed are wrong. The question of how to determine whether a given action was in accord with ṛta had a ready answer. Elders in the family, priests, kings and ministers, and village assemblies—all relying heavily on tradition—could provide the necessary interpretations of the requirements of ṛta. In addition, since ṛta was conceived as providing the basis for the fullness and harmony of existence, peace and harmony in family and social life were important indicators of ṛta.

Upholding and maintaining ṛta is not always easy; sometimes it requires effort. Evil must be resisted, and evil-doers punished. Āryan warriors were referred to as protectors of ṛta, suggesting that fighting for the sake of justice and righteousness was accepted practice. The model is Indra, upholding ṛta by fighting and destroying its enemy, the terrible Vṛtra who is holding all existence in bondage.

By following ṛta one becomes established in *satya*, or true existence, achieving a fuller and more harmonious existence, deeply in tune with the fundamental energies and rhythms of existence. Being in accord with the fundamental movements of existence is a cardinal Vedic virtue. The Yajur Veda says, "Through dedication one obtains consecration; by consecration is obtained grace. By grace one acquires faith, and by faith one attains true existence [satya]" (19.30).

Turning from basic religious and moral values to questions of social organization, it appears that the village was the primary unit of society and that a large number of villages were ruled over by a king. A threefold classification of society into priests (*brāhmaṇas*), rulers and guardians (*kṣatriyas*), and producers and traders (*vaiśyas*, "people") appears to have been in effect already in early Vedic society, although there is no evidence that these classes were closed at this time. Late in the Vedic period a fourth class, the *śūdra*, or servant, class, was also recognized, as evidenced by the Hymn to the cosmic Person, where the feet of the Person are regarded as the symbolic origin of the servant class. Perhaps with the increasing dominance of the Āryan peoples and the absorption of other groups into Āryan society, the divisions between classes, especially between śūdras and the other three classes, began to harden as a way of protecting the traditions and values of the Āryans.

## Classical Values

By the time of the first Upaniṣads (700 B.C.?), the earlier Vedic optimism and affirmation of life had given way to a preoccupation with suffering and bondage. There was a growing tendency to devalue the bodily self and material world in favor of a spiritual self and a spiritual world. Wealth, enjoyment, and morality continued to be important aims in life, but they were now subordinated to the aim of *mokṣa*—liberation or freedom from the bondage of matter, body, and mind. Knowledge, as a form of spiritual realization, was now regarded as the key to the ultimate good—mokṣa. Ritual was still praised as important but was clearly subordinated to knowledge. The knowledge sought was that by which the reality that never dies and is never born can be realized, for only thereby can *saṁsāra*—the cycle of repeated births and deaths that subjects the individual not merely to one death but to innumerable deaths—be stopped.

The idea of saṁsāra appears to be the result of a natural progression of thought. Birth here, in this world, is followed by death, which is followed by re-birth in another, heavenly, world. But if birth here is followed by death here, will not birth there also be followed by death there? And will not that be followed by yet another birth and another death in another place? Notice that it is not the prospect of re-birth that is troublesome, but the likelihood of re-death. Indeed, it was this prospect of bondage to repeated dying that drove the sages and seers to seek a way out of the cycle. Since everything tangible and material is subject to death and destruction, it was logical to seek a solution to the problem of re-death in an intangible or spiritual reality, with which the true self could be identified, thus making it immune to the ravages of repeated births and deaths.

This kind of thinking led to a preoccupation with spiritual existence and, since ritual utilized physical actions and material goods, to a de-emphasis of religious ritual in favor of knowledge as a way to spiritual realization. It also led to the development of individual and social norms that would be effective in securing not only the principal moral and social values, but that would also facilitate the spiritual aim of mokṣa.

The story of the search for a reality and self immune from repeated deaths and births will be told in the next chapter when we examine the Upaniṣads. Here we wish to outline the main ideas and values that have determined the course of Indian society and directed the moral and social life of the individual since approximately the sixth century B.C.

Indian society was never static, of course. It was constantly changing, with new ideas, values, and practices emerging and old ones undergoing modification. But the majority of these changes occurred within a generally accepted framework that has persisted through the centuries. It is possible, therefore, to present the ideas and values that have provided the underlying framework that has endured for nearly twenty-five hundred years without denying the historical fact of continuous changes occurring within this framework. The ideas of *saṁsāra* and *karma*, the aims of *dharma* and *mokṣa*, the organization of society into classes (*varṇa* and *jāti*), and the ideal organizatin of life into four distinct stages (*āśrama*) have contributed much to the enduring Indian way of life. It is within this framework that ritual action, faith and devotion, yoga, asceticism, morality, and knowledge have provided the primary ways of coping with the human situation and seeking liberation over the last twenty-five centuries or more.

## KARMA

Karma, the principle according to which a person's future life is determined by present actions, underlies and energizes Indian morality and the quest for liberation. Karma is literally "action." But as a principle of the interconnectedness of actions and events, it goes deeper, ensuring that every action, physical, mental or moral, good or bad, large scale or imperceptible—no matter how subtle—will have its effect. Nothing other than the effects of previous actions has determined the present state of affairs, and nothing other than present actions will determine the future state of affairs. There is no room for chance or divine intervention; everything is inexorably determined by the law of karma. In the realm of human action karma constitutes a moral law of cause and effect. As the Bṛhardāraṇyaka Upaniṣad says, "By good actions one becomes good; by bad actions one becomes bad" (4.4.5).

As a principle of moral determinism, karma says, "what you sow, that will you reap." But karma is almost universally interpreted also as a principle of freedom, for although conditioned by previous actions, a human being is free to act now in such a way as to determine his or her life in the future. Only two, relatively minor, schools of thought—the Ājīvikas and the Cārvākans—interpreted karma in a completely fatalistic way. They concluded that one's whole life is predetermined and that nothing one might attempt to do could make the least difference in what happened in life. All the other Indian schools of thought recognized the possibility of influencing the course of one's life by the deliberate choice of actions and thoughts (knowledge).

There is, of course, a paradox here, as any thinker who has struggled with the issues of freedom and determinism knows well. Freedom is not meaningful unless the actions a person freely undertakes have the power to determine future events. If following a diet and exercise plan are powerless to determine my future state of health, there is no point in doing so and it is meaningless to talk of freedom to act. On the other hand, if the determinism accepted as a necessary basis for freedom is total, it is difficult to see where choice and freedom enter in at all. Most Indian thinkers have concluded that, although human existence is conditioned and determined by circumstances, situations, and past actions, this conditioning is not total. Choice itself can interject a new determining force into a situation, thus giving human beings a degree of control over, and responsibility for, their own lives.

It should be kept in mind, therefore, that, although most Indians accepted that their birth was determined by events of a previous lifetime, this did not prevent them from also accepting that they could, through their own volition and effort, influence and affect the course of this life as well as the conditions of birth in the next life. Thus, except for Ājīvikas and Cārvākans, everyone agreed that good conduct and right knowledge were effective in transforming one's condition from bondage to a liberated state.

Since it is karma that binds one to the cycle of repeated births and deaths, to achieve liberation a way must be found that will not accumulate any further karmic forces and that will "burn up" all karmic forces already accumulated. The Jaina, Buddhist, and Hindu ways all agree that bondage to saṁsāra can be broken only by a way of life that accumulates no further karmic forces. They also agree that only nongrasping and nonattached modes of actions are immune from the law of karma and therefore advocate nonattachment and nongrasping as the principal means of liberation. They disagree, of course, on how to achieve nongrasping and nonattachment, differing on the relative importance of conduct, knowledge, and faith.

The universal acceptance of karma and the overriding concern to break the bondage of saṁsāra meant that the norms guiding social structure and individual behavior would need to serve a dual purpose. In the first place they must provide for a coherent, well-ordered society and the fulfillment of the ordinary biological, psychological, and social needs of individuals. But, second, they must also provide for a way of transcending these needs and achieving liberation from the bondage they impose on the spirit. This dual demand shows up clearly in each of the three sets of basic norms guiding social organization and human action: *puruṣārthas, varṇas,* and *āśramas.*

## SOCIAL IDEALS

The idea of *puruṣārtha* or basic human aims informs a person of what may legitimately be pursued in life and establishes priorities regarding different aims. The first three puruṣārthas direct a person's energies to (1) moral rightness (*dharma*), (2) the various goods of life (*artha,* money, fame, power, etc.), and (3) enjoyment (*kāma*)—the three ordinary, universal, and legitimate aims in life. But the fourth aim, overriding the others, is that of *mokṣa*, or liberation. The effect of accepting mokṣa as the paramount aim is to allow the other aims as legitimate but to subordinate them to the requirements of spiritual liberation.

The idea of life stages (*āśrama*) is to devote specific portions of one's life to satisfying the various needs and aims that all humans share. The second stage, that of the householder, is common to every society. It is here that the various goods of life are accumulated and enjoyed (according to the requirements of morality, of course), making it the locus of the first three aims in life. The first stage, that of the student, is devoted to preparation not only for the householder stage but also for the two stages that follow—the forest-dweller and the stage of renunciation. The forest-dweller devotes his time and energy to the preparation and training required to spiritually outgrow the lower needs of body, mind, and society. In the fourth stage all attachments are renounced, as mokṣa becomes the sole preoccupation of life. The āśrama scheme clearly assumes the overriding importance of activities aimed at liberation, providing for over half a person's life to be devoted to this end.

Classification of persons into one of the four recognized classes according to the needs of society and the qualifications of the individual, does not necessarily assume the subordination of the other aims to that of mokṣa. But the prevailing social attitude regarding brāhmaṇas and saṁnyāsins (renounced ones) as superior to kings and ministers (kṣatriyas) clearly reveals the priority accorded the aim of liberation. This is seen also in the attitude that regards birth as a śūdra (worker) to be spiritually lower than birth as a vaiśya (producer), an attitude that is painfully obvious in the widespread idea that only brāhmaṇas, kṣatriyas, and vaiśyas are "twice born." This means that, since the śūdras are regarded as having been born biologically but not spiritually, they are denied many of the religious privileges and opportunities of the so-called upper three classes, on the grounds that they are spiritually unqualified and further removed from the possibility of liberation.

Since puruṣārtha, varṇa, and āśrama have provided Indian society with enduring rules of living, we will now examine each of these ideas in greater detail. Of course, in every society there is some discrepancy between what people think they ought to do and what they actually do. India is no exception, and the following discussion should not be mistaken for a description of historical social practice. The focus is on the basic normative ideas that have guided life in India, for ultimately it is these ideas—along with an understanding of the various material and social forces involved—that renders the historical practice intelligible.

## Human Aims

*Puruṣārtha* is literally "a person's aim." All people have four legitimate basic aims in life according to the classical Indian vision. The first three of these, morality, goods of life, and enjoyment, were recognized already in Vedic times. The fourth, liberation, was added to the earlier three values more than twenty-five hundred years ago. These four aims have constituted the basis for Indian values since the time of the Upaniṣads. They are discussed in the great texts on moral and social values (Dharma Śāstras), by Kauṭilya in his treatise on politics and power (Artha Śāstra), and in the Mahābhārata, the encyclopedic epic of India. Practically all the literature concerned with moral and social life accepts these four aims as the fundamental norms of life. Taken together, these aims define the good life, informing every person of what he or she may and may not aim at in life.

### DHARMA

Traditionally, *dharma* is the first of the aims to be explained, because it is more fundamental than artha and kāma and provides for their regulation. There is no satisfactory simple translation of dharma. In its broadest sense it is whatever is right to do. Foreigners called the people who lived in the land of the Indus River Hindus and called the major religion of these people Hinduism. But these people did not describe themselves as practicing Hinduism; they were simply following the eternal dharma. "Hinduism" is thus a synonym for the eternal dharma that every person must follow to live well and fully. Referring to specific requirements of life, dharma is used in more restricted ways to refer to religious ritual, to the obligations of justice and morality, and even to rules of personal hygiene and food preparation. Used in a legal sense, it refers to the laws and traditions governing society, informing every citizen of the rules governing social life. This is closely related to the moral sense, which prescribes the obligations of personal and social morality for the individual.

Dharma is usually classified according to the requirements of one's position in society and stage in life, for these represent the main factors of time, place and circumstance that determine one's own specific dharma. Thus, *varṇa dharma* refers to the duties attending one's class and social position, stipulating, for example, that studying, teaching, and officiating are the primary duties of a brāhmaṇa. *Āśrama dharma* refers to the duties attending one's particular stage in life. For example, the householder stage requires marriage, raising a family, producing the goods necessary for society according to one's profession, giving to those in need, and serving the social and political needs of the village and kingdom.

There is also a universal dharma that applies to a person regardless of social class or stage in life; just in virtue of being human everyone has certain requirements of action. For example, telling the truth, avoiding unnecessary injury to others, respecting the possessions of others, not cheating, and so on are common dharmas that all human beings share. The texts also refer to those dharmas that are determined by particular circumstances and therefore cannot be identified in advance. But the rule for determining the specific requirements of action in unusual or unpredictable situations is that the higher dharmas and values should always prevail. Noninjury and compassion are basic moral principles to be used in adjudicating cases of conflicting moral duties, and what is detrimental to spiritual progress should never be done.

Although dharma has these various senses, they all have a common element. The word "dharma" is derived from the verbal root *dhṛ*, which has the sense of "to support" or "to maintain." The various senses of dharma all refer to what must be done to maintain and support the individual, the family, social class, and the whole society. Since what must regularly be done constitutes a rule of action, the various dharmas are simply so many different rules of action—the rules that apply to a stage in life, to a social class, to being a king, to being a human being, and so on.

One of the reasons why it is difficult to find adequate English equivalents for dharma is that the thought and practice of Indian society differs considerably from that of Greco-European society. In the West, norms for human behavior have usually been conceived as rationally derived from human needs and aspirations. The Protagorean dictum that "man is the measure of all things" and the Aristotelian conviction that to be human is, above all else, to be rational have encouraged thinking of norms of action in terms of their rational design to facilitate human aims. In India, on the other hand, human existence is regarded as a manifestation and expression of a deeper reality that constitutes the ground and measure of human existence. The fundamental norm of the universe (ṛta) is the orderly coursing of this deeper reality in its central being. Moral and social rules are partial expressions of this highest norm and not autonomous conventions of human reason. Unlike the typical Western conception of the universe as a collection of three kinds of beings—divine, human, and natural (the last two created by the first)—India has tended to see all reality as one in being and function. The diversity found in the universe represents merely different expressions of the same underlying ultimate reality, which, in its deepest center, is hidden from ordinary experience and reason.

Within this unified conception of reality the various norms of life participate in the order of ultimate reality. The order of the deepest reality is the fundamental norm, and the norms for individual beings are given by their very being to the extent that they participate in the ultimate reality. This is extremely important for a correct understanding of dharma: the dharma of an individual is given by its very being through its participation in the central and ultimate reality of which it is a manifestation; it is not something added onto the being of the individual in order that certain aims might be achieved.

In the Vedic age, dominated by ritual action, yajña was seen as establishing connection with the ṛta of the higher unmanifest reality from which this world has evolved. The effects of yajña, called dharma (*yajña dharma*), maintained the order and function of this world. Indeed, yajña has continued to be seen as a way of supporting and maintaining the world right up to the present time. Throughout the ages doing one's dharma was seen as a kind of yajña, and yajña was seen as a dharma one must perform. But as yajña became only one way among many—rather the exclusive way—of maintaining existence, the ideas of dharma and karma gradually came to replace the concept of ṛta, and the word is used infrequently after the time of the early Upaniṣads.

But the underlying idea is continued, for karma refers to the total interconnectedness of events, and dharma refers to the normative dimensions of this interconnected reality. As noted, the law of karma guarantees the relatedness of all events in the world, but it does not provide for the regulation of events. The ordering or regulation of relations between events is accomplished by dharma. Just as in the Vedic view yajña regulated the various functions of the cosmos, so later, when attention was concentrated on social activities, dharma was viewed as the regulator of human relations. The term *dharma* does not come to mean something radically different; it merely is extended to refer to additional and detailed aspects of the world in a specifically social sense.

The vision of a deeper reality providing for the being and regulation of this ordinary world continues to dominate Indian thought, at least through the period during which the Dharma Śāstras and other works on social dharma were compiled. The fact that attention is focused more sharply on the individual and his or her relation to other individuals in this later period should not be allowed to obscure this fact, for, when attention shifts to the individual, that person comes to be seen as a microcosm of all reality.

Dharma is the expression of cosmic ṛta in human life, providing the identity of the individual reality with the higher reality. This is why the highest authority on dharma is generally recognized to be the person who knows the Veda and is established in dharma. This is, of course, a continuation of the Vedic recognition that the seers were able to see into the deeper reality that is the source of this world and discern there a truth or law governing all existence and sustaining the various levels of beings, providing for the deepest connections between things. This universal aspect of dharma is not lost when the concept takes on greater social significance, for all ordinary human dharma is only an aspect of the universal dharma and is justified not in itself, but only in the function of the universal dharma, the ṛta of the Ṛg Veda.

Doing one's dharma means functioning in accord with reality. Since there are various levels of reality, a distinction must be made between levels of dharma. The higher dharma means being in accord with the higher reality out of which the lower evolved. The lower dharma means being in accord with the lower manifested reality of ordinary experience. Mokṣa dharma, as the higher dharma, represents harmony with the higher distinctionless reality, which is not only the source but also the inner being of the individual. The lower dharmas represent a harmony of the various aspects of manifested reality (especially social aspects) with each other. But since all beings have their source and inner being in a higher distinctionless reality, there is no conflict between the social dharmas of varṇa and āśrama and the extra-social dharma of mokṣa.[1]

## ARTHA

The second aim in life, *artha*, refers to the various means or goods of life. Money, food, shelter, clothes, possessions, fame, and power are all forms of artha. Along with social recognition and influence, they are regarded as necessary to a full social existence. Kauṭilya's famous work

[1]See J. M. Koller, "Dharma: An Expression of Universal Order," *Philosophy East and West*, April 19, 1972, Vol. 22, no. 22, 131–144.

on artha represents the perspective of a king's minister. For a king, power and influence are the most important kinds of artha, and Kauṭilya's work is concerned with the various ways in which a king can get and maintain power. This shrewd advisor to the great Chandragupta Maurya, the Magadhan king who unified and ruled all of northern India from 324 to 301 B.C., was a master of realpolitik. He probably authored the core of the Artha Śāstra (although additions and revisions continued to be made for centuries afterwards). This text presents the same kind of pragmatic analysis of the strategies by which power is to be gotten, used and maintained that more than a thousand years later appears in *The Prince.* The general principle governing political power, acknowledged at the beginning of the Artha Śāstra, is that force is to be used only in accord with established moral rules; the development and use of political power is precisely to eliminate "the law of the fishes," where might determined right and where "the big ones eat the little ones."

For producers and merchants, money and property are the chief forms of artha. Although there is not a single text devoted exclusively to obtaining and maintaining wealth, this kind of wisdom has never been lacking in India. Although much of the rest of the world regards Indians as having deliberately chosen poverty as a way of life, this is historically not true. The Pañcatantra, a popular collection of wisdom in the form of fables and stories reflecting India's folk wisdom, puts it this way: "The smell of wealth [artha] is quite enough to wake a creature's sterner stuff. And wealth's enjoyment even more. Wealth gives constant vigour, confidence and power. Poverty is a curse worse than death. Virtue without wealth is of no consequence. The lack of money is the root of all evil.[2]

Since without wealth the priests have no support, the rituals cannot be performed, and society cannot be maintained, artha has been regarded as a requisite for dharma and has frequently been described as the basis for all the other aims in life. The Mahābhārata says, "What is here regarded as dharma depends entirely upon wealth [artha]. One who robs another of wealth robs him of his dharma as well. Poverty is a state of sinfulness. All kinds of meritorious acts flow from the possession of great wealth, as from wealth spring all religious acts, all pleasures and heaven itself. Wealth brings about accumulation of wealth, just as elephants capture elephants. Religious acts, pleasure, joy, courage, worth, and learning; these all proceed from wealth. From wealth one's merit increases. A person without wealth has neither this world nor the next" (Mahābhārata, 12.8.11). It is assumed, of course, that no artha be pursued in violation of dharma.

## KĀMA

*Kāma*, the third aim in life, has two senses. In the narrower sense kāma is sexual desire or love, symbolized by Kāma, the Love God. The

[2] *The Pañcatantra,* trans. A. W. Ryder (Chicago: University of Chicago Press, 1925), p. 210.

Kāma Sūtra, along with a number of other less well-known texts, is devoted to kāma in this sense, providing instruction on how to obtain the greatest possible sexual pleasures. It includes advice on sexual preparation, sexual positions, love potions, how to acquire a wife, and how a wife should conduct herself. There is a chapter on courtesans and another on how to make oneself attractive to others.

The prudishness that Victorian England introduced to India has, figuratively speaking, thrown up a screen of fig leaves, hiding sexual activity, creating an atmosphere in which educated people pretend either that sex is nonexistent or that it is a furtive and dirty thing. Traditionally, however, sexual activity was considered not only legitimate but an important and valuable activity and aim in life, treated with frankness and respect in the popular literature. Without a general acceptance of the value and importance of human sexual activity, the great erotic poems, songs, and sculpture of India would not have been accepted and certainly would not have become important vehicles and expressions of religious devotion.

As a basic human aim, kāma goes beyond this narrower sense of sexual enjoyment to include all forms of enjoyment, including the enjoyment of fame, fortune, and power. Again, the modern stereotype that presents the Indian people as so single-mindedly intent on pursuing religious salvation that there is no room for laughter, fun, or games gives us a false picture. Traditionally and currently, stories, games, festivals, and parties filled with music, laughter, and fun are highly prized by most of the people. As a recognized basic aim in life, kāma legitimizes the human need for enjoyment; it recognizes that not only are the various goods necessary for life but that they are to be enjoyed in life as a way of fulfilling human nature. As in the case of artha, however, only those activities aiming at kāma that are in accord with dharma are allowed. Enjoyment at the pain and expense of other creatures or persons is not allowed. Sexual activity is to be restricted to one's spouse; drugs and intoxicating beverages are regarded as wrong and sinful because of the injury they do.

## MOKṢA

The fourth aim, that of *mokṣa*, has priority over the others. Ultimately, dharma, artha, and kāma must serve to aid the individual in his or her efforts to destroy the bondage of saṁsāra. Human beings are assumed to be more than biological and social animals. At the very core of their being they are seen as identical with that primordial energy and being from which all existence originates. The aim of mokṣa is to realize this deeper level of existence and to live in the full awareness of one's identity with the ultimate reality. Identification with the lower and more manifest levels of existence must be transcended, for they are incomplete and can never satisfy the deeper yearning for unity and fulfillment.

One of the clearest and most influential statements of the multileveled nature of human existence comes from the Taittirīya Upaniṣad (2.1–5). There a person is said to consist of five layers of reality. (1) Nonliving matter, called "food," is the outermost and shallowest layer. This is the lowest level of human existence as is clear from the usual uncertainty as to whether to refer to a deceased person as a dead person or as the body of a dead person. (2) The next layer is life, for living matter is a higher level of reality. (3) But a person is not simply a living body, for people are able to feel and perceive, thus revealing a third level of reality. (4) The fourth layer is constituted by intelligence, for thinking and willing constitute a still higher level of reality. (5) But the story does not stop here, for higher than even intelligence is the level of reality upon which the integrated functioning of all the other levels depends. This innermost layer is regarded as the ultimate level of reality, supporting the other levels, but remaining independent of them. (See illustration, "Penetrating the Layers of Self with Yoga," p. 178.) Although words cannot describe it, since it is the ultimate, it is said to consist of infinite bliss, for infinite bliss is the most profound level of reality humans can envision.

The aim of mokṣa is progressively to free oneself from the exclusive identification with the lower levels of the self in order to realize the most profound level of existence. Since at this deepest level the self is identical with ultimate reality, once this identity has been realized there is nothing that can defeat or destroy the self. Thus, here one puts an end to saṁsāra and overcomes death.

Of course, a person is constituted by all five layers of existence, and it would be a mistake to deny that the lower levels constitute actual dimensions of human existence, just as it would be a mistake to identify the self exclusively with only the lower levels. It is because the lower levels of the self are recognized as important functional dimensions of human existence that the aims of artha and kāma are recognized as legitimate. This is also why dharma is recognized as a regulatory principle to be interiorized by each person and used to direct not merely the fulfillment of the needs of these lower dimensions of human existence but also the transcendence of these needs for the sake of fulfillment of the needs of the higher self.

The perfection of human existence is to realize the ultimate identity of personal existence with the primordial creative energy from which all existence originates. Awareness of the separation from the source of existence provides motivation for the religious quest for fulfillment; freedom from exclusive identification with lower forms of existence enables a person to realize this deeper unity and therefore constitutes the ultimate aim in life.

Both the concept of basic human aims and the institution of āśramas or life-stages to facilitate achievement of these aims embody the recognition that biological, economic, and social needs are legitimate and must be fulfilled in order to go beyond them. But it is also recognized that because of the deeper nature of human existence the thirst for freedom and fulfillment cannot be satisfied by pursuing the lower needs of life. Their acquisition only increases the thirst for more and more of these goods. Achieving contentment by acquiring the objects of desire is regarded as equivalent to trying to put out a fire by throwing fuel on it.

### PRIORITY OF MOKṢA

The Indian attitude that regards fame, fortune, power, and pleasure as shallow and fleeting, incapable of satisfying the human yearning for fulfillment and immortality, is succinctly and clearly expressed by Naciketas. The story of Naciketas describes the encounter of a brāhmaṇa's son—cursed and sent to hell by his father for criticizing the paucity of his father's sacrificial offerings—with Yama, death personified. When Naciketas arrived in the underworld, Yama was absent, and his servants failed to provide the food and water that dharma required be offered to a guest. In compensation for this failure, Yama offers Naciketas three boons. First, Naciketas asks that his father might forgive him for having criticized his offering and angering him to the point of cursing his own son. Second, he asks for the secret of the fire ritual whereby deathlessness in heaven is achieved. Upon the fulfillment of these requests, he asks what happens after death to a person who achieves mokṣa.

Now Yama tries to beg off, saying that this knowledge is most difficult: "Choose another boon. Choose sons and grandsons who will live a hundred years, lots of cattle, horses, elephants, and gold. Choose great areas of land and as many years of life as you want. Choose wealth and long life if you like this kind of boon. You will prosper on this great earth and I will make you an enjoyer of all your desires. All the desires that are hard to attain in this world of mortals—all these you shall have. Noble maidens with chariots and musical instruments beyond what can be attained by ordinary humans" (Kaṭha Upaniṣad, 1.1.23–25).

Naciketas replies with the wisdom of one who knows that the objects of desire are fleeting and can never satisfy the yearning for eternal life: "Fleeting are these, O Yama, and they wear out the vigour of the senses. All life is brief. Yours, Death, are the chariots [of time]; yours the song and the dance. Humans cannot be satisfied with wealth. How shall we enjoy wealth when we have seen you? What decaying mortal on this earth, knowing the pleasures of love and beauty will delight in a lengthened life when undecaying immortality has been glimpsed?" (1.1.26–28).

Failing to dissuade Naciketas, Yama keeps his promise and instructs him about the nature of the self that is untouched by death and the means for realizing this self. This inner self is described as "without sound, touch, form, taste or smell; without beginning or end, eternal and undecaying. It is beyond the great and unchanging. Knowing that self frees one from the jaws of death." But the way is not easy: "The sages say that the path is sharp as a razor's edge, hard to cross and difficult to tread" (1.3.14, 15).

We see now why, although the aims of dharma, artha, and kāma are legitimate, they are subordinated to the aim of mokṣa. It is the aim of mokṣa that guides one's efforts to realize identity with the ultimate reality. But mokṣa does not repudiate the other aims; indeed, it calls for fulfilling these aims as a preparation for achieving complete freedom and fulfillment. There is no conflict between mokṣa and the other three aims because the different levels of existence are seen as manifestations of the ordering of the ultimate reality of undivided wholeness rather than as separate realities. Although different aims are appropriate to different levels of manifested existence, this does not create an opposition between them because these levels are themselves part of the ordered unity of ultimate reality. Even when the distinction between worldly and spiritual existence becomes prominent, there is a tendency to see the distinction in terms of higher and lower levels of the same reality rather than to postulate two different and opposed realities.

The relations between the various aims in life can be compared with the different aims appropriate to a person at different times in life. In all societies children need to play with toys, youths desire sex, adults want power and fame, and old people seek wisdom and salvation. Just as adults outgrow the immature needs for toys and sex, so does a mature person outgrow the need for fame and power. Artha and kāma are legitimate goals of life up to a certain point. When a person reaches this point of maturity, these aims properly give way to the aim of mokṣa, which alone can satisfy the deeper yearning of human beings.

## Social Classes

Caste may well be the phenomenon most frequently associated with India. Over the years I have asked students to jot down the first four words that come to mind when I say "India." Not only does "caste" appear on nearly all the lists, but its appearance is more than twice as frequent as the next word. Although different people understand different things by caste, it is almost universally understood to refer to limited social mobility. "Caste" is the English translation of the word "casta," which the Portugese used to translate *jāti*, meaning "birth." Jāti, or birth, has indeed been the dominant basis of social classification for thousands of years in India. But it rests upon another basis of classification called *varṇa* ("class," literally, "color"). To understand the duties and rules that apply to a person because of social class and position, we must examine the ideas of both varṇa and jāti.

The ideal of four social classes (varṇas) was established already in late Vedic times, for the Hymn to the Cosmic Person (Ṛg Veda, 10.90) presents the four classes as originating from the primordial yajña from which the whole world issued. The three functional classes of brāhmaṇas, kṣatriyas, and vaiśyas were established early in Āryan history and are assumed in the earlier portions of the Ṛg Veda. It may be that the fourth class, the śūdra, represents an accommodation of peoples conquered and absorbed by the Āryans into their society. There is, however, no solid evidence behind this speculation, although we do know that by the time of the Upaniṣads the four varṇas were clearly accepted as an established feature of Indian society.

As traditionally interpreted, the Vedic verse proclaiming the origin of the brāhmaṇas in the mouth of the cosmic Person, the kṣatriyas in the arms, the vaiśyas in the legs, and the śūdras in the feet establishes three important features of varṇa. First, it is not a human creation or convention but a divinely ordained institution, not subject to modification for secular reasons. Second, the basis of classification is the nature of the person, for the nature of the mouth is different from that of the feet, and the nature of that which issues from the mouth—the brāhmaṇa—will differ from that which issues from the feet—the śūdra. Third, the functions of the different classes are given according to the part of the Person from which they originated. Thus, the brāhmaṇas are priests and teachers, for with the mouth one recites and chants; the kṣatriyas rule and protect, for with the arms one defends and administers; the vaiśyas produce and trade goods, for the legs enable one to tend cattle, till fields, and transport goods; the śūdras serve the other three classes just as the feet serve the rest of the body.

Manu, after explaining the origin of all existence and the divine ordination of the four classes for the sake of the prosperity of the world, succinctly states the principal duties that the Lord assigned each class as follows:

> To brāhmaṇas he assigned studying and teaching, performing sacrifical rituals for themselves and for others, and giving and receiving donations. He commanded the kṣatriya to protect the people, give gifts, perform yajña, study, and abstain from attaching himself to sensual pleasures. Vaiśyas are to tend cattle, cultivate the land, trade, lend money, give gifts, perform yajña, and study. The only occupation the Lord prescribed to the śūdras was to meekly serve the other three classes.
>
> Manu Smṛti, Book X

From the statement in Manu and in many other texts that the four classes were established for the sake of the prosperity of the world, we may assume an underlying rationale of ensuring the activities required for successful social functioning. The essential functions of preserving and renewing the culture and instilling it in the hearts and minds of the young, providing security against enemies and maintaining law and order, producing and trading goods, and providing menial labor are charged to brāhmaṇas, kṣatriyas, vaiśyas, and śūdras, respectively, as their ordained dharmas.

The insistence that each class stick to its own duties and not usurp those of another class suggests that a second underlying rationale is that the fulfillment of each individual will be enhanced by doing the kinds of things for which he or she is best suited by nature. Indian society has always assumed inherent differences between individuals and consequently has recognized that different requirements and privileges are appropriate. Varṇa is a way of grouping individuals according to their own natures and qualifications so that they might make a maximum contribution to the social order while at the same time enhance their prospects for fulfillment and liberation. As Krishna tells Arjuna in the Gītā, "Better is one's own dharma, even though difficult to fulfill, than the dharma of another which is easier to do. Better is death in the fulfillment of one's own dharma. Adopting the dharma of another is fraught with great peril."

Although ideally classification according to the nature and qualifications of the individual will provide a sufficient number of people to fulfill the four necessary kinds of social function, it is recognized that this does not always work out. Manu says, for example, that "if a brāhmaṇa cannot live by following his proper occupation, then he may live according to the rule of the kṣatriyas, for they are next in rank. If it be asked, 'But what if he cannot maintain himself by either of these occupations?' the answer is that he may adopt a vaiśya's mode of life" (10.80). He also allows that "a śūdra unable to find service with the twice-born and threatened with the loss of his sons and wife through hunger, may maintain himself by handicrafts [a vaiśya's occupation]" (10.100).

Occupation determines the majority of jāti classifications. Of the nearly three thousand jātis enumerated by British census takers, more than two thousand clearly represented occupational divisions. Among the many theories of the origin of the jāti system, none suggests a divine origin. One extremely influential theory (put forth in the Mahābhārata and by Manu) sees the jātis as originating in the intermixing of the classes. Another theory sees jāti as a separate occupational system of classification that was later subsumed under the varṇa scheme. Whatever the truth about the origins of jāti, it has been related closely to the varṇa system since the time of the Mahābhārata at least, and jāti duties have inherited the sacred and inviolable character of varṇa dharma.

It is not surprising that in practice birth will determine one's class and occupation, for lacking independent objective criteria for determining the nature and qualification of a person, birth becomes the criterion. For the most part this probably worked out rather well, for heredity and environment will generally combine to produce a person who will have the characteristics and qualifications of the parents. However, this does not always work, and using birth as the only criterion has the unfortunate effect of putting some individuals into situations for which they are poorly suited and in which they are oppressed. The recognized conflict between the ideal of classification according to qualification and the practice of classification according to birth shows up in the many stories about persons whose birth would place them in one varṇa, but who, because of their actions, are recognized as belonging to another varṇa. One of these stories is from the Chāndogya Upaniṣad (4.4.1–5) and concerns a boy named Satyakāma Jābāla.

Satyakāma wished to go into the forest to study with a guru. Since this practice was reserved for members of the brāhmaṇa class, he went to his mother to ascertain the particulars of his birth. To his great dismay, he was informed that his father was unknown. This meant, of course, that he was not entitled to any of the privileges of the brāhmaṇa (or any other) class. But determined to try anyhow, the young man went into the forest and, with fuel in his hands, approached the teacher. Upon being asked about his family and his birth, the boy admitted that he did not know to what class his father belonged, that in her youth his mother traveled about a great deal and did not know what man had fathered him. The teacher did not reject him on the grounds that his birth did not allow him this privilege of class, but accepted him, saying that anyone who would tell such an embarrassing truth in these circumstances surely is a brāhmaṇa, regardless of his birth.

This story, like many others, shows clearly that the intended basis of social class is the qualification of the individual. But it reveals just as clearly that it was accepted social practice to determine a person's class by birth. Although there are always some exceptions, it was birth that came increasingly to determine one's class and position in society and to be the primary focus of the various rules of life regarding marriage, occupation, ritual, food, and relations to other jātis. But since most of the jātis are also grouped under the traditional varṇa headings, hundreds of jātis belonging to the same varṇa will have common varṇa duties and privileges as well as distinct jāti duties and privileges.

Westerners are often surprised by the willingness of the Indian community to accept social classification according to birth. Because of assumptions about the equality of all persons, emphasis on upward mobility, and the ideal of a classless society, we may fail to notice the Indian assumptions that people are in fact unequal, that social classes are designed to accommodate these differences, and that one's birth is determined by actions (karma) in a previous life, thus being "earned."

Although these assumptions are quite different from the assumptions underlying Western ideals of social organization, this does not automatically make them wrong. To show them wrong requires showing that the underlying view of the nature of human beings and society is mistaken—a challenge taken up by many nineteenth- and twentieth-century Hindu reformers, with varying degrees of success.

Any discussion of Indian social organization would be incomplete without reference to the outcasts or untouchables—of whom there were about eighty million when the Indian government banned the practice and legislated against the wholesale discrimination against these persons. The untouchable was cast out of the society, usually for offenses against the established dharmas of society and enjoyed none of the usual social privileges and benefits. The children of outcasts were automatically outcasts too, and thus their numbers increased, making them an extremely large dispossessed class. Mahatma Gandhi did much to direct attention to their plight and to allow their re-entry into society, calling them Harijans or "children of God." Their situation has frequently been compared with that of blacks in America prior to the Civil War, for neither group had any rights or privileges but were expected to work for and serve everyone else.

Although in practice there is still considerable discrimination—despite the laws prohibiting such discrimination—much progress has been made over the last thirty years in removing the stigma of untouchability and providing economic and social opportunities for former untouchables, allowing them to take their place in society. One of the problems is that, since they do not belong to any of the four varṇas, they have difficulty fitting into the Hindu social scheme. Consequently, since Buddhism never accepted the caste system, a number of former untouchables have recently become Buddhists.

## Stages of Life

Unlike varṇa which is intended to promote the stability, well-being, and progress of the entire society, the institution of āśrama, or stages in life, is designed to serve the individual in the progressive attainment of the basic aims in life. Ideally, the life of every twice-born male (śūdras and women are excluded) is to be divided into four distinct stages of approximately equal length. The student stage (*brahmacarya*) provides an opportunity to study the Veda, learn the requirements of dharma, and learn a trade or profession. In the householder stage (*gṛhastha*) young adults marry, raise a family, and produce the various goods and services required by the rest of society. (The duties of this stage apply to women and śūdras throughout their lives.) When a man's social obligations are satisfied and his children grown and married, he takes up the activities of the forest-dwelling stage (*vānaprastha*). Gradually he withdraws from society, intent on establishing himself in dharma and achieving an attitude of nonattachment. Finally one becomes a saṅnyāsin, concerned only with attaining mokṣa.

The root *śram* from which the word *āśrama* is derived means "to exert oneself." Derivatively, it means both the action of exerting oneself and the place where the exertion takes place and gives us the meaning of āśrama as a stage in life where a concentrated effort is made to achieve certain goals. The goals, of course, are the four basic aims in life, and the āśramas are stages of training and effort aimed at living well—first within this world and then, in the last two stages, in freedom from this ordinary world.

**Student Stage.** Since dharma governs one's entire life, it is appropriately the special focus of the first stage, for, unless a child learns the requirements of dharma early in life and develops the appropriate attitudes and character that will allow him to consistently do his dharma for the rest of his life, none of the other aims can be achieved.

The student stage begins when the young boy leaves his parents' home to study in the house of his teacher. An important sacred rite (*upanayana*) initiates him into this stage and marks his spiritual birth into the class of the twice born. The teacher is like a father to the boy, and the close relationship between the two is a familiar theme both in the classical literature and the popular stories. Studying the Vedas and learning the requirements of dharma are the most important subjects. But music, archery, science, and medicine—along with practical arts and crafts—are taught as well. This system of education enabled the religious-philosophical basis of Indian culture to be renewed and transmitted to each generation, fostering the continuity of tradition, and providing a strong center of ideas and values to guide the life of the community.

**Householder Stage.** The completion of the boy's studies is celebrated with a sacred homecoming rite (*samāvartana*). He is now ready to embark on the householder's stage of life. All Indian literature recognizes the central importance of this period of life, for the whole society depends upon the goods and services provided by the householder. Marriage and family are sacred duties as well as sources of great joy and security. Many important rites can be performed only by a householder and his wife; children are a great blessing, for they ensure the continuity not only of the family but also of the sacred rites.

To appreciate the importance of this stage, we must consider the Indian attitude toward life. Life in this world is seen as a wonderful opportunity to gain liberation from the round of births and deaths that torments all creatures. This opportunity comes as a precious gift, placing the individual in the debt of the giver. A debt is owed the Gods, for they provide the gift of life in this world. Parents and ancestors make possible the birth of an individual in a family and are therefore owed a great debt. The third debt is incurred by the gift of the seers and teachers who, by preserving and teaching "what is worth knowing," provide for a second birth, a birth into the world of culture and spirit. In the householder stage the debt to seers and teachers could be satisfied by studying the Vedas, the debt to parents and ancestors by having children, and the debt to the Gods by offerings and ritual performances, making it the only stage in which all three debts can be satisfied simultaneously.

Before noting some of the important duties of husband and wife, we should mention that marriage was usually monogamous, although a second wife was permitted if the first was unable to bear children. Divorce was impossible among the three higher classes, because the marriage sacrament created an irrevocable bond. Widows were not allowed to remarry, although widowers might. However, the practice of virtue (*sāti*) by voluntary self-immolation of a widow upon her husband's funeral pyre is not referred to in the early texts; it is a later practice not enjoined by dharma.

Although the position of women in Indian society has been far from enviable by Western standards, they were accorded high respect in the home and frequently ruled the household like queens, controlling purse strings and making all domestic decisions. Even Manu declared that "children, proper performance of religious rites, faithful service, greatest conjugal happiness and heavenly bliss for the ancestors and oneself depend entirely on one's wife" (9.25–39). He included among a wife's duties serving her husband, collecting and spending his money, keeping everything clean, performing religious acts, preparing food, and taking care of the household" (9.10–13).

The dependence and subservience of women is highlighted by the fact that the young bride ordinarily left her parental home and went to live in the home of her husband's family. Here she was completely subservient to her mother-in-law as well as to her husband. Of course, the time would come when her sons would bring their brides into her home and she would rule the household. But even for this she was dependent on husband and sons.

A husband must protect and provide for his wife, see to his sons' education and his daughters' marriages, perform religious rites every morning and evening, study the Vedas, and accumulate and disburse artha according to his occupation. Yājñavalkya sums up these duties by declaring, "Learning, religious performances, age, family relations, and wealth—on account of these, in the order mentioned, are men honored in society. By means of these, if possessed in profusion, even a śūdra deserves respect in old age" (1.97 ff.).

A man is advised to cherish his wife as a goddess, knowing that she is half of him, to look on her as his best friend, and to remember that she is the source of dharma, artha, kāma, and even mokṣa. And "never, even in anger, should a man do anything disagreeable to his wife, for happiness, joy and virtue all depend upon her." Together, husband and wife must take care of the household and offer prayers and oblations. "Children, married daughters living in the household, old relatives, pregnant women, sick persons, girls, guests and servants should all be fed before husband and wife eat the remains" (Yājñavalkya Smṛti, 1.97 ff.).

**Forest-dweller.** When the duties of the householder stage have been fulfilled, a person may proceed to the third stage, that of a forest-dweller. "A householder may leave for the forest when his skin is wrinkled, his hair white, and he sees the sons of his sons," says Manu. Having fulfilled his social dharma, a man—with his wife, if she wishes—may leave his home and village and turn his attention to performing rituals and studying the scriptures as he seeks to establish himself in dharma and acquire an attitude of nonattachment to all the things of this world. This period of "retirement" from social life is one of asceticism aimed at achieving the self-control and spiritual strength needed to attain mokṣa. Honored and respected by nearly everyone, these forest-dwellers are sometimes sought out for their wise counsel and therefore still constitute a vital part of the social fabric.

**Saṁnyāsa.** The fourth stage, that of the *saṁnyāsin*, is one of complete renunciation of worldly objects and desires. Manu says, "He should always wander alone, without any companion, to attain mokṣa. He should have neither fire nor dwelling place, being indifferent to everything, of firm purpose, meditating and concentrating on Brahman" (Manu Smṛti, Book VI). So complete is the saṁnyāsin's renunciation that he is usually regarded as having died already. Indeed, upon termination of his biological life, the usual funeral rites and cremation are not performed. Instead, special *samādhi* rites are performed in recognition that personal and social death had occurred earlier, upon entry into this stage of life.

## Political Rule

So far we have focused on social life as guided and regulated by the four aims in life and the institutions of class and stages in life. We now turn to the question of how Indian society was ruled and administered and how this affected the individual and the community. It appears that a combination of kingship and village councils constituted the basis of political rule throughout India until recent times, when electoral democracy made an appearance. Throughout most of history India was not unified under a single king or administrative system, but consisted of numerous kingdoms, frequently vying with each for power and control. The notable exceptions to this pattern occurred during the Mauryan and Gupta dynasties and under the foreign rule of the Mughals and the British.

The first unification was achieved by the Mauryans, who under the great Chandragupta (reigned 324–301 B.C.) unified the whole northern part of the subcontinent and who under Ashoka's rule (269–232 B.C.) extended their domain to all but the southern tip of the peninsula. Following Ashoka's reign, which encouraged all religions, but especially Buddhism, the kingdom began to break up. It was not until the Gupta dynasty (A.D. 320–550) that the greater portion of the subcontinent again came under one rule. With the decline of this great dynasty a glorious period in Indian history slowly came to a close, although it enjoyed a late flowering under the extraordinary ruler Harsha Vardhana (reigned A.D. 606–647), who encouraged a great revival of Hinduism that lasted until the Muslim conquests of the ninth and tenth centuries. For the next thousand years India was to come under the domination of foreign rule, first by the Muslims and then by the British, who rather easily extended their rule over the politically divided subcontinent, frequently playing one kingdom against another.

There is no doubt that the power struggles between kings affected the lives of the people, for sometimes, when the wars were long, many kṣatriyas died and the royal demand for revenues caused severe poverty. Also, India's political and military inability to resist Muslim and British invasions led to incalculable effects on the people, as the occupation and rule by both these groups of foreigners constituted a serious threat to the religion and culture of India. On the other hand, it is truly amazing that the frequent military and political conquests, and even foreign rule, had relatively little impact on the values, life-styles, and attitudes of most of the people.

The relative imperviousness of Indian culture to political activity and changes in government is linked to the religious basis of the culture and to the prevailing conception of the function of government. No sharp line was drawn between secular and religious matters or between spiritual and temporal power. The ultimate aim in life for everyone was extrasocial, requiring detachment from the social and political spheres of life, making the affairs of government subordinate to this religious concern. In addition, the ruling class, the kṣatriya, was regarded as lower than the brāhmaṇa class, providing another obvious basis for the subordination of the political realm to the religious. This subordination of the political to the religious helps to explain the absence of priest-kings in India and the relative lack of rivalry and struggle between political and religious leaders.

Not only was political rule regarded as subordinate to religious concerns, but the proper function of government was to preserve order and to provide security against external threats (from neighboring kingdoms). Ordinarily the government would not attempt to regulate the life of the individual or the community. The king's duty (dharma) was to preserve order by ensuring the performance of dharma. Since dharma is not legislated by kings, but issues from class, life stage, and moral requirements, government has nothing to do with the internal workings of society unless things begin to break down because of individual and group failures to regulate human action. Because the foundation of dharma is religious, the king's primary duty was actually to assist the religious leaders in their efforts to encourage the people to fulfill their duties. At the same time the priests were assisting the king in fulfilling the requirements of his office. This partnership usually worked smoothly and well, probably because the king had his wealth, power, and fame and the priests their status and respect. In any event, because government was generally conceived of as a conservative force, functioning to maintain the existing social order that was generated and maintained by the self-regulation of individuals and groups, villages and families were allowed to function autonomously—as long as they paid their taxes.

## Sacramental Rites

Much more important than government in maintaining the attitudes and ideas that constituted the basis of Indian values were the rituals making sacred important events in the life of every individual. Authoritative texts such as the Gṛhya Sūtras and the Gautama Dharma Śāstra list from forty to forty-eight *saṁskāras* or sacraments—ritual means for purifying life and making it sacred. The widespread practice of initiating and celebrating life's great moments with sacred rituals that employed approximately the same formulas, liturgy, and actions from generation to generation and from region to region has been one of the great cohesive and stabilizing forces in Indian history. The following sacraments are among the more important and regularly practiced sacred rites of passage and constitute important varṇa and āśrama dharmas.

The first sacrament in the life of the individual is the *garbhādhāna* or foetus-laying rite. Performed at the consummation of marriage, it celebrates the gift of life, emphasizes the obligation to have children, and sanctifies the conception of a new human being.

During the third month of pregnancy the "male-making" (*pumsavana*) rite is performed, sanctifying the foetus and emphasizing the continuity of the family through a male heir.

At birth the father touches and smells the infant, uttering mantras in its ears, prays for intelligence and long life, feeds it with honey and butter, and then gives it to the mother for nursing. After being thus sanctified by the birth ceremony, the umbilical cord is cut, and the infant is ready to begin life as a separate person.

On the tenth or twelfth day after birth the child is to be named. Because a name is considered to determine a person's behavior in various ways, it is important that a person's name be sanctified by holy rituals.

In the fourth month the child is ritually presented to the sun, the symbolic embodiment of all the great natural forces, to sanctify all contacts and relations with nature.

In about the sixth month the "rice-eating" sacrament is performed. The primary visible sign of this sacrament is the cooked rice (or other food) that the child eats as his first solid food. Eating is made a sacred act by means of this ritual.

Sometime between the first and third year the "hair-cutting" ritual is observed, emphasizing the importance of discipline in life. The hair is cut for the sake of dharma, symbolizing the need to discipline and regulate one's body and mind.

One of the most important and solemn sacraments is that of "spiritual entry" or *upanayana.* At early adolescence or slightly before, males of the so-called upper classes are initiated into a new life—a spiritual life as opposed to a merely natural life. This begins the first stage of conscious religious activity, celebrated with the investiture of the sacred thread that marks the boy as "twice born" (once biologically, once spiritually). The ritual is impressive for the entire family and awesome for the boy, laying on him—in the symbol of the sacred thread—the obligations of spiritual striving for himself and for the whole society.

Usually performed as a concluding portion of the upanayana sacrament, the *sāvitṛ* (sacred words) ritual emphasizes the power of sacred words to make life itself sacred.

The sacred point between the first and second stages of life is ritually celebrated with the "homecoming" *(samāvartana)* sacrament, which emphasizes the sacredness of study and the qualifications required for taking on the responsibilities of family life.

Life in the second stage, that of the householder, is launched as a sacred journey with the elaborate marriage (*vivāha*) ritual. For the bride this sacrament constitutes her upanayana or initiation into spiritual life and thus has a double significance. Together, bride and groom vow to love each other for life, to have children, to perform the required rituals, to keep the sacred hearth fire burning, and to fulfill all the dharmas pertaining to family.

The last sacrament, *antyeṣṭī,* is performed at death, signifying the end of this earthly career and sanctifying the journey on into the world of the ancestors and beyond.

Although the form and style of the sacramental ceremonies have varied somewhat according to time and place, an amazing continuity endures. The mantras recited today are the same ones used twenty-five hundred years ago, most of them taken from the Vedas. There is the same recognition of the sacredness of each important moment of life and the same emphasis on the duties imposed by the ceremonially marked phases of life. Indeed, the sacramental character of life, emphasizing duties, obligations, and debts rather than rights and freedom, has been the dominant force shaping the attitudes and expectations of the individual and giving Indian society its distinctive character over the centuries.

## Summary

The two main continuing themes from the Vedic age to the formative and classical age of the great texts on dharma and on to the present are those of sacrificial celebration (yajña) and ṛta/dharma. Yajña continues as a primary obligation and opportunity. It is an obligation because without it neither human life nor the cosmos can function properly, but it is also a wonderful opportunity, because through yajña human and cosmic fulfillment are possible. The ritual offering of oneself and all the prized goods of life to the fundamental creative powers of existence continues to be regarded as a precious way of renewal, even though the form of the yajña changes over the ages from ritual preoccupied with external actions to ritual dominated by the symbols and intentions of the celebrant. Life in India today is still thought of as a sacrificial celebration of life; indeed, performing one's dharma is commonly seen as a yajña.

The emphasis on dharma that has dominated Indian thought and practice for thousands of years is rooted in the Vedic vision of ṛta—the normative coursing of reality at its very center that determines the inner law and requirements of action of everything that exists. Gradually the concept of ṛta was taken over by the twin concepts of karma and dharma. Karma, the law of interconnectedness of all actions, provides a basis for both human bondage and freedom. Dharma, the normative dimension of the central reality, constitutes the basis for the regulation of life in accord with the inner being of each creature. Ultimately, dharma provides for freedom from all of the determining effects of action (karma) by bringing the whole life of the individual up to the highest level of being where there is no distinction between the individual and the source of existence. It is this level of life—mokṣa—that the dharmas of varṇa and āśrama are intended to help each person achieve.

The primary rules of life determining a person's lifelong obligations and daily duties were the requirements of social class and stage in life. The purpose of these dharmas, which governed the whole life of the individual, was to facilitate achievement of the four great aims in life—virtue, means of life (wealth, power, fame, etc.), enjoyment, and liberation. No sharp distinction was made between religious duties, such as performing rituals, making offerings, and making donations; moral duties such as telling the truth, avoiding hurting others, honesty, and fairness in all dealing with people, and social duties, such as paying the king's taxes, participating in village council decisions, or educating one's children. All the requirements of life that aimed at achieving the four legitimate aims in life had a religious character and fulfilling them constituted both the practice of religion and the fulfillment of social duty.

Concern for achieving mokṣa—liberation from the round of births and deaths—was paramount from the time of the Upaniṣads on. Prior to that time, during the Vedic age, the good life was defined in terms of the requirements for a full life in this world, with longevity, wealth, family, and honor among the primary aims. Only with the development of the idea that life in the next world would terminate in death—even as life does in this world—did the emphasis begin to change from living the fullest possible life in this world to achieving liberation from the continuing round of births and deaths that threatened every person. With this change in emphasis, mokṣa came to be the overriding aim in life and the classic institutions of varṇa and āśrama, structured in terms of the four aims in life, were developed during the period from 800 to 200 B.C. The normative patterns established during this time have continued to shape society and guide the individual right up to the present time.

## Suggestions for Further Reading

*Hindu Social Organization: A Study in the Socio-Psychological and Ideological Foundations*, by Pandharinath H. Prabhu, 4th ed. (Bombay: Popular Prakashan, 1961), first published in 1940, remains one of best presentations of both the underlying ideas and social practices that have constituted the practice of Hinduism.

*Hindu View of Life*, by the late Sarvapalli Radhkrishnan (New York: Macmillan Publishing Co., Inc., 1964), has been an influential little book ever since first published in 1927 and continues to be widely read. The first forty pages place Hinduism in the broader context of world religions. The concluding forty-six pages present a vision of dharma that takes into account both the underlying metaphysical and the social assumptions.

*The Mahābhārata* is a storehouse of information about Indian values, social practices, and ideals. Encyclopedic in scope and size, it runs to eleven volumes in Roy's English translation. A one-volume English version based on selected verses by Chakravarthi V. Narasimhan (New York: Columbia paperback) does a good job of presenting the story of the ancient rivalry between the Pandu and Kuru cousins, the main narrative theme around which are woven the discussion of artha, dharma, and mokṣa that have made the epic a guide to life over the centuries. A masterful new English translation with superb introductions to each main topic by the late J. A. B. Van Buitenen (University of Chicago Press) is under way. The first three volumes were published before his untimely death in 1979, and plans call for completion of the project by his students and colleagues. The reader seriously interested in this epic is encouraged to consult this new translation if at all possible.

*The Rāmāyana* is a poetic epic of twenty-four thousand couplets telling the story of the hero Rāma, the abduction of his wife Sītā by Rāvaṇa, and successful rescue by Rāma and Hanuman. The whole is a discourse on dharma, and Rāma and Sītā have frequently been taken as models of virtue, to be emulated as closely as possible. Many partial translations are available, including the retelling by William Buck in *The Rāmāyana* (New York: New American Library, Mentor ed., 1978).

*Four Families of Karimpur*, by Charlotte V. Wiser (Syracuse, N.Y.: Syracuse University Foreign and Comparative Studies/South Asian Series No. 3, 1978), is the wonderful true story (by the author of *Behind Mud Walls*) of three generations of life and change in four village families over a fifty-year period beginning in 1925. Providing an unusual entry into the lives of typical families, the book enables the reader to enter into a sympathetic relationship with members of these families, achieving a nearly experiential understanding of how dharma operates in practice. If you can read only one book about Indian social life, this is the one to read.

# 5

# Liberating Knowledge: The Upaniṣads

In their hermitages in the quiet of the forest, Indian sages shared their reflections on the ultimate nature of self and existence with qualified learners. These profound teachings were known as Upaniṣads because they were imparted to students who sat (*sad* = "to sit") down (*ni* = "down") near (*upa* = "near") the teacher to receive these secret teachings. Departing from the ritualistic traditions of the earlier Vedic age, the Upaniṣadic sages were engaged in a radical rethinking of the nature of self and reality that was destined to deeply influence the course of religion, philosophy, and life in India and beyond. Radical and profound, their discoveries were shared only with qualified learners, thereby creating a body of secret knowledge. According to the Chāndogya Upaniṣad, even Indra, king of the Gods, had to live with his teacher for 101 years practicing self-discipline before Prajāpati thought him prepared to receive the highest knowledge about the self.

The earliest collections of these forest teachings, the Bṛhadāraṇyaka, Chāndogya, Aitareya, Taittirīya, Kena, Kaṭha, Kauṣitākī, Praśna, Muṇḍaka, Māṇḍūkya, Śvetāśvatara, and Īśa Upaniṣads, were probably composed between 800 and 500 B.C. and have been commented on by most major Indian thinkers. Actually there are many more Upaniṣads: Indian tradition counts a total of 108, and modern scholarship reveals more than 200. However, since the early Upaniṣads have been most influential, we will examine only those listed. Most are parts of Āraṇyakas and belong to Brāhmaṇas appended to the Vedas, thus revealing the textual continuity of the Vedic tradition.

The central Upaniṣadic concern is reflected in three questions: What

**Figure 1.** Hermitage Scene: Two sages in conversation. Early 19th century. (Courtesy, Museum of Fine Arts, Boston. Ross Coomaraswamy Collection.)

am I, in the very depths of my being? What is the ultimate basis of all existence? and What is the relation between my deepest self and the ultimate reality? With some simplification, we can say that the conclusion of the meditations and speculations constituting the Upaniṣads is that each person, in the most fundamental depths of his or her existence, is identical with the ultimate power and reality of the universe. This is expressed in the great sayings, "I am Brahman," and "You are That [Brahman]."

Before examining these teachings, we will look at the transition from Vedic to Upaniṣadic thought. The growing conviction that birth and death are not unique events, that each rotation of the wheel of life brings a new birth and another death to each person, was central to this transition. How can one get free from this seemingly endless round of repeated deaths? It is this urgent question that motivated the sages to seek a power beyond death (Brahman) and a Self (Ātman) independent of Saṁsāra, the birth-death cycle.

In the first part of this chapter we will examine the idea of re-death and the search for a Self that while consistent with ordinary experience nevertheless is not intrinsically subject to the cycle of repeated dying. We will then explore the concepts of Brahman and Ātman and the discovery of their identity—the central teaching of the Upaniṣads.

## Transition from Vedas to Upaniṣads

Although the Upaniṣads represent a significant departure from the Vedas, the transition from Vedas to Brāhmaṇas to Āraṇyakas to Upaniṣads is gradual, and a definite continuity is maintained. Their designation as "the end of the Veda" (Vedānta) indicates the general acceptance of the Upaniṣads both as the concluding portion of the Veda and as the highest and most profound statement of the truth of all prior scriptures. What sets the Upaniṣads apart from the earlier scriptures is their emphasis on knowledge as a means of liberation. The rituals of yajña come to be regarded as taking a person only as far as the realm of the ancestors. To go beyond that, to achieve complete fulfillment and immortality, meditative knowledge is necessary. But the movement from ritual to knowledge as the way of salvation is by way of a gradual transformation of yajña into meditative wisdom through a process of internalization.

The Bṛhadāraṇayaka Upaniṣad (part of the Śatapatha Brāhmaṇa, which belongs to the Yajur Veda) shows how ritual is transformed into meditative knowledge. It begins with a description of the great horse sacrifice, which it then proceeds to interpret as being really an internal meditative act through which the whole world (not just a horse) is sacrificed. By this sacrificial act of renouncing the world, the individual achieves spiritual autonomy (rather than earthly sovereignty).

Meditation is the means of transforming ritual into knowledge in the Chāndogya Upaniṣad as well. This text, part of the Chāndogya Brāhmaṇa, which belongs to the Sāma Veda, is named after the singer, Chāndoga. Appropriately enough for a text named after a singer, the Upaniṣad begins with a meditation on AUM, the essential sound of liturgical song, the sound with which each chant is begun. This sound is identified as the essence of all sound, containing all wisdom, breath of life, the sun, and the entire cosmos. Describing the whole world and the entire self as grounded in the holy sound, the sage declares that, indeed, the syllable AUM is this entire existence. Furthermore, "One who knows this, knows all. Therefore one should meditate on this: 'I am the All' " (Chāndogya Upaniṣad, 2.21.4).

In the third chapter of the Chāndogya, sacrificial celebration is seen as a symbolic expression of human life. The first twenty-four years are the morning offering, the next twenty-four years are the midday offering, and the last forty-eight years are the third offering. Hunger, thirst, and nonenjoyment are the initiatory rites; eating, drinking, and enjoying are the milk ceremonies; eating, laughing, and sexual activity constitute chanting and recitation; and austerity, donations, uprightness, nonviolence, and truthfulness are the gifts to the priests (3.16, 17). By the time we come to the seventh chapter, the internationalization and transformation of yajña has reached the point where the Self (Ātman) is identified as the ultimate reality and the ground of all existence, including the empirical self. Now the seeker can be advised that one who finds the Self obtains all worlds and fulfills all desires, including the desire for immortality (8.12.6). As we shall see (pp. 92 ff.), the key to this liberating knowledge is the distinction between the ordinary self constituted by the processes and contents of consciousness, and the Self (Ātman) which is the ultimate ground of these processes and contents.

## RE-DEATH

To understand the transition from Vedic to Upaniṣadic thought, and why the shift from worship and external ritual to its internalization and meditative expression as knowledge occurs, we must attend to (1) the changing conception of death and suffering and the related conceptions of salvation and (2) changes within the idea of ṛta that led to emphasis on karma, dharma, and Brahman. These changes occurred over a relatively long period of time, from the composition of the earliest Ṛg Vedic hymns, perhaps around 1500 B.C., to the completion of the early Upaniṣads, around 600 B.C., and can be traced through the Vedas, Brāhmaṇas, Āraṇyakas, and Upaniṣads.

During this time the Āryans settled into a new home, moving from the Indus to the Gangetic plains, achieving political control and establishing their culture. Transition from a seminomadic rural society with a herding and primitive agricultural economy to an increasingly less mobile society with more complex forms of production and trade, urban centers of commerce and culture, and increasing domination by priests with their complicated and costly rituals may well have spurred the reflections underlying the changing ideas of life, salvation, and reality and made the forest retreats an enticing refuge for persons seeking an alternative way of life and salvation.

From the time of Brāhmaṇas on (1000 B.C.?), the idea of re-death becomes dominant, and life comes to be seen increasingly in terms of its misery and incompleteness, marking a departure from the Vedic attitude that emphasized the happiness and fullness of life. Why the emphasis on re-death occurs in Vedic thought at this time is not clear, but it may well be due to the increasing influence of an earlier indigenous culture—perhaps the Indus—that accepted liberation from the torment of repeated dying as the ultimate goal of life.

By the time of the Upaniṣads, life in both this world and the next was regarded as temporary; death was sure for whatever was born. Suffering and evil now came to be regarded as abnormal, but inevitable in life as it is usually lived (i.e., in ignorance). Because it is abnormal, it could be eliminated if the right way could be found, although it would have to be an extraordinary way. This prospect of interminable suffering, symbolized by the unceasing turning of the wheel of re-birth and re-death, motivated an increasing number of recluses and teachers to seek a way of liberation.

Although in this chapter we will focus on the teachings of the Upaniṣads, it is the urgency of this same problem of suffering and repeated death that motivated the Buddha, Mahāvīra, Gośala, and the leaders of other sects of this time, or slightly later (seventh to fifth centuries B.C.), to seek their own liberating ways of life. While the Buddhists, Jainas, and Ājīvikas repudiated the entire Vedic ritual tradition, this is not true of the majority of Upaniṣadic sages. Indeed, the acceptance of ritual action as the way of creating and maintaining oneself in the world initially paved the way of knowledge that characterizes the Upaniṣads.

## FROM ṚTA TO BRAHMAN

We need to recall that the way of ritual is rooted in a vision of existence grounded in and controlled by ṛta, the fundamental rhythm and norm. In the Ṛg Veda, ṛta unites the different kinds of existence, constituting the very basis of their being and function; all existence is grounded in and controlled by this divine energy. Liturgical hymns, prayers, and offerings celebrate and evoke this controlling energy, allowing all beings to participate in the rhythmic energy that is the normative basis of existence. Ṛta controlled everything in the universe; it was the power of powers, beyond even the Gods. The rhythmic chants and prayers and the carefully controlled actions of offering and worship constituting the yajña were regarded as penetrating to the heart of ṛta, sharing in this ultimate power. Consequently, the priests, who with their sacred mantras and actions controlled the ritual, were regarded as controlling the universe through the power of yajña.

In the early Vedic age, the efficacy of yajña was undoubted, and the emphasis was on the order of the ritual whereby the orderliness of personal and cosmic life could be ensured. Appropriately enough, it was the controlling and regulating dimensions of ultimate reality that were emphasized. But as the power of prayer and priest came to be emphasized, so did the power dimension of ṛta. At first this dimension was recognized as Brāhmaṇaspati, Lord of the Holy Power. Later, when the ultimate ground of existence was recognized to be ontologically prior to either existence or non-existence—"Then [originally] there was neither existence nor non-existence"—it came to be called simply Brahman ("great-making power").

Power was not the only dimension of ṛta to be emphasized. As the idea of repeated dying gained acceptance, it became important to understand the linkages between one life and another. Consequently special attention was focused on karma, the causal dimension providing the basis for the interconnectedness of all existence. The normative and regulative function of ṛta remains important, but as it comes to be thought of increasingly in social and moral terms—with an emphasis on the obligations of individuals and groups to maintain the world through performance of their duties—this dimension comes to be thought of as dharma.

Distinguishing between the various features and functions of ṛta enabled the sages of the Upaniṣads to focus on the realization of Brahman as the solution to the problem of suffering and repeated death, for if somehow one could achieve the power that is the source of all power, then no other power could control life, and death would be defeated. The search for Brahman, the underlying ground and power of being, thus becomes an important Upaniṣadic quest. (But this quest is still frequently thought of as a kind of yajña, though now internalized and performed through meditation).

The other Upaniṣadic quest, for the ultimate Self (Ātman), also has its roots in the ritual tradition and the emergence of the problem of re-death. Faced with the prospect of repeated deaths, the task of determining the nature of the individual self who is subject to repeated births and deaths became urgent. So did the task of discovering the connections between one life and another. What energy and what process transforms the activities of this life into the next life?

A common image used in thinking about this problem was that of a plant and its seed. A plant, which grows from a seed, in maturity concentrates its energy in the enveloping seed before dying and is thereby re-born again from its own seed. In a similar way, it was thought that there must be an inner self, which like a tiny seed, carries the concentrated vital energies beyond the death of this body into a new life. This idea of an inner or core self, coupled with the requirement that only the changeless could be immortal, led to a search for an inner Self (Ātman) that was essentially unchanging.

## IDEAS OF SELF

The sages recognized that, to achieve immortality, the grip of saṁsāra (the cycle of repeated births and deaths) must be broken. This, in turn, required knowledge both of the inner Self that transmigrates from life to life and of how this Self can be liberated from the transmigratory cycle. We have here the central question of the Upaniṣads: What is the Self that survives death, that can be liberated from saṁsāra?

The concern behind this question provided incentive for inquiring into the nature of the Self and also set important parameters for this inquiry. The Self must be subtle, for since it survives the death of the body and mind, it must be subtler than either. Furthermore, it must be capable of taking on various forms, features, and sizes, for re-birth could be as a God, human, or animal. What kind of reality could fit these requirements? The most promising candidates were water, breath, fire, and knowledge. Each of these was integral to human life, enduring, and sufficiently subtle to assume the many forms required by the idea of saṁsāra. It is not surprising that each became the basis of a different theory about the nature of the Self.

**Self as Water.** The theory of the self as water appears to be grounded in the observation that water is essential to life and that it is sufficiently subtle—changing states from liquid to solid to "ether" (upon evaporation)—to take the variety of forms required by the theory of saṁsāra. It is also sanctioned by tradition, for it is rooted in an older theory, which sees the departed spirit rising to the heavenly world through the gateway of the moon. In ancient times the moon was seen as a huge drinking bowl, filled with the liquid of life. When the moon tipped on its side the liquid poured out and descended as rain, bringing life to the earth. Using this older image, advocates of the water theory of the self speculated that, when a person dies and is placed on the funeral pyre, the life moisture evaporates and rises heavenward to the moon in the form of smoke. There it is collected and periodically returned to earth to provide renewed life. But in the case of those persons qualified for liberation from the cycle of death and birth, the door in the moon is opened so they can pass through to achieve their heavenly reward.

**Self as Breath.** The breath theory begins with the observation that all creatures have breath, which is assumed to be a form of wind omnipresent in the world, extremely subtle, capable of taking the form of the breather. Since without breath one dies, it could be taken as the foundation of life. Thus, the inner self was identified with breath: when it left one body it could enter another, bringing life to it.

The sage Raikva presents the breath theory to king Janaśruti in the fourth chapter of the Chāndogya in a concise form: "Wind is that which gathers everything together, for when a fire goes out, it enters the wind.

When the sun sets it goes into the wind, when the moon goes down it enters into the wind, and when water dries up it enters the wind. All these are gathered into the wind; this is the way it is with the Gods (who occupy the cosmic realms). With reference to the self, breath is that which gathers everything together. When one sleeps, speech enters into breath; sight enters into breath; hearing enters into breath; and mind enters into breath. All these are gathered into the breath" (4.3.1–3). When the breath departs from a dying person, it is assumed to take all the life functions with it, returning that person to a home in the omnipresent wind.

**Self as Fire.** The third theory of the self finds the subtle essence to be fire. This is no doubt connected to the idea of the ritual fire carrying the offering to the Gods in heaven, transforming food offerings into the new life promised by the yajña. It probably is also connected with the observation that when life leaves a body it becomes cold. Heat, associated with fire, is required to digest food, to cook food, to hatch eggs, and to make plants grow. In addition, heat consummates the sexual generative act. According to a very old idea, fire is identified with the sun, and the rays of the sun interact with the veins and arteries of the body, receiving and returning the sun's life heat. The person in the sun with the golden teeth was originally seen as Agni. But now, with the idea of re-death, he is seen as Mṛtyu, the God of Death, who uses the rays of the sun to bind a person to the continued cycle of birth and death. The fire theory provides a way of liberation, since the sun contains a door to immortality that Mṛtyu cannot block for one who possesses the liberating knowledge.

Fire, breath, and water theories of the self all rely on older ideas about the source of life and the power of transformation. Thus, they have the weight of tradition behind them, even though they are now being employed in a new way. Furthermore, they all identify the self in terms of natural elements, thus paving the way for the eventual identification of the Self with Brahman, the ultimate reality of the universe.

**Self as Knowledge.** But it was the idea of Self as knowledge that really made possible the idea of Ātman. One of the problems with the other ideas was that, while they could account for re-birth, they did not provide a very satisfactory solution to the problem of liberation from saṁsāra. Although extremely subtle, the selves identified with water, breath, or fire—inevitably subject to repeated births and deaths—were continuously changing. Immortality required something beyond this, something permanent. Knowledge had for long been held to be indestructible, and the eternal yajña itself regarded as a kind of knowledge—indeed, the highest kind. Although knowledge might take the form of the knower, and although it might be die and be re-born in its personal form, in its own nature it was indestructible, making it an ideal candidate for the inner Self.

With the identification of the Self with knowledge, the way of liberation naturally emphasized *knowledge over ritual action*, and thus was born the *way of knowledge*. Because the ideas of self as breath, water, or fire had already prepared the way for identifying the deepest self with the ultimate power and ground of existence, it was possible to regard the Self whose essence is knowledge as also identical with Brahman, for the power of knowledge is the greatest of all powers.

## Quest for Brahman

Having examined the transition from Vedic to Upaniṣadic ideas of self and reality, we are ready to turn to specific teachings about the nature of Brahman and Ātman in the Upaniṣads. But before considering the search for an unchanging ultimate reality and an imperishable self, a word of caution about the texts is in order.

The various Upaniṣads, even taken together, do not contain a single coherent vision. Furthermore, each individual Upaniṣad contains a number of different, sometimes conflicting, views. Different sages and teachers, each seeking a way of liberation, reflect on their experiences as they meditate on and speculate about Ātman and Brahman. These reflections, of many sages, were shared with students and eventually collected into Upaniṣads. They reflect the great diversity of their origins.

Our aim in this chapter is to present the dominant ideas that have been stressed by the great teachers throughout the years and that have had significant influence on subsequent ideas and attitudes—not to compile an encyclopedia of Upaniṣadic ideas. In India these teachings have always been received as reports of the experiences of wise and holy people; only very recently have they been taken (mistaken?) to be theories testable by science or to be justified by philosophical arguments.

It is also important to point out that, although the Upaniṣads record spiritual quests for liberation, they do not repudiate wealth, fame, or power; indeed, the sages seek these also, but they recognize that ultimately they cannot satisfy the yearning for fulfillment and immortality. When the renowned sage Yājñavalkya comes to King Janaka's court and is asked whether he comes for wealth or wisdom, he replies, "For both, your majesty!" The teacher's prayer, with which the Taittirīya begins, shows clearly that these teachers of wisdom understood also the importance of worldly things: "Bring me increasing amounts of food, drink, clothes and cattle. May students of sacred knowledge who are self-disciplined, peaceful and well-equipped come to me from every side. May I become famous and even more renowned than the extremely rich!" (1.4).

The same Upaniṣad reveals the importance attached to social and moral activity. Students of sacred knowledge, upon leaving their guru to return home, were given this advice: "Speak the truth, practice virtue, continue your study, seek prosperity, have children, and attend to religious activity. Treat your parents, teachers and guests as Gods. Loving virtue, do only what is blameless" (1.11.1–6, condensed). Incidentally, this same timeless advice is still often quoted to students when they finish their university education. Because of the stereotype that presents Indian spirituality as an extreme form of asceticism, it is important to note that according to the Upaniṣads spiritual fulfillment does not require the ascetic rejection of normal physical, mental, and social activities and enjoyments. Both the material and spiritual worlds could be enjoyed by the wise.

## SIX QUESTIONS ABOUT REALITY

The Praśna Upaniṣad typifies the Upaniṣadic quest for Brahman. It begins by naming six young men, "devoted to Brahman, intent on Brahman, seeking the highest Brahman, [who] approached the revered Pippalāda with fuel offerings in their hands, hoping that he would explain everything to them." Pippalāda's response was, "Live with me another year in faith, austerity and purity and then ask whatever questions you desire answered. If we know, we will tell you everything." After a year they approach and ask their questions.

Kabandhī wants to know the source of all the creatures that exist. Pippalāda explains that, through austerity, Prajāpati, the Lord of Creation, produced the elemental forms of matter and life-force. Through their interaction all the present forms of existence were produced. Those who think the material force is primary and seek it through ritual and piety are following the path of the ancestors. Although they gain a great reward in the realm of the ancestors, they will be subject to re-birth and re-death. "But those who seek for the Self by austerity, purity, faith and knowledge reach the sun, the [symbolic] foundation of the primordial life-force. That is the final goal, unending and without fear, from which there is no returning. That is the stopping [of saṁsāra]" (1.12).

Bhargava wants to know what powers support and illumine this world, and which among them is the greatest power. Pippalāda identifies wind, water, earth, and fire as primary elements supporting everything in this world and ear, eye, mind, and speech as powers illumining all things. But greater than any of these, he explains, is the primordial life-force (*prāṇa*) without which there would be nothing to support or illumine.

Kausalya follows up on this reply, asking for both the source of the life-force and the process by which it comes to be associated with this body and this self. Pippalāda acknowledges that these are profound questions, but because Kausalya is extremely well qualified and devoted to Brahman, he agrees to answer them. The life-force is born from Ātman and enters this body according to capacities determined by all previous activities. The Ātman, dwelling in the heart, takes form in all the vital functions of the mind and body and also in the external elements of wind, fire, earth, and sun that support this existence.

Now Gārgya asks how waking and sleeping consciousness are produced and in what they are grounded. Using the imagery of ritual and likening the life-force to the sacred household fire that is the basis of all religious practice, Pippalāda answers that consciousness is grounded in Ātman. Through an evolutionary process this consciousness comes to be diffused among the various organs of sensation and perception, which are subtler forms of the material force of which external objects consist. In waking experience, consciousness reaches out through the eye, ear, nose, tongue, skin, and mind, re-establishing contact with the elements of air, fire, water, earth, and ether. In sleep, consciousness is not diffused through the organs into the external world, but concentrates itself into a greater force whereby whatever has been experienced previously can be re-experienced, and where new experiences can be had directly without the mediation of the senses. Finally, in deep sleep, consciousness is concentrated totally and illumined fully. Here in the purity of the Self there are no experiences and no dreams; there is only the total bliss of the highest Self. "One who knows that Imperishable Self, in which are grounded the intelligent self, the life-forces, the elements of existence, and all the Gods, becomes all-knowing, my dear, and enters into all existence," concludes Pippalāda.

Throughout his teaching up to this point, Pippalāda has made generous use of the imagery of ritual and has frequently couched his explanations in the language of religion. But at the same time he has made it clear that, worthy as the way of ritual is, only through knowledge can one can be liberated from saṁsāra. It is probably to get him to take a clear stand on the relative merits of the way of ritual and the way of knowledge and to reveal what relationships, if any, exist between these two ways, that Satyakāma asks the next question: "What does he gain, who meditates on A–U–Ṁ until the end of his life?" Pippalāda's answer reveals how ritual has been internalized and transformed into the way of knowledge in the Upaniṣads. The chants are no longer taken to be liturgical offerings, but are devices for focusing meditative attention on Brahman. "The sound A–U–Ṁ," he tells Satyakāma, "is Brahman, in both its lower and higher form." He goes on to explain that a person is assured a speedy re-birth as a human being and enjoys greatness in this world by meditating only on the sound of "A." By meditating on two sounds, "AU," the chants can lead him to the intermediate world between the realm of Brahman and the realm of humans. But by using all three sounds, "A–U–Ṁ," to meditate on the highest Person (Ātman), the meditator comes to see the Person dwelling in the body who is higher than the highest life. This is how the chants lead to the realm of Brahman from which there is no returning. "In this way a wise person, using only the sound A–U–Ṁ as a support, achieves that existence which is peaceful, unaging, undying, fearless and supreme."

The final question is Sukeśa's, who wants to know who the person with sixteen parts is. The question refers to a teaching, current at the time, about how the individual self came to be separated from the universal Self and the means by which it became established in this world. Pippalāda explains that initially life was created from the universal Self. From this primordial life came the other fifteen parts of the individual person: faith, ether, air, light, water, earth, sense organs, mind, and food. From food came strength, austerity, hymns, action, and the world. In the world, names or individuals were established. The separation of these distinct features of existence out of the universal Self and their coming together to form the individual person make possible human life in this world. Liberation is the reverse process, the process of reuniting these separate parts in the universal Self from which they originated. Pippalāda uses the image of many streams of water, all originating from the same water that falls upon the earth in different forms and in different places, reuniting in the mighty ocean: "Just as these flowing rivers tending toward the ocean, on reaching the ocean, disappear, their individuality being destroyed so that they are simply called 'ocean,' even so will the seer established in these sixteen parts tending toward the universal Person, upon reaching that Person, lose all individuality, and be called simply The Person. That One, without parts, is immortal" (6.5). Because the individual person originates in the undivided universal Self, the loss of individuality in returning to the "Source" is not something to be dreaded or feared. It is, instead, a joyous homecoming, a return to primordial greatness that cannot be comprehended in terms of individual beings and qualities.

## BRAHMAN AS ULTIMATE GROUND

The quest for Brahman as the ultimate ground of all existence and the consequent identification of Brahman with Ātman, the ultimate ground of personal existence, is clearly exhibited also in the debate between Yājñavalkya and Gārgī in the eighth section of the third chapter of the Bṛhadāraṇyaka. This debate takes place in the context of a royal contest. King Janaka of Videha called for the celebration of a great yajña. Priests and wise persons from all over the kingdom were in attendance, so Janaka, always interested in spiritual knowledge, declared a contest to find out who was the wisest of all the wise people gathered. As a prize he offered a thousand cows, each with ten gold coins fastened to the horns, saying to the assembly "Venerable Brāhmaṇas, let the wisest one among you take away these cows." When no one else dared claim them, Yājñavalkya ordered his pupil, Sāmaśravas, to take the cows. Thoroughly angered by his boldness, the other priests quickly challenged Yājñavlkya's right to the cattle and gold. One after another, they put to him the most difficult questions they could conceive. But Yājñavalkya was equal to the challenge, answering every question to the satisfaction of the whole assembly.

Finally, the renowned Gārgī Vācaknavī challenged him, telling the assembly that she will ask two questions. If Yājñavalkya can answer these two questions, then it must be admitted that he cannot be defeated, and he may keep the cows and the gold. The first question concerns the foundation of all existence and all time. Using the imagery of woven cloth, where the cloth is contained in the warp and woof woven on the loom, she asks, "That which is said to be above heaven and beneath the earth as well as in between these two, and that which is called the past, present, and future—across what is that woven, like warp and woof?" Yājñavalkya answers that space is the foundation of existence, for all things are contained in space: "Across space is that woven, like warp and woof."

The next question is more difficult. Indeed, Gārgī has laid a trap for Yājñavalkya. Attempting to get him to describe Brahman, the ultimate reality in which everything else, including space, is grounded, she asks, "Across what is space woven like warp and woof?" She knows that if he says this cannot be known he will be judged to lack knowledge. On the other hand, if he identifies something else as the ground of existence he will have opened up an infinite series in which another ground can always be postulated by the simple arithmetical process of adding one more unit. He will thus reveal his ignorance by claiming that Brahman is not the ultimate. His dilemma is caused by the fact that, if Brahman is ultimate, then it is its own ground. The question of what it is grounded in cannot be answered by postulating yet another ground, for to do so would constitute a denial of the fact that Brahman is the ultimate reality, grounding all existence, including itself.

Yājñavalkya finds a way between these two alternatives. Space, as the container of all existence and time, is grounded in something, but not in a particular kind of being. "That ground," says Yājñavalkya, "is called the Imperishable (*akṣara*). It is neither coarse nor fine, neither short nor long, neither glowing nor adhesive, without shadow or darkness, having neither air nor space, untouchable, odorless, tasteless, without eye, ear or voice, without mind, radiance, life-force, or mouth, immeasurable, without inside or outside. It neither eats nor is eaten." Yājñavalkya here denies that Brahman is a being that could have particular characteristics while at the same time he maintains that Brahman is that in which all existence is grounded.

He then goes on to identify the Imperishable Brahman, ground of the universe, with the Imperishable Self (Ātman), ground of personal existence: "Truly, Gārgī, that Imperishable [Brahman] is unseen, but is the seer; is unheard, but is the hearer; is unthought, but is the thinker; is unknown, but is the knower. There is no seer but this; there is no hearer but this; there is no thinker but this; there is no knower but this. Across this Imperishable [Brahman], Gārgī, is space woven like warp and woof."

Acknowledging the profundity of his reply, Gārgī turns to the assembly saying, "Venerable Brāhmaṇas, you may think it a great thing to get off with merely bowing to him. No one of you will defeat him in arguments about Brahman!"

Because Brahman is ultimate it cannot be reduced to anything else, for everything else is derived from Brahman. Nor can it be adequately described, for whatever descriptions might be applied are taken from specific features of experience and the world that represent the undivided ultimate ground of existence only partially and in a fragmented way. Understanding this, the student in the Kena asks his teacher how it is possible for anyone to be a teacher of Brahman: "We do not know how one can teach that to which the eye does not go, to which speech does not go, to which the mind does not go" (1.3). The teacher praises his understanding, saying that it is indeed different from the known, but above the unknown. It is not knowledge in the ordinary sense, but, since it is the ground of everything that exists and all that we are, we experience it directly, although dimly and partially, in our everyday activities and existence. As he explains, Brahman is not what is expressed by speech but, rather, the power making speech possible; not what the mind thinks but, rather, the power by which the mind thinks; not what is seen by the eye but, rather, the power by which the eyes see; not that which is heard by the ear but, rather, the power by which one hears; not that which is breathed but, rather, the power by which one breathes.

He then challenges the student to go beyond rational understanding, telling him, "If you think that you have understood Brahman well, then you know it only slightly, whether it refers to [the ground of] your self or [the ground of] the Gods" (2.1). When the student returns, he says, presumably on the basis of insight and direct intuitive knowledge gained through meditation, "I think it is known, for neither do I think I know it well nor do I think that I do not know it." Commending this recognition that though Brahman knowledge is quite unlike ordinary knowledge, still it is a kind of knowledge, much more precious than ordinary knowledge, the teacher responds, "To whomever it is not known, to him it is known; to whom it is known, he does not know. It is not understood by those who understand it; it is understood by those who do not understand it" (2.3).

Although as the undivided ground of reality Brahman cannot be conceptualized or described, still it can be known directly through the Self, for the inner Self, the ground of personal existence, is identical with Brahman—this is the great secret of the Upaniṣads. As the great teaching of Śandilya proclaims, Brahman is the source, sustaining power and life of all existence, and the Self within the heart. First, he refers to Brahman: "Indeed, this whole world is Brahman, from which it comes forth, without which it would dissolve, and by which it breathes." He then describes the Self: "This is my Self within the heart, smaller than a grain of rice, than a barley kernel, than a mustard seed, than a millet seed or than the kernel of a millet seed. This is my Self within the heart, greater than the earth, greater than the atmosphere, greater than the sky, greater than these worlds." Having indicated that the Self simultaneously dwells within a person and transcends personal existence, he explicitly affirms the identity of Self with Brahman: "Containing all actions, all desires, all odors, all tastes, embracing this whole world, without speech, without concern, this is the Self of mine within the heart; this is Brahman. On departing from here I shall enter into Him. One who believes this will have no more doubts" (Chāndogya, 3.14).

## Quest for Ātman

The identification of Ātman and Brahman would have been impossible without profound discoveries about the self. Questions about the self—Who suffers? Who is reborn and subject to re-death? Who can be liberated from saṁsāra?—motivated a variety of attempts to discover the ultimate ground of personal existence.

### PRAJĀPATI TO INDRA

The criteria of the Self are put succinctly in the parable where Prajāpati (Lord of Creation) tells the Gods and demons that "That Self who is free from evil, free from old age, free from death, free from grief, free from hunger and thirst, whose desire is the Real, whose intention is the Real—he should be sought; him one should desire to comprehend. One who finds and knows this Self obtains all worlds and desires" (Chāndogya, 8.7–12).

When the Gods and demons heard this teaching, they resolved to seek that Self to obtain all the worlds and all their desires. With fuel in hand, Indra, delegate of the Gods, and Vairocana, representative of the demons, came to Prajāpati, asking to be accepted as students. After they had shown their seriousness by living the disciplined life of students of sacred knowledge for thirty-two years, he asked them what knowledge they were seeking. Upon being told they wanted to know the Self that was free from old age and death, that participated in the Real, and that satisfied all desires, he instructed them to look at the image seen in the eye of another person or a mirror and to report back whatever of the Self they failed to understand. When they told him that they saw themselves so clearly that even the nails and hairs appeared distinctly, he told them to look at themselves in a mirror again, when they were well groomed and well dressed. Doing so, they told him that now they saw themselves "well adorned, wearing their best clothes and neat. . . ." That is the Self," he said, "That is the immortal, the fearless; that is Brahman."

When he saw them go away, well pleased and satisfied with this teaching, Prajāpati said, "They leave without knowledge of the Self.

Whoever follows such a teaching, whether God or demon, will perish." Vairocana returned to the demons teaching that the Self is this body, and that one will obtain the best of both this world and the next world by serving this bodily self. That happiness is found in satisfying this bodily self is indeed the teaching of the demons, observed Prajāpati.

But Indra realized that if the Self is identical with the bodily self, then whenever the body changes, so does the Self. Furthermore, when the body perishes, so does the Self. Knowing that this cannot be the immortal Self he was seeking, Indra returned to Prajāpati for further instruction. After another thirty-two years of the disciplined life, Prajāpati told him, "He who moves happily about in a dream is the immortal, the fearless; that is Brahman" (8.10.1).

Again, Indra was dissatisfied with Prajāpati's teaching and returned, protesting that not only is the dream self subject to many disagreeable experiences, but it is subject to death within the dream world. Prajāpati agrees that this is not the highest teaching and tells Indra that, if he lives another thirty-two years of disciplined life with him, he will instruct him further about the Self.

The teachings up to this point have suggested to Indra that the Self is to be identified neither with external objects nor with internal objects (dream objects) of consciousness. Now, another thirty-two years later, Prajāpati tells him that the real Self is found in dreamless sleep: "When a person is sound asleep, composed, serene, and knows no dream—that is the Self. That is the immortal, the fearless; that is Brahman" (8.11.1).

Before reaching the Gods, Indra saw a serious problem with this teaching also: "Surely, this Self in the condition of deep sleep is not aware of himself or of anything around him. It is as though he were annihilated. I see no good in this teaching." Prajāpati agrees with this assessment, telling Indra that if he lives with him as a student for another five years he will reveal the final teaching about the Self.

Having prepared himself by living the austere disciplined life of a student for 101 years, and having reflected on the lower teachings about the Self, Indra is now ready for the highest teaching. "O great one," said Prajāpati, "This body is surely mortal; it is taken over by death. But it supports the bodiless, deathless Self. Indeed, the embodied Self is taken over by pleasure and pain and there is no freedom from pleasure and pain for the embodied Self. The wind, clouds, lightning and thunder are without bodies. Now just as these, when they arise from yonder space and reach the highest form, appear each with its own form, so does this serene Self, when it rises up from this body and reaches the highest light, appear in its own form. That Self is the Supreme Person" (8.12.2).

The teaching concludes with the advice that, by realizing the Self as a spiritual person independent of the body and consciousness, a person obtains all worlds and all desires—just as the Gods who dwell in the realm of Brahman control all worlds and desires by meditating on that Self.

This entire account is typical of a number of important attitudes: (1) Nothing else is as important as sacred knowledge, for it is the key not only to immortality and unending bliss after death, but also to happiness in this world. (2) Sacred knowledge is practical rather than theoretical. It must be realized in human experience and therefore requires the careful preparation of a dedicated and disciplined life. (3) This knowledge is exceedingly difficult to achieve; even Indra, king of the Gods, required 101 years of disciplined living and learning to comprehend the highest teaching of the Self. (4) A spiritual teacher and guide—a guru—is necessary because this knowledge is personal and experiential. (5) Self-knowledge is gained progressively. Indra must first understand that, although the bodily self participates in Ātman existence, it does so incompletely. The Self is more than body; it is mental as well. But the mental self, identified with the dream self by Prajāpati, is also incomplete, for a person continues to exist even in deep sleep, where there is awareness of neither external objects nor internal objects.

At a still deeper level, Prajāpati suggests that the Self should be thought of as the power that underlies and makes possible consciousness itself. But Indra, assuming mistakenly that awareness of objects is the only kind of consciousness possible, does not understand how the Self can be the ultimate ground of subjectivity. He complains that realizing a Self beyond objective consciousness is no better than death—in either case all consciousness is lost, he protests. In the final stage of understanding, Indra presumably realizes that the "form" of the highest Self cannot be reduced to any other form—not bodily form, not mental form, not even the form of consciousness itself. The Ātman is its own form; it is the self-less Self.

## SELF AS PURE SUBJECT

There is no explanation of the Self that is beyond consciousness in this chapter of the Upaniṣad, but in the fourth section of the second chapter of the Bṛhadāraṇyaka, Yājñavalkya explains this idea to his wife, Maitreyī. In preparation for entering the third stage of life as a forest-dweller he tells her that he will make a final settlement, giving her her share of his wealth and property. "Would all the wealth on the earth make me immortal?" asked Maitreyī, knowing that he was renouncing these inferior material things in favor of greater spiritual treasure. "No," replied Yājñavalkya, "wealth will enable you to live like the rich, but it will never bring immortality." Telling him that she is interested in immortality, not wealth, Maitreyī asks him to tell her whatever he knows of the way to immortality.

"My dear wife," said Yājñavalkya tenderly. "You have always been dear to me and now you speak precious words. Come, sit down, and I will explain it to you." In what follows, he explains that the Self is the basis of all value and worth. Husband, wife, sons, wealth, social class, the world, the Gods, existence itself—"all these are dear not for their own sake, but for the sake of the Self. Truly, Maitreyī, it is the Self that should be seen, heard of, reflected on and meditated upon. Through seeing, hearing, thinking of and understanding the Self everything is known."

To emphasize that everything that exists has its basis in Ātman, Yājñavalkya proceeds to tell her that the various forms of existence are not different from the Self and that even the Gods ignore a person who thinks that they (the Gods) are different from the Self: "This brāhmaṇa, this kṣatriya, these worlds, these Gods, these beings and everything are this Self." He then gives a number of examples to illustrate that, although the Self is the basis of all existence, it is so subtle that it cannot be grasped by ordinary means; only an extraordinary knowledge can reach the Self. "As a lump of salt dissolves when thrown into water leaving no salt to grasp, but making water salty wherever one may taste it, *so does this great being [Ātman] consists in nothing but knowledge. Arising out of the various elements, one vanishes into them. When he has departed there is no more knowledge*" (italics added).

Maitreyī is confused by this explanation of immortality. First she is told that the Self is knowledge, then that, when the Self is realized, there is no more knowledge. Yājñavalkya's explanation of self-realization sounds like self-annihilation. "How can this be?" she asks.

Yājñavalkya replies that this teaching is confusing only when knowledge is assumed to be dualistic, the result of the interaction of a subject with an object. But in the case of Self-knowledge, since the Self is everything, there is no object to be known, and hence knowledge in the ordinary dualistic sense is impossible. Since the Self is of the nature of pure knowledge, when the confusion and ignorance surrounding the Self is removed, it stands revealed in its own luminosity.

This insistence on the nondualistic nature of reality and the self-luminous quality of ultimate reality is so basic and important to the whole Indian tradition that Yājñavalkya's explanation deserves to be quoted in full: "Where there is duality, as it were, there one smells another, there one sees another, there one hears another, there one speaks to another, there one thinks of another, there one understands another. Where, indeed, everything has become the Self, then by what and by whom should one smell, then by what and by whom should one hear, then by what and to whom should one speak, then by what and on whom should one understand? By what should one know that by which all this is known? By what, my dear, would one know the knower?" (2.4).

Yājñavalkya is here affirming the identity of the Self as pure intelligence with the ground of the world. Since they are identical, there can be no question of Ātman coming to know Brahman. This Ātman-Brahman is of the nature of pure intelligence and, when its fullness and purity is realized, then all is immediately and spontaneously illumined by Ātman's own light. There is no object to be known, and no separate subject seeking knowledge; dualistic knowledge at this level, the level of undivided reality, makes no sense. The challenge is not to discover a new reality but, rather, to recover the reality that grounds all existence but that has been obscured and lost through ignorance.

## Tat Tvam Asi

This identity of the ground of personal existence with the ground of external existence is revealed by Uddālaka to his son, Śvetaketu, in the most famous teaching of the Upaniṣads: *Tat Tvam Asi* (*tat* = "that," Brahman; *tvam* = "you," inner or Ātman Self; and *asi* = "are"). This teaching begins when the son returns some after twelve years of Vedic studies with his guru, proud of his learning and arrogant. "Śvetaketu, since you think yourself so learned and are so conceited, I presume you asked for that instruction by which what is unheard becomes heard, what is unthought becomes thought and what is not understood becomes understood?" his father asks. When Śvetaketu admits that he does not know that, and asks how there can be such a teaching, Uddālaka replies, "My dear, just as by knowing one lump of earth everything made of earth becomes known—the various distinctions arise only from speech, while the truth is that even the modifications are only earth." He gives other examples, such as things made from gold and iron, pointing out that in all these cases, although there are many things made of iron or gold, when one knows the gold or iron of which they are made, then one knows all these things insofar as they are gold or iron.

The examples are similar in spirit to the modern physical explanation of all material existence which maintains that, when the one-hundred-plus basic elements and the laws of their combinations are known, then the composition of the entire material world is known. Of course, Uddālaka is not concerned primarily with the physical universe; he is looking for a single unified ground of all existence. Uddālaka explains that all the myriad forms of existence constituting the entire world are unified in their ground and origin. Through the manifestations of heat, water, and food energy—and the resulting differentiation by shape and form—this original Brahman appears to be a multitude of distinct existences. But the wise know that all these different forms of existence have the same Brahman as their ultimate ground. From this Brahman they originate and to it they return at the end of their separate existences.

Uddālaka tells Śvetaketu, "When a person departs from here his speech enters his mind, his mind enters the life-force, the life-force enters heat, and heat enters the highest divine power [Brahman]. That which is the ground of all existence this whole world has as its self; that is the Real, that is the Self. You are That [*Tat Tvam Asi*], Śvetaketu!" (Chāndogya, 6.8.6–7).

Eight more times Uddālaka tells Śvetaketu that in his inner Self he is identical with the ultimate ground of all existence. The first three times he repeats the identity formula, he prefaces it with parables illustrating how Brahman constitutes the underlying unity of all existence: as bees combine all the nectars they collect into the one honey they make, as all the rivers merge in the one great ocean, and as all of the parts of a great tree are united in a single life, even so all forms of existence are united in Brahman as the ground of their being.

The next two parables illustrate that, although the ultimate power, Brahman, is imperceptible, it is nonetheless real. As salt dissolved in water can no longer be seen, but is present everywhere in the water, and as the life of the great Banyan tree is contained in the imperceptible kernel of the seed, so is the Brahman that is present in all existence and that is the source of all existence imperceptible.

Before repeating the formula a sixth time, Uddālaka suggests that seeking Brahman without a teacher is like going around blindfolded. But a good teacher can help a person to get rid of the blindfold and arrive at the goal (Ātman realization).

Before the seventh repetition Śvetaketu is advised that for a wise person death is the gradual absorption into Brahman. Finally, before being told for the ninth time that he is identical with the ground of all existence, he is told that the practice of truthfulness is the greatest safeguard of the Self and best guide to final release from bondage.

## FIVE LEVELS OF REALITY

Although the sages of the Upaniṣads seek the most profound level of existence, they do not repudiate the lower levels as mere appearance or illusory existence. Instead, they recognize a number of distinct levels of reality, distinguished according to their permanence and power to produce effects. One of the clearest examples of the tendency to distinguish between levels of reality occurs in the Taittirīya Upaniṣad where five different levels of reality comprising the Self are identified.

At the lowest level the Self is material and is identified with food. At the next level the Self is identified with life: "Different from and within that which consists of the essence of food is the Self consisting of life." Identifying a still higher level of reality, the text goes on to say, "Different from and within that which consists of the essence of life is the Self which consists of mind [rudimentary forms of awareness that humans share with other animals]." Next, a fourth level of reality is recognized. Here is a still deeper source of consciousness and existence: the Self said to be of the nature of understanding (*vijñāna*). Finally, Self is identified with joy as the fifth and ultimate level of reality. Joy (*ānanda*) or bliss is regarded as the root or source of all existence, the foundation of higher consciousness, lower consciousness, life, and matter. (See illustration, p. 178.)

The joy of life and the bliss of salvation stem from the very heart of existence itself, according to this teaching. This is, of course, no ordinary joy or bliss, as the text points out by comparing the bliss that is Brahman with ordinary bliss. "Take a young man, well educated, quick in action, steady of mind and strong of body. If this whole earth is filled with wealth for him, that is one unit of bliss." Then, in a series of comparisons with the bliss of divine beings and the Gods, the bliss that is Ātman is declared to be $10^{10}$ greater than the initial unit of bliss! (Taittirīya, Chap. 2).

A similar teaching, this time with respect to Brahman, occurs in the third chapter, in the dialogue between Varuṇa and his son Bhṛgu. When Bhṛgu approached his father and asked for instruction about Brahman, Varuṇa explained the nature of matter, life, the senses, understanding, and speech, and how the various forms of existence are comprised of these elements. Then he went on to say "Indeed, that from which these beings are born, by which they live, and into which they enter when dying, endeavor to know that as Brahman," emphasizing that Brahman is the origin, the support, and return point of all existence.

Varuṇa now instructs his son to practice austerities to prepare him for the deeper understanding of Brahman, as he describes the levels of Brahman as matter, life, lower awareness, higher consciousness, and, finally, as Bliss. "Having performed austerities, Bhṛgu came to know that Brahman is Bliss, for truly, beings are born from Bliss, live by Bliss, and enter into Bliss when they leave (this existence)."

Lest this teaching of the highest level of reality as the bliss of Brahman be misunderstood to be a repudiation of the lower levels, Varuṇa immediately goes on to emphasize the importance of the lowest level of reality saying, "Do not speak ill of matter. That shall be the rule. Life, indeed, is matter. The body is the eater of material food and life is established in the body."

## UNITY OF EXISTENCE

It is important to recognize that the various levels of reality distinguished in the Upaniṣads are distinctions within a unified organic whole; they are not separate realities. Brahman, as the pure ground of all existence, is said to be beyond all possible description. When Śakalya asks, "What is the Brahman that you know? What is the basis of your Self?" Yājñavalkya replies, "The Ātman can only be described as *neti, neti*—not this, not that—for it is ungraspable, unattached and irreducible" (Bṛhadāraṇayaka, 3.9.26). But this should not be taken to mean either that it is separate from the world or that it is a mere negation of existence. Yājñavalkya emphasizes this in the conclusion of his debate with the assembly of Brāhmaṇas in King Janaka's court. "From what does a person grow forth when he is cut down by death?" he asks. Answering his own question, he declares, "Brahman, which is Knowledge and Joy, is that root, the supreme refuge of the generous giver who stands firm, knowing Brahman" (Bṛhadāraṇyaka, 3.9.28).

It might seem that, if Brahman is indescribable, then it should not be described as "existence, knowledge, and joy" (*sat, cit, ānanda*). But the Upaniṣads do not approach their inquiry into Brahman with this kind of exclusive logic; instead they recognize the complementariness of differing descriptions and views, emphasizing that different perspectives and parameters yield different visions and claims. When the ground of existence is referred to as it is in itself, prior to any manifestations and without characteristics, it is called *nirguṇa* (Brahman without qualities), and all descriptions are rejected with the formula *neti, neti*. Seen as the creative matrix or womb out of which existence issues, this ground is called *Hiraṇyagarbha* (golden womb). Seen in terms of personal qualities Brahman is *Iśvara*, the Lord, embodying supreme wisdom, joy, and creativity. From yet another perspective the world itself is Brahman, for all the myriad forms of existence emerge from this source through its creative energy. Viewed this way, Brahman is *Virāj*, the life-world.

The identification of Brahman with Hiraṇyagarbha, the golden womb of existence, and with Virāj, the entire life-world, links the Upaniṣadic notion with the Vedic ideas of the ultimate reality, thus providing a continuity, despite the remarkable transformation the concept undergoes. Indeed, the identifications with Hiraṇyagarbha and Virāj are transitional, having relatively little significance once the idea of Brahman as pure ground of being without any qualities (nirguṇa Brahman), and the idea of Brahman with qualities (saguṇa Brahman) personified as the Lord, become established. Of course, one of the reasons why Brahman conceived as Virāj or Hiraṇayagarbha loses significance is that the idea of Brahman as both the creative matrix of existence and as the ground of all manifested existence becomes incorporated in the idea of saguṇa Brahman as the Lord of the Universe. While Brahman in itself, completely unmanifest and totally without characteristics, proves to be a philosophical idea of great importance to the developing tradition, it is the conception of saguṇa Brahman, especially when conceived of as the Lord of Existence, that most profoundly affects religious and social life.

## BRAHMAN AS GOD

We must be careful not to overdraw the distinction between nirguṇa and saguṇa Brahman, for these are not two separate realities. They are the same reality seen from two different, though not exclusive, perspectives. By analogy, we can think of nirguṇa Brahman as energy in its undisturbed ground state and saguṇa Brahman, the creative power of the universe, as energy in motion. This idea is beautifully expressed in the symbol of the Lord of the Dance (see Figure 8, p. 248). Here Shiva, as Lord of the Dance, is transforming the energy of Brahman into the various forms of existence through the energetic motion of his creative dance. The countenance of the Lord shows the pure passionless face of nirguṇa Brahman, but the rhythmic lightning movements of his legs and arms reveal the transformation of Brahman into the moving energy of manifest existence in the world.

The Īśa Upaniṣad, Gandhi's favorite, presents a classic statement of the unity of Brahman and the world in the highest Lord (Īśa). "All this, whatever moves and changes in this changing world is enveloped by the Lord," declares the poet, in the first of the eighteen short verses constituting this Upaniṣad. Describing this reality in both its unmanifested ground and in its manifested existence in the world, he goes on to say, "Undivided, motionless, it is swifter than the mind. It is always beyond the senses which never reach it. It moves and remains motionless; though far, it is near; within all this, it is also outside of all this."

In the next two verses he presents a vision of all existence united in the highest Lord, which is also the Self within each person. "He who sees all beings in his own Self and who sees his Self in all beings because of this view is not repelled by anything. Indeed, for one who truly knows, all beings have become one with his own Self. What sorrow or delusion can come to one who has seen this oneness?"

"Those who worship only the unmanifest reality are said to enter into darkness, while those who worship only the manifested reality are said to enter into even greater darkness." On the other hand, "he who knows these two together as a unity crosses over death brought by ignorance, and through knowledge attains unending life."

In the Īśa and Śvetāśvatara we come upon a fully developed theism for the first time. There are hints and suggestions in some of the earlier Upaniṣads, but for the most part they are concerned either with the inquiry into the nontheistic power constituting the ground of all existence or else their notion of the Gods is still Vedic. The theism that developed in India after the Īśa and Śvetāśvatara Upaniṣads, eloquently expressed in the Bhagavad Gītā, is not the result of consolidation of Vedic deities. The Vedic deities, as noted in Chapter 2, were symbolized powers of existence. They were regarded neither as existing prior to everything else nor as creators of existence. Rather, they were seen as manifestations of a deeper power, the power underlying the yajña, making it an effective means of transformation and control of life. This power, the rhythmic norm of the universe known as ṛta, was regarded as superior to the Gods. As the effort to seek out and understand the fullness of this underlying power led the sages of the Upaniṣads to the idea of Brahman as the underlying ground of all existence, the old Gods and Goddesses, already subservient to the ritual and ṛta by the late Ṛg Veda, became obsolete and died a death of neglect.

But the human tendency to endow the greatest conceivable reality with human characteristics and the human need to relate to the ground of being through faith and devotion allowed new Gods to be born that personified and symbolized the newly discovered ultimate power called Brahman. And since this Brahman was identical with the inner Self, these new Gods were regarded as dwelling within the hearts of people as well as having their abode in the highest heavens of reality.

The transformation of the old Vedic deities into aspects of Brahman can be glimpsed in the dialogue between Śakalya and Yājñavlakya in the Bṛhadāraṇyaka. "How many Gods are there?" asked Śakalya. "As many as are invoked in the praise hymns to the All-Gods, namely, three hundred and three and three thousand and three," replied Yājñavalkya. Upon being asked again how many Gods there are, Yājñavalkya reduces the number to thirty-three, then to six, to three, to two, to one and a half, and finally to one. Asked to explain how three thousand and three Gods can be only one, Yājñavalkya explains that the larger number represents only the various differentiated powers of the one. When asked what the one God is, Yājñavalkya answers, "The one God of which these are the manifested powers is Brahman, whom they call That."

Having identified the old deities with different aspect or functions of Brahman, it became possible to regard Brahman itself as God. Since Brahman is the ultimate power and reality, when personified as deity, it becomes the Supreme Lord, the Īśa or Īśvara. But because Īśvara is only a partial aspect of the manifested Brahman, no particular personal symbol of Brahman ever came to be regarded as the exclusive God. Consequently monotheism as understood in the Judaic, Christian, and Islamic traditions did not develop in India. Different people see the Lord in different ways. Some see Shiva, some Vishnu, others Kālī or Krishna, to name only a few of the many symbols of the personal Brahman that have captured the imagination and dominated the life of faith and devotion in India over the centuries.

## Summary

The Upaniṣads are a splendid testament to the human effort to seek a spiritual foundation for existence. They mark a transition from the way of ritual to the way of knowledge through the discovery that the inner Self of each person is identical with the ultimate ground of all existence. In their quest to overcome the continuous round of births and deaths known as saṁsāra, the sages of the Upaniṣads sought a permanent reality underlying the processes and forces of this continuously changing existence. The Vedic Gods symbolized the changing powers of existence; the sages asked, "What is there deeper and more profound than the Gods, that is impervious to all change—indeed, what is the source of change itself?" The question reveals that the Gods were viewed as something less than ultimately or absolutely real, making it possible now to identify them with each other and to regard them as the symbolic manifestation of a deeper ground of existence. This process is begun already in the Ṛg Veda, especially the later portions, which include the Hymn of Origins (10.129), the identification of Prajāpati as the sole creator and the embodiment of all the Gods (10.121), and the construction of the abstract principle, the "All-Maker" (Viśvakarman), as the unifying source of all existence.

The emphasis on the reality and power behind the Gods goes hand in hand with a gradual shift away from ritual activity centering on the Gods to a way of knowledge that internalizes ritual and focuses meditation on the power (Brahman) behind the Gods and the ritual. Brahman is the ultimate ground of all existence, the source, the support, and the return point of everything. But because it is prior to all forms of existence, it cannot be reduced to anything else or be adequately defined in terms of anything else, and thus is not knowable in any ordinary ways.

Fortunately, the second great discovery of the Upaniṣads provides a solution to the problem of knowing Brahman. Seeking an imperishable, undying Self, the sages found that older ideas of the inner self as fire, water, or breath were inadequate. But in their search they discovered that the Self is ultimately the ground of consciousness. Since Brahman was conceived of as pure intelligence, this idea of the inner self as the ground of consciousness made possible the third great discovery, the identity of Self and Brahman. With the discovery of this identity a way of liberation from death and re-death was established, for the ultimate reality, beyond the grasp of death, is as close as one's own self. Because Brahman-Ātman is pure intelligence, the way of knowledge was seen as a way of recovering the original and unchanging self.

Finally, near the close of the great Upaniṣad period, around 400 B.C., a distinction between the unmanifest nirguṇa Brahman and the manifest saguṇa Brahman was made. This distinction, coupled with the eclipse of the Vedic deities by the emerging idea of Brahman as ultimate ground and power of existence, made possible the conception of the Supreme Lord of the Universe. This opened the door for the development of a way of faith and devotion to complement the way of knowledge, a development that we will explore later, in the chapters on the Gītā and the Devotional Way.

## Suggestions for Further Reading

*The Principal Upaniṣads,* ed. and trans. Sarvapalli Radhakrishnan (London: George Allen & Unwin, 1953), contains the Sanskrit text and excellent readable translations of all the early Upaniṣads. This work, by the late Dr. Radhakrishnan, professor at Oxford and Madras and president of India, also has a good, although somewhat Advaitic, introductory essay. (Other translations may also be consulted. Those by R. E. Hume and Juan Mascaro are especially recommended.)

*The Beginnings of Indian Philosophy*, by Franklin Edgerton (Cambridge, Mass.: Harvard University Press, 1965), is the summary of a great scholar's lifetime's work on early Indian thought. An excellent thirty-page introduction is followed by careful translations from the Ṛg Veda (twenty-five pages), Atharva Veda (fifty-three pages), Upaniṣads (fifty-seven pages), Gītā (fifty-two pages), and the Mahābhārata (seventy-eight pages).

*Man in the Universe*, by Norman W. Brown (Berkeley: University of California Press, 1970), is an excellent little book presenting four major ideas that have greatly influenced Indian thought and culture. The language is simple and straightforward, making the ideas intelligible to laypersons and students beginning their study of Indian thought.

*The Vedic Experience*, by Raimundo Panikkar (see Chapter 2), contains translations of important passages from all of the early Upaniṣads and provides excellent introductory remarks and comments.

# 6

# The Jaina Vision

It is August, 1955. On the holy mount of Kunthalagiri, in the state of Maharashtra in India, an old man called Śāntisāgara (Ocean of peace) is ritually fasting to death. He is the ācārya (spiritual leader) of the Digambara Jaina community; now, after thirty-five years as a mendicant, he is attaining his mortal end in the holy manner prescribed by the great saint Mahāvīra almost 2,500 years earlier. Śāntisāgara has owned nothing, not even a loincloth, since 1920. He has wandered on foot over the length and breadth of India, receiving food offerings but once a day, and then with only his bare hands for a bowl; he has spoken little during daylight hours and not at all after sunset. From August 14 until September 7 he takes only water; then unable to drink without help, he ceases even that. At last, fully conscious and chanting the Jaina litany, he dies in the early morning of September 18. The holiness and propriety of his life and of the manner of his death are widely known and admired by Jainas throughout India.[1]

Why did Śāntisāgara choose this way of extreme asceticism? And why is he so widely admired for his ascetic life and ritual death fast—not merely among the four million Jainas but also among millions of other people living in India? To answer these questions, we will have to explore the Jaina vision of life, for Śāntisāgara was simply following the example of the Jaina saints who, for thousands of years, have been attempting to conquer human bondage in this way.

[1]Padmanabh S. Jaini, *The Jaina Path of Purification* (Berkeley: University of California Press, 1979), p. 1.

# Overview

Literally, a Jaina is a follower of a *Jina* (spiritual victor), sometimes also called a "Ford Builder" (*Tīrthaṅkara*) because he shows the way across the ocean of suffering. But the Jinas are neither divine incarnations nor originators of a religion; they are ordinary human beings who have the capacity to purify themselves sufficiently to follow the eternal way of release. Although they are teachers and propagators rather than Gods or God-men, they are highly honored within the community for their extraordinary purity, wisdom, and teaching and are venerated as omniscient and perfect human beings. Thus, the recent twenty-five-hundredth anniversary of Mahāvīra, the last Jina of our time cycle, was celebrated with great festivities and his statues and pictures highly honored. Indeed, even though the scriptures assert that Mahāvīra, like all Tīrthaṅkaras, is an ordinary human being, born of human parents, legends have grown up depicting him as a superhuman being, and the lay community frequently honors him as a deity. This is also a well-known story with the Buddha as well as with other extraordinary persons in India. It represents neither ignorance nor hypocrisy, but the projection of a strong and warmly felt honor and appreciation for a great person who has shown the way.

Jainism is a way of compassion and ascetic self-restraint designed to liberate the *jīva* or soul from the bondage of karmic matter. No Creator God or initial act of creation is recognized. Existence is without beginning or end, and the eternal way of liberation is possible only through human effort. The Jinas, like Mahāvīra, have shown the way by their examples and teachings.

Jainas see the universe as a vast organism, pulsating with life. Countless billions of jīvas (souls) pervade the universe. Some are ensnared in the bodies of humans, gods, animals, or plants; others are trapped in air, earth, or fire bodies. But all are inherently pure and capable of omniscient knowledge—which means that liberation is possible for all. These jīvas have always been ensconced in matter, but since they are inherently pure, the person who can check the defiling and obstructing influx of karmic matter and exhaust the already present accumulations of karma can achieve liberation from the bondage that subjects a person to the round of births and deaths and the accompanying suffering.

Bondage occurs when karmic matter, which pervades the entire universe, enters a person through the channels provided by speaking, thinking, and acting. This karmic matter defiles the purity, limits the energy, and obscures the knowledge of the soul. Every act, physical and mental, attracts a certain amount of karmic matter, but those that are prompted by desire or hate and those that hurt other living beings are the worst, attracting the greatest amounts of defiling and obstructing karma. Because of the original defilement of the soul's bliss, the karmic matter attracted by human action "sticks" to the soul, like dust sticks to a beautiful gem, obscuring its purity and brilliance.

Liberation requires knowledge of the true nature of the soul, knowledge gained through (1) faith in the teachings of the Jinas, (2) actions devoid of any taint of desire or aversion and that bring no harm to other creatures, (3) ascetic practices designed to burn up the already accumulated karmic matter, and (4) ultimately, the cessation of all actions whatever. It must be noted that liberation is not for the human person, but for the soul; the personality must be left behind, for ultimately it is a hindrance to the soul.

In this chapter we will examine the early historical context of Jainism and explore the dominant ideas of bondage and liberation. What were the dominant ideas structuring the intellectual climate in the days of

**Figure 2.** Mahāvīra, A Jaina Tīrthaṅkara. 11th century. (Courtesy, Philadelphia Museum of Art: Given by National Museum, New Delhi, India.)

Parśva and Mahāvīra? How did the early Jaina way differ from other influential ways vying for attention twenty-five hundred years ago? What are the key features of the Jaina concepts of bondage and liberation that have sustained the Jaina way over the centuries? And, finally, in what ways did Jainism contribute to the developing Hindu way?

## Historical Context

The beginnings of Jainism are lost in the dim reaches of antiquity, perhaps rooted in an indigenous Indian culture prior to the coming of the Āryans and the Vedic age. Mahāvīra, twenty-fourth and last Tīrthaṅkara of the present cycle, is reckoned to have lived in the sixth century B.C., while his immediate predecessor, Parśva, lived in the middle of the ninth century B.C. according to Jaina tradition. But the twenty-two previous Tīrthaṅkaras claimed by tradition are entirely beyond the reaches of historical scholarship.

Clearly, the time of Mahāvīra and the Buddha and the several preceding centuries were filled with intellectual excitement, culminating in the great and enduring ways of Jainism, Buddhism, and Hinduism by the fifth century B.C. The Brāhmaṇas and Āraṇyakas (1000–700 B.C.) may be seen as conservative responses to a series of new challenges to the way of yajña. But even though a number of new ideas may be found scattered throughout their pages, the entire tone is so conservative—not to say reactionary—that it is difficult to feel the intellectual excitement that must have been present. However, the Upaniṣads (800–500 B.C.) are another matter; here are great debates and brāhmaṇas seeking wisdom from kings and princes—a situation most unlikely unless the Vedic tradition was being seriously challenged by other ideas and practices.

Perhaps the most impressive evidence of a vigorous religious and philosophical pluralism in the sixth and fifth centuries B.C. comes from the Dīgha Nikāya, one of the oldest Buddhist texts, in a passage describing the views of six teachers advocating ideas and practices clearly outside the Vedic way. King Ajātaśatru, a renowned seeker of wisdom, is describing to the Buddha the doctrines of the other famous teachers whom he has consulted—all of whom, he explained, had failed to convince him that following the life of renunciation provided any benefits for this worldly life. Kassapa, the first teacher, taught that the distinction between moral and immoral action was baseless because everything is totally determined and a person has no control over actions. A second teacher, Gośala, was a contemporary of Mahāvīra and the Buddha. He was a leader of the Ājīvikas, a major and long-established sect of the time which endured for almost two thousand years after his death. In agreement with Kassapa, he held that asceticism and virtue are completely ineffectual because everything is predetermined: "There is no question of virtuous conduct, purity, vows or penance bringing unripe karma to fruition or of exhausting already ripened karma; that is impossible. The round of births and deaths is measured as with a bushel, with its joy and sorrow and its appointed end. It can be neither increased nor decreased, nor is there any surplus or deficit of it."

A third teacher, Ajita Kesakambala, proclaimed a doctrine of materialism, denying the efficacy of religious practice and the possibility of life after death. "Those who preach almsgiving are fools and those who claim the existence of spiritual beings speak vain nonsense and lies. When the body dies both fool and wise alike are cut off and perish. They do not survive death." These sound like the teachings attributed to the Cārvākans by Madhva in his eleventh-century summary of Indian philosophies and may very well represent an early version of this worldly and materialistic view of life.

The fourth teacher, Kacchāyana, taught an atomistic doctrine that may represent the foundations of the later Vaiśeṣhika atomistic theory of existence. Seven atoms, each of them eternal and unchangeable, simple and uncaused, constitute the basis of all existence: these minute bodies of earth, water, fire, air, joy, sorrow, and life are the fundamental building blocks of all existence.

The fifth teacher is Nātaputta, generally agreed to be none other than Mahāvīra, who taught that "A person free from bondage [a *nirgrantha*] is restrained with a four-fold self-restraint. He lives restrained with respect to evil; he has washed away all evil; he lives filled with the knowledge of evil held at bay."

The sixth and last teacher referred to in this section of the Dīgha Nikāya is a skeptic by the name of Sañjaya Belaṭṭhiputta who said, "If you ask me whether or not there is another world I would say so if I thought it was so. But that is not what I say. I say neither that it is so, nor that it is not so; nor that it is otherwise, or not otherwise." There is no evidence of any group or sect that embodies and carries forth these skeptical views, but Sañjaya's position suggests that serious questions were being raised about the possibility of showing that a given theory of reality is true or false. This reveals concern with rather sophisticated epistemological issues, suggesting ongoing controversy over long-established points of view.

Not only is the existence of such a diversity of views among the famous teachers of the day suggestive of a period of great intellectual ferment, but the fact that a king was actively seeking out teachers suggests a sociopolitical atmosphere encouraging this kind of religious and philosophical quest. King Ajātaśatru's succinct and lucid summary of the various competing views suggests further that his whole court was involved in this quest and that it occupied a significant portion of the court's time and energy, providing a kingly example for the people to follow.

Unfortunately, there is no surviving literature from this period to which we can turn to piece together and assess the origins, developments, and arguments of these different views of life and reality. The information and references contained in later works like the Dīgha Nīkaya and Jaina writings are obviously biased in favor of their own systems and only hint at the richness and complexity of earlier views.

Despite the paucity of reliable historical documents, it appears that the currents that gave the Indian way definite shape were operating at full strength already between 800 and 500 B.C. Not only do the powerful Jaina, Ājīvīka, and Buddhist movements emerge with their comprehensive philosophies at this time, but the great synthesis of the ways of knowledge, ritual, and devotion that the Bhagavad Gītā bequeathed to Hinduism undoubtedly also has its beginnings at this time. We have chosen to discuss the Gītā after Jainism, Buddhism, and Yoga because the text of the Gītā itself appears to be later than the beginnings of these other systems and because it provides a valuable entry into the later devotionalism of the Hindu tradition. But the Gītā's vision may very well predate the text, going back even as far as the early Upaniṣads.

We are probably safe in assuming that Māhāvira, a contemporary of Gośala of the Ājīvikas and the Buddha, was heir to long-established ways of ascetic practice and sophisticated doctrines of life. The fact that in the Upaniṣads kṣatriyas such as Janaka, Ajātaśatru, Asvapti Kaikeya, and Pravahana Jaivali are depicted as authorities on spiritual matters, and are shown revealing secret knowledge to brāhmaṇas, strongly suggests that the old Śramana traditions, to which Mahāvīra, Gośala, and the Buddha belonged, were an important influence on the evolution of the Upaniṣadic teachings. Indeed, in the Bṛhadāraṇyaka, Pravahana addresses the highly respected brāhmaṇa, Gautama Aruni, who comes to him as a student, with words that directly state that the nonbrahmanical origin of these new teachings: "Truly, never before has this knowledge been the possession of any brāhmaṇa whatsoever. But I will tell it to you, for who can refuse one who comes as a student of sacred knowledge?" (6.2.8).

It may well be that the Śramana tradition originated not with the Āryans, but with earlier indigenous people. Indeed, it is tempting to identify the Jaina way with the Indus people, for animal emblems associated with the Tīrthaṅkaras are reminiscent of those depicted on Indus seals; the Jaina practice of yoga recalls the lotus-postured figure on some of the Indus seals; and the older Jaina sculptures strongly resemble nude terra cotta figures found in the Indus Valley. Although Mahāvīra and Parśva are both thought to have lived in the Ganges, rather than the Indus Valley, it is possible that their predecessors lived in the Indus Valley and migrated ahead of the approaching Āryans. If this were the case, then perhaps the transformations in the Vedic way noted in the last chapter could be seen as at least partially occasioned by contact with the ancient Jaina and Ājīvika ways—which may have seen saṁsāra as a natural component of the cyclical nature of all existence.

## MAHĀVĪRA

Although twenty-three Tīrthaṅkaras are said to have preceded Mahāvīra, he is *the* teacher of the present era. Little it known about his personal life, for the biographical facts that were deemed important concerned only his practice and his teachings—his accomplishments in overcoming saṁsāric bondage and presenting a path to be followed by other persons. The tradition embellishes his biography with all sorts of achievements and accomplishments to illustrate important Jaina attitudes and teachings, but most of these accounts are legend rather than fact. The outline of his personal life appears to be this: He was born in 599 B.C. at Kundagrāma (near modern Patna). At twenty-eight, upon the death of his parents, he joined the followers of Parśva, living a severely austere life for the next twelve years. In the thirteenth year he achieved omniscience (*kevala*) and came to be recognized as a Jina and Tīrthaṅkara.

For the next thirty years he led the community through teaching and example, gathering around him a great many monks, nuns, and devoted laypersons. Also, according to tradition, one of his first disciples, Indrabhuti, collected and compiled the teacher's words into the Aṅgas constituting the Jaina scriptures. According to tradition, Mahāvīra's followers included some 14,000 monks, 36,000 nuns, 159,000 laymen, and 318,000 laywomen at the time of his death. Although this number has seemed greatly exaggerated to many non-Jaina scholars, it may actually be a reasonably accurate estimate, for once Mahāvīra was recognized as a Tīrthaṅkara he probably inherited most of Parśva's followers. As for the great number of women followers, there is a ready explanation. In the first place, the wives of many Jaina monks may have joined the order. Female relatives—especially widowed sisters and aunts—may have also found the Jaina community a welcome refuge from the difficult life of widowhood. Unlike many other monastic orders, the Śvetāmbara Jainas welcomed women into the religious community.

## JAINA SCRIPTURES

The Aṅgas compiled by Indrabhuti constitute the heart of Jaina scriptures. Altogether there are about forty-five volumes of canonical scripture, collected, composed, and compiled during the thousand-year period between the death of Mahāvīra and the Valabhi Council in the fifth century. The eleven Aṅgas or "limbs" are basic, and the first two of these, *The Book of Conduct*, which spells out the rules for living, and *The Book of Critique*, which examines the "heretical" views opposed to Jaina teachings, are especially important.

The subsidiary canonical works include the twelve Upāṅgas ("secondary limbs"), which are narrative instruction addressed to the lay followers; six volumes of ecclesiastical law spelling out Jaina discipline for both monastic and lay communities; four collections of basic teachings concerned mainly with the practices of nonhurting, restraints, and austerities; ten short "miscellaneous texts" describing rituals and providing hymns for use in preparing for a holy death—like that of Śāntisāgara's; and two volumes of appendices, the *Book of Blessing* and the *Door of Inquiry*, both containing summaries of material from the rest of the canon.

In addition to the canonical scriptures, there are numerous commentaries and philosophical writings by Umāsvāti (second century), Bhadrabāhu (fifth century), Siddhasena (fifth century), Jinabhadra (sixth century), Haribhadra (seventh century), Jinasena (eighth century), and Hemacandra (twelfth century), among others. Since the scriptures embody the teachings of enlightened human beings—rather than revelations of God—it has always been important in the Jaina community to interpret, develop, and apply the teachings of the Jinas. Great effort went into compiling biographies of the Jinas, developing the moral basis of good conduct and the system of monastic discipline, studying the nature of existence through astronomy and cosmology, and developing the study of logic, psychology, epistemology, and metaphysics. It is for good reason that Jainas have always been respected by the other sects and traditions in India, not only for their honesty and moral uprightness, but also for their scholarship. In addition, they produced impressive epic narratives, legends, and devotional poetry that were extremely effective in educating the laity and providing vehicles for their religious and philosophical development and expression.

## HISTORICAL CONTINUITY AND SCHISM

What is completely amazing to a Westerner, accustomed to thinking of the "progress of time" and the rapid change in beliefs and practice from generation to generation, is the continuity of basic Jaina ideas and practice over more than twenty-five centuries.

There was, however, one major schism that occurred shortly after Mahāvīra's death (there is even a possibility that it occurred before his time), dividing the community into the two major sects that comprise Jainism today. The Digambaras (sky clad), to which Śāntisāgara belonged, insist on total nudity, for clinging to clothing, even a loin cloth, is a form of attachment creating passions—as evidenced in the apparent sense of shame that prevents the Śvetāmbaras (white clad) from going naked. For their part, the Śvetāmbaras protest that external signs, such as clothing or the lack thereof, are insignificant and evidence nothing of the interior attainments necessary for liberation. They view Mahāvīra's own nudity as providing the option of going nude, but not as requiring nudity as a condition of true monastic renunciation. Discussions attempting to resolve this issue met with no success, and to this day the practice of nudity is the major issue dividing the two sects.

There are other differences also, although they do not affect the almost total doctrinal agreement between the two sects. The issue next in importance to nudity is whether women should be allowed into the monastic life. The Śvetāmbaras believe that women can become Tīrthaṅkaras and should be allowed to live the monastic life as nuns. Digambaras maintain that women can become Tīrthaṅkaras only after re-birth as men and should not be allowed entry into monastic life. Of course, the Digambara insistence on total nudity for the mendicant life itself constitutes a bar to admitting women, for, while India has approved of nudity for men taking up the religious life, it has never approved of female nudity for religious reasons. For example, although Śevetāmbara monks have the option of nudity, nuns do not.

Practices concerning the presentation of the Jina symbols, accounts of Mahāvīra's life, and collections of canonical scripture also divide the two sects but, as in the case of differences over women and nudity, do not affect their agreement on the basic doctrines concerning bondage and liberation, to which we now turn.

## Bondage

Of course, it is impossible to understand the ideas of bondage and liberation without exploring Jaina views of the self, matter, knowledge, and morality. But these views, philosophically important and interesting in themselves, take on life and meaning for the Jaina community precisely to the extent that they explain the fact of bondage and render intelligible the possibility of liberation. It is the experience of human bondage that we must first come to appreciate if we are to understand the Jaina way.

**The Man in the Well.** There is probably no better illustration of the Jaina conception of the human plight than the parable of the man in the well. This story, focusing on the bondage of karma, is not unique to Jainism, although the version we are following is that of the great seventh-century Jaina writer, Haribhadra. He tells us of a man, greatly oppressed by poverty, who decided to find a new life in another land. After several days he lost his way in a thick forest. Hungry and thirsty, surrounded by wild animals, stumbling along the steep paths, he looked up to see a mad trumpeting elephant charging straight at him with upraised trunk. Simultaneously, a hideous and wicked demoness, laughing madly and brandishing a sharp sword, appeared in front of him. Trembling with fear, he searched for a way to escape. Seeing a great banyan tree off to east of him, he raced across the rugged terrain to its refuge. But when he reached it his spirits sank, for it was so high that not even the birds could fly over it, and its great trunk was unscalable.

Finally, looking all around, he saw an old grass-covered well nearby. Frightened of death and hoping to prolong his life, even if for only another moment, he leaped into the dark hole, grasping a clump of reeds growing from its wall to support himself. As he clung to these reeds he saw beneath him terrible snakes, enraged by the sound of his falling, while hissing at the very bottom was a huge black python, thick as the trunk of a heavenly elephant, mouth wide open, looking at him with its terrible red eyes. More frightened than ever, the man thought, "My life will last only as long as these reeds hold."

But raising his head he saw two large mice, one white and one black, gnawing at the roots of the clump of reeds. In the meantime, the enraged elephant charged the great banyan tree overhanging the well, battering its trunk with his mighty head, dislodging a honeycomb swarming with bees. While the angry bees were stinging the poor defenseless man, a drop of honey chanced to fall on his head and roll down his face to his lips, giving him a moment's sweetness. Forgotten were the python, elephant, snakes, mice, bees, and the well itself, as he became possessed by the craving for still more drops of sweet honey.

Haribhadra interprets the parable with forceful clarity. The journeying man is the soul or life-principle (*jīva*) and his wanderings are the four types of existence in which the life-principle dwells: divine, human, animal, and lower than animal. The wild elephant is death, the wicked demoness old age. The banyan tree represents salvation, for it is out of reach of death, the elephant. But no person attached to the senses can achieve this refuge. The well is human life itself and the snakes are the passions that craze and confuse, preventing a person from knowing what to do. The clump of reeds is a person's allotted lifetime during which the soul is embodied in this form. The mice are the weeks and months that destroy the support of life, and the stinging bees are the many afflictions that torment a person destroying every moment of joy. The terrible python at the bottom of the well is hell, which seizes the person ensnared by sensual pleasure and imposes pains by the thousandfold. The few drops of honey are the pleasures of life that bind one to terrible suffering. "How," concludes Haribhadra, "can a wise person want them in the midst of such peril and suffering?"

## CAUSES OF BONDAGE

To Haribhadra it is clear that the aversion to pain and suffering and the desire for pleasure that direct our lives are rooted in ignorance. But what is the source of this ignorance? How do we get caught up in this ignorant, wasteful, and destructive life? Who or what creates the human bondage that manifests itself in untold suffering and the repeated deaths and births that string out this torment for a seeming eternity? The Jaina answer places the responsibility for our condition—and the hope for liberation—squarely upon ourselves. It is we who, through thought, speech, and action, create and perpetuate our own bondage.

Each present moment of existence is "earned" by our past actions and each future life is "earned" by our present life. If my next birth is in the form of a less capable person in less fortunate circumstances, or as an animal, plant, or even a still lower simple organism having only air, fire, or water for a body and possessing only the sense of touch, it will be so because my own greed, hatred, and anger, expressed in hurtful and dishonest activity, will have merited this increased bondage. It is the conduct of our own thoughts, speech, and actions that causes bondage.

To understand how immoral conduct causes bondage and how moral conduct can effect liberation, we must investigate the Jaina vision of reality. According to the Jainas, reality consists of two fundamentally different kinds of substances, each with its own distinctive qualities and modes. These two kinds of substance, souls and material atoms, operate within a spatiotemporal context through which their movements cause the creation and destruction of things constituting the world around us.

The essence of the soul (jīva) is life and its chief characteristics are knowledge, bliss, and energy. In its pure state—not associated with matter—its knowledge is omniscient, its bliss pure, and its energy unlimited. But the matter that embodies the soul defiles its bliss, obstructs its knowledge, and limits its energy. This is why matter is seen as a fetter binding the soul.

The word for matter, *pudgala* is derived from *puṁ*, meaning "coming together," and *gala*, meaning "coming apart," and reveals the Jaina conception of matter as that which is formed by the aggregation of atoms and destroyed by their disassociation. There is an infinite number of these invisible, and indivisible atoms, each possessing the qualities that make possible seeing, tasting, touching, and smelling when the atoms are aggregated to constitute an existing thing. These atoms of matter come together to form all the perceptible objects of experience. Most significantly, they also constitute the senses, mind, and speech that form the subtle body of the soul through which experience is possible. The matter constituting the senses, mind, speech, and volitional faculty is thought to be especially subtle and fine (in distinction to the coarse matter making up the physical objects in the world) and is called karmic matter.

This view of karma as a material force distinguishes the Jaina view from other Indian views that take karma to be only a psychological or metaphysical force. Jainas do not deny the moral, psychological, and metaphysical dimensions of karma, but they insist that the primary dimension is that of a subtle material force. Thus, Jainas share with other Indian thinkers the idea of karma as a determinant of future existence, agreeing that each action leaves a residual force that inevitably expresses itself as a determinant of existence at a future time. They also accept the common analogy of this residual karmic force to a seed, which, given the right conditions, will grow and bear fruit according to its own nature. The implication is that each person will reap the results of his or her every action, in the form of either reward or retribution, and either immediately or in the future. This is the inexorable law of karma as understood by nearly every Indian thinker.

The uniqueness of the Jaina view of karma is in the insistence on the material basis of this law of life. According to them, the universe is filled with tiny imperceptible particles of karmic matter, indistinguishable from each other and floating about freely until attracted to an embodied soul. In a way, their view of karma is similar to our view of the atmosphere as pervaded by tiny indistinguishable molecules of air that can only be felt when aggregated and set in motion as wind.

It is important to understand that the Jainas view embodiment as karmic: the body, senses, mind, intelligence, and volitional faculty are all constituted by karmic matter and are not part of the soul itself. Instead, they obscure the omniscient knowledge, defile the pure bliss, and limit the energy that are the soul's natural qualities, thereby constituting the bondage that limits the expression of these qualities.

Although we are inclined to think of the senses and the mind as windows on the world or doorways to knowledge, from the Jaina perspective they are actually blinders and filters, obscuring the natural luminosity of the soul. Real knowledge is obtained not from the senses or the mind but from the soul's inherent luminosity. The difference between a wise person and an ignorant person is that a wise person's mind blocks out less of the soul's natual knowledge than does the ignorant person's mind. A popular analogy suggests that as when the fog and clouds are cleared away the light of the sun illuminates the entire world, even so, when the karmic obstacles are removed from the soul, its natural omniscience will reveal everything.

But why, if the soul is inherently pure and omniscient, does it come to be embodied in matter and thereby subjected to the bondage of repeated births and deaths? The Jainas really have no answer to this question, for they do not look at it in this way. For them embodiment is the beginning point; it is the condition in which we all find ourselves. None of us has the experience of being perfect, free, or omniscient. The assumption is that souls have always been embodied, just as gold has always been embedded in ore. Indeed, this analogy is taken a step farther: as gold can be separated from the ore containing it by a refining process, so can the soul be liberated from karma by a process of purification, for the nature of neither gold nor the soul is changed by its association with ore or karma. A later analogy with heat and iron makes a similar point. Just as heat can combine with iron, softening it and removing its strength without changing its nature, so can karma combine with the soul, defiling its bliss, obscuring its knowledge, and limiting its energy, without changing its nature.

For the Jainas, what is important is not the origin of karmic bondage, but its removal. Only when this bondage is removed can the perfection inherent in the soul be realized. Of course, bondage extends far beyond the human condition, reaching out to the countless billions of souls trapped in animal, plant, fire, water, or air bodies that make up the great community of life. But human embodiment is special, for it represents a wonderful opportunity to achieve liberation. Only human actions can effect liberation, and consequently Jainas, like all other Indian thinkers, regard human life as a precious gift. However, this gift carries with it a responsibility to use it well, for in the struggle for liberation there is no divine grace or superhuman help to turn the tide; nothing but human effort counts toward stopping the cycle of torment. Therefore human beings must come to understand the forces and agencies of bondage in order to chart a path to freedom. Elaborate theories of how karmic bondage works have been developed, describing the karmic process in great detail, for understanding the process of bondage is the first step toward eliminating it.

As we have noted, embodiment is a beginningless process that defiles the inherent bliss of the soul. Because of this initial defilement, the soul's natural energy, flowing out through the body by the conduits constituted by thoughts, speech, and actions, is obstructed and forms an energy field around the soul that attracts the freely floating particles pervading the universe. When the soul is infected with the passions of desire and hatred, these particles stick to it, like dust sticks to a moist jewel, obstructing its natural brilliance. Fettered by these new accumulations of karma, every human action accumulates a certain amount of additional karmic matter, with those prompted by desire or hate and those that hurt other living beings attracting the greatest amount of defiling and obstructing karma. It is a most difficult cycle to break, for the initial impurity leads to actions producing yet additional impurities in the soul, which lead to still more karma-producing actions, which, in turn, even further obstruct the knowledge, limit the energy, and defile the purity of the soul. It is as though a blazing fire were to attract its own fuel through burning, so that, although its fuel were constantly being used up by the burning process, this same process would continually replenish the fuel supply, keeping the fire burning.

Indeed, Jainas usually assume that each jīva will pass through innumerable births, occupying at some time or other all of the various kinds of bodies, ranging from those of the Gods and humans to those of plants and lower—such is the difficulty of breaking the karmic cycle.

**Kinds of Karma.** Although the subtle karmic particles pervading the universe are indistinguishable from each other in their free condition, when they are attracted to the soul they take on the characteristics of the acts that attract them, making possible a classification of different kinds of karmas according to the actions producing them and the effects that they will have on a person.

The worst kinds of karma are those that are attracted to the soul by actions proceeding from ignorance and a desire to hurt others. These are said to be destructive, for they destroy the soul's insight into its own nature, generating false views of itself and the material world, and cause the passions of desire and aversion. Desire—expressed as greed, dishonesty, and pride—and aversion—expressed as hatred and anger—destroy pure conduct and lead to further karmic entanglement.

Because the destructive karmas defile the soul's purity, limit its energy, and obscure its knowledge, they allow the entry of a variety of secondary karmas to surround the soul, producing yet additional bondage. These secondary karmas produce the feelings of pleasantness and unpleasantness that help to direct actions along the paths of desire and aversion; determine the particular birth of a soul (i.e., determine whether it will be born plant or human, male or female, black or white, etc.); establish the life span of a particular incarnation; and determine the particular circumstances that will either promote or hinder the quality of spiritual life in a particular incarnation.

It is not necessary to go into the minute details of karmic classification to appreciate the main point: all karmic bondage is earned by the actions producing it. Furthermore, the specific characteristics and effects of the attracted karma are determined by the nature of the act attracting it. For example, if the act proceeds out of jealousy and consists in withholding information from someone, then the attracted karma will take the form of bondage that will eventually cause the loss or obscuring of one's own knowledge. Or, if desire in the form of greed leads to robbery, then the attracted karma will take the form of bondage that will eventually cause the loss of one's own possessions.

The length of time the attracted karma will bind a person is determined by the intensity of the passions motivating the act as well as the nature of the act itself. If, for example, an action performed to help a neighbor is motivated, even slightly, by lust for his wife, then the intensity of this lust will determine the length of time that he will be bound by the resulting karma. Of course, once the karma has produced its full effects, it falls away from a person "like ripe fruit" and returns to a free and undifferentiated state where it is available for attraction to another soul or to this same soul at another time.

But those karmas that have not yet produced all their effects continue to adhere to the soul, constituting a subtle body within the physical body. When the karmically determined life span is up, the soul departs from the physical body and, embodied by the unspent karmic forces, is re-born into another physical body of precisely the kind merited by the accumulated karma. There is no difference between the souls of plants and humans; the differences are only between the karmic and gross bodies that surround the souls. This is why Jainas recognize all living things as part of the same family, regarding the harm done to even the simplest life body as hurting a brother or sister.

This is also why the goal of liberation dominates Jaina life, for karmic bondage means not only the relatively pleasant and blessed life of a human being, but also the untold lifetimes spent embodied as lower forms of life. We need to recall that according to Jaina teachings every soul passes through tens of thousands of incarnations, ranging from fire, mineral, air, or vegetable bodies to those of plants, animals, humans, and Gods. The intense sufferings of the soul in these various embodiments is revealed with great feeling in an eloquent speech of the young prince, Mṛgaputra, in which he begs his parents to allow him to leave home and take up the religious life to cut the bonds of suffering. A few brief excerpts from this speech will make the point far more effectively than will a conceptual description:

From clubs and knives, from stakes and maces, from broken limbs,
have I hopelessly suffered on countless occasions.
By sharpened razors and knives and spears have I these many times
been drawn and quartered, torn apart and skinned.
As a deer held helpless in snares and traps,
I have often been bound and fastened and even killed.
As a helpless fish I have been caught with hooks and nets,
scaled and scraped, split and gutted, and killed a million times . . .
Born a tree, I have been felled and stripped, cut with axes and chisels
and sawed into planks innumerable times.
Embodied in iron, I have been subjected to the hammer and tongs
innumerable times, struck and beaten, split and filed . . .
Ever trembling in fear; in pain and suffering always,
I have felt the most excruciating sorrow and agony . . .
(Uttarādhyāyana Sūtra, 19.61–74)

## Path of Liberation

For someone who, like Mṛgaputra, has felt the sufferings of karmic bondage, the quest for a means to end this bondage takes on an existential intensity that energizes every act of life. Some, like Śāntisāgara, will abandon family, home, worldly possessions, and, through the holy death fast, the body itself. But every Jaina mendicant and layperson, even though not going to the extreme of fasting to death, will make the quest for liberation the central focus of life, undetaking the four restraints—of body, senses, speech, and mind—and taking the five great vows of nonhurting, nonstealing, sexual purity, truthfulness, and nonpossession to check the inflows of karma. In addition, every Jaina will undertake a variety of penances to burn up the karmic forces already accumulated, for Jainism is essentially a quest for liberation through pure conduct and ascetic practice.

Fourteen stages of purification along the path of liberation mark the individual's progress from bondage to omniscience and liberation. These stages are achieved by a combination of deep faith, right knowledge, and pure conduct—the "three jewels" of Jaina practice by which the influx of destructive karmas caused by delusion, false views, and the passions can be halted. Remember, Jainas do not recognize any savior Gods or any divine grace; only human understanding and conduct is available to check the torment of karmic bondage. For this reason Jainas have paid special attention to the nature of knowledge and the norms of conduct. But the individual is not totally alone in the quest for liberation; the Jaina community—lay and monastic—and the examples and teachings of the Tīrthaṅkaras support and nurture the efforts of every faithful Jaina.

Faith is traditionally considered the first of the three jewels because its realization marks the moment in life that decisively turns the individual away from the path of further bondage and toward liberation. We will consider the Jaina view of knowledge first, however, in order to appreciate both the nature of, and the need for, faith.

## KNOWLEDGE

We have seen that the worst kinds of destructive karmas are caused by actions proceeding from ignorance and a desire to hurt others. Ignorance produces karmas that destroy the soul's insight into its own nature and generate false views of itself and the world. This ignorance, caused by the soul's initial defilement, obscures its omniscient knowledge and makes it dependent on perception, reason, and the authority of others for its knowledge. But these kinds of knowledge are extremely limited, obscuring more than they reveal. Even worse, when the limits of these kinds of knowledge are not recognized, and the knowledge claims generated are taken to be the truth about the self or the world, serious falsehood and self-deception occur.

According to Jaina metaphysics, reality is constituted by the innumerable material and spiritual substances, each of which is the locus of innumerable qualities. Not only are there innumerable substances, each with innumerable qualities, but each quality is susceptible to an infinite number of modifications. Clearly our ordinary knowledge (non-omniscient) cannot comprehend this complex reality, for ordinary knowledge is limited by the perspectives adopted by the knower as well as the conditions of space, time, light, and so on. Recognizing the rich and complex nature of reality and the relative and limited nature of ordinary knowledge, the Jainas developed the notion of the "many-sidedness" (*anekānta*) of existence. Our ordinary knowledge only gives us access to one aspect of reality at a time, with the result that in making claims about what is true, we usually resemble the five blind men confronting an elephant.

According to a popular Jaina story, a king once brought five blind men into his courtyard where he had secured a large elephant and asked them to tell him what he had fastened there. Each man touched the elephant, and on the basis of his perceptions, told the king what he knew this thing to be. The first felt the trunk and declared that it was a huge snake. The second touched the tail and said that it was a rope. The third felt the leg and called it a tree trunk. The fourth took hold of an ear and called it a winnowing fan, while the fifth felt the side of the elephant and declared it to be a wall. Because each insisted that his claim was correct and truly described the object in question, they were soon in the middle of a heated argument, each saying the others were wrong and calling them ignorant.

Like the blind men, we too use only what is available from our own perspective, determined by sociocultural conditioning, particular place, time, light, hopes, fears, and, of course, subject to the limitations of our sensory receptors and reasoning power. The moral of the story is clear: any knowledge we claim about reality is limited and partial and should not be mistaken for the whole truth. Indeed, no claim can be said to be unqualifiedly true. Assertions and denials based on ordinary human knowledge are at best true conditionally, that is, true only with respect to the conditions and limitations of the perspective assumed. Just as the blind men should have been more circumspect and have said, for example, "Standing here, feeling the object with my hands, it feels like a winnowing fan. It may be a winnowing fan," so should we understand that our knowledge claims should be asserted only conditionally.

Analyzing the logic of conditional assertion, the Jainas came up with a sevenfold schema for making a truth claim about any particular object. For example, the following assertions are possible with respect to, say, the temperature of a pan of water: (1) It may be warm (to someone coming in from the cold); (2) it may not be warm (to someone coming from a very warm room it will appear cold); (3) it is both warm and not warm, depending upon certain conditions; (4) independent of all conditions, the water is indescribable (all knowledge rests on certain conditions); (5) indescribable in itself, the water may be said to be warm subject to certain conditions (a combination of 1 and 4); (6) indescribable in itself, the water may be said not to be warm, subject to certain conditions (a combination of 2 and 4); and (7) indescribable in itself, the water may be said to be warm and not warm, depending upon certain conditions (a combination of 3 and 4).

The reason why the last three assertions all begin with the claim "indescribable in itself" is that every substance known and described possesses an infinite number of qualities—each of which also possesses an infinite number of modifications. Although knowledge reveals some of these qualities and modifications, it cannot reveal them all. Thus, our descriptions of reality are only partial. The substance itself, with its infinite qualities and modifications, can never be fully known or described.

The sevenfold scheme of conditional assertion forces us to recognize the partial and incomplete nature of our knowledge. This is an important initial step in overcoming the passions, for desire, hatred, pride, anger, and greed stem from a partial and one-sided understanding of things that are dogmatically presumed to be the whole truth. How many times have we embarrassingly realized the inappropriateness of our anger, jealousy, pride, or greed when we came to see the "full picture"? Greed for money vanishes when its attendant evils are recognized. Excessive pride gives way to humility when we come to appreciate the wonderful qualities and accomplishments of others. Anger and hatred disappear when we realize that other objects, situations, or persons are no threat to us. To the extent that we appreciate that the knowledge from which these passions stem is partial, we are encouraged to restrain ourselves until our understanding increases.

**Awakening Vision.** Understanding the partial nature of ordinary knowledge makes Jainas more appreciative of the knowledge of the Tīrthaṅkaras, encouraging faith in their teachings and motivating effort to emulate their lives in the hope of achieving similar omniscience, purity, and bliss. The attendant longing for true insight and knowledge may serve as a catalyst to activate the soul's natural inclination to freedom and direct its energies toward recovery of its omniscience, making possible the momentary flash of insight (*samyak darśana*) that marks the beginning of the way out of bondage.

This first step occurs when the soul glimpses its own true nature because of a temporary suppression of the great masses of obscuring karmas—an enlightenment achieved through faith.

Through faith, the soul's natural yearning for insight into the true nature of existence makes a person more open and receptive to instruction, capable of learning from ordinary experiences (which up to now had been meaningless), as well as from scriptures and teachers, and, most dramatically, from a Jina. Receiving these teachings releases the energy needed to recognize both the presence and source of the defiling and obscuring karmas. This recognition leads to further energetic activity reducing the intensity and duration of the karmic matter holding the soul hostage, releasing a great surge of energy that allows the soul to glimpse, just for a moment, its own pure state and to have a vision of reality as it really is—that is, as the omniscient see it.

Although this awakening experience is only the first stage on the path of liberation, no other attainment except the permanent achievement of mokṣa is of the same order of significance. It is this momentary flash of insight and achievement of purity that directs the energies of the soul to overcoming bondage, guaranteeing eventual liberation. This momentary illumination of the soul is thus the critical turning point. And, although this initial insight into the soul and the true nature of all things is achieved by suppressing, rather than eliminating, the karmic forces, and is therefore only temporary, it should not be underestimated, for it provides the impetus and releases the energies needed for the liberation effort.

Most importantly, this momentary vision of the true nature of the soul enables a person to cease identifying with the body and its actions, bringing the realization that the soul's only pure and proper activity is that of knowing. This realization brings an inner peace that fosters the pure conduct needed to overcome the tendencies toward anger, hatred, pride, deceitfulness, and greed that characterize the unenlightened person's grasping for karmic existence.

This flash of insight also reveals the universal community of souls, engendering a strong feeling of brotherhood for all beings. The great differences between, say, a person and a cabbage are seen to be at the level of qualities and karmic processes, not at the level of soul, where the possibility of omniscience resides in all beings. This realization generates a pure compassion, which expresses itself in the urge to avoid hurting any beings and, more positively, in the urge to help all beings to salvation.

Unfortunately, the achievements of this initial illumination are only temporary, because the karmas have not yet been permanently eliminated, but only momentarily suppressed. When they resurface, the soul finds itself backsliding into its former false views and bondage-producing passions. But once a soul has had a true vision of itself, eventual liberation is assured, for now the energies required for the prodigious effort of eliminating the karmas have been released and a faith has been awakened that guides the person's actions toward liberation rather than bondage.

## FAITH

Faith, awakened in a momentary flash of insight, is constituted by an affirmative attitude toward life and liberation. It is rooted in the soul's momentary insight into its true nature and is nourished by the knowledge taught by the Jinas such as Mahāvīra or Parśva or the accomplished Jaina teachers. It replaces skepticism about the teachings of the Jinas with a positive, though critical, outlook that affirms the truth of these teachings and eliminates desires for gain and profit as sources of motivation. Aversion to ordinary kinds of evil and suffering are replaced with a deeper feeling that regards as unpleasant only that which produces bondage. Faith also frees a person from false beliefs on which worship of Gods and Goddesses is based, from superstitious religious practices such as sacrifice and prayer, and allows recognition of false teachers and doctrines. Positively, faith moves a person who has attained true initial insight to become protective of the Jaina order, provides security in Jaina beliefs and practices, and motivates one to act in a way that will illuminate and exemplify the Jaina teachings and, ultimately, to follow the example of the Jinas in every way possible.

It must be emphasized that, although faith is indispensable to the Jaina way, this is not a blind faith in scriptures or persons. The basis of faith is an experience of a momentary flash of insight into the true nature of the soul, which introduces a positive approach to life and motivates one to work for liberation.

But the understanding of faith needs to be clarified and tested carefully by experience and reason. No other religion has placed more emphasis upon philosophical vision and reasoning as a means of salvation than has Jainism. And no religion has placed more emphasis on personal effort and right conduct as means to salvation, for, while faith provides direction for life and releases the soul's energies needed to stop the karmic accumulations, only prodigious human efforts of moral and ascetic practice can eliminate bondage.

## CONDUCT

The faith and knowledge generated by the initial flash of insight takes one from spiritual blindness and false views (first stage) to the fourth stage of liberation where the new vision reveals the falseness of presently held views and the harmfulness of actions proceeding from these views. But the passions, which have not yet been brought under control, will quickly cloud this new vision and the person will sink back into his or her old ways (second stage). However, because the initial awakening directs the soul's energy toward liberation, this second stage is far preferable to the original blindness, for it makes possible a return to the insight of the initial vision through the oscillating efforts of faith and knowledge (third stage).

Although faith and knowledge prepare the way and provide the necessary direction, it is right and pure conduct that brings a halt to the passions causing karmic bondage and achieves the progress toward liberation marked by stages five, six, and seven. This understanding has resulted in a Jaina commitment to moral principles and practice that may be unique in the world. Not only is the honesty of Jaina businessmen proverbial, but the high moral standards of the entire Jaina community has affected and influenced all the peoples of India and many outside of the subcontinent.

*Ahiṁsā*, or nonhurting, is the basis of Jaina morality, for ultimately all questions of good and evil and right or wrong come down to whether or not the thought, speech, or action in question hurts any life-form. Thus, the five great vows of moral conduct that a Jaina is moved to take upon initial insight into the true nature of the soul are headed by the vow not to hurt any living being; nonhurting is the cardinal rule of Jaina life.

Although Buddhists and Hindus also recognize the principle of nonhurting as a fundamental rule of life, the Jainas have developed this principle most fully and have carried its application the furthest. The term "nonhurting" is negative, but the principle is entirely positive, being rooted in a philosophy that recognizes the community of all living organisms and sees love as the basis of a relationship between all the members of this community. The prohibition against hurting has nothing to do with the fear of eating one's own grandmother (who now may have been re-born as a pig or a cow). Rather, it embodies the realization that all life is one and that to hurt others is to destroy the community of life, which is the basis of all sacredness.

Ahiṁsā implies both action and intention. Hurting is defined as harming other living organisms either deliberately, or by carelessness or neglect, or through actions motivated by pride, greed, hatred, prejudice, or desire. But the very intention of harming others, even if the physical action is not carried out, is regarded as hurting them. All actions rooted in anger, pride, hatred, greed, and dishonesty are regarded as forms of violence and must be renounced and abandoned. Of course, since the whole universe is alive, it is impossible to completely avoid injuring life-forms if one is to act at all. But the degree and extent of hurtful activity can be greatly reduced, and the higher life-forms, which are capable of greater suffering, can be treated with special care and kindness.

Since meat eating requires the slaughter of animals, Jainas are strictly vegetarian. Indeed, they criticized the Buddhists severely for allowing meat eating, pointing out that, although Buddhists were prohibited from killing animals for food or from eating meat from animals that had been killed especially for their food, still eating any meat at all made them partially responsible for the sins of the butchers: if they refused all meat, the butchers would cease killing animals. In a similar vein they criticized the Hindu practice of making sacrificial offerings of animals, pointing out that the wrongness of killing animals could not be alleviated by the fact that the act was performed in the name of religion.

Every Jaina takes vows not to injure any living beings, but the monastic community carries its vows to a further extreme than do laypersons. Both groups refrain from occupations and acts that are particularly hurtful, such as hunting, fishing, making war, or dealing in drugs and alcohol. But monks do not dig in the earth lest they hurt earth bodies; they avoid swimming and bathing or walking in the rain lest they hurt water bodies; they neither light nor extinguish fires lest they injure fire bodies; they avoid sudden movements lest they injure air bodies; and they are extremely careful in walking to avoid injuring vegetation growing along the path. Usually, they sweep the path ahead of them to remove small living beings so that they don't get trampled, and they wear a cloth across their nose to avoid breathing and destroying life-forms in the air.

Jainas also avoid alcohol and honey, which are regarded as literally swarming with life-forms. Figs and other fruits with many tiny seeds and plants with sweet sticky tissue are not eaten because they are regarded as hosts for millions of life bodies. Undoubtedly, the widespread practice of vegetarianism and the general aversion to alcohol in the larger Indian community owe much to the Jaina elevation of non-hurting to the position of the central moral virtue.

The second great vow is that of truthfulness (*satya*), which requires that great care be taken to ensure that speech is always used to promote the well-being of the great community of life. The virtue of truthfulness is closely related to that of ahiṁsā, for the rule is that speech resulting in hurting is to be avoided. Lying is generally considered to lead to hurtful acts, but in cases where deliberately issuing false statements would avoid harmful action, it is allowed. For example, if a hunter asks about the location of an animal he wishes to kill and you lie, sending him in the opposite direction, this action is preferable to telling the truth and contributing to the killing of animals and is required by the vow of truthfulness.

Truthfulness requires complete honesty in all business and professional activity, encouraging the scrupulous behavior of Jaina businessmen that has earned them the respect of nearly everyone. Also precluded by truthfulness are speech acts that might hurt others through unkindness, harshness, rudeness, gossiping, breaking confidences, slander, or even idle chatter.

The third vow, nonstealing (*asteya*), requires that a person refrain from taking what belongs to another, whether in the form of outright theft or in more subtle forms, such as adulterating a product, tax evasion, black marketing, providing improper weights and measurements for exchanged products, failing to provide full value of goods or services exchanged, and so on. One must not accept stolen or lost goods or buy goods at a lower price if they were obtained wrongfully in the first place. The general rule is not to take anything that is not offered to one. Stealing, in any form, is regarded as hurtful activity stemming from greed, and the positive virtue of nonstealing consists in being completely satisfied with what you have so there is not the slightest desire for somebody else's possessions.

The fourth vow is that of sexual purity (*brahmacarya*). The Jaina ascetic abstains not only from all sexual activity, but from all thought about sex as well. Obviously, this virtue could not be practiced in its extreme form by laymen and laywomen. For them, celibacy means that no sexual activities or thoughts were allowed outside of their relationship with wife or husband. The rationale for this vow is that sexual activity proceeds from and feeds desire and the other passions that produce bondage.

The fifth vow taken by every Jaina is that of nonattachment (*aparigraha*). An attitude of nonattachment must be cultivated to put an end to action that seeks identification with the external world of karmic bodies. Thus, aparigraha is much more than simply nonpossession, though this is the most obvious external sign and the first requirement. The mendicant is required to give up all wealth and possessions upon joining the order and the layperson must observe numerous restrictions and conditions on wealth and possession and their means of acquisition. But physical renunciation by itself is not the goal. The goal is to get rid completely of all thoughts and attitudes that are the agents and vehicles of the desire and aversions proceeding from a perspective distorted by karmic accumulations. The vow to eliminate thoughts and actions rooted in desire or aversion is based on the insight that this is an effective way of eliminating the desires and aversions themselves.

These five basic vows are strengthened and expanded by a series of secondary vows that (1) curtail travel; (2) prohibit drinking unfiltered water, certain kinds of food, and certain methods of preparing foods; (3) proscribe brooding, mischiefmaking, giving harmful advice, and watching or listening to unedifying events or performances; (4) obligate fasting; (5) require meditation; (6) enjoin almsgiving; (7) temporarily restrict one's activities to a given location; and finally (8) commit one to a holy death through meditation and fasting.

Through increasingly strict observation of the primary and secondary vows a person can achieve the fifth, sixth, and seventh stages of purification. Now one can, under the guidance of a teacher, take up the meditational discipline required to release the additional energies of the soul needed to eliminate even the subtle secondary passions that are ordinarily hidden from consciousness. If these subtle secondary passions are actually eliminated in the eight, ninth, and tenth stages, the person is ready for the twelfth stage of activity in which the roots of the secondary karmas are destroyed. But if the secondary passions are only suppressed—rather than eradicated—a person will fall from this eleventh stage back to the lower stages.

Once the roots of all the secondary karmas have been eliminated, it becomes possible to eliminate the roots of the subtle primary karmas that defile, obstruct, and limit the soul. In this stage one achieves omniscience and is called variously an Arhat (Noble One), Kevalin (Isolated from Karma), Jina (Conqueror), or Tīrthaṅkara (Ford Builder).

Only one higher stage remains prior to mokṣa, or complete liberation. This fourteenth stage can only be achieved by an Arhat in the moment prior to death, for it requires the coincidence of the total exhaustion of all previously acquired karmas and the complete cessation of all life activities. Thus, for Jainas, unlike Buddhists and Hindus, total perfection is not possible during life, but comes only upon the final death.

## Impact of Jaina Thought

Finally, it should be pointed out that this remarkable way of liberation, whose doctrinal purity over twenty-five hundred years offers valuable insights into the thought of ancient India, has made important cultural contributions to Indian life. Emphasis on the importance of human knowledge led to important accomplishments in philosophy, logic, literature, and the sciences, encouraging non-Jainas to develop and refine their own systems and methods. The contributions of Haribhadra (seventh century), Hemacandra (twelfth century), and Malliṣeṇa (thirteenth century) to Indian logic were impressive enough to stimulate the thinking of major Buddhist and Hindu philosophers and resulted in important conceptual breakthroughs.

Using the vernacular languages to create stories, narratives, and poems to present Jaina teachings to the lay community, Jaina monks contributed a great deal to the development of literature in the vernacular languages—especially Gujarati, Prakrit, and Canarese. Mallinātha's commentaries on Kālidāsa's works have been used and praised by practically all scholars of India's greatest poet. The Jaina penchant for writing and collecting texts resulted in impressive libraries serving the larger community and saved many ancient texts on astronomy, mathematics, and grammar from destruction. Hemacandra's poetic history of the world as contained in myth and legend, his Sanskrit and Prakrit dictionaries and grammar, and his science textbooks, for example, contributed much both to the ongoing study of these subjects and to their preservation.

But perhaps the greatest contributions to Indian life were made by Jaina examples of moral virtue and careful reasoning. Their migrations from the Ganges Valley to the southern tip and over the western borders of the subcontinent allowed them to spread the best of Indian culture to these parts of India through their exemplary lives. Jaina adherence to the rule of non-hurting has been a major factor in the importance that this moral principle has assumed in Buddhist and Hindu life over the centuries. Mahatma Gandhi, whose adherence to non-hurting in the successful efforts he led to throw off the yoke of British colonial rule, brought the principle of non-violence to the admiring attention of the whole world, gratefully acknowledged the great impression made on him by the Jaina ascetics he knew as a youth.

## Summary

Originating sometime before the eighth century B.C., Jainism has deeply influenced Indian life through its philosophical models of bondage and release, exemplification of virtuous conduct, and emphasis on human experience and reason. But these accomplishments are incidental, for the primary aim has always been to help all who can be awakened to the plight of their suffering existence achieve the omniscient knowledge and pure bliss that inheres in the human soul.

Rejecting belief in God as a false view, Jainas have also abandoned the superstitious and magical practices that accompany most religions, relying, instead, on their own efforts to follow the path charted by those wise and good human beings who have achieved liberation, and are therefore venerated as spiritual conquerors and Tīrthaṅkaras. This spirit of self-reliance, and the consequent emphasis on the need to understand the conditions of bondage and the way of release, led the Jainas to develop sophisticated philosophical models and a rationally based ethics.

Bondage is caused, as we have seen, by the accumulation of karmic particles that are attracted by impure and harmful thought, speech, and action. These karmic particles constitute a subtle body that surrounds the soul, defiling its inherent purity, obscuring its natural omniscience, and limiting its energy.

The only way to liberate the soul from this karmic body is to stop the further accumulation of karma and exhaust the karmic forces already accumulated. To this end the Jainas set out an elaborate path of purification consisting of knowledge, moral conduct, and ascetic practice.

Knowledge includes faith based on insight and trust in the teachings of the Jinas and qualified preceptors, as well as the understanding achieved through experience and reasoning, for both kinds of knowledge are needed to destroy the false views that lead to karma-producing actions.

Moral conduct requires eliminating desires and aversions as the motivating forces of actions through the practices of nonhurting, truthfulness, nonattachment, nonstealing, and sexual restraint.

Ascetic practices involve restraining the body, senses, speech, and mind through fasting, nonmovement, yogic activities, and a long list of specific forms of penance.

Through the successful practice of asceticism and moral conduct, and the acquisition of insight and knowledge, the soul can be freed from the karmic bondage chaining a soul to countless births and deaths in every conceivable life-form, subjecting it to untold suffering in these various incarnations. Freed, the soul rises spontaneously to the very top of the universe to enjoy eternal omniscience, absolute bliss, and unlimited power.

## Suggested Readings

By far the best book on Jainism is *The Jaina Path of Purification*, by Padmanabh S. Jaini (Berkeley: University of California Press, 1979). Sympathetic, unbiased, and scholarly, it is written in clear, straightforward English, simple enough for the beginning student of Jainism, yet accurate and profound enough to help the more advanced student. It contains an excellent bibliography, a glossary of Sanskrit and Prakrit terms, and a very useful index.

*Sources of Indian Tradition,* ed. William Theodore De Bary, Vol. I (New York: Columbia University Press, 1967), contains fifty-five pages of translated Jaina tests and explanation by the great scholar A. L. Basham. Topics covered include cultural background, ideas of bondage and liberation, and philosophical and political thought.

Heinrich Zimmer's *Philosophies of India* (Cleveland: World Publish Company, 1961) contains a long illuminating chapter on Jainism. The dozen pages (accompanied by eight plates) on Jaina images are especially informative. Zimmer was convinced that Jainism was pre-Āryan, and he marshalls considerable evidence to support his view. This book, edited by his student, Joseph Campbell, after Zimmer's death in 1943, and published originally in 1951, remains one of the best and most insightful available on Indian philosophical and religious thought.

One of the best books on the more technical aspects of Jaina philosophy is N. Tatia's *Studies in Jaina Philosophy* (Varanasi: Jaina Cultural Research Center, 1951.)

# 7

# The Way of the Buddha

In about 525 B.C. an event occurred in northern India that was to transform the history of Asia. Siddhārtha Gautama, son of Suddhodana and Māyā, underwent a profound spiritual experience that illumined the fundamental causes of human suffering and revealed the way to achieve an existence entirely free of suffering. It was this experience that transformed Siddhārtha into the Buddha—"the Enlightened One."

Of course, if Siddhārtha, the Buddha, had simply become enlightened and freed himself from all the sufferings and anxieties of life, no radical historical change would have occurred, and we probably would never have heard of him. But he did more; moved by compassion for all who suffer, he presented his way of deliverance from suffering to all who would listen.

The teaching caught on, and by the end of King Ashoka's rule in 232 B.C., Buddhism had spread over practically the entire subcontinent, enduring as a major religious, philosophical, and cultural force in the land of its origin for the next thousand years. By the time of its decline in India, in the eighth and ninth centuries, it had already spread to most of the rest of Asia, where it has continued to exert a major influence on the lives of hundreds of millions of people right up to the present. In its Mahāyāna form Buddhism came to dominate religious life and philosophical thought in China, Tibet, Korea, Vietnam, and Japan, and in the twentieth century it has become a minor but important force in Europe and the Americas. In its Theravāda form Buddhism spread to Sri Lanka (Ceylon), Thailand, Cambodia, and Burma, where it has been the major religious and cultural force for most of the last two thousand years.

Our approach to this long and complex story of the development of Buddhism will be to focus on the *three jewels*—the Buddha, his Teachings, and the Buddhist Community—that constitute the core of the Buddhist way. Every Buddhist vows to take refuge in these three jewels as a formal act of becoming a Buddhist. Who is the Buddha? What are the Teachings? What is the Community of Buddhists (*saṅgha*)? These three questions structure our examination of the Way of the Buddha.

We will begin with the Buddha's first sermon and a sketch of the cultural context of his life and message. Our attempt to understand who the Buddha is and what his teachings are will be guided by the vision and understanding that Mahāyāna and Theravāda hold in common. Presumably their shared teachings reflect a core of understanding going back to very early Buddhism—perhaps as far back as the community in which the Buddha himself lived. Finally, in examining the development of the Buddhist Community, we will sort out some of the major differences between the Theravāda and Mahāyāna forms of Buddhism.

## First Sermon

Since his first sermon summarizes the content of the Buddha's enlightenment experience, it is an appropriate place to begin. This concise description of his insight into the conditions of human suffering and the way in which to remove these conditions was presented initially to five skeptical monks who had been Siddhārtha's companions during his experimentation with extreme asceticism. When he abandoned asceticism for the middle way between indulgence and ascetism, they deserted him, however, thinking that he had given up the quest for liberation. Even now they challenged his claim to enlightenment, saying, "By those [extreme] observances, friend Gautama, by those [extreme] practices, by those [extreme] austerities, you have not achieved power surpassing that of men, nor higher knowledge and vision. How will you now, living with full habit, having given up your efforts, having turned to luxury, be able to obtain power surpassing that of men, and the higher knowledge and vision?"

Siddhārtha corrected their wrong impressions of him, asserting that in abandoning asceticism he had not abandoned his efforts to achieve liberation; indeed, in his efforts to follow the middle way he had found enlightenment. He now insisted that he had been transformed by the enlightenment experience and that out of respect for his enlightenment they should no longer call him friend, but Tathāgata—"one gone thus" (to enlightenment).

Perceiving that a radical change had indeed overcome their former companion, the five monks willingly listened as the Buddha preached his first sermon, setting in motion the wheel of teaching that was to bring Buddhism to all parts of India and the rest of Asia—indeed, to the whole world. The heart of this teaching is the middle way that leads beyond suffering to enlightened living:

There are two extremes, monks, which are to be avoided. What are these two extremes? A life given to pleasures, dedicated to pleasures and lusts—this is degrading, sensual, vulgar, unworthy, and useless. And a life given to self-torture—this is painful, unworthy, and useless.

By avoiding these two extremes, monks, the Tathāgata has gained the knowledge of the Middle Path which leads to insight, which leads to wisdom, which produces calm, knowledge, enlightenment and nirvāṇa.

Having emphasized that, unlike other ways being advocated in India at this time, his was a moderate way, eschewing all extremes, the Buddha went on to indicate the fourfold truth concerning suffering that he had discovered.

This, monks, is the Noble Truth of suffering: birth is suffering; decay is suffering; illness is suffering; death is suffering; presence of objects we hate is suffering; separation from objects we love is suffering; not to obtain what we crave is suffering: In short, the five attachment groups are suffering.

This, monks, is the Noble Truth concerning the origin of suffering: it originates in that grasping which causes the renewal of becomings, is accompanied by sensual delight, seeking satisfaction now here, now there; the grasping for pleasures, the grasping for becoming, the grasping for not-becoming.

This, monks, is the Noble Truth concerning the cessation of suffering: It is the complete stopping of this grasping, the elimination of passions so that grasping can be laid aside, given up, harbored no longer and gotten free from.

This, monks, is the Noble Truth regarding the Path which leads to the stopping of suffering: it is, indeed, this Noble Eightfold Path. That is, right understanding, right resolve, right speech, right action, right livelihood, right effort, right mindfulness, and right meditation.

(Mahavāgga)

Our main concern in this chapter will be to understand this fourfold truth: (1) that the anxiety and suffering experienced in life proceed from a basic defectiveness called *duḥkha*; (2) that duḥkha is caused by attachments; (3) that the way to get rid of the attachments is to remove their conditions; and (4) that the way to remove the conditions of duḥkha is to follow the eightfold noble path.

## Background

Although the Buddha's teaching was new, it was achieved and presented in the context of a variety of views competing for acceptance in the sixth century B.C.. The dominant view was still the Vedic, which emphasized ritual as the effective means of securing the help of the Gods and achieving re-birth in heaven. But the older ideal of ritual practice was being challenged and modified by the way of knowledge being worked out in the Upaniṣads.

However, as we saw in the chapter on Jainism, both the Vedic way of ritual and the Upaniṣadic way of knowledge were being seriously contested by a number of alternative visions that rejected savior Gods, divine help, sacrifical ritual, and the orthodox priesthood as erroneous beliefs and useless for attaining freedom from death. Despite this commonality, the non-Vedic views were widely divergent. There were determinists and indeterminists, nihilists and eternalists. It is interesting that the same philosophical positions that are clamoring for our assent today—theism, materialism, and agnosticism—were being advocated with much enthusiasm twenty-five hundred years ago in India!

There were two pairs of extreme views that the Buddha particularly wished to avoid, for they ruled out the possibility of human action that could remove human suffering by removing its conditions. The first pair of views were those held by the hard determinists and by the indeterminists. The former, represented by Purana Kassapa, were similar to modern-day behaviorists, holding that all behavior is totally determined by the forces of nature and environment. The latter held that everything happens purely by chance, that there are no conditioning or determining factors at work in the world at all. For both groups human effort to eradicate suffering is ruled out. The indeterminists deny all causality whatever, thus leaving no basis for the efficacy of human action. The determinists, on the other hand, claim that everything is causally determined, denying the possibility of freedom and the possibility of human choice and control.

The other pair of extreme views that Siddhārtha wished to avoid were those of the eternalists and nihilists. The former see the self as a spiritual substance existing eternally, in itself unchanging, achieving liberation upon permanent separation from the body. The problem with this view is that the self, being an unchanging spiritual substance, is not in any way involved in action. However, action that does not involve the self is not really action, but merely bodily behavior, totally unaffected by the self. Reciprocally, since the self is essentially separate from the body, the conditions of the body cannot really affect the self. How, on this dualistic view, can the conditions responsible for suffering be affected and removed by human action?

On the other hand, the nihilists deny both the existence of a self that survives death and the continuity of the individual. Since nothing continuous exists from moment to moment, there is no possibility of doing something in one moment of existence to influence the next moment, rendering human choice and action meaningless.

Buddhism, like Jainism, emphasizes wisdom, meditation, and moral conduct as effective means of overcoming suffering and death. Although Buddhists eschew the extreme asceticism of the Jainas, they agree that the monastic order—rather than either the priesthood or the lay community—centers the religious community and anchors the religious life.

Buddhists also accepted the familiar sixth-century Indian cosmological vision that sees the universe extending incredibly far in space and time. Time is measured in aeons and kalpas (billions of years) rather than in centuries and millenia. According to a well-known analogy, the length of time this universe has existed is innumerable times greater than the length of time it would take to wear a solid rock mountain, higher than Mt. Everest, down to sea level by touching it ever so lightly once every hundred years with a piece of the very softest Banaras silk. And so great is the extent of the universe that our earth is like one small drop in a great ocean of planetary bodies.

Also like Jainas, and most other groups in India at this time, Buddhists assumed that most beings die and are re-born innumerable times, sometimes in human form, other times in plant or animal forms, and sometimes as Gods and Goddesses. But until freedom from this round of births and deaths is achieved, there is no end to torment and anguish. Buddhists also agree that karma drives this whole process of birth and death, but contrary to the Jaina view of karma as a form of material existence, they see it as a volitional force.

The Buddhist monastic community, like the Jaina, served the dual purpose of creating an environment conducive to undisturbed practice of the way of perfection and—unlike most other monastic orders—providing both religious and social assistance to the lay community. Buddhists went further, however, in providing a great variety of social services, such as clothing the poor, feeding the hungry, and educating the children.

Coming to views of reality, we note that Buddhists rejected the Jaina idea of permanent selves and things. According to Buddhism, whatever exists is a stream of becoming; nothing that exists is permanent. A beautiful but fragile blossom best exemplifies the Buddhist view of existence, for beautiful as it may be, it is clearly a passing phenomenon, as all who have seen the wind and rain driving newly opened cherry blossoms to the ground know very well. For one who thinks that these blossoms should be permanent this may seem tragic, but for someone who understands that change—the continuous arising and falling of existence—is the very nature of existence, the joy of seeing the beautiful blossoms is not destroyed by their falling. Only when this vast stream of becoming is mistaken for a conglomeration of *permanent things,* subject to various modifications, but nonetheless unchanging at their very core, does change threaten to destroy existence.

Unlike Jainism, which has remained relatively unchanged and confined to India throughout its long history, Buddhism underwent many changes in teachings and practices as it spread throughout Asia and beyond, influencing non–Indian Asian civilizations, much as Christianity influenced European civilization. As we must now distinguish between devotional and gnostic Christianity, and between Catholics and Protestants, so must we distinguish between the Buddhism of devotion and ritual piety and the Buddhism of meditation, and between Theravāda and Mahāyāna Buddhism. The doctrinal uniformity of Jainism—despite the split into Digamabara and Śvetaṁbara sects—does not apply to Buddhism, whose numerous sects have disagreed over many doctrinal, scriptural, and philosophical issues as well as over practices.

# The Buddha

"Who is the Buddha?" This is the first question to be raised as we begin our examination of the "three jewels."

## THE THREE BUDDHAS

To understand the place of the Buddha in Buddhism, we must make some initial distinctions, for the Buddha is simultaneously three beings. First, he is the historical person, Siddhārtha Gautama. Second, he is the ultimate spiritual reality that resides in all beings as their hidden perfection. Third, he is both the historical person and the ultimate spiritual reality incarnate, for Siddhārtha embodied the ultimate spiritual reality of existence awakened through innumerable lifetimes of spiritual effort. Thus, although only a particular embodiment of the ultimate spiritual reality, the Buddha (Enlightened One) is not simply the historical son of King Suddhodana and Queen Māyā.

While the historical Siddhārtha is shown to be a wise and compassionate person, the legends of the Buddha attempt to reveal the enlightened reality incarnate in this person. But history and legend cannot be neatly separated, for Siddhārtha Gautama is both the historical person and the enlightenment reality.

As the enlightenment reality, the ultimate spiritual reality residing within all beings as their hidden perfection, the Buddha is capable of being manifested innumerable times in innumerable forms. Mahāyāna stresses this in its recognition that we are all Buddhas already and that the "achievement" of Buddhahood is simply the awakening to the fullness of our existence, which for most of us is dormant and hidden. Theravāda stresses the same thing in its insistence that we can achieve enlightenment through our own efforts—that we are our own best refuge.

Thus, it is not the historical Siddhārtha, limited to a certain physical body and mind, that is of primary interest to the Buddhist, but this historical person as glorified by the in-dwelling enlightenment reality (*dharmakāya*) as emphasized in Mahāyāna, or this historical person as embodying the enlightenment reality as emphasized within Theravāda. Consequently, in our efforts to see the historical Siddhārtha Gautama, born in about 560 B.C. in northeastern India, we must bear in mind that for Buddhists he is also the enlightenment reality.

**The Historical Buddha.** The strictly historical information about Siddhārtha is distressingly scant. His father, Suddhodna, was the ruler of the small Śakya republic in northern India, and his mother was Māyā, from Devadaha. At about age sixteen he was married to the princess Yaśodharā, with whom he shared his life of luxury in his father's palace. Their only child, Rāhula, was born about twelve years later, shortly

**Figure 3.** Standing Buddha. Bronze, Gupta period, 320–647. (Courtesy, The Asia Society: Mr. and Mrs. John D. Rockefeller 3rd Collection.)

before Siddhārtha, distressed by and filled with compassion for the suffering beings he encountered, took up an ascetic's life in search of a way to eliminate suffering.

After six years of severe asceticism and studying with the most renowned religious teachers of his day, Siddhārtha rejected the ascetic way, just as earlier he had rejected the way of pleasure. Resolved to avoid these extremes, he forged his own way of conduct and contemplation, achieving, at age thirty-five, the illumination that was to mark him as the Buddha (The Enlightened) from that day forth. Shortly after his enlightenment, he preached his first sermon at the deer park near Banaras. For the next forty-five years he taught all who would listen, sharing his insights and wisdom equally with men and women, outcasts and brāhmaṇas, rich and poor. He died at age eighty—of food poisoning, according to many accounts—at Kuśinara (near Gorakhpur).

Even this brief account goes slightly beyond the strictly historical knowledge we have, drawing upon universally accepted legends. But these legends are more important to a Buddhist than is the strictly historical information, for in legend it is possible to represent features of the universal reality of enlightenment that the Buddha embodied. The legendary Buddha is more than simply a wise historical person; he is a person who embodies the very essence of enlightenment and whose teaching is capable of awakening in all of us the same enlightenment that made him the Buddha. Although this feature of Buddhism becomes more pronounced in the later, Mahāyāna, forms of Buddhism, it is clearly present from the beginning, and is an important part of Theravāda Buddhism as well.

It is important to note that, although the Buddhists regard the Buddha as enlightenment incarnate, they do not think of him as a God; and, of course, he never claimed to be anything more than a human being. But in his humanness—as in ours—there is a deep and wonderful fullness, which can become the basis for a new life when we are awakened to it. It is this overcoming of the shallowness of ego existence—an existence that reveals itself in the grasping for new being and the clinging to old being that lies at the heart of human anxiety and suffering—that the Buddha taught as the path to enlightenment. Since the basis of this enlightment is not something apart from or different from our own being, Buddhists hold that each one of us can achieve it if we will but follow the way of wisdom, pure conduct, and meditation taught by the Buddha.

**The Four Signs.** The awakening of Siddhārtha to the pervasiveness of suffering in the world and the arousal of a deep compassion for the suffering of all beings are touchingly depicted in the legend of the four signs recorded in the Dīgha Nikāya.

According to this legend, at Siddhārtha's birth a wise old man had predicted that, when the child grew up and witnesssed the breadth and depth of suffering in the world, he would renounce his father's kingdom, take up life as a recluse, and become enlightened. King Suddhodana, not wanting to lose his son in this way, arranged everything so that Siddhārtha would never witness suffering in the world. Every possible delight was provided for the growing boy, and he was protected from the sights of evil, sickness, old age, and death. But one day the young prince persuaded the charioteer to take him for a ride outside the palace grounds. There he saw an old man, "gnarled and bowed as a rafter, decrepit and sorely afflicted, long past his prime, leaning on a staff, tottering as he walked."

Shocked at this sight, Siddhārtha asked his driver what was wrong with this man: "Why is he so different from the other men?" Upon being told that this was an old man and that this is what happens to people when they get old, Gautama could not understand, for he had no experience with old age. But when the driver explained that being old meant suffering, being nearly finished, and about to die, the young lord began to understand and became increasingly troubled. "Tell me, my good driver, am I too subject to old age? Have I not gotten past old age?" he asked.

"You, my lord, and we too, we are all of a kind to grow old. We have not gotten past old age," replied the driver.

Shocked and horrified at the prospect of all people having to endure life in the miserable condition of this decrepit old man, Siddhārtha returned to his palace. There he found no relief or comfort in all the gaiety and delights surrounding him, for he now knew how temporary all this was; old age lay ahead for everyone.

Later, on a second ride outside the palace grounds, Siddhārtha encountered "a sick man, suffering and extremely ill. Having fallen down he was weltering in his own urine, being lifted up by some and being dressed by others." Turning to his driver for an explanation of this distressing sight, he was informed that this man was ill, that illness comes to everyone, and that the suffering of illness is unavoidable: "You, my lord, and we too, we are all subject to illness. We have not gotten past the reach of illness."

Returning to his palace, Siddhārtha reflected on this encounter with sickness, wondering how people could find pleasure in life when constantly threatened with illness. Deeply troubled by these encounters with old age and sickness, he got his first sight of death a few days later while driving to the park. Observing a large group of people constructing a funeral pyre, he asked his driver what they were doing. Upon being told that they were preparing to cremate a dead man, the young prince demanded to see the corpse. Shocked by the sight, he wanted to know if this thing called death came to only some people or to everyone. His driver's answer was to the point: "You, my lord, and we too, we are all subject to death. We have not gotten past the reaches of death. When you die neither the king nor the queen, nor any of your relatives will ever see you again, nor will you see them."

Going back to his palace the Buddha-to-be again reflected on what he had witnessed. "Shame on this thing called birth," he thought to himself, "for to one who is born comes decrepitness, disease and death."

Aware of his son's encounters with old age, disease, and death, King Suddhodana attempted to surround him with even more pleasures and delights. But to no avail, for Siddhārtha could not forget what he had witnessed, and the implications of suffering for life loomed larger and larger in his reflections.

Finally, many days later, he again persuaded his charioteer to take him for a drive outside the palace grounds. Now he encountered a yellow-robed recluse, with shaved head and a contented look. "What has this man done," he asked the driver, "that his head is unlike other men's heads and his clothes unlike those of others?"

Upon being told that the man shaved his head and wore the yellow robe because he had become a recluse, having gone forth from his home into a homeless condition, Siddhārtha asked to be driven up to the recluse so he could question him. "What does it mean to have 'gone forth,' to have become a recluse?" he asked the recluse.

"It means, my lord, being thorough in the religious life, being thorough in the peaceful life, being thorough in worthy conduct, being thorough in nonhurting, being thorough in kindness to all beings," came the reply.

So delighted was the young prince with the way of life of the recluse that he too decided to take up this alternative life-style, directing his charioteer to return to the palace without him, announcing that he would shave his head and put on the yellow robe right then and there.

After this decision, most accounts agree that Siddhārtha underwent intensive training in yoga and took up a life of extreme asceticism. Seeking out the best teachers he could find, Siddhārtha studied with both Arāda Kālāma and Udraka Rāmapūtra, but discovered when he had achieved a level of yogic attainment equivalent to theirs that he had not achieved the calm and peaceful condition of nirvāṇa wherein the passions of desire and aversion were extinguished.

To awaken the enlightenment being deep within human existence requires constant vigilance and untiring effort. The legends emphasize this by depicting the Buddha-to-be, who had spent untold previous lifetimes in spiritual preparation for this final enlightenment, as now undertaking the most extreme forms of asceticism. Finally, almost dead, he realized that extreme asceticism does not by itself lead to enlightenment and reflected that, even as the extreme of indulgence in pursuing the world of desire should be avoided, so should the extreme of ascetic denial be avoided.

But the Buddha-to-be was not discouraged by the failure of his teachers or ascetic practice to reveal a more profound level of existence free from duḥkha. Instead, he increased his resolve to continue his efforts. But in his recognition of asceticism as an extreme to be avoided he had gained two very important insights. First, the spirit cannot be liberated by torturing the body; for a person is not two things, a soul or spirit trapped in a body, but a single organic whole of many dimensions.

Second, happiness is not the enemy of liberation or enlightenment. Contrary to the accepted opinion of the ascetic community, there was nothing wrong with happiness. Indeed, happiness free from desire and turmoil, free from grasping and clinging, is good and conducive to enlightenment. These insights underlie his resolve to practice a middle way, avoiding the extremes of indulgence in pleasures and the denial of happiness.

**Temptations and Enlightenment.** The great resolve and effort required to rise above the conditionedness of an ego-centered existence is dramatically presented in the legends of Siddhārtha's temptations by Māra, the personification of death and chief of demons. Knowing that fear of death and annihilation underlies the clinging to self that sustains ego-centered existence, Māra attempts to frighten Siddhārtha, threatening him with the most dreadful forces and weapons imaginable. But having overcome all ego attachment, fear found no foothold in the Buddha-to-be, so Māra turned to desire to topple the Buddha's resolve. Knowing that desire, the grasping for ego through pleasures, nourishes the illusion of self, Māra presented Siddhārtha with the most delightful and tempting of pleasures, attempting to seduce him with the attractions of the world personified as beautiful nymphs. But again, having overcome all attachments to ego, Siddhārtha was untouched by lust and desire, and Māra was forced to withdraw in defeat.

Now, the legend continues, free from temptation, strong in resolve, and calm, the Buddha-to-be entered deeper and deeper into meditation. During the evening of the May full moon (525 B.C. ?), he achieved insight into all his former existences, seeing how they were conditioned by previous existence and how they conditioned succeeding existence. As the night wore on, this insight deepened and he was able to penetrate the mysteries of the birth-death process. He became aware of the conditionedness of all existence and realized that wholesome conduct leads to happiness and unwholesome conduct to suffering. During the early hours of the morning his meditation deepened and his insight increased even further. Now he saw how the terrible suffering that wastes human life is caused and how it can be eliminated, recognizing the fourfold noble truth that was to become the basis of his teaching. This fourfold truth declares (1) that suffering exists, (2) that it depends on certain conditions, (3) that these conditions can be removed, and (4) that the way to remove these conditions is to practice the eightfold way.

But this illumination left Siddhārtha Gautama—now the Buddha—with a dilemma: witnessing the suffering of all existence awakened a great compassion that moved him to reach out and help his fellow beings. But this awakening had been so difficult to achieve, and the truths it revealed were so profound, that he did not see how it could be put into words and made intelligible to anyone not having the experience.

Legend says that initially he felt that what he had realized could not be taught, and that he resolved to say nothing, lest he be misunderstood. But eventually his compassion overcame this initial reluctance and after forty-nine days he set in motion the "wheel of teaching" by preaching his first sermon.

For the next forty-five years his compassion and wisdom were expressed in his teaching and example and the organization of the Buddhist community. This deep sense of compassion—of wanting to help all living beings progress toward enlightenment and to eliminate suffering—is the single most important factor in the development and spread of Buddhism from a small band of followers of the Śākyamuni to a world religion of tremendous cultural, spiritual, and philosophical importance.

This ideal of compassion is embodied in the ideal of the Bodhisattva. Literally, a Bodhisattva is a being whose essence is shining enlightenment. The Bodhisattva ideal embodies the Buddha's compassion and encompasses the resolve not to cease, even for a moment, one's effort to help all beings to nirvāṇa. This ideal came to dominate Mahāyāna Buddhism, even as the ideal of individual liberation dominated the Theravāda tradition. The ideal of individual salvation is found in the Buddha's teachings—accepted by both Mahāyānists and Theravādins—while the basis for the Bodhisattva ideal is found in the *example* of the Buddha, to which Mahāyāna has given great emphasis.

But both the Theravāda and Mahāyāna traditions embrace the Buddha as the perfect human being, the embodiment of the Teaching, of liberation and the incarnation of the enlightenment reality that constitutes the basis of all existence. The refusal for many centuries to portray the Buddha in art or sculpture testifies to the acknowledged inexpressible grandeur of his enlightenment being and to the inexpressibility of the content of his enlightenment in ordinary form—and also to the great reverence and respect held for the Buddha as the embodiment of the enlightenment reality. When artists did begin to render images of the Buddha, every effort was made to subordinate the human characteristics to the transcendent reality of enlightenment being, thereby illuminating the Teachings of the Buddha rather than his psychophysical being.

## The Teaching of Liberation (Dharma)

How can the fear, anxiety, and suffering that torment most of us throughout our lives be eliminated? Ultimately the entire teaching of the Buddha is no more and no less than the answer to this question. As we have seen, in his first sermon the Buddha outlined his answer to this question in four parts, first, analyzing the nature of suffering, second, analyzing the conditions that give rise to suffering, third, examining how these conditions can be removed, and finally, like a good physician, prescribing a way of living that will eliminate suffering through removing its conditions. We will follow this same outline, examining the Buddha's statement of each of these four noble truths in the light of other canonical statements, as well as Buddhist practice and philosophy.

## DUḤKHA

What is suffering (duḥkha)? What did the Buddha mean when he said, "This, monks, is the noble truth of duḥkha; birth is duḥkha; decay is duḥkha; illness is duḥkha; death is duḥkha; presence of objects we hate is duḥkha; separation from objects we love is duḥkha; not to obtain what we desire is duḥkha. In short, the five attachment groups are duḥkha"? Although we have been translating duḥkha as "suffering," this word, as usually understood, does not exactly coincide with the Buddhist understanding of duḥkha. Since no other translation of "duḥkha" is any better, we will continue to call it "suffering" but will show how the ordinary meaning of this word will have to be extended to include the various levels of duḥkha pointed out by the Buddha.

There are actually three distinct, though connected, levels of suffering: ordinary suffering, change, and the attachment groups. Ordinary suffering includes the sorrow of separation from those we love through absence or death; the presence of persons and things we hate; frustration of our desires; sickness; degeneration of our faculties; and fear, anxiety, and the prospect of death. This level of suffering is easy to understand, for it is part of everyone's life experience. But these kinds of suffering are counterbalanced by the joys and happiness that we all experience, as, for example, when we are in the presence of persons we love, our health is good and we have the most important things we desire. Surely, if the Buddha had meant suffering only in this ordinary sense, he would not have made it the cornerstone of his Way.

But there is a deeper level of suffering, where suffering is equated with change. At this level even the pleasant and joyous moments of life are a form of suffering, for hidden in them is the poison of temporariness. Every moment of happiness, love, or joy will pass away. Not only does their passing bring suffering, but even the presence of these happy moments is tinged by the sorrow, fear, and anxiety that the underlying awareness of their temporariness produces. Frequently we are successful in pushing this awareness into the deeper recesses of consciousness that we call the subconscious or the unconscious. But still it works its evil, creating unconscious fears and anxieties that dominate our lives to a much greater extent than most of us realize.

Duḥkha, in this second sense, is a basic anxiety. Like a black hole at the center of our being, it threatens to devour our existence, undermining every attempt to achieve security and permanence either through clinging to what we have experienced and become or through grasping at what we might become in the future. Surfacing as a fear of death or annihilation, it destroys even the pleasures and joys of life, showing them to be only fleeting moments. Since all existence is constantly changing, our craving for eternal life and happiness is inevitably doomed to frustration. It is for this reason that Buddhists characterize existence not only as impermanence (*anitya*) but as duḥkha. As we shall see later, however, it is not the simple fact of change by itself that is duḥkha, but only change in the context of a self seeking permanence.

The third level of duḥkha is indicated clearly in the Buddha's summary statement, "In brief, the five attachment groups are duḥkha." This level of suffering is much harder to understand than is ordinary suffering or change. But it is this level that is most important, for it underlies and makes possible the first two levels.

What are the attachment groups? Stated as simply as possible, they are the five groups of factors that constitute a person, when these groups are experienced as attached to a self.

The following schema shows the five basic groups of activities that make up a person on the right and the supposed *owner* of these groups on the left. The *attachment groups* are the five groups *as attached* to the self that is thought to exist independently of them. The Buddhist analysis is intended to show that there is no self separate from the groups, that the self is nothing more (and nothing less!) than these five groups in their interrelated functioning. But then "ownership" and attachment lose their basis, which is precisely what the analysis is about.

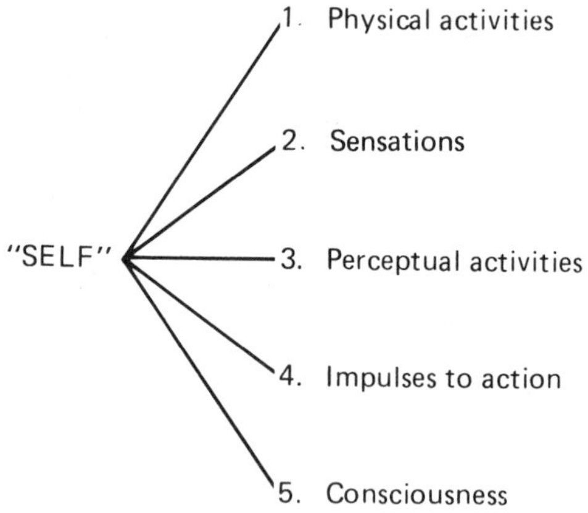


The first group includes the material factors responsible for all physical existence. This includes all the fundamental elements of material existence and their derivatives, namely, the body and sense organs and the objects of the external world.

The second group includes all our physical and mental sensations that give rise to rudimentary feelings that are pleasant, unpleasant, or neutral. These sensations and feelings arise when the eye makes contact with visible form, the ear with sound, the nose with odor, the tongue with taste, the body with tactile objects, and the mind with ideas and thoughts.

The third group is constituted by perceptual activities, those of the five senses as well as the mind. In Buddhist psychology the mind is thought of as being like the other senses except that its objects are ideas and thoughts rather than material factors. Here the sensations and feelings constituting the second group become the basis for recognition of objects and events, generating perceptual knowledge.

The fourth group includes the various mental formations, the most important of which are the volitional activities, which direct the senses and the mind in the direction of the good, bad, or neutral. It must be pointed out here that it is only these volitional activities that the Buddhists call karma. Even the results of volitional activities are not called karma, but only "the fruit of karma." Thus, karma, as a condition of suffering, is not some blind material or mechanical force, but human volitional activity. Among the fifty-two mental formations that provide impulses to action and constitute the basis of habit, character, and personality are attention, confidence, doubt, will, ignorance, hate, desire, compassion, and idea of self.

The fifth group is constituted by the various activities of consciousness that make possible both knowledge and delusion. Buddhists do not regard consciousness as a separate faculty or power but, rather, as a response to the perceptions of the senses and the mind that relates these perceptions to their external objects and to each other in a conceptual way. Thus, there are only six kinds of consciousness, corresponding to the five senses and the mind: body consciousness, eye consciousness, ear consciousness, taste consciousness, smell consciousness, and mental consciousness.

It is important to note that, although the self is nothing over and above these five groups of factors in all their interactions, it is neither their owner nor is it to be identified with any one of these groups. In India, as in the West, it has proved tempting to identify the self with consciousness, but the Buddha left no doubt about the erroneousness of this view.

One of his disciples, Sāti, was going about saying that the Master taught that it is consciousness that transmigrates and experiences the cycle of births and deaths. When confronted by the Buddha and asked to explain what he meant by consciousness, Sāti replied, "It is that which expresses, which feels, which experiences the results of good and bad deeds here and there."

"Stupid one, to whom have you ever heard me explaining the doctrine in this manner?" retorted the Buddha. "Have I not always explained consciousness as arising out of conditions?" He then goes on to explain that the conditions of visual consciousness are the eye, the visible form, and the contact between them; the conditions of mental consciousness are the mind, the ideas and thoughts, and the contact between them, and so on. The Buddha's point is that consciousness is rooted in the first four groups of factors, and apart from them there is no consciousness. As he said, "Were a person to say: I shall show the coming, the going, the passing away, the arising, the growth, the increase or the development of consciousness apart from matter, sensation, perception and mental formations, he would be speaking of something that did not exist" (Majjhima Nikāya).

Confronted with these five groups of factors as the constituting features of a person, we might be tempted to say that the most important feature has been left out, for nowhere has the self been mentioned. After all, do not consciousness, volition, sensation, perception, and bodily activities all *belong* to a self? The Buddhist answer to this last question is an emphatic "No!" The whole point of the analysis is to show that everything that belongs to personal existence can be accounted for in terms of these five groups. Over and above the five groups, there is no real self. The self taken to have an independent existence as the owner of the groups is only a construction of the five groups. It is this self, originating as a mental formation, that becomes attached to the groups, thinking, "they are mine" or "I am this."

This attachment is at the heart of duḥkha, for the groups are of the nature of process, never remaining, even for a second, the same. But the self constructed out of these groups grasps at and clings to them, trying to create an existence that will not suffer anguish and sorrow, that will not grow old and decrepit, that will not die. This effort is clearly doomed to failure, for change is the very nature of existence, and clinging and grasping will not change that; grasping and clinging can only produce frustration, fear and anxiety—along with a few brief moments of happiness and joy.

## CONDITIONS OF DUḤKHA

We are now in position to understand what the Buddha meant when he said that duḥkha "originates in that grasping which causes the renewals of becomings, is accompanied by sensual delight, seeking satisfaction now here, now there; the grasping for pleasures, the grasping for becoming, the grasping for not-becoming."

Grasping for pleasures is the most obvious form of grasping, for we all reach for pleasure, and achieving it, hang on, not wanting to let go. This is true not only for the sensual pleasures of food, drink, or sex, but also for the pleasures of music, understanding, and virtuous activity—and even the pleasure that accompanies insight, compassion, and trance. Grasping for vanished youth in middle age; grasping for life in the face of inevitable death; grasping for power to control all the conditions of life—all these kinds of grasping cause suffering. It is our grasping for friendship that underlies the hurt when a friend turns on us, and it is our grasping for love that threatens to destroy us when a loved one dies.

But what are we really grasping for in the examples just given? Is it not for our own being? Are we really not, either consciously or unconsciously, seeking to secure and enlarge our own self? From the Buddhist perspective, the idea of self, which is merely a mental formation, attaches itself to the groups of processes constituting the individual person. So attached, it is mistaken for the agent of conscious activity, volitions, perceptions, sensations, and physical activity, and it is regarded as an independent reality underlying these five groups of processes. Attaching itself to the powerful will to live that expresses itself through the five groups, this self attempts to appropriate more and more of the world to itself to satisfy this will. Whatever is not identified with the self stands outside it as a threat to its continued existence. Either it must be incorporated into the self through love, friendship, or utility, or else feared as an enemy and hated for the threat to the self that it represents.

Thus, when the Buddha talks of "grasping for becoming," he refers to just this attempt of the self to appropriate the five groups of processes for its own being. The "grasping for not-becoming" refers to the aversion to whatever cannot be so appropriated, an aversion expressed in hatred, fear, and anxiety.

A moment's reflection reveals the acuteness of the Buddha's analysis, for most of us do indeed think that we are a self over and above the various groups of activities constituting our empirical being. And through this self we are continuously trying to appropriate the world, reaching out through our sensations, feelings, knowledge, and actions to make contact with, embrace, and bring into our own being as much of the world as we can. What resists these efforts—the great unexperienced and unknown—is like an enemy confronting and challenging us, constituting the root of our fears and anxieties.

The human effort to embrace the whole world in experience, feeling, and knowledge—the human quest to become co-terminus with the world—is by itself not the chief cause of duḥkha. Indeed, it may well be taken as the crowning glory of human existence. However, when this human quest is distorted by the delusive self into a frantic effort to render feeling, knowledge, happiness, and peace permanent and unchanging through identification with a self that is ultimately unchanging, duḥkha is inevitable. Unceasing change is the rule for all existence. Nowhere does anything remain, even for a moment, the same. The creation of a self—in ignorance—that grasps for permanence, especially its own permanence, in this world of continuous change puts us at odds with our own existence. This "out-of-jointness" is the core of duḥkha, and it produces all the various forms of suffering that we experience.

## CONDITIONED ARISING

Some interpreters of Buddhism have assumed that craving and grasping for permanence issue from a basic defect in the self—analogous to the defectiveness that Christians impute to human nature in the doctrine of original sin. Other interpreters have focused on ignorance as the basic defect, assuming it to be a primordial aspect of reality, with an independent ontological status outside the five groups. Both interpretations are wrong, as can easily be seen by looking at ignorance and grasping as conditions of suffering in terms of the principle of conditioned arising (*pratītya samutpāda*).

Insight into the conditioned arising of all existence is at the heart of the Buddhist vision; indeed, it is frequently said to encapsulate the whole Teaching. The Buddha recognized that the two commonly accepted views of causality prevalent in his day did not allow room for human effort to eliminate suffering. The hard determinists postulated entities such as God, soul, or matter that rigidly determined every event in the universe, leaving no room for human choice and action. On the other hand, the indeterminists claimed that nothing caused anything else; everything just happened randomly or by chance, and human resignation to whatever happened was suggested as the appropriate response.

The idea of conditioned arising is midway between these extreme views. Patterns and relationships between various events and between various moments of the same event are recognized as conditions that affect and influence the arising and ceasing of each moment and each event. But no one condition is seen as totally determining, for there are innumerable determining conditions; each condition contributes something to the event in question, but is itself subject to countless other determining conditions. On the Buddhist view there are neither first nor final causes and no independent beings or substances. Existence is constituted by innumerable interrelated processes, with each moment in each process determined by the countless conditions constituted by all the various related processes.

The general formula of the conditioned arising of all existence, stated abstractly is, "This being so, that is so" and "This not being so, that is not so." Stated dynamically, in relation to the actual world of change, the principle of conditionality is, "This arising, that arises; this not arising, that does not arise."

This principle can be applied to every conceivable aspect of existence, leading to statements expressing the conditions dominant in any kind of change. Formulated as "basic laws," these statements form the basis of our knowledge of physics, biology, psychology, and so on. But it is the application of this general principle of conditionality to the continuous arising of the self in relation to the groups of processes that is of particular concern, for it explains how suffering arises in the life of the individual and suggests how this suffering can be ended by eliminating its conditions. This, of course, was the concern of the Buddha. Beginning with the present moment of existence, with suffering here and now, he sought both the conditions upon which it depends and a way to remove these conditions.

## CONDITIONS OF SUFFERING

The application of the principle of conditioned arising to individual existence is done traditionally in terms of the twelvefold chain of conditionality and depicted by the Wheel of Becoming, an ingenious way of diagramming the endless continuum of processes constituting a person. The rim of this twelve-spoked wheel is divided into twelve segments, each representing a group of important conditions upon which suffering

WHEEL OF BECOMING

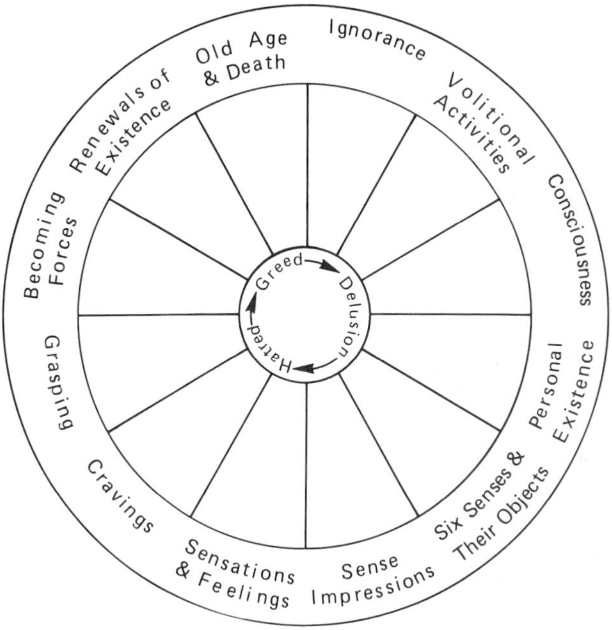


depends. The nave, regarded as the driving force, is constituted by hatred, delusion, and greed, for these are the driving forces of suffering. The twelve groups of conditions, in the traditional order, are

1. Ignorance, which conditions volitional activities,
2. Volitional activities, which condition consciousness,
3. Consciousness, which conditions personal existence,
4. Personal existence, which conditions the mind and the senses,
5. Mind and senses, along with their objects, which condition sense impressions,
6. Sense impressions, which condition sensations and feelings,
7. Sensations and feelings, which condition cravings,
8. Cravings, which condition grasping,
9. Grasping, which conditions new becoming forces,
10. Becoming forces, which condition renewals of existence,
11. New existence, which conditions old age and death, and
12. Old age and death, which condition ignorance (with the series repeating itself ad duḥkham).

As with all illustrations, there is a certain arbitrariness in the choice of conditions represented by the wheel of becoming. Old age and death are by no means the only forms of duḥkha; yet on the wheel they stand for suffering and the other eleven factors stand for the conditions that give rise to suffering. Of course, there are not precisely eleven conditions of duḥkha; there are innumerable conditions, only a few collections of which are chosen as especially significant—and these are viewed from only one of a vast number of possible perspectives. In addition, although turning the wheel in either a forward or reverse direction suggests that what conditions is also conditioned, it does not capture the full reciprocity that obtains between conditioned and conditioning forces. Despite these limitations, the wheel of becoming serves quite well to illustrate the arising (and ceasing) of duḥkha in the life of the individual according to the twelvefold chain of conditionality.

Because we control our existence through volitional activities, and because volitional activities are conditioned by beliefs, it is customary to begin with the link constituted by false views or ignorance. From the Buddhist perspective, two features of the relationship between beliefs and choices are especially important. First, beliefs—whether true or false—do condition our choices. For example, if we believe that we have control over our lives we will live one way, but, if we believe that we have no control over our lives, we will live in quite a different way. Second, wrong beliefs condition our choices in the direction of unwholesome existence, whereas right views condition our choices in the direction of wholesome existence.

By ignorance is meant not some primordial or generic feature of human nature but, rather, simply the presence of incorrect views and the absence of correct views about the nature of existence. More specifically, ignorance is frequently said to be ignorance of duḥkha, its conditions, cessation, and the path leading to its cessation. In artistic portrayals ignorance is frequently depicted as a blind man with a stick, for just as a blind man sometimes chooses the right path and sometimes the wrong path, so without right views our choices are blind, sometimes resulting in good actions, sometimes in bad. But even when he chooses the right path, the blind man does not know it. In the same way, even when the ignorant man chooses the right action he is unaware that it is right and, therefore, cannot adhere to the path of right living.

From the perspective of the arising and ceasing of suffering, however, the especially injurious ignorance consists in the false view that we are or have a self (or soul) that, though attached to the processes, is essentially independent of them. Convinced that we are or have such a self, we grasp at the groups of processes, trying to identify them with the self to give them permanence and independence. Or else we repudiate and reject the processes as not-self to preserve the illusion of an independent and imperishable self. Both these alternatives, grasping for becoming and grasping for not-becoming, are choices of actions and lifestyles that follow upon the ignorance constituted by a false view of self.

Of course, belief is not the only cause or condition of volitional activity. While beliefs guide and direct our choices, it is obvious that desires and aversions provide much of the motivation. But in actuality there are innumerable conditions affecting mental formations and choices. Climate, health, education, sociopolitical conditions, friends, habits, and character are just a few. Although not as prominent as beliefs and desires, they nevertheless do condition human choices.

It is also important to realize that, although beliefs condition volitional activity, the relationship between the conditioned and the conditions is interactive, mutually affecting all the terms and providing for a reciprocity wherein choices are simultaneously the conditions of our beliefs and conditioned by them.

Turning to the next link, where volitional activities are seen to condition consciousness, we need to keep in mind both the reciprocity of conditions and the conditioned and the fact that all conditioning factors are themselves subject to the conditioning forces of numerous other factors. Thus, volitional activities should not be thought of as totally free and unconditioned, completely within our control. On the other hand, the fact that we *can* give direction to life through our choices—even though these choices receive much of their momentum from psychological or physiological conditions—should not be overlooked.

The artistic depiction of volitional activities as a potter with wheel and pots illustrates this very nicely, for what the potter can do is dependent upon the clay and the wheel. The clay determines what the potter can do with it, even as the potter determines what is done with the clay. Yet he introduces a guiding hand, using the force of the wheel to shape the lump of clay into a pot, just as we can shape the materials and forces constituting our existence into a wholesome human life through our choices. There is also an analogy between the pot and human life, for as pots are created by bringing together and shaping a variety of bits of clay, so is human existence created by bringing together and shaping a variety of processes of existence. And as pots break into fragments when the cohesive force of clay weakens, so a person dies and disintegrates into a series of simpler processes when the interrelationships between the processes disintegrate.

The statement that volitional activities condition consciousness is clearly not intended to deny that other factors—heredity and environment, for example—also condition consciousness. The intention is rather to emphasize that, among all the various factors conditioning consciousness, there is one factor—our volitional acts—over which we do have control and that through our choices we can enter creatively into the shaping of our consciousness and our whole existence. This claim rests on the insight that choices and decisions not only give consciousness a certain quality or tone, inclining it toward wholesomeness or unwholesomeness, but also provide a basis for its continuity, contributing to the arising of consciousness in the next moment and lending it the tone or color acquired in the previous moment of existence.

The color and tone of consciousness, in turn, conditions the individual person, for the continuous development of a person depends upon the changes in consciousness resulting from volitional acts (among a great variety of conditional factors). What is called "continuous development of a person" is traditionally thought of as including also renewed birth, for it has been customary for people believing in reincarnation to interpret the renewal of personality as re-birth in a succeeding incarnation.

But this interpretation is by no means essential. It is quite obvious that each person is constantly changing—constantly dying and being reborn—and that this continuous renewal is dependent upon, among other factors, the current state of consciousness.

Only if personal existence is thought of as something static or permanent is one forced to interpret the Buddhist texts as insisting that the new becomings of a person can apply only to reincarnated persons. It is quite consistent with the Buddha's teachings to interpret all these conditioning and conditioned states of existence as occurring in the present life. Indeed, since he denied the existence of a self that could transmigrate from one body to another, this is the most obvious interpretation.

Personal existence, in turn, conditions our sensory and mental receptors and their contents or, more simply, our experience of the external world. The point here is that what we take to be the external world around us to be is very much dependent upon the kind of person we are. For a blind person the world is without color; for a deaf person it is without sound; for a confident person it is full of challenges; for an insecure person there are only obstacles and problems. This link in the chain serves to point out that what we feel, hear, see, think, and so on depends not only upon external objects or events, but also upon the sensory or mental receptors and upon a great deal of psychological and social conditioning.

The next two links are fairly obvious, for clearly our sense impressions are conditioned by our senses and the external objects, and our sense impressions condition our sensations and feelings. It is also obvious that our desires or cravings are conditioned by sensations and feelings—this is the principle behind all advertising! But the Buddhist understanding of craving (*tṛṣṇa)* includes not only the more obvious cravings for the objects of the senses and cravings for fame and power but also the cravings for selfhood and permanence or immortality. We crave and grasp at the objects, persons, and experiences that promise pleasure, while simultaneously fearing and hating whatever threatens pain. In either case we become hopelessly entangled in our passions, as the self "seeks satisfaction, now here, now there," in a vain attempt to make permanent either the attainment of pleasure or the elimination of pain.

The link between craving and grasping seems intuitively clear, for when our cravings are strong we grasp their objects, sometimes even creating objects to grasp. For example, a person craving water in a desert may grasp at any appearance, finding an oasis in a mirage.

By clinging to wealth one becomes a miser or by grasping at every opportunity to steal one becomes a robber. Similarly, our grasping at, and clinging to, independent selfhood conditions what we become in the next moment of life. Here again, although it has been customary for people believing in reincarnation to interpret this becoming as the becoming of a new person in the next life, there is no good reason why this new existence should be interpreted as the next bodily incarnation rather than as the next moment in the present life. Thus, instead of regarding the becoming forces as the vehicle carrying the life-force from one incarnation over into the next, we can see them as the determining conditions of the arising of the next moment of life, interpreting the next link, birth, as a moment in the continuous arising (and ceasing) of individual existence.

Coming to the twelfth link, it probably goes without saying that the totality of conditions present in the birth of each new moment of our existence brings about the suffering that is represented on the wheel by old age and death. Furthermore, the experienced suffering is an important factor conditioning how we view the world, producing yet additional ignorance, and so on.

By illustrating how the various conditions of suffering arise, the principle of the conditionedness of all existence depicted by the wheel of becoming leads naturally to the third truth, the cessation of suffering through elimination of its conditions.

## CESSATION OF SUFFERING

The third noble truth, that suffering can be eliminated by removing the conditions on which it depends, follows upon recognition of the general principle of the conditionedness of all existence and insight into the specific conditions on which the suffering individual person depends. The Buddha's statement that the cessation of suffering "is the complete stopping of this grasping, the elimination of passions so that grasping can be laid aside, given up, harbored no longer and gotten free from" is clear enough in terms of the foregoing analysis of the conditions of duḥkha. It means that all grasping for self and grasping for not-self must be overcome by eliminating the conditions on which it depends—the conditions represented schematically by the twelvefold chain of conditionality.

But given that individual existence is nothing other than the groups of processes, if they are removed will not the individual cease to be? Is this not nihilism? This question is brought up so frequently—and by so many people who should know better—that it is easy to overlook how ill-founded and silly it really is. Nowhere does the Buddha say that the groups of factors constituting individual existence should be removed; nowhere does he say that the way to remove duḥkha is to eliminate existence. Such a teaching would have never caught on, for surely the cure is worse than the disease! What the Buddha says is that the conditions or factors within the groups that are responsible for duḥkha should be removed. What are these factors? As we have just seen, they are ignorance, wrong intentions, impure consciousness, the illusion of self, the attachment of self to the processes, the resulting craving and grasping that lead to the renewal of attachment, ignorance, and so on.

We need to recall that suffering is equated not with the groups but only with the *attachment groups*. The difference is all important, for if the groups constituting existence are themselves duḥkha, then duḥkha cannot be eliminated without eliminating existence. On the other hand, if it is not the groups themselves, but *attachment* of these groups to a self that constitutes duḥkha, then duḥkha can be eliminated by getting rid of attachment. The Buddha left no doubt in his teaching that it is attachment that must be eliminated, saying, "Therefore I say that the Tathāgata [Buddha] has attained deliverance from and is free from attachment, because all imaginings, agitation, or proud thought concerning a self or anything pertaining to a self, have perished, have faded away, have ceased, have been given up and relinquished" (Majjhima Nikāya, 72).

Thus, nirvāṇa, the cessation of suffering, is not the extinction of existence. On the contrary, it is the full perfection of existence that is achieved by eliminating all forms of grasping and attachment. Free from attachments, life can be lived in the full richness of the present moment, without fear, hatred, or anxiety.

## THE PATH

Although understanding the truths about suffering, its conditions, and its cessation is important to Buddhist practice, the fourth truth—that of the way to live to eliminate the conditions of duḥkha—is the heart of the Buddhist way. Understanding is important, not because it satisfies intellectual curiosity, but because it affects and transforms life. While Buddhists have spent a great deal of time and energy memorizing, copying, and commenting on the Buddha's teachings, they have generally understood that the real point is fully to incorporate these teachings into one's whole life and embody them in every moment of existence. The Brahmajāla Sūtra makes the point dramatically: "Peeling your own skin for paper, with blood for ink, and spinal fluid for water to mix it, using your bones for a pen you should copy out the teachings of the Buddha."

The way of life set forth as the fourth noble truth, the middle way, was declared by the Buddha in his first sermon. It consists in

| | |
|---|---|
| 1. Right understanding<br>2. Right intention | Wisdom |
| 3. Right speech<br>4. Right action<br>5. Right livelihood | Moral conduct |
| 6. Right effort<br>7. Right mindfulness<br>8. Right concentration | Contemplation |

As indicated by the headings on the right, these eight norms are customarily grouped under the three basic axioms of the middle way: wisdom, moral conduct, and contemplation.

Because this eightfold way is called a path (*marga*), people sometimes think that practice should proceed sequentially, beginning with right understanding, right intention, and so on until the concluding practice of right concentration is taken up. This is a serious mistake, however, for these eight norms of wholesome living need to be followed simultaneously, as they are interrelated and mutually supportive. Although it is true that, without at least an initial understanding of the nature of existence as well as the existence, conditions, and way of eliminating duḥkha, a person would have no reason to practice the eightfold way, this understanding may be quite shallow and incomplete. But if it serves to activate the intention of avoiding all forms of evil and unwholesome actions to pursue a moral and wholesome life, thereby giving rise to the practices of contemplation, then this initial understanding will be deepened and the initial intention strengthened. Gradually, as compassion replaces desires and aversions as the basis of all action, and right effort, mindfulness and concentration develop a higher meditative insight, a complete understanding based on direct insight can replace the partial understanding based merely on confidence in reason or someone else's word.

But these three axioms of the middle way—wisdom, moral conduct, and contemplation—are interdependent, with progress in any one area dependent upon progress in the other two. Without moral control over the passions and the replacement of desire with compassion as the mainspring of action, the self-discipline of right effort, mindfulness, and concentration leading to contemplative insight cannot be achieved. But without self-discipline and insight, it is impossible to achieve moral conduct—right speech, action, and livelihood. And of course, without right understanding and right intention—which cannot be acquired without practicing moral conduct and contemplation—one cannot achieve moral purity or contemplative insight. Thus, although it is customary to begin explanations of the path with right understanding, it must be understood that in the practice of the middle way these eight norms are to be followed simultaneously as the basis of a completely integrated life.

Wisdom, the guide to wholesome living whereby suffering is overcome, comprises both the right understanding of existence and the intention to act in accord with this understanding, that is, the intention to act only out of love, compassion, goodwill, and selflessness. That wisdom is thought of as including the resolution to live in this wholesome way shows that this is not merely theoretical knowledge. Indeed, the Buddha described right understanding variously as (1) understanding of the four noble truths; (2) understanding what is conducive to wholesome and unwholesome existence; (3) understanding that the formations of existence are impermanent, without self, and (when attached to a self) duḥkha; (4) understanding the conditionedness of all existence; and (5) understanding how the fetters that bind one to the wheel of suffering (self-illusion, skepticism, attachment to mere rule and ritual, sensual lust, ill will, craving for material existence, craving for immaterial existence, conceit, restlessness, and ignorance) can be removed.

Clearly, although right understanding does not exclude theoretical knowledge, it should not be equated with metaphysical theories about the self and the self and the world—theories that the Buddha described as a jungle or wilderness. The parable of Māluṅkyāputta contained in the Majjhima Nikāya illustrates the Buddha's attitude toward metaphysical theories very nicely.

One day while meditating, it occurred to the monk, Māluṅkyāputta, that the Buddha had set aside and left unanswered a whole set of important metaphysical questions—whether the world is eternal or not, whether the world is finite or infinite, whether the self and the body are separate or identical, and whether a saint exists after death or not. So he approached the Buddha, angrily declaring that, unless the Blessed One answered these questions, he would abandon the monastic life. After reminding Māluṅkyāputta that he had never promised to answer these questions if Māluṅkyāputta took up the religious life with him, the Buddha explained that these questions rested on a great many theoretical distinctions and assumptions and could not possibly be answered in the relatively short time before a person died. Furthermore, these questions were beside the point: "It is as if, Māluṅkyāputta, a man had been wounded by an arrow thickly smeared with poison, and his friends and companions, his relatives and kinsfolk, were to procure for him a physician or surgeon, and the sick man were to say: 'I will not have this arrow taken out until I have learned whether the man who wounded me belonged to the brāhmaṇa, kṣatriya, vaiśya, or śūdra class; the name of the person who wounded me and the clan to which he belongs; whether he was tall, short, or medium in height; whether he was black, yellow, or brown; what village, city, or town he was from; what kind of wood the bow was made from; what kind of material the bow-string was made of; what kind of arrow it was, and with what it was feathered; what kind of sinews it was bound with; and what kind of point it had.' That man would die, Māluṅkyāputta, without ever having learning this."

The Buddha goes on to say that, in the same way, a person who refused to begin religious practice until the Buddha answered all the metaphysical questions posed by Māluṅkyāputta would be dead before he got the answers. "The religious life, Māluṅkyāputta, does not depend on the dogma that the world is eternal; nor does the religious life, Māluṅkyāputta, depend on the dogma that the world is not eternal. Whether the dogma obtains, Māluṅkyāputta, that the world is eternal, or that the world is not eternal, there still remain birth, old age, death, sorrow, lamentation, misery, grief, and despair, for the extinction of which in the present life I am prescribing." Then the Buddha repeats this for each of the other questions posed by Māluṅkyāputta, pointing out that he has not elucidated any of these theories because this kind of speculation "profits not, nor has to do with the fundamentals of religion, nor tends to aversion, absence of passion, cessation, quiescence [of duḥkha], the supernatural faculties, supreme wisdom, and nirvāṇa; therefore have I elucidated it.

"And what, Māluṅkyāputta, have I elucidated? Duḥkha, Māluṅkyāputta, have I elucidated; the origin of duḥkha have I elucidated; the cessation of duḥkha have I elucidated; and the path leading to the cessation of duḥkha have I elucidated. And why, Māluṅkyāputta, have I elucidated this? Because, Māluṅkyāputta, this does profit, has to do with the fundamentals of religion, and tends to aversion, absence of passion, cessation, quiesence [of duḥkha], understanding, supreme wisdom and Nirvāṇa; therefore I have elucidated it. Accordingly, Māluṅkyāputta, bear always in mind what it is that I have not elucidated, and what it is that I have elucidated."

Because right understanding is seen as a kind of practical knowledge of the conditions of duḥkha and the elimination of these conditions, it naturally leads to the resolve to free oneself from the attitudes and intentions that lead to ill will, lust, and hurting. Put positively, right intention is the intention or resolve to cultivate selflessness, goodwill, compassion, and love for all beings.

The right understanding and right intention of wisdom lead directly to moral conduct, for wrong speech, actions, and means of livelihood spring from wrong understanding and wrong intentions. The third norm, that of right speech, requires telling the truth, speaking in kind and friendly ways, and saying only what is useful. The principle is that speech should be used to bring about wholesomeness. Speech that leads to unwholesomeness should be avoided. Thus the norm of right speech prohibits (1) lying; (2) slander, character assassination, or talk that might bring about hatred, jealousy, enmity, or discord among others; (3) harsh or rude talk, including all kinds of impolite, abusive, and malicious language; and (4) idle chatter and gossip.

Right action means that all of one's action should respect the well-being of others, fostering the peace and happiness of all living beings. Negatively, it prohibits killing or hurting living beings, stealing, dishonesty, and illegitimate sexual activity.

Right livelihood extends the norms of right speech and action to one's means of earning a living. Only those means of livelihood that promote peace and the well-being of oneself and others are allowed. Occupations and professions that bring harm to others, such as trading in firearms, liquor or drugs, killing, and sexual procurement, are prohibited.

The third group of norms—right effort, mindfulness, and concentration—aims at inculcating a steady discipline of consciousness that brings about self-awareness and insight. Right effort includes cultivating a strong will capable of (1) preventing evil and unwholesome states of mind from arising; (2) overcoming evil and unwholesome states of mind (e.g., greed, anger, selfishness, ill will, lust, and delusion) that have already arisen; (3) bringing about good and wholesome states of mind; and (4) developing and maintaining good and wholesome states of mind already present. It is suggested that the appropriate attitude toward right effort on the part of a person who has penetrated the Buddha's teaching and is possessed of faith is reflected in the thought, "Though skin, sinews and bones wither away, though flesh and blood of my body dry up, I shall not give up my efforts till I have attained whatever is attainable by courageous perseverance, energy and endeavor" (Majjhima Nikāya, 70).

Right mindfulness consists in being carefully aware of and attentive to the activities of (1) the body, (2) sensations and feelings, (3) the mind, and (4) thinking and conceiving. Mindfulness of the body can be attained through attention to breathing, to bodily positions and activities, and to the various internal processes. Mindfulness of sensations and feelings is achieved by attending to whether they are pleasant, unpleasant, or neutral and to how they arise and disappear within oneself. Mindfulness of mental activities is achieved by being attentive to all the activities of the mind and becoming aware of whether or not one's thoughts are greedy, lustful, hateful, deluded, distracted, concentrated, and so on. Mindfulness of thinking and conceiving is achieved by attending to how thoughts and ideas arise, how they disappear, and how they are developed or suppressed and the conditions on which they depend.

The practices of right mindfulness are intended to enable a person to live as completely as possible in the present moment of existence in complete self-awareness, overcoming both distractedness and self-conciousness. Because this kind of meditation leads to direct insight into oneself and into the nature of things, the self-consciousness and distancing that most modes of self-awareness entail are avoided, and a sense of wholeness is achieved. In a way this practice of the fourfold right mindfulness is the heart of the Buddhist way. In the discourse on the "Setting Up of Mindfulness" (Dīgha Nikāya, 22), the Buddha brings the understanding of the four noble truths and the practice of the eightfold noble path within the practice of right mindfulness. Why this should be so is expressed with a certain elegance in the opening verses of the Dhammapada, where the insight that ignorance and suffering on the one hand, and happiness and enlightenment on the other, are dependent upon one's mental states is formulated as follows:

> Mind precedes all unwholesome states and is their chief; they are all mind-wrought. If with an impure mind a person speaks or acts, misery follows him like the wheel that dogs the foot of the ox. Mind precedes all wholesome states and is their chief; they are all mind-wrought. If with a pure mind a person speaks or acts, happiness follows him like his never departing shadow.

But to achieve the purity of mind that dispels misery and unwholesomeness, right mindfulness needs to incorporate the practices of concentration or *dhyāna*. Four stages of concentration can be distinguished. (1) First is the stage where thoughts of lust, ill will, worry, anxiety, doubt, and laziness are eliminated and are replaced with a sense of joy and well-being. (2) In the next stage all forms of mental activity and thinking are left behind, and one's existence is pervaded by joy and a sense of well-being. (3) In the third stage of absorption the mental activities responsible for the feelings of joy are transcended, and one achieves equanimity pervaded by happiness. (4) Finally, in the fourth stage, direct insight replaces all activities of the mind, and a perfect equanimity is achieved beyond the dualities of grief and joy.

This insight is the basis of the wisdom that sees the conditionedness and interrelatedness of all existence: a pervasive interdependence leaving no foothold for selfishness and ill will. Now sympathy and compassion replace selfishness and utility as motivation for speech, thought, and action. Ignorant grasping for self and things is replaced by an equanimity that frees a person from fear and anxiety, permitting life to be lived to its fullest possible extent—here, now, in this present moment of existence.

## Development of the Buddhist Community (Saṅgha)

Our examination of the Buddha and his Teachings up to this point has focused on the understanding that is more or less common to all Buddhists sects, in different lands and at different times. The scriptural sources for this common understanding are the Discourses of the Buddha as contained in the Pali Nikāyas of the Theravādins and the Sanskrit Āgamas (preserved in Chinese and Tibetan translation) of the Mahāyānists. These Discourses, as preserved in Pali, were collected into five groups or *Nikāyas*: Long Discourses (*Dīgha*), Medium Discourses (*Majjhima*), Connected Discourses (*Saṁyutta*), Item-more Discourses (*Aṅguttara*), and Little Texts (*Khuddaka*).

Despite major differences between the thought and practice of Theravāda and Mahāyāna, there is very close agreement on the contents of the first four of these five collections of sayings of the Buddha in their respective canons. Their interpretations of these discourses also agree with respect to the fundamentals of the middle way—the four noble truths and the eightfold noble path—suggesting a common ground going back to the beginnings of Buddhism. But differences in emphasis and minor differences in interpretation—both of doctrines and of rules for living—occasioned disagreements within the early community, leading to schism and the formation of various sects and subsects.

Within a hundred years of the Buddha's death a major schism occurred, and by 100 B.C. eighteen or more sects had arisen, differing over interpretations of teaching or rules of discipline. Of the major sects, Theravāda has a continuous history of development from the beginnings of Buddhism up to the present, being the dominant form of Buddhism in Southeast Asia. The other two major early sects, the Mahāsaṅghikas and the Sarvāstivādins, contributed much to the development of Mahāyāna, into which they were absorbed about the beginning of the Common Era. Two thousand years of Mahāyāna Buddhism have left their mark not only on North India, but on China, Tibet, Japan, Korea, and Vietnam, and to a lesser extent on other parts of the world as well.

It is clearly beyond the scope of this chapter to detail the development of Buddhist thought and practice across more than twenty centuries and almost as many countries. But in our efforts to understand the Saṅgha—in which, as the third jewel of Buddhism, hundreds of millions of people have taken refuge over the centuries—we cannot ignore this historical development, for it has shaped the Buddhist community into these two distinct forms of Theravāda and Mahāyāna.

From the beginning, the influence of the Buddha and the practice of the Dharma occurred in the context of the Buddhist Saṅgha—the community of monks, nuns, laywomen, and laymen. Although frequently the term "saṅgha" is used only with respect to the monastic assembly, this is a mistake. It extends to the lay community as well, even though the monastic order has historically been regarded as the center of the religious community and the lives of its members seen as exemplary and paradigmatic for Buddhism as a whole.

Monastic communities were common in the Buddha's time, and it is not surprising that he accepted into his company those who accepted his teachings and wished to follow his way. But unlike most religious communities, admission to the Buddha's group was open to all who were willing to accept the teachings and the rules of living laid down. Rich and poor, male and female, brāhmaṇa and outcast, merchant and thief—none were excluded if they accepted the Buddha, the Teachings, and the rules of living within the community.

Apparently there was some initial hesitation over admitting women to the monastic community. But according to all indications, the order of nuns was established within the Buddha's lifetime, even though from the beginning nuns were regarded as being somewhat inferior to monks and subordinate to them. And historically the order of monks—not of nuns—was the great center of Buddhism, spreading it from region to region and from country to country, interpreting the teachings and exemplifying the Buddhist way of life.

Initially the Buddhist community was loosely structured and unbureaucratic, with entry a simple and relatively informal matter. One simply indicated acceptance of the Buddha as the teacher, willingness to follow his teachings, and respect for the Saṅgha. Since Siddhārtha himself had "gone forth" into the homeless state and had, like many others of his day, given up possessions and adopted begging as a way of survival, it was natural for his followers to imitate his example. They also followed his example of moderation in eating and sleeping and adopted the moral code of non-hurting, truthfulness, honesty, and sexual purity. But these practices were not immediately codified into formal requirements. The only entrance formality was the Buddha's acknowledgment of acceptance: "Come, bhikṣu [monk]."

On the instruction of the Buddha, these monks traveled their own separate ways, explaining the four noble truths and practicing the eightfold path wherever they went, converting many people to the way of the Buddha as they journeyed throughout the country. As they traveled farther and it became increasingly difficult for the new converts to come to the Buddha for acceptance into the order, the monks were given permission to accept new people into the Buddhist order on their own. Soon it became clear that the rapid growth and expansion being experienced required certain procedures to protect and safeguard the community and the Teachings. Now rules were developed to govern (1) admission into the community, (2) the conduct of life, and (3) ordination of teachers. Gradually the distinction between those practicing the middle way as laypersons and those dedicating their whole life to practice and teaching—symbolized by adopting the robe and begging bowl—came to be accepted as a difference between a partial and inferior way suitable for laypersons and the full-fledged superior way of the monastics, a differentiation that has continued to characterize Buddhist attitudes in most countries for the last twenty-three hundred years.

As the distinction between lay and monastic Buddhists hardened and the monks, self-assumed superiority relegated lay practice to an inferior status, a quarrel developed within the monastic community. Those who championed the worthiness of lay practice advocated a concept of Saṅgha that embraced both lay and monastic Buddhists. These "Great-Assembly-ests" (Mahāsaṅghikas), as they were called, were opposed by the Elders (Sthaviras), who claimed that the true Saṅgha included only Buddhists who had joined the celibate monastic order.

The issue is more basic than it first appears. At stake is the whole question of what constitutes an *arhant*—"a worthy one." Is a person worthy because of spiritual attainments—insight and enlightenment? Or because of strict observance of the disciplinary rules of the community? Furthermore, is worthiness due to one's compassionate efforts to lead all beings out of suffering, or is it due to success in overcoming suffering in one's own life?

The controversy over who is a "worthy" follower of the Buddha that divided the early community into Sthaviras and Mahāsaṅghikas—the predecessors of Theravādins and Mahāyānists—was rooted also in differing interpretations of the Buddha's teachings. While the Buddha was alive, questions concerning the understanding and interpretations of his teachings could be appealed to him directly. But after the Buddha's death there was no one in a position of central authority to whom the community could appeal in cases of disputed interpretations. Even as he felt death approaching he refused to appoint one of his favorite monks as his heir to lead the community. Instead he recommended that after his death the community be guided by his teachings and discipline. This refusal to appoint a successor to himself expressed the Buddha's confidence in the ability of his teaching and practice to win acceptance on their own merits, thereby providing a greater safeguard against corruption than could be secured by creating an ecclesiastical authority.

But replacing the Buddha with his teachings and discipline put great pressure on his followers to ensure correct interpretation of the teachings and proper application of disciplinary rules. Since the Buddha's Teachings were now the Teacher, nothing was more important than ensuring the accuracy of analysis and interpretation of the discourses. No detail was too small or insignificant to escape careful and painstaking analysis, and a thoroughgoing scholasticism soon permeated the Buddhist community. But because the Buddha had avoided all metaphysical positions, the disputes arising concerning the basis of differing analyses and interpretations could not be settled by appeal to his words on the subject. The initial controversy over strictness of disciplinary observance and criteria for an arhant quickly broadened to include issues of interpretation of the teaching and claims about metaphysical presuppositions underlying the teachings, splitting the community into two opposing sects. Apparently the differences could not be resolved, and within a few centuries, without a strong center claiming their allegiance, new groups split off from each of these two sects. Soon there were some eleven sects of Sthaviras—of which the Theravādins survived as the dominant "southern" sect—and seven sects of Mahāsaṅghikas—which gradually merged into the dominant "northern" form of Mahāyāna.

## DIFFERENCES BETWEEN THERAVĀDA AND MAHĀYĀNA

The major differences between the Mahāyāna and Theravāda forms of Buddhism can be seen most easily by examining their answers to five controversial questions. The first question is, "What is the Saṅgha?" Mahāyānists have, for the most part, accepted the Mahāsaṅghika's view that anyone—layperson or monastic—who accepts the Buddha as Teacher and agrees to follow the middle way is a worthy member of the community. Theravādins have tended to deny the status of arhant to lay Buddhists. After all, the laity do not observe total nonpossession or complete celibacy. Furthermore, they take only five of the ten moral vows required of monastics. Laypersons who take refuge are recognized as Buddhists, of course, but greatly inferior to members of the monastic orders, who alone are considered truly worthy.

The second question is, "What are the essential teachings of the Buddha?" While both sects agree that the four noble truths and the practice of the eightfold path are central teachings, the Theravādins tend to stress the literal word as contained in the collections of Discourses, whereas the Mahāyānists stress the example of the Buddha. Accordingly, the Mahāyānists have accepted as canonical many texts that stress the awakening of faith and the development of compassion on the grounds that they embody the Buddha's teaching by example—even though they go beyond his actual words as recorded in the Discourses.

As we saw earlier, the Buddha avoided metaphysical questions, concerning himself only with the overcoming of suffering. But in their zeal to substantiate their interpretations of the Buddha's teachings, his followers tended to adopt metaphysical positions on which to base their views. Although almost every shade of metaphysics was explored or adopted along the way, on the whole Mahāyānists tended to emphasize that ultimately reality is undivided; the differences and distinctions that characterize the ordinary world are nothing but conventions. However convenient for practical purposes, these conventions are ultimately barren of truth.

On the other hand, undivided reality transcends all conventions and distinctions and therefore cannot be known by any ordinary means. The Prajñāpāramitā Sūtras (Texts of Wisdom That Goes Beyond), devoted to elucidating this transcendent reality, continually engage in a dialectic of paradox, where teachings are said to be nonteachings, Buddhas are called non-Buddhas and nirvāṇa is identified with saṁsāra. The intent of this dialectic is to coax or shock the hearer into going beyond the dualities of conventional truth. For example, in the Diamond Sūtra, the Buddha asks Subhuti whether there is any reality (dharma) that has been fully known by the Tathāgata as "the utmost, right and perfect enlightenment" or whether any reality has been demonstrated by the Tathāgata. In impeccable Mahāyāna fashion, Subhuti replies: "No, not as I understand the Lord's teaching, for the reality which has been fully known or demonstrated by the Tathāgata cannot be grasped or talked about. It is neither reality nor non-reality."

Theravādins, on the other hand, tend to emphasize the reality of processes constituting this ordinary world. Although things and persons are held to be without self or "own-being," when correctly seen as processes they are accepted as real. Analysis of the processes constituting persons and things reveals innumerable dharmas or elemental forces, which in their movements and associations with each other give rise to the connected processes that we call things or persons. As worked out in the Sarvāstivādin philosophies, this means that there really are no selves or things. Selves and things are just conventional designations for arbitrary collections of elemental existence forces (dharmas). Ultimately only these dharmas are real. It is this view that underlies the Theravāda meditational practice of dissolving self and things into processes of dharmas as a way of achieving wisdom and overcoming grasping.

The third question is, "Who is the Buddha?" The Theravādins emphasize the historical Śākyamuni, Siddhārtha Gautama, who differs from other arhants principally in that he is the originator of the path and the first teacher. Mahāyāna accepts the historical Śākyamuni as one of many appearances of the ultimate enlightenment reality, stressing the ultimate undivided reality in which all reality participates. Because all beings participate in the undivided reality, all are potentially Buddhas; they need only become awakened to their true reality. From the higher standpoint of absolute truth in which conventional distinctions are overcome, there are no Buddhas—the appearances of Buddhas at the conventional level are only manifestations or appearances (*Nirmāṇakāya*) of the undivided Buddha reality.

The fourth question is, "What is the goal toward which one should strive?" The Theravādins, emphasizing the Buddha's advice to "be your own refuge" and to "work out your salvations with diligence," regard liberation of the individual from duḥkha as the primary goal. Mahāyānists, emphasizing the Buddha's own untiring efforts to help others overcome duḥkha, regard the goal of individual liberations as limited and selfish, preferring the ideal of the Bodhisattva. A Bodhisattva vows not to cease diligent effort until all beings have been liberated and not to accept nirvāṇa until then.

The Bodhisattva ideal is given succinctly in the following passage from the Diamond Banner Sūtra.

> A Bodhisattva resolves: I take upon myself the burden of all suffering, I am resolved to do so, I will endure it. I do not turn or run away, do not tremble, am not terrified, nor afraid, do not turn back or despond.
>
> And why? At all cost I must bear the burdens of all beings, in that I do not follow my own inclinations. I have made the vow to save all beings. All beings I must set free. The whole world of living beings I must rescue, from the terrors of birth, of old age, of sickness, of death and rebirth, of all kinds of moral offense, of all states of woe, of the whole cycle of birth-and-death, of the jungle of false views, of the loss of wholesome dharmas, of the concomitants of ignorance—from all these terrors I must rescue all beings. . . . I walk so that the kingdom of unsurpassed cognition is built up for all beings. My endeavours do not merely aim at my own deliverance. For with the help of the boat of the thought of all-knowlege, I must rescue all these beings from the stream of Saṁsāra, which is so difficult to cross, I must pull them back from the great precipice, I must free them from all calamities, I must ferry them across the stream of Saṁsāra. I myself must grapple with the whole mass of suffering of all beings. To the limit of my endurance I will experience in all the states of woe, found in any world system, all the abodes of suffering. And I must not cheat all beings out of my store of merit. I am resolved to abide in each single state of woe for numberless aeons and so I will help all beings to freedom, in all the states of woe that may be found in any world system whatsoever.
>
> (*Vajradhvaja Sūtra* of the Sikṣasamuccaya, 280–281)[1]

The fifth controversial question concerns strictness of discipline. Theravādins, following the Buddha's advice to work out their salvation with diligence and emphasizing the primacy of moral conduct in achieving nonattachment and wisdom, have tended toward extremely strict observance of the disciplinary rules. Mahāyānists, on the other hand, because of their emphasis on the Bodhisattva and understanding of the Buddha as the inner reality of all beings, have given primacy to the awakening of faith and the development of compassion. This emphasis on faith and compassion finds it fullest expression in the Mahāyāna sect of Pure Land Buddhism where it is believed that simply invoking the name of the Buddha in faith and devotion will effect a person's salvation. The origins of devotional Buddhism of faith are not entirely clear, but it has been widespread, with the invocation to the Buddha of

[1]As translated by Edward Conze in *Buddhist Texts Through the Ages* (New York: Harper & Row, Publishers, 1964), pp 131–132.

infinite light found in the Sanskritic Indian form: "Om! Namo Amitabhaya"; in the Chinese form: "Om! O-mi-to-fo"; and in the Japanese form: "Namo Amida Butsu."

Of course, members of the Pure Land sect are also expected to lead pure lives, even though their practice is dominated by the activities of awakening faith—activities that include praising the Buddha's virtue, giving gifts, honoring his wisdom and compassion, invoking his name, and expressing confidence in the power of the acts of the various Buddhas and Bodhisattvas to bring all beings to salvation. The Mahāyāna of faith and devotion may seem a long way from the Buddha's teaching of the eightfold noble way as the way to overcoming duḥkha, but in fact the Buddha himself laid the groundwork for this development. Shortly before his death, in recognition of the needs of his followers for an expression of their faith and trust, he instructed them to visit and honor the four auspicious places associated with his career, telling Ananda,

> There are four places which should be seen by, and which create emotion in the clansmen with faith. Which four? "Here the Tathāgata was born . . . Here the Tathāgata attained supreme and perfect enlightenment . . . Here the Tathāgata set the incomparable wheel of the Teaching rolling . . . Here the Tathāgata passed away in the element of nirvāṇa without any substrate left."
>
> (Dīgha Nikāya, 2.140)

This advice, along with the Buddha's own example of compassionate and self-less effort to deliver all beings from suffering, nourished the Mahāyāna development of the Bodhisattva ideal and the practice of faith and devotion that proved so appealing to ordinary people who were inclined neither to asceticism nor to yoga.

These differences between Theravāda and Mahāyāna should not be exaggerated, for their common core of agreement far exceeds their disagreements. Buddhists of both persuasions share the common understanding of the Buddha and his Teachings outlined in the previous pages. But because of different emphases and interpretations, they have developed this basic understanding into two wings, which, though sharing a common base, extend in opposite directions. The original meaning of Saṅgha—the community of all those who, because of personal worthiness, acceptance of the Buddha and his Teachings, and practice of the eightfold way, stand in a spiritual relationship to the Buddha reality and to each other—remains the basis of the Buddhist community, whether the sect is Theravāda, Jodo, Zen, or somewhere in between.

## Summary

Setting in motion the wheel of teaching with his first sermon in approximately 525 B.C., the Buddha proclaimed his insight into four truths: (1) the nature of human suffering, (2) its conditions, (3) the elimination of these conditions, and (4) the way to overcome these conditions, thereby eliminating suffering. These four truths were declared to be a "middle way," for they charted a path midway between the positions of complete determinism and complete indeterminism—neither of which allowed room for human effort to overcome suffering—and midway between a life of extreme asceticism and a life of indulgence in the passions and pleasures of life. Its moderation in these two respects distinguished the way of the Buddha from other ways prevalent twenty-five hundred years ago in India and contributed to its widespread appeal.

The insight underlying the four noble truths is that suffering arises only when certain conditions are present. Distinguishing between ordinary kinds of suffering, suffering as change and suffering as attachment to the processes of existence, the Buddha declared all three to be subject to a variety of conditions. But these conditions—in particular the critical conditions of ignorance and grasping—can be eliminated by practicing the eightfold way of wisdom, morality, and contemplation, thereby bringing about the calm, peace, and insight of nirvāṇa.

As a result of its popular nonsectarian appeal, diligent missionary activity, and the patronage of state—in particular, the support of Ashoka, India's greatest king, who from 269 to 232 B.C. ruled almost the entire subcontinent—Buddhism caught on, spreading throughout India in the first three centuries after the Enlightenment. Although they shared a common understanding of the basic teachings concerning the four noble truths and the eightfold noble path, differences in interpretation of who the Buddha is, and how the Buddhist way ought to be practiced, split the Buddhists into numerous sects by the end of Ashoka's rule. The teachings of two of these sects—the Mahāyāna and the Theravāda—proved decisive for the religious and philosophical life of most of Asia. Between 200 B.C. and A.D. 500, Theravāda became a dominant cultural force in most of Southeast Asia. In the meantime, Mahāyāna was taking hold in China, from where it would begin its movement to Japan, Korea, and Vietnam, becoming a major religious-philosophical force in the lives of the people in those countries. Although by A.D. 1000 it was no longer a vital force in India, it had now found its way to Nepal and Tibet, where it has continued as the primary religious vehicle up to the present time.

While both Mahāyānists and Theravādins recognize and honor the historical Buddha, the former regard him as merely one among many manifestations of the underlying enlightenment reality, recognizing many other Buddhas and Bodhisattvas. For the Theravādins, the historical Buddha is unique. They attempt to follow his advice to be their own refuge and to seek out their salvation with diligence, aiming at the goal of arhantship—the elimination of suffering in their own lives. Mahāyānists, on the other hand, emphasizing the compassion that the Buddha felt for other suffering beings and the dedication of his life to rescuing others from suffering, see the Bodhisattva as the ideal Buddhist. The Bodhisattva renounces the goal of individual liberation from suffering, vowing not to enter into nirvāṇa until all beings have been delivered from suffering. For a majority of Mahāyāna Buddhists this knowledge that countless Buddhas and Bodhisattvas are working to deliver them from suffering leads to an emphasis on faith rather than the Theravāda reliance on individual effort.

## Suggestions for Further Reading

*The Buddhist Way,* by Kenneth Inada (New York: Macmillan Publishing Co., Inc., forthcoming, 1983), is best overall account of the central teachings and development of Buddhism.

*What the Buddha Taught,* by Walpola Rahula, 2nd ed. (New York: Grove Press, 1978), is a splendid little book. In ninety pages of text the author, a Buddhist monk, does an admirable job of explaining the four noble truths, the idea of no-self, and the practice of mindfulness from the Theravāda perspective. The accompanying translation from key scriptures and the seventeen carefully chosen plates combine to make this one of the best introductions to the basic teachings of Buddhism available.

*Buddhist Philosophy: A Historical Analysis,* by David J. Kalupahana (Honolulu: University of Hawaii Press, 1976), is a brief, clearly written, straightforward account of key ideas of early Buddhism and their development in the Theravāda and Mahāyāna schools. The appendices on metaphysics and Zen are gems.

*Buddhist Thought in India,* by Edward Conze (Ann Arbor: University of Michigan Press, 1967), is a very good account of key ideas of Indian Buddhism as they developed among the various sects. The chapters on Mahayana, especially the chapters on the Mādhyamikas, are particularly good. Conze's earlier *Buddhism: Its Essence and Development* (New York: Harper Torchbooks), though written thirty years ago, is still a good place for a Westerner to begin studying Buddhism.

*Buddhist Sects in India,* by Nalinaksha Dutt (Calcutta: Firma KLM Private, 1977), does an outstanding job of tracing the similarities and differences among the eighteen sects of Indian Buddhists. Like his earlier books, *Mahāyāna Buddhism* and *Early Monastic Buddhism,* this is a work of careful scholarship, good organization, and clear presentation.

*The Buddhist Religion,* by Richard Robinson and Willard Johnson, 2nd ed. (Encino, Calif.: Dickenson Publishing Co., 1977), is an introductory account of the development of Buddhism by the late Richard Robinson, one of the great students of Buddhism of our times, revised by his student. It contains a good bibliography that will direct the reader to the more important works dealing with the various historical phases of Buddhism.

# 8

# Yoga

## The Power to Transform Existence

Despite major differences among the Buddhist, Jaina, and Upaniṣadic visions, there is agreement that life as it is usually lived is permeated by suffering and that liberation from suffering requires a radical transformation of existence. Furthermore, all three visions find that at the root of human suffering lies a deep ignorance of who we really are—a case of mistaken identity of the profoundest kind that binds us to repeated suffering and death. How can this ignorance be overcome and liberation from bondage achieved? This extremely urgent question motivates and guides almost all Indian thought. Although no two thinkers agree in all of the details of their answers, almost all agree that the techniques of yoga are central to liberation. Indeed, the common acceptance of yoga as an indispensable means of liberation by the many different systems constitutes one of the great unifying forces of Indian thought and practice.

The origins of yoga are lost in antiquity. Judging from the figures seated in classic yoga positions on the seals discovered at Indus sites, it appears that yoga was already practiced in India before the Vedic age. In the intervening four thousand years yoga has been associated with a great variety of metaphysics, and its many techniques have been employed for quite different purposes. But throughout its known history yoga has remained faithful to the underlying ideal of self-transcendence through self-control, an ideal combining the two great cultural ideas of power through self-discipline and liberation from bondage and suffering.

The idea of power through self-discipline reflects the conviction that we control our own destiny. By harnessing and controlling the deeper powers of reality, we can control this saṁsāric existence, effecting our liberation from the bondage that we have unwittingly created for ourselves. This idea is captured in a frequently presented analogy by the image of a chariot driver. The author of the Kaṭha Upaniṣad presents the image in these words: "The body is like a chariot. Know the Self as its owner, intelligence [*buddhi*] as its driver and mind [*manas*] as the reins. The senses are said to be the horses, and the world of sense-objects their arena. The Self, associated with body, senses, and mind, is the Enjoyer—so say the wise. But for one without understanding, whose mind is always unrestrained, his senses are out of control—just as wild horses are uncontrolled by the charioteer" (1.3.3–5).

The idea of liberation from suffering is presented by the author of The Knife Upaniṣad in the image of a migrating bird:

> As a migratory bird
> Imprisoned within a net
> Flies upward toward the heavens
> When the captive's cords are cut;
>
> So the Self of the adept
> Set free from passion's bondage
> By the keen knife of yoga
> Escapes saṁsāra's prison.
> (Kṣurika Upaniṣad, 1.25)

**BONDAGE**

Together, these two images reflect the widely shared understanding that, for the sake of liberation from lower levels of existence, characterized by suffering and bondage, the various energies of life must be harnessed and directed toward a higher and more profound mode of existence.

We should recall that the quest for Ātman in the Upaniṣads—a quest embodied in various forms in almost all the succeeding Indian ways of salvation—was motivated by the urge to achieve freedom from repeated deaths in the saṁsāric cycle. Despite all its pleasures and joys, life was clearly seen to terminate in death. And, granted acceptance of transmigration, it was not only one death, but innumerable deaths, that had to be faced. How could death be overcome? This question, based on the underlying attitude that emphasized bondage to the cycle of life and death, motivated the sages of the Upaniṣads to seek both the ultimate ground of being and self and the methods of realizing life at this deepest level where suffering and death could not reach.

Repeated dying or bondage to saṁsāra eventually came to symbolize all kinds of suffering, representing the entire defectiveness of human existence. Our studies of Jainism and Buddhism have shown clearly that the experience of suffering furnishes both the starting point and the motivating energy for these otherwise quite different ways of thought and practice. The Jaina parable of the man in the well (see p. 116) and the Buddhist wheel of becoming, shown grasped in the clutches of death personified are dramatic representations of this pervasive Indian concern to recognize the impermanence and unwholesomeness of human life and to achieve a transformation of existence so radical and profound that all forms of suffering are left behind.

The Bhagavad Gītā, which accommodates many Vedic, Upaniṣadic, Jaina, and Buddhist ideas and ways of practice in the ways of salvation called Hinduism, also assumes this radical defectiveness as its starting point. Its three primary ways of liberation—the yoga of knowledge, the yoga of action, and the yoga of devotion—assume that saṁsāric existence is the embodiment of evil and defectiveness. This widespread Hindu attitude that pain, fear, anxiety, and death are our constant companions on an interminable journey through the cycles of life and death is captured brilliantly by Bhatṛhari in verse 197 of the *Śatakatraya*:

> Birth is scented by death,
> Youth's brilliance shadowed by old age.
> Contentment is menaced by ambition;
> Calm, by bold women's amorous glances;
> Virtues, by human malice;
> Woodlands, by serpents;
> Kings, by criminals.
> Rich treasure
> Is plundered by transience.
> Is anything spared the threat of destruction?

If this were the vision of a person oppressed by poverty, struck down by disease, a victim of crime and injustice, or cruelly lacking in talents and accomplishments, we might be tempted to dismiss it as unwarranted pessimism born of frustration. But Bhartṛhari, a fifth-century philosopher and court poet, was rich and famous. Depending on the legend believed, he was either a king or a high official in the king's court. In either case he enjoyed a royal life of great opulence and courtly pleasures—all of which he renounced in favor of the joyful calm of a hermit's life long before age had robbed him of the capacity to indulge his senses and enjoy his fame. His indictment of life did not issue from failure to achieve money, power, pleasure, or fame; of these riches he, like Prince Siddhārtha Gautama a thousand years earlier, had a surfeit. But compared with the joys of inner contentment, spiritual fulfillment, and deathlessness, all these worldly blessings seemed no better than a curse.

Paradoxically, it is optimism, not pessimism, about life's possibilities that underlies the Indian recognition that, for one who truly knows, this saṁsāric life is only duḥkha. Almost all Indian thinkers have been convinced that we are capable of radically transforming our existence in such a way that suffering is overcome by joy and death by immortality. Furthermore, the techniques by which this transformation is accomplished are available to every person who will make the necessary effort. Too often people look at only the starting point of the Indian analysis—the recognition that life in its usual modalities is inevitably accompanied by suffering—and conclude that Indian thought is pessimistic. If they were to accept the Indian vision of transformed existence and acknowledge the effectiveness of the techniques that have been worked out over millenia for achieving this transformation, these same people would laud India's optimism rather than decry her pessimism.

Knowing that a spiritually fulfilled existence is possible and confident of achieving the bliss of mokṣa or nirvāṇa, Indian thinkers have had the courage to face the human condition realistically, analyze its defectiveness, and prescribe for its cure. For someone convinced that this saṁsāric condition is all there is, that there is no alternative to this present mode of life, it may not be possible to perform a careful and realistic analysis of the human condition. It may be necessary to hide the ugliness and suffering of life, to pretend that all is well, when in fact it is not. If we know that there is a cure for the cancer that afflicts us, we want an examination that will reveal the full extent of the illness, no matter how ugly and distressing it may appear at the moment. But if we are convinced that nothing can be done about the disease, we would probably prefer to remain ignorant of its nature and effects, pretending, as well as we can, that everything is really all right, putting on a cheerful face.

## CONTROL

Whether the Indian diagnosis of the human condition is regarded as pessimistic or optimistic depends entirely upon whether or not one accepts the possibility of a radically transformed mode of existence and the effectiveness of the techniques for achieving this transformation. Accepted on its own terms, the Indian vision is not pessimistic, just realistic. The condemnation of the saṁsāric mode of life is an effective way of both celebrating a contrasting mode of life, free from suffering, and creating motivation to work for the attainment of this liberated existence. This contrast, evident in practically all India's great thinkers, is expressed in another verse of Bhartṛhari's, a verse that, in its last three lines, reflects the Indian confidence in the yogic techniques of transformation:

> Pleasures are as fleeting as lightning
> Flashing through a cover of clouds;
> Life as fragile as a rain-cloud
> Blown by the wind.
> Youth's gentle touch from mortals flees.
> You who are wise, reflect on this;
> Hasten to establish your minds in yoga,
> Purest fruit of meditation and calm.
> (Śatakatraya, 178)

Although the primary meaning of "yoga" is that of a method of control, Bhartṛhari's use of the word to refer to the result of this method ("yoga, purest fruit of calm and trance") is not unusual. In fact, many Indian thinkers, when deriving the word "yoga" from its verbal root *yuj*, suggest that this root has the double meaning of controlling and joining. The basis for this dual derivation is easily seen in the example of harnessing a horse to a chariot. The harness is essentially a means of control. But this means of control joins the horses to each other and to the chariot. The energy by which the chariot is transformed from a stationary collection of pieces of wood to a swift and efficient mobile instrument of battle comes through this union with the controlled power of the horses. The analogy suggests that, in a similar way, the power whereby the lower self can be controlled and life transformed comes through joining one's existence—by means of yogic control—to the deepest powers of ultimate reality coursing deep within the body, senses, mind, and intelligence.

The image of the chariot is particularly apt, for the task of yoga is to harness the energies of existence, guiding a profound transformation of life by making available the spiritual energy of the deepest level of reality.

Although nothing is known of Indus yoga or of the indigenous words used to describe it, it is significant that the Sanskrit word by which the name of this practice was translated in ancient India is the same word—"yoga"—that the Vedic people used for harnessing wild horses to their war chariots. As we have seen, the warrior-owner of the chariot completely transforms his situation on the battlefield by having a good driver who can harness and control the war chariot powered by wild horses.

Skeptics may find it hard to believe that the yogic techniques of self-control can transform human life in a radical way, empowering it with an undreamed of energy. But for a person with no experience in training and driving, it would also be hard to believe that, with a few scraps of leather, a good chariot driver could transform wild horses into chariot power. The secret is the *discipline* that channels the available energies into useful power. The driver uses the harness to guide and control; while it is used to restrict the horse's activities that interfere with the goal of pulling the chariot well, it is also used to encourage increased power and speed. Similarly, the techniques of yoga are used to restrict undesirable activities and to facilitate the activities of illumination. Discipline can be used to restrict, but also to release, energy. The successful yogin and the successful driver know how to do both, using their control to transform one kind of existence into another, more desirable, kind.

We must take care not to be misled by the analogy of the chariot, however, for whereas horse, driver, harness, and owner are all separate realities, the human individual is an undivided unity, not separate from the deepest powers of reality. A person is a microcosm of the whole universe, and the powers enabling the yogic transformation to occur are not separate but, rather, a deep dimension of human existence obscured by shallower modes of being. Thus, yoga is not a joining of two separate realities, but an awakening and realization of what was already there. Even here the analogy of the chariot is suggestive, however, for though initially the owner, horses, chariot, and driver are separate, when joined together by harness they function as a unit.

The image of control in the analogy of the chariot and driver suggests also that degrees of control are directly related to levels of reality. The body, a lower level of reality, is controlled by the mind, a higher level reality. The mind, in turn, is controlled by a still higher reality, the intelligence (*buddhi*), while all of these are controlled by and work for the highest reality, the Self. When the power of the highest level of reality reaches down into the lower levels of reality, disciplining and controlling them, they are transformed by the highest power—even as wild horses are transformed into chariot power by the power and control of a skilled driver.

The concept of degrees or levels of reality is extremely important, for it makes intelligible the presupposition of yoga that a person is really (i.e., at a more profound level of reality) a quite different kind of being than is usually assumed. Our usual attachment to, and identification with, a particular body-mind complex is the result of ignorance of the nature of the deepest level of the self. Of course, this ignorance is not merely intellectual; it is not a lack of information. Rather, it is a lived ignorance constituting our entire way of experiencing and relating—our whole way of being in the world. When a person achieves a living realization of the truth that everything springs from a deeper level of reality—a level that in the Upaniṣads is known as Ātman or Brahman—and that all the lower levels of existence are grounded in the highest Self that is beyond all spatio-temporal conditionings and all manifestations, then a profound transformation is experienced. As the Chāndogya Upaniṣad says, "Knowing that everything springs from this Self, and knowing this Self as everything, one experiences neither fear, nor suffering, nor death" (7.26).

The bondage caused by mistaken self-identify, and the liberating transformation made possible by the knowledge of one's true nature, are aptly illustrated by an old Indian story. The story tells of a little tiger raised from birth by wild goats. Having lived his whole life with goats this little tiger mistook himself for a goat, until one day, as a result of a direct experience of his true being, he realized that he was a tiger, not a goat.

The tiger's mother had died giving birth, and the infant was left all alone in the world. Fortunately, the goats were compassionate and adopted the little fellow, teaching him how to eat grass with his pointed teeth and how to bleat like they did. Time passed and the tiger assumed that he was just like the rest of the band of goats. But one day an old male tiger came upon this little band of goats. They all fled in terror, except for the tiger-goat, now about half-grown, who for some unknown reason felt no fear. As the savage jungle beast approached, the cub began to feel self-conscious and uncomfortable. To cover his self-consciousness he began to bleat a bit and nibble some grass. The old tiger roared at the little one in amazement and anger, asking him what he thought he was doing eating grass and bleating like a goat. But the little one, too embarrassed by all this to answer, continued to nibble grass. Thoroughly outraged by this behavior, the jungle tiger grabbed him by the scruff of his neck and carried him to a nearby pool. Holding him over the water, he told him to look at himself. "Is that the pot face of a tiger or the long face of a goat?" he roared.

The cub was still too frightened to answer, so the old tiger carried him to his cave and thrust a huge chunk of juicy, red, raw meat between his jaws. As the juices trickled into his stomach the cub began to feel a new strength and a new power. No longer mistaking himself for a goat, the little tiger lashed his tail from side to side and roared like the tiger he was. He had realized his true being. He no longer took himself to be what he appeared to be in his ignorance, but realized his true nature, which had nothing to do with the world of goats.

The idea that the individual embodies all the levels of reality and all the powers of existence, that the individual is, as it were, the whole universe in miniature, is a very ancient Indian idea. We saw earlier, in our examination of the Hymn to the Cosmic Person (Ṛg Veda, 10.90), that the Vedic people envisioned the universe as originating in the sacrificial celebration of the cosmic Person, with his various powers coming to manifest themselves as the different parts of the cosmos. Here the universe is a microcosm of the cosmic Person. Since the cosmic Person is the human prototype, it is not surprising that the individual should be seen as, in some way, embodying the reality of the whole universe.

Perhaps the clearest teaching of the hierarchically ordered levels of reality constituting both the universe and the individual is presented in the "sheath theory" of the Taittirīya Upaniṣad. As we have seen (pp. 102–104), according to this teaching the Self is pure bliss at the deepest level of reality, or innermost core, of being. But this inner core of being is covered over and hidden by consecutive layers or sheaths of reality that allow the Self to be taken to consist exclusively in these lower levels of reality. Thus, the Self is thought to be of the nature of food, or simply a material mode of being. Penetrating this outermost layer the Self is identified with life; and by penetrating the layer of living matter, the Self consisting in awareness is recognized. But within this layer is a more profound mode of existence, that of consciousness and understanding. Going deeper still into the core of being, one discovers the ultimate level of reality in the Self that is pure bliss, identical with Brahman, the ground of the universe—which is also declared to be pure bliss. See illustration following page.

If these various sheaths of reality are thought of as a series of concentric layers, with the most profound and powerful reality at the core, then the task of yoga can be seen as that of progressively harnessing and controlling the powers of the outermost layers to penetrate to the inner layers, until finally the innermost core is reached. This experience, the lived realization of Ātman, frees one from the bondage and suffering of the lower, conditioned self.

## Classical Yoga

Before we move on to consider the various techniques by which the yogin gains control of the powers needed for liberation, we need to point out that the monistic view of reality just sketched, a view typical of the Upaniṣads and Vedānta, is by no means universally accepted.

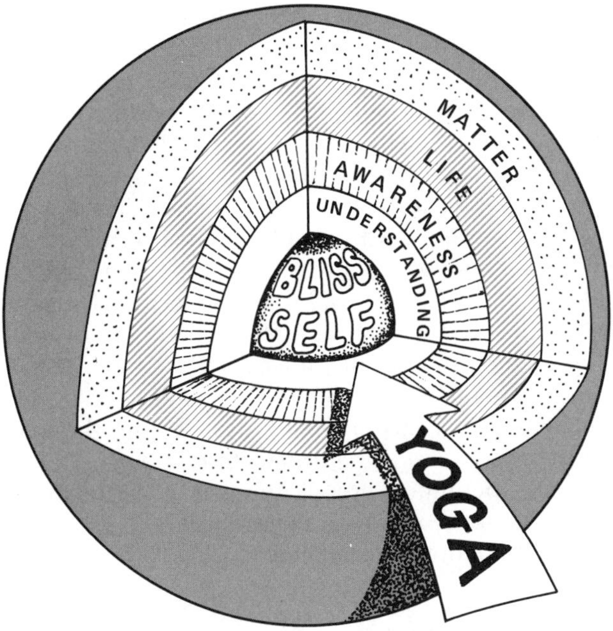


PENETRATING THE LAYERS OF SELF WITH YOGA

Yogic thinkers are just as likely to accept a dualistic view of reality. Because of the difficulty of reconciling the idea of Self as the blissful ground of all reality with the experience self as the subject of countless deaths and limitations, the ultimate Self is frequently thought to be fundamentally different from the physical and psychic matter in which it is embodied. Seen in these dualistic terms, the task of yoga consists in controlling the powers of embodied existence to effect the liberation of the pure Self from embodiment, thereby overcoming all limitations and suffering. Although the metaphysics changes, the central aim of yoga remains the same—as do the basic techniques of discipline and control.

Not surprisingly, yoga has undergone many changes in its long history and has been viewed from many different perspectives. It has been seen in both dualistic and monistic terms, in purely atheistic terms, and as an instrument of religious devotion. Some have seen the techniques as a means of mental control; others have seen them as means of bodily control. Still other thinkers have seen them as means for both bodily and mental control. Depending upon association with differing ideas and techniques of salvation, there have been Buddhist, Jaina, Tantric, and Hindu yogas. The Gītā distinguishes among the yogas of action, knowledge, and devotion. But regardless of associated ideas or emphasis, *yoga has always represented the control of deeper powers of existence for the sake of transformation and liberation.* Furthermore, since the time of Patañjali (200 B.C.?), the techniques of yogic control have been systematized into a royal or kingly way (*rāja yoga*) that has been normative for practically all the yogic developments of the last twenty-five hundred years.

We now turn to this classical vision of yoga, preserved in the Yoga Sūtras of Patañjali, for not only has it been normative for almost all succeeding writers on yoga, but it is also a systematic summary of the various ancient yoga traditions to which this great scholar of yoga was heir. Although for the sake of clarity and convenience we anchor our investigation of yoga in the teachings of Patañjali, it must be understood that yoga neither begins nor ends with him. Standing somewhere in the historical middle of this great tradition, he brought together all the important teachings on the subject with which he was familiar, systematizing them according to the ideas, techniques, and attainments involved.

Patañjali begins with a definition: "Yoga is the elimination of the fluctuations of consciousness [*yogaḥ citta vṛtti nirodaḥ*]." The crucial questions raised by this definition are (1) What is consciousness (*citta*)? (2) What are the fluctuations of consciousness (*vṛtti*) to be eliminated? and (3) How are the fluctuations eliminated (*nirodaḥ*)?

## PRAKṚTI-PURUṢA DUALISM

To understand Patañjali's view of consciousness, we must explore the underlying metaphysics that he takes for granted. This is the frankly dualistic metaphysics of the Sāṁkhya philosophy, according to which there are two fundamental kinds of reality. *Prakṛti*, sometimes translated as Nature, is the reality of experienceable existence—including the contents and structures of consciousness. *Puruṣa*, on the other hand, is the ultimate Self, the transcendent subject, which itself can never be an object of experience. Both prakṛti and puruṣa are ultimately real and in no way reducible to each other.

Care must be taken not to confuse this dualism with the typical body-mind dualism so familiar in the West. Body and mind are regarded by Sāṁkhya and Yoga thinkers as being ultimately the same. Consciousness, conceived in terms of mental structures, contents, and processes, is not only inseparably linked with physical structures and processes but is actually of the same nature, for both body and embodied consciousness belong to prakṛti. The dualism of prakṛti and puruṣa is based on the fundamental difference between the subject and object of experience, not on the difference between body and mind. Prakṛti refers to whatever can possibly be an object of experience. Since the objects we experience change, are caused, and appear as objects in consciousness, prakṛti is characterized as changing, caused, and objectively experienceable. Puruṣa, on the other hand, is pure consciousness, unembodied, uncaused, eternally unchanging, and completely unaffected by experience.

The Sāṁkhya-yoga insistence on this transcendent consciousness is rooted in the recognition that a particular object is an object only for a self, that the world (prakṛti) is a world only for a self. The self of which we are aware must, therefore, be a self for a more basic self. Unless a self as subject that does not appear as an object is admitted, it is impossible to account for experience. And since without experience there can be neither an object nor a world, Sāṁkhya thinkers posit this fundamental duality of puruṣa and prakṛti as a condition of experience and existence.

The most difficult problem for Sāṁkhya is the relationship of puruṣa to prakṛti, a problem that appears in Yoga in terms of the relationship of pure consciousness to embodied consciousness. The embodied consciousness is aware of the various kinds of suffering; it experiences and fears death and the entire saṁsāric cycle of repeated deaths and births. How can this embodied consciousness be liberated from the conditions of existence that result in untold suffering? If the very nature of consciousness is to be embodied, changing, and ever determined by experience, then liberation is impossible, for to liberate consciousness from the very conditions of its existence would be, in effect, to eliminate consciousness itself.

Fortunately, however, it is not of the nature of consciousness itself to be determined by experience and change, according to Sāṁkhya and Yoga philosophers. In itself consciousness is purely an illuminating and witnessing of existence, unembodied and totally unaffected by what is illuminated and witnessed. An example sometimes given is that of the moon, totally unaffected by its illumination of a pond of water. The image of the moon reflected in the pond can, however, be easily obscured by foam and debris and fragmented and distorted by the waves. If this embodied reflection of the moon, shining not by its own light, but by the light of the unembodied moon, were to mistake itself for the moon, it would think itself affected by everything that happens to the water and would suffer all the changes undergone by the water. In a similar way, the analogy continues, the consciousness of puruṣa, though reflected in prakṛti, is actually independent of prakṛti. But when the reflected consciousness embodied in prakṛti mistakes itself for puruṣa and thinks that it is affected by everything that happens to prakṛti, then it suffers all the afflictions and changes undergone by prakṛti. Only when the reflected consciousness is purified sufficiently can it see that it is not puruṣa, but merely the reflection of puruṣa. Now, not being mistaken for prakṛti, the pure consciousness of puruṣa is freed from the illusory bondage by prakṛti. It is this removal of ignorance that both Sāṁkhya and yoga strive to achieve.

Despite the fundamental difference between pure and embodied consciousness, however, the activities of embodied consciousness are made possible only by the presence of pure consciousness. The energizing power that illuminates embodied consciousness belongs ultimately to puruṣa, whereas the structures, processes, and contents of consciousness proceed from prakṛti. Ordinarily the power of consciousness is found together with the energized structures and processes, leading one to the uncritical and mistaken conclusion that they are identical or inseparable and, therefore, that the self is ultimately of the nature of prakṛti. The witnessing function of consciousness in self-awareness signals their ultimate difference, however, for the self of which there is awareness constitutes an *object* of awareness and therefore must be distinguished from the subject that is aware of the self as object. This recognition of the difference between the pure witnessing and the embodied consciousness provides a basis and motivation for the yogic task of isolating the pure consciousness from its reflected prakṛtic embodiment.

## FORCES OF BONDAGE

According to modern psychologists, most of the processes and structures of consciousness are hidden from us in the depths of the subconscious and the unconscious. Ancient Yoga thinkers did not use the language of Freud or Jung, but they clearly recognized that consciousness operates on many levels and that most of these levels are usually hidden from our awareness. For simplicity's sake, we will reduce the levels of consciousness to two, the attentive and the residual. The attentive mode corresponds to those structures, processes, and contents illumined by witnessing consciousness. This is the level of self-awareness, analogous to what we commonly think of as the fully aware or "conscious" level of mental life—as opposed to the subconscious or unconscious levels. The residual mode of prakṛtic consciousness, corresponding roughly to the subconscious and unconscious levels, features the traces (*vāsānas*) and impressions (*saṁskāras*) of the totality of human experience. It is much deeper and more pervasive than is the attentive mode of consciousness, and it accounts for most of our conditioning. It is at this hidden level that the primary forces shaping our personality and creating our personal identity operate. Unless these powerful forces can be brought out of the darkness and illumined by increasing self-awareness, they will keep us in their bondage.

We can now see that the purpose of eliminating the movements of consciousness is to increase awareness of each of these levels of consciousness, moving progressively from the more superficial to the more profound modalities of conscious being. The first task is to fully illuminate and transcend the most superficial level, that of attentive consciousness. From there one can go on to control and illuminate the deeper levels that we have called residual consciousness. As the power of the witnessing consciousness is gradually developed so that it pervades and illumines every aspect and dimension of existence, the pure consciousness of puruṣa comes finally to stand revealed in its own nature, independent of the prakṛtic movements of consciousness at either the attentive or residual levels.

To understand the yogic discipline established for achieving this freedom from prakṛti, it is necessary to understand the agencies by which embodied consciousness, operates. Patañjali describes five major conditioning agencies underlying the various movements of embodied consciousness. The first is *unknowing (avidyā)*—the lack of awareness that the self is of the nature of puruṣa rather than prakṛti. The result of this unknowing is that human existence comes to be identified exclusively with the various modalities (*guṇas*) of prakṛti. The second agency is the incessant urge to build and maintain an ego (*asmitā*). Because of ignorance of puruṣa, there is a desperate attempt to establish the self in prakṛtic activities, with the continual transformation of all activities into "mine" and "not mine." Third, in the attempt to establish the self in prakṛti, there is an infatuation with and grasping for things (*rāga*) that shows up in attachments. The fourth agency is the negative drive creative of the "not mine." It is the dislike of and aversion to (*dveśa*) that which threatens the prakṛtic self. It reveals itself in hatred and retreat from the hated. Rooted in ignorance and feeding upon ego, attachment and aversion (*rāga* and *dveśa*) are the propelling forces of the personality, pushing and pulling against each other, creating a continuously agitated state of being for the individual. The fifth agency is deeper than the pairs of opposites and overrides aversion and retreat. This is the will to live forever (*abhiniveśa*) in the modalities of prakṛti.

Although from the ordinary, prakṛtic, perspective these five conditioning agencies of consciousness are regarded as normal and healthy, from the yogic point of view, which regards puruṣa as the true Self and the ultimate energy of consciousness, they are impairments or defilements of consciousness, for they obscure the light of puruṣa. Thus, the yogic techniques for deconditioning consciousness aim at eliminating these agencies and thereby stilling the movements (*vṛttis*) of consciousness they cause.

## Techniques of Discipline and Control

Initially only those conditionings of consciousness that are relatively superficial and predominantly external can be attacked, for the individual is unaware of the deeper conditionings. For this reason the eight sets of techniques or aids (*yoganga*) of yogic practice begin with the "external" efforts to control the activities of consciousness. The five 'external' sets of techniques include (1) the moral restraints (*yama*), (2) disciplines (*niyama*), (3) bodily postures (*āsanas*), (4) regulation of the breath energy (*prānāyāma*), and (5) sense withdrawal (*pratȳahāra*).

**External Techniques.** The key to the moral restraints and disciplines (yama and niyama) is contained in the concept of *ahiṁsā* or "nonhurting." As in Jainism, ahiṁsā means not only avoiding hurting any living beings but also overcoming all forms of hatred and ill will toward other creatures. The other moral restraints—truthfulness, nonstealing, sexual restraint, and nongrasping—are all practiced to perfect the virtue of nonhurting, which in its positive sense is a universal love for all beings. Developing this compassionate love for all beings is a powerful means for overcoming selfishness and the bonds of ego.

The second restraint is to avoid speech that will hurt others. A person's intentions and words should promote the good of all living beings. Speech that is empty, confused, or deceptive cannot be used to help others and therefore should be avoided. But even speech that avoids meaninglessness, confusion, or deception is regarded as falsehood if it brings harm to others, for the underlying principle is that speech be used to avoid hurting and to bring about the well-being of others.

Nonstealing obviously precludes taking what rightfully belongs to someone else. But the restraint against stealing cuts deeper, for it aims to eliminate the desire for possessing what belongs to another person. Wanting to take from others is a kind of intentional hurting that must be avoided not only by refraining from action but, more important, by eliminating the desire itself. Nongrasping, the fourth restraint, carries the principle of nonstealing even farther, for it consists in eliminating the desire for all goods whatever, or in a positive sense, the cultivation of complete nonattachment. Even gifts should be refused.

Wrong sexual activity not only involves the appropriation of another person's body for one's own pleasure, but also nourishes the growth and domination of the ego, which by virtue of its will to assert its independence of other creatures threatens injury to the whole community of living beings. For this reason sexual activity is to be restrained. This restraint is also regarded as the conservation of the life-forces for higher purposes.

From the yogic perspective the activities to be eliminated by these five restraints are all forms of hurting encouraged by the forces of socialization. In a way, lying, stealing, grasping, and illicit sexual activity are all forms of hurtful behavior encouraged by the social pressures to succeed as an individual. To stand out, to get ahead, to be noticed, one pits oneself against the rest of the world. In extreme cases we even turn other living beings, especially other persons, into our opponents. Even though not intentionally wanting to hurt others, human beings in this situation cannot help but hurt others; success, even survival, are seen as dependent upon our "victory" over others. The nearly universal moral proscriptions against lying, cheating, stealing, undue violence (murder), and illicit sex constitute a tacit recognition by almost all societies that the combination of human nature and processes of socialization encourages people to engage in these kinds of activities. Although usually encouraged by socialization, these proscribed activities are recognized as a threat to the society itself and therefore in need of social regulation by moral (and legal) norms.

Since yoga is primarily interested in the liberation of the self, rather than in the preservation of society, it goes beyond mere regulation of these hurtful activities and recommends not only their complete elimination, but the elimination of the drive behind them as well. This drive, as we have seen, is the urge to create and maintain an ego—at any cost. But since the activities that nourish ego existence bind one all the more closely to the lower modalities of prakṛti, they must be eliminated as the first step in the deconditioning of consciousnes. Only by weakening—and eventually destroying—the support system of prakṛtic consciousness constituted by the kinds of social conditioning reflected in the various forms of hurtful activity can the purity of consciousness wherein Self is recognized to be independent of prakṛtic existence be achieved.

The five disciplines (niyama) of (1) purity, (2) calmness, (3) asceticism, (4) study, and (5) devotion are intended to aid in eliminating the forces of social conditioning by providing a sense of independence of these conditions. Purity in reference to the body means keeping it scrupulously clean. In terms of personal existence, one must avoid all forms of social and ritual pollution, taking care to purify oneself with sacrificial offerings. Inner purity, which is most important, consists in cleansing the mind. Not only must all impure thoughts be eliminated, but the residual effects of all previous thoughts and actions must be washed away—especially those thoughts and residual impressions that foster ego attachment.

Contentment is being satisfied with whatever one has, undisturbed by circumstances and environment. This discipline helps a person to realize that the Self is essentially independent of other persons and natural forces.

Asceticism involves going beyond the pairs of opposites (heat and cold, hunger and thirst, etc.), freeing oneself from the pulls and pushes of likes and dislikes. A variety of practices involving self-denial and self-mortification not only help to remove impurities and ego attachment, but generate power enabling one to experience a sense of independence of ordinary bodily and sensory limitations.

Study, the fourth discipline, refers to the effort to understand the means of liberation. Although sometimes the emphasis is on the guru's teachings, sometimes on the texts of yoga, and other times on the Vedas, the practitioner must always be completely humble and open to the teachings.

The fifth discipline is devotion to the Lord. Patañjali, and those who follow his theistic interpretation of reality, see devotion as a means of eliminating personal motives and attachments by making God the motive of all thought and action. To surrender oneself to Kālī, for example, is to eliminate one's own will in favor of Her Divine Will. Even the skeptic who is keenly aware of the risks and dangers in religious devotionalism—especially cultic devotionalism—must admit that it is an extremely effective way of overcoming the bonds of ego attachment.

The practice of these various restraints and disciplines is aimed at eliminating the prakṛtic consciousness rooted in social conditioning. But social conditioning is only one of the many interrelated support systems of embodied consciousness. The physiological conditions of consciousness must also be subjected to yogic discipline. Consequently, the third set of techniques works toward deconditioning consciousness through a series of disciplined bodily postures and exercises (*āsanas*). Aimed at controlling consciousness through bodily control, these techniques presuppose the complete interrelatedness of consciousness and the body.

Hundreds of different bodily postures are referred to in the yoga texts, and some of the several dozen that are explained in detail are extremely difficult to master. Difficult as the practice of various āsanas may be, however, the reasoning behind it is simple: bring the body under the control of consciousness instead of allowing it to control consciousness. Controlled by consciousness, the body can become a vehicle of liberation rather than of bondage.

The various postures must be practiced until they become totally effortless. At first one's entire attention is focused on the bodily postures, but as control increases it becomes possible to completely transcend bodily awareness. At this point bodily activities no longer constitute conditioning factors of consciousness, for freedom from the physical support system has been achieved. Every well-conditioned athlete experiences, at least partially, a sense of this physical freedom.

Breath is the key to life, for by breathing one takes in the vital energy of organic life. The entire organism, bodily and mentally, is conditioned by breathing, being completely dependent upon the flow and rhythm of the vital breath energy. For someone in a deep state of awareness, each inhalation feels like an internal explosion, fragmenting ideas and feelings into a confusing disarray. Each exhalation scatters the contents and energies of consciousness like fallen petals in a storm. Only in the calm between exhalation and inhalation is consciousness collected and concentrated. (Did you ever notice that when you concentrate intently on something you instinctively hold your breath?) In recognition of this, yoga has developed techniques for controlling and regulating breathing as a means of deconditioning the breath-energy support system.

Sense withdrawal (pratyāhāra) comprises the set of techniques used for eliminating the conditionings of consciousness by sensory stimulations. Ordinarily the movements of consciousness are stimulated by the senses and follow the patterns of sensory activities. But through withdrawal of the senses from external objects, consciousness becomes free to illuminate the external world according to its own intents—rather than in accord with the dictates of the senses.

**Internal Techniques.** At this point, having eliminated the need for the external support systems upon which consciousness depends and which condition its activities, the yogin turns his attention to the "internal" techniques or aids. These—*dhāraṇā, dhyāna,* and *samādhi*—have as their object the elimination of internal support systems of residual consciousness. These techniques follow the recognition that all activities of consciousness leave residual traces (vāsanās). Although not present in attentive consciousness, these traces nevertheless are the seeds of future consciousness conditioning. The fruition of these seeds constitutes an internal conditioning agency of consciousness, parallel to the external conditioning factors of bodily activity, social activity, breathing, sensation, thought, and action. Now the inner core of consciousness, as witness, must withdraw from the conditioning forces of the residual traces and actions. Dhāraṇā, or concentration, consists in fixing consciousness on a single point for the sake of comprehending consciousness itself through the object being concentrated upon.

However, since the success of this technique still leaves consciousness conditioned by the object of concentration, it is necessary to move to a deeper level, that of objectless concentration. This requires sustaining the concentration and turning it upon itself, that is, away from an external object to itself as object. This constitutes the meditative condition known as *dhyāna*. Here the only conditioning factor is that of the illumining (*sattvic*) mode of prakṛitic consciousness as a "seat" for the pure witnessing consciousness.

In samādhi the support (*sālambana*) or seed (*bīja*) of prakṛti is eliminated, and consciousness shines by its own light, that is, by the light of puruṣa, which is the true self. Liberated from all the conditions of prakṛti, this self cannot be described in ordinary ways. From the ordinary human point of view, the self has ceased to exist, though from the perspective of puruṣa it has now come into its full being. As the concluding sūtra of Book Three puts it, "Then the Self, having its light within itself becomes undefiled [by prakṛti] and isolated [from prakṛti]." The yogin is now totally free from the world. Having "died" to this world, he is described as being "reborn into that [spiritual] world." Here words and descriptions do not follow, for they belong to the world of prakṛti, with respect to which the yogin has ceased to exist.

## Summary

Yoga refers to the techniques of discipline and control used to achieve power over ordinary limited modes of human existence to gain liberation from bondage and suffering. Practiced long before the time of the Buddha, its beginnings may go back to Indus civilization, four thousand years ago. As the central core of most Indian ways of salvation, yoga has been one of the great unifying forces of the Indian tradition and one of India's most precious gifts to the world.

The underlying idea is that ignorance of the spiritual nature of true existence leads human beings to identify themselves with lower and superficial modes of being. By practicing yoga the various movements of consciousness through which this mistaken identity is created and reenforced can be stilled, allowing the light of pure consciousness—the real Self—to shine through, illuminating and transforming one's entire existence.

Patañjali, the great authority on yoga, identified five basic agencies of ignorance that operate through consciousness to produce the mistaken identification with the non-self. The first is the lack of awareness that the self is of the nature of pure consciousness (puruṣa) rather than experienceable existence.

The result of this ignorance is that human existence comes to be identified exclusively with objective existence, thereby obscuring the true subjective self. Because of this mistaken identity, there is an incessant urge to build and maintain an ego, transforming the world into "mine" and "not mine." The third agency is the ego's infatuation with and grasping for things as support for its claim to selfhood. The fourth agency is the complementary dislike of and aversion to whatever threatens the ego's existence. Finally, there is the ego's will to live forever in the modalities of prakṛti, the non-self.

These five agencies of embodied consciousness that condition us to mistake our true identity must be eliminated by stilling the involved movements of consciousness. To this end the eight sets of techniques known as "aids to yoga" are practiced. These aids are essentially techniques for deconditioning consciousness and eliminating the support system that underlies our mistaken self-identity, the cause of bondage and suffering. The first two, the moral restraints and disciplines, aim at destroying the ego support system constituted by social conditioning. Control of the breath and the bodily processes work to free consciousness from its dependence on breath-energy and physiological processes. Withdrawing the senses from their natural objects aims at independence of sensory domination of consciousness.

The last three sets of techniques—concentration, meditation, and samādhi—aim at freeing consciousness from the deeply embedded traces and impressions of all previous conditioning by illuminating even the deepest levels of consciousness. When finally, in samādhi, all the conditionings and supports of prakṛiti have been eliminated, consciousness shines by its own light, the light of puruṣa, the true Self. Now bondage has been broken and liberation achieved.

## Suggestions for Further Reading

*Yoga and the Hindu Tradition,* by Jean Varenne and trans. Derek Coltman (Chicago: University of Chicago Press, 1976), can be heartily recommended to the reader interested in learning more about both the techniques of yoga and the place of yoga philosophy in the larger context of the whole Hindu tradition. The book, which is clear, brief, and to the point, is divided into four parts. The first part explores the underlying Indian conception of the universe and human nature, focusing on the sense of bondage and suffering that leads to the quest for liberation. Part Two concentrates on the idea of liberation and the role of knowledge and control in achieving liberation. These first ninety pages provide an excellent introduction to Indian thought. The next forty-five pages are devoted to an explanation of the eight aids to yoga, and the last part deals with Tantric yoga. As a special treat, the last twenty-two pages contain a translation of the complete Yoga Darśana Upaniṣad.

*Yoga: Immortality and Freedom,* by Mircea Eliade and trans. W. R. Trask, 2nd ed. (Princeton, N.J.: Princeton University Press, 1969), remains the most thorough study of yoga easily available in English. Do not be dissuaded by its size and scholarly trappings. The first one hundred pages give a relatively clear picture of both the philosophy and the practical techniques of yoga. By this time your appetite may be sufficiently whetted to go on to Eliade's excellent discussions of the relationships between yoga and the other spiritual traditions of India. The more advanced reader will especially appreciate the extensive notes at the end.

Another useful introduction to yoga in the larger context of the whole Indian tradition is provided by Georg Feuerstein's *The Essence of Yoga* (New York: Grove Press, 1976.) The subtitle, "A Psychohistorical Examination of Indian Thought Through the Lens of Yoga," indicates the approach.

For the reader who wants to go directly to the sources, the translations of Patañjali's sūtras and commentaries by Vyāsa and Vācaspati Miśra in James Haughton Woods, *The Yoga System of Patañjali,* 2nd ed. (Cambridge, Mass.: Harvard University Press, 1927; authorized reprint, Motilal Banarsidass, 1966), is recommended. It is well organized and the translations are excellent.

Although there are scores of books available on yoga practice, none have been recommended. For all but the simplest techniques a qualified teacher is needed. Even accurate textbooks—if you can find one—are inadequate guides for practice.

# 9

# The Bhagavad Gītā

## Introduction

The techniques of yoga that we examined in the previous chapter are central, of course, to both Jaina and Buddhist practice. The eightfold path taught by the Buddha is clearly an adaptation of these techniques. And the fourteen stages of purification marking the Jaina path to liberation also incorporate these techniques. Indeed, despite the great differences between them, both Jainism and Buddhism agree that the way to eliminate suffering is through insight, pure conduct, and meditation. In departure from the earlier reliance on ritual, or the help of the Gods, Jainas and Buddhists rejected both the Gods and rituals as significant means of liberation. Instead, they relied on human effort, effort enhanced by the techniques of yoga.

Influential as Jainism and Buddhism were, however, they by no means replaced the earlier emphasis on ritual and deities. Probably at about the same time that Mahāvīra and the Buddha were exhorting their followers to seek liberation from suffering through disciplined action, meditation, and insight, a great new synthesis, that of Hinduism, was being forged. Devotion, ritual, and knowledge were being integrated into a single comprehensive way that combined the strengths of these previously separate ways of salvation. The key to this integration was yoga, for what the three ways had in common was an insistence on discipline, an insistence that helped shape the Hindu way.

In this chapter we will explore the Hindu synthesis as it is presented in the Bhagavad Gītā. Undoubtedly, the Gītā itself is centuries later than the beginnings of this synthesis, for the vision presented in this text is almost certainly the culmination of a long process of synthesis and integration. Consequently, since the Gītā could hardly have been composed later than the second century B.C., it is reasonable to assume that the integration it represents was probably underway already by the sixth century.

## The Text and Its Message

The Bhagavad Gītā or "Song of the Lord" is the single most important scripture of Hinduism. Most Hindus regard it as containing the essence of the teachings of the Vedas and Upaniṣads. Indeed, it is frequently called an Upaniṣad and each of the eighteen chapters concludes with the remark, "Here ends the Bhagavad Gītā Upaniṣad . . .".

The Gītā is frequently called the New Testament of Hinduism by modern commentators because it occupies a place in Hinduism similar to that of the New Testament in Christianity. Unquestionably, the Gītā has thoroughly permeated Hindu consciousness from one end of India to the other. Like the New Testament, it is also part of a larger scriptural tradition, for it appears both as a fulfillment of the Vedas and the Upaniṣads and as an important new teaching modifying the older teachings in significant ways. Unlike the New Testament, however, the Gītā was not seen as so radically different from the older tradition that it required a new religion. Indeed, the Gītā, rather than becoming the inspiration for a new religion, became a great unifying force, drawing together different visions of reality and accommodating the diverse ways of salvation that had developed within the older tradition.

We do not know who composed the Gītā or exactly when it was composed. It forms a small but extremely significant part of the world's longest epic poem, the Mahābhārata, whose author(s) and dates are also unknown, though tradition attributes it to Vyāsa, and modern scholars are inclined to think of it as a composite work, composed between 500 and 100 B.C. Judging from internal evidence, it is likely that the Gītā was composed in the second or third century B.C. It may well have been a separate work inserted into the great epic to give it the epic's authority. But for Hindus who accept the Gītā as divine wisdom, questions about authorship and dates of composition are unimportant, for spiritual truths are timeless and authorless.

Because of its central importance in Hindu life, the Gītā has been subject to continuing interpretation and commentary. Many of India's great religious and philosophical thinkers have written commentaries on it, and it constitutes one of the pillars of Vedānta, which, by general consensus, is the most vigorous and important philosophical tradition of the last thousand years.

In recent times important commentaries have been written on the Gītā by Gandhi, Aurobindo, Telang, and Radhakrishnan, to mention only a few of the better known interpreters. Translations of the Gītā and major commentaries are available in all of India's major languages, and there may not be a single Hindu who is unfamiliar with at least part of the Gītā, while many know it by heart.

I know from my own experiences in Indian villages what a joyous and blessed occasion it is when a visiting holy man and storyteller comes and recites the verses of the Gītā. Old and young alike gather together at the village meeting place (frequently at the well) to receive the gift of these precious words that are treasured for life. My impression is that most Hindus know their Gītā better than most Christians know their Bible.

It is difficult to say precisely why the Gītā has come to exert so much power over Hindu consciousness and life. Its appeal may be due to a number of different factors. First, it is a poem of great splendor and power. It appeals as much to our feelings and will as it does to our minds. Although many Westerners, especially those whose acquaintance with the text is limited to reading a translation or attempting to locate a coherent system of philosophy within the text, do not appreciate this point, it remains true that for most Hindus the beauty and power of the poetry moves their hearts fully as much as the message moves their minds.

Second, Arjuna's dilemma is universal. Everyone knows what is like to be caught in a conflict of duty: should I tell the truth and betray my friend? Or should I be loyal to my friend and tell a lie? Arjuna's dilemma is such a conflict of duties: does his duty require that he engage in acts of war, fighting for his country in a war that is clearly just? Or does his duty demand that he refrain from acts of violence and bloodshed? Confused by this conflict, Arjuna turns to Krishna for help. Krishna's advice, given in a universalized form that addresses not only this conflict, but any human conflict, constitutes the Gītā's message.

Caught in a conflict of fundamental duties, it is only natural to seek a rule of action stemming from a vision of life that will enable us to overcome the conflict. What is the self? What is ultimately real? Is human salvation to be found in following the way of knowledge? The way of action? Or the way of devotion to God? These are the questions Arjuna asks as he seeks a way out of his dilemma. Because the answers to these questions are important to everyone, the Gītā has a relevance that transcends a particular place or time. Most Hindus to whom I have talked indicate that the Gītā contains a message directed to them personally.

On a broader cultural level, the Gītā has managed to combine the ways of yoga, ritual, work, knowledge, asceticism, and loving devotion in a manner that allows each person to choose a particular path most appropriate to his or her own needs and circumstances. The older Vedic way had emphasized ritual and moral activity as the way to salvation. The Upaniṣads advocated knowledge rather than action. In addition, yogins recommended self-discipline and asceticism, whereas cultic religion followed the way of devotion to the Lord.

The split between knowledge and action was especially acute, for the Vedic emphasis on ritual and moral action rested on a vision of self as doer or agent, whereas the Upaniṣadic insistence on the way of knowledge grew out of a vision of self not as agent but as pure consciousness. No doubt, at some level we are both agents and knowers, but the question is, "What are we ultimately, at the deepest level?" If we are doers or agents, then our deepest being must be that of embodied consciousness, for action requires a body. If we are knowers, then our essential being may be that of unembodied consciousness, for the body is seen as a hindrance to consciousness. The Gītā manages to take seriously both the embodied self as agent and the self as pure consciousness, attempting to reconcile them in a higher divine reality.

Another divergence reconciled by the Gītā was that between the monistic emphasis of the Upaniṣads and the dualistic emphasis of Sāṁkhya and Yoga. Is Brahman the sole indivisible ground of all reality? Or are there two kinds of ultimate reality, a material ground and a spiritual ground? The Gītā recognizes a fundamental difference between mind and matter (prakṛti) on the one hand and spirit (puruṣa) on the other, but finds them reconciled in a higher unity, the Supreme Lord.

Many modern interpreters have pounced on the fact that from a rational point of view the Gītā's attempt to accommodate all these differing views and ways of salvation is logically inconsistent. I agree that it is impossible to find a single all-embracing philosophical system within the Gītā that is logically coherent and consistent. But it might be a mistake to look for such a system in the first place. The Gītā, like most religious texts, is concerned to speak to the condition of the hearer, to reach into the heart as well as the mind, opening it to the divine power and the in-dwelling spiritual life. This the Gītā does, speaking to many different kinds of persons of differing backgrounds, qualifications, and abilities, assuring them that, although their way may be different from someone else's, it is not therefore wrong. What counts most, insists the Indian tradition, is not logic, but whether the way leads to inner transformation, to the joy and freedom of divine life.

## Arjuna's Dilemma

The Gītā opens with two opposing armies facing each other on the battlefield, preparing to fight a great civil war. One side is led by the five Pāṇḍu brothers, the most famous of whom is Arjuna. On the other side are their cousins, the Kurus, sons of Dhṛtarāṣṭra. The opening verses of the first chapter describe the two mighty armies on the battlefield. Hoping to assess their strengths and weaknesses, Arjuna orders Krishna, his driver, to stop his chariot midway between them. What he sees troubles him deeply, for, although justice is on his side and it is his duty to fight this just war for his kingdom, he realizes also the wrongness of the hurting and suffering that this civil war will entail. In the words of the Gītā,

> Stationed there Arjuna saw
> Fathers and grandfathers,
> Teachers, uncles and brothers,
> Sons, grandsons and also comrades;

Fathers-in-law and friends too
In the two armies.
The son of Kuntī [Arjuna]
Seeing all these kinsmen so arrayed,

Filled with the utmost compassion,
Spoke despondently:
O Krishna, seeing my own kinsmen
Drawn near and eager to fight,

My limbs collapse,
My mouth becomes dry,
There is trembling in my body,
And my hair stands on end.

Gāṇḍīva [the bow] falls from my hand
And my skin is burning.
I am unable to stand still
And my mind is whirling.

(1.26–30)

It is not that Arjuna is afraid to fight but, rather, that both alternatives facing him seem evil and sinful. Clearly it is his duty to fight this war. He is a professional warrior, and righteousness is on his side; if ever there was a just war, this it. Further, he knows that the very maintenance of society depends upon every class and every person performing their duty to the best of their ability.

Telling Arjuna that this is a wonderful opportunity, an opportunity that opens heaven's door and that would make any warrior happy, Krishna admonishes Arjuna as follows:

But if you will not wage
This righteous battle, then
Having abandoned your duty and glory,
You will incur sin.

(2.33)

If fighting this righteous war is clearly his duty and the abandonment of his duty wrong, why does Arjuna hesitate? Because he sees that it is also wrong to kill other people, especially friends and relatives. Besides, war is destructive of the very social fabric that it is his duty to protect.

Telling Krishna that he foresees no good in slaying his own kinsmen in battle, Arjuna protests that victory, kingdom, and happiness are all meaningless when family and friends are destroyed. Only sin and evil can result from fighting this war.

What happiness can come to us, O Krishna
Through slaying the sons of Dhṛtarāṣṭra?
Only evil will fall on us
If we kill these murderers.

Therefore we should not slay
The sons of Dhṛtarāṣṭra, our own relatives.
For having killed our relatives
How could we ever be happy, O Mādhava [Krishna]?

Even if they, intelligence destroyed
By greed, do not see
The sin caused by destruction of family
and the crime committed by injuring a friend,

Why should we not have the wisdom
To turn back from this evil,
We who see the sin of destroying
The family, O Janārdana [Krishna]?

(1.36–39)

Here is Arjuna's dilemma: not to perform his duty as a warrior is clearly wrong, but performing this duty seems fully as wrong. What should he do? Every one of us who has experienced a similar conflict of duties (and who has not?) knows the confusion and agony involved. What Arjuna is seeking is the knowledge that will enable him to overcome his dilemma.

## Krishna

Fortunately for Arjuna, he does not have to worry about which sacred scripture, philosophical treatise, or wise person to consult. Krishna, his chariot driver, is clearly no ordinary driver! Although throughout most of the Mahābhārata he appears simply as Arjuna's cousin, in the Gītā he reveals himself to be none other than the Lord, the Supreme God incarnate in human form. As he tells Arjuna, whenever there is need of him in this world he crosses over from the ultimate unmanifest level of reality into this realm of manifested existence.

Although I am the unborn, eternal Self,
Although I am Lord of all beings, still
Through establishing Myself in My own material nature,
I come into being through My own mysterious power.

Whenever righteousness declines and
Unrighteousness flourishes
O Son of India, then
I send forth Myself.

For the preservation of the good,
For the destruction of evil,
To establish a foundation for righteousness,
I come into being in age after age.

(4.6–8)

Here we encounter, for the first time in Indian thought, a clearly stated concept of *avatārana*, the crossing over of the supreme spirit of the universe into this material world. God's descent into the world in human form is an extremely effective way of bridging the gap between God and humans, a truth recognized by Christians as well as by Hindus. Jesus, the adorable little baby; Jesus, the wise teacher who loved and cared for sinners and the poor; Jesus, the man who so loved us that he gave up his own life—who cannot relate to God when He appears in these forms? In a similar way, Hindus, while acknowledging that Brahman, the ground of all existence and our innermost Self, is completely unmanifest, beyond all possible characterization, realize the human need for a Supreme Reality to which they can relate personally. Recognizing the unlimited power of the Ultimate Reality to take on an infinite variety of forms, it seems entirely appropriate to them that the Supreme Spirit should take on forms that will inspire human beings and allow them to experience their own inner divinity through personal relationships with God. Thus, they readily acknowledge the actuality of God's incarnation—not just once, but many times. And not just in human form, but in a great variety of forms.

According to Hindu tradition the incarnations of Vishnu, who as Supreme Lord and Sustainer of the universe, symbolizes the ultimate Brahman, include Matsya, half man, half fish; Kūrma, a tortoise with human trunk and head; Varāha, the boar; Narasiṁha, half man, half lion; Vāmana, the dwarf who swells to the size of a giant; Paraśurāma, the fierce mustached brāhmaṇa who put the kṣatriyas in their proper place of subordination to the brāhmaṇas; Rāma, the beloved hero of the Rāmāyana; Krishna of the Gītā; the Buddha; and Kalkin, rider of the white horse who will appear at the end of the present heavy age of the Kālī *yuga*. In addition, his power is present in Rādhā, divine lover of Krishna, and in the Goddesses Shrī (Lakshmī) and Bhū, his divine consorts. The idea of many forms and incarnations of Vishnu is celebrated in the litany of his names. According to tradition, Vishnu has 1,008 names, a number suggesting the infinity of forms that the Supreme Spirit of the universe assumes.

In the Gītā, however, we hear neither of these other incarnations of Vishnu nor of Krishna the playful child, always up to mischief and playing pranks on everyone. Arjuna is a warrior on a battlefield making it appropriate that the Lord appear to him in the guise of Krishna, his chariot driver. Having confided his confusion and despondency to his driver, and realizing that Krishna is none other than the Lord Himself, Arjuna requests a vision that will guide him in doing the right thing.

> My very being is afflicted and weakened by compassion;
> My mind is confused about my duty.
> I ask Thee, which is better? Tell me definitely.
> I am your pupil; teach me who comes to Thee.
>
> (2.7)

## Self and Body

As we have seen, Arjuna's confusion results from a clearly perceived conflict of duties. His duty to fight this war and win back the kingdom that rightfully belongs to his family conflicts with his duty to protect and maintain the well-being of society, for by satisfying the duty to fight he will destroy the well-being of society by killing husbands, breaking up families, turning family members against each other, and so on. What we expect—especially in light of our knowledge of the central place that the principle of nonhurting occupies in Indian morality—is some moral advice on how to resolve this conflict of duties. But to our surprise (and Arjuna's, most likely!), Krishna shifts the discussion to an entirely different level, telling Arjuna about the eternal indestructible reality that is the ground of all being and that is embodied as the Self of all persons.

It is not the innermost eternal Self that is confronted with conflicting duties, but only the embodied self. The real Self does not act; it neither kills nor is killed. Making sure that Arjuna understands this distinction between the embodied self that acts and the inner self that is beyond all action, Krishna echoes the teachings of the Kaṭha Upaniṣad:

> He who thinks this [Self] a slayer,
> And he who thinks this [Self] slain,
> Are both ignorant.
> This [Self] neither slays nor is slain.
>
> Neither is it born nor does it die;
> Nor having come to be will it ever cease to be.
> Unborn, eternal, everlasting, this primeval one
> Is not slain when the body is slain.
>
> (2.19–20)

Arjuna views his problem only from the perspective of the embodied self. Krishna wants him to see it from the perspective of the eternal unembodied Self as well. This shift in perspective enables the Gītā to speak to the central existential conflict within the Indian tradition, the conflict between knowledge and action.

This conflict between the way of action and the way of knowledge is rooted in two differing philosophies of self. The Vedic people tended to see the world in terms of action. For them the self is ultimately a doer or agent who achieves salvation through actions in the world that conform to high moral standards and that participate ritually in the continuing creation of existence. The seers of the Upaniṣads, however, in their concern to find an ultimate self not subject to death and rebirth, evolved a different philosophy of self. Seeing action as a source of bondage, these seers rejected the agent self as ultimate. Instead, they equated the ultimate nature of the self with Ātman, the eternal unchanging ground of all existence, of the nature of pure consciousness or knowledge. But if the self is pure consciousness rather than an agent, then knowledge, not action, will bring about self-realization and liberation from suffering and death. Actions, because they are taken to produce bondage, must be renounced in favor of knowledge, and all the residue and effects of past actions must be exhausted to attain mokṣa.

Arjuna, like every other Indian, is caught up in this conflict between the obligation to act in fulfillment of his dharma and the need to refrain from action to eliminate bondage. Nothing is more important than acting to fulfill one's dharma, for thereby society is maintained and the universe itself supported. On the other hand, action is seen as a cause of bondage. Liberation can be achieved only through knowledge; all action must be renounced and abandoned.

The strong emphasis on family and society and the insistence on dharma derive from a conception of the self as agent. On the other hand, the emphasis on yoga, asceticism, and liberation through knowledge presupposes that the self is ultimately of the nature of knowledge or consciousness. What Krishna is telling Arjuna, in effect, is that to resolve the conflict between the way of action and the way of knowledge he must first determine whether he is ultimately a doer or a knower, and then come to understand how knowledge and action are related to each other.

The conflict between knowledge and action had been recognized before the time of the Gītā, of course, and an uneasy solution worked out—a solution that, modified by the teachings of the Gītā, continues as a guiding principle of life up to the present time. This solution, as we have seen, is to accommodate the requirement to act and the requirement of renunciation sequentially. According to the principle of life stages, the first half of a person's life is devoted to action, as the aims of dharma, artha, and kāma are pursued. Then, following a transitional stage, the last quarter is giving over to renunciation. Here, as a saṅnyāsin, a person goes beyond action, family, and society.

The uneasiness of the sequential accommodation of the ways of action and knowledge in the ordering of life stages is reflected in the ambivalent attitude displayed toward the saṅnyāsin. On the one hand, since he is fulfilling the highest aim in life, he is honored and greatly revered—though from a distance. At the same time, when he is near, he is feared and regarded as a threat to society. As though recognizing that the rejection of dharma is implicitly a rejection of society, people see the saṅnyāsin as a potential source of personal pollution and social corruption, and therefore regard him as an untouchable when, on rare occasion, he comes within the village.

The Gītā does not reject the sequential accommodation of both action and renunciation provided by of the life stages but, rather, presents a different solution. Preserving the Vedic injunction to act, while at the same time accepting the Upaniṣadic vision of the self as ultimately identical to the pure consciousness that is Ātman, Krishna informs

Arjuna of a higher truth by which a person can act in the world without incurring the binding effects of action. The key to this kind of actionless action is the renunciation of all desire for the results of action and the abandonment of identification with the doer of action. To achieve this renunciation of desire and the abandonment of ego, Krishna recommends complete surrender to God in loving devotion, performing all works and actions in a spirit of sacrifice to Him. How this vision is worked out and how it accommodates the three ways of knowledge, action, and devotion can best be seen in terms of Krishna's own words in the Gītā.

Krishna advises Arjuna that he should discriminate between the eternal and the embodied selves, for by knowing that they are distinct and that the eternal self is neither killed nor a killer, he can perform his duty and fight without fear of incurring sin. This confuses Arjuna, for it sounds as if Krishna is telling him that salvation is through knowledge but at the same time advising him to engage in action. "If you think that knowledge is superior to action, then why urge me to do this violence? Tell me decisively, what is the single best way to my well-being?" he asks (3.1–2). Krishna responds that His teaching, from old, is that both the way of knowlege and the way of action are needed, that

Not by refraining from actions
Does a person attain freedom,
Nor by renunciation alone
Does he attain perfection.
(3.5)

Why does He not recommend the renunciation of action in favor of the way of knowledge? Because the person seeking liberation is an embodied self, and for an embodied self action is inevitable:

No one, even for a moment,
Can remain inactive.
All are helplessly forced to act
By the guṇas born of prakṛti.
(3.6)[1]

On the other hand, the Ātman, being separate from the guṇas of prakṛti, is not involved in or affected by the actions of the guṇas. If Arjuna realizes this, then not identifying himself with prakṛti he will no longer think of himself as doer or attach himself to the results of action. As Krishna says,

Actions are performed only
By the guṇas of prakṛti

[1]The guṇas are the constituent threads of the fundamental matter of existence.

But he who is deluded by the ego
Thinks, "I am the doer."

He who knows the truth, O Arjuna,
Of the separation [of the Self] from both the guṇas and action,
Knows that it is the guṇas that act upon the guṇas,
And is not attached [to action].

(3.27–28)

These verses summarize Krishna's teaching that attachment and bondage result from the ignorance wherein the prakṛtic self is mistakenly embraced as the Ātman. Knowing their separation, the actions of the prakṛtic self produce no bondage. But when Arjuna is deluded into identification with the prakṛtic self, desire, springing from rājas, the guṇa of passion, obscures his self-knowledge—as smoke covers fire or dust a mirror, according to Krishna—and his actions produce bondage (3.36–39).

## ACTION WITHOUT DESIRE FOR RESULTS

But if, as Krishna maintains, action is inevitable for the embodied self, then the question changes from *whether* one should act to *how* one should act. The choice between action and nonaction is illusory, for the guṇas in which the Self is embodied force a person to act unceasingly. On the other hand, since what produces bondage is not action itself, but only action rooted in desire and grasping for results, there is no need to abandon action to eliminate bondage. What must be abandoned is the desire for, and attachment to, the results of action.

Anticipating Arjuna's question about this strange kind of action that appears so unlike the actions with which he is familiar, Krishna Himself raises the question, What kind of action is it that does not aim for any results?

What is action? What is inaction?
Even the wise are confused about this.
Therefore I will explain action to you
So that knowing this you will be freed from evil.

(4.16)

Having abandoned attachment to the results of action
Always content and independent,
Even when engaged in action
He does nothing whatever.

(4.20)

Without desires, self and mind controlled,
Abandoning all possessions,

Engaging in action with only the body,
He does not commit sin.

(4.21)

For a person who is free from attachments, who is liberated,
Whose mind is firmly established in knowledge,
Who performs actions only as sacrifice [yajña]
For him [the bondage of] action is completely dissolved.

(4.23)

"Sacrifice" might be a misleading translation of yajña. As we noted in Chapter 2, yajña does not connote a costly or painful surrender of something precious, but refers instead to the offering of our own existence to the primordial forces of creation so that life may be renewed through the infusion of the divine energy of existence. In the theistic terms of the Gītā, the exchange involved in yajña is Arjuna's offering of himself to Krishna so that his life might be filled with, and directed by, the Divine Life of God.

Whatever you do, whatever you eat,
Whatever offering you make, whatever you give,
Whatever austerities you perform, O Arjuna,
Make that an offering to Me.

(9.27)

By surrendering his ego existence to God, Arjuna is told that he will find his true Self. Here is no room for desire or attachment, and consequently his action will produce no bondage. Identifying himself with Brahman, Krishna says,

Having placed his actions in Brahman,
Having abandoned attachment,
One is no more affected by sin
Than a lotus leaf is affected by water.

(5.10)

Because the embodied self, society, and the world are maintained by action, action cannot be abandoned. In Chapter Three, Krishna tells Arjuna that he should perform the actions required by his dharma.

Therefore, perform all action that must be done
Without attachment,
For by performing action without attachment
Man attains the Supreme.

(3.19)

Applying this teaching to Arjuna's moral and social duty to maintain justice and protect righteousness in society, Krishna tells him how to act:

> Surrendering all your actions to Me,
> With your consciousness fixed on the highest Self,
> Being free from desire and selfishness,
> Fight, freed from your grief.
>
> (3.30)

There can be no doubt that Krishna's teaching is that the actions required by dharma must be performed, for even in this difficult test case, where the evil consequences of acting in accord with dharma have been carefully pointed out, the judgment is that the required action must be performed.

## Ritual Action

Social action in the performance of one's dharma was not the only kind of action threatened by the extreme emphasis on knowledge as *the* way of liberation that developed in India during the centuries preceding the Gītā. Ritual action, the key to Vedic yajña, was also threatened by the emphasis on knowledge. Yajña had apparently degenerated into something approaching magic, where it was thought that the ritual actions of calling upon the Gods, chanting the sacred verses, and making the offerings of melted butter and other materials would of themselves transform this life and this world through the divine power of the higher reality, forced into service by the ritual. The Upaniṣads themselves, though clearly in the Vedic tradition, questioned the usefulness of the way of ritual, increasingly emphasizing the way of knowledge, while Jainas, Ājīvikas, and Buddhists openly criticized and rejected the ritual way of liberation, preferring the means of knowledge and yoga.

The Gītā is aware of and accepts this criticism of degenerate ritual, for Krishna says

> The ignorant, delighting in the
> Letter of the Veda, O Arjuna,
> Saying there is nothing else,
> Utter this flowery speech
>
> Which fills many ritual performances that
> Aim at attaining power and enjoyment, but
> Which result in re-birth, for their natures
> Consist of desire and they are intent only on heaven.
>
> (2.42–43)

But the great value of ceremony and ritual, when done in a spirit of self-offering as a way of opening one's existence to the divine transforming power of a higher reality, is clearly recognized, for Krishna also says:

Know that action [ritual] arises from Brahman
And Brahman springs from the Imperishable.
Therefore, the universal Brahman
Is ever established in yajña.

(3.15)

In the final chapter Krishna recommends the performance of ritual actions in the strongest of language:

Acts of yajña, gift, and austerity
Should not be abandoned; rather, they should be performed.
Yajña, giving and austerity
Are purifiers of the wise.

These actions ought to be performed
With abandonment of fruits and attachment.
This, O Arjuna,
Is my definite and highest judgment.

(18.5–6)

Here is Krishna's answer to Arjuna's question, "How can I act in fulfillment of duty without committing sin?" as well as an answer to the question embodying the long-standing conflict between the way of knowledge and action, "How can I perform my required social and ritual action without incurring further bondage?" The answer is as simple as it is profound. It is not actions but intentions and desires that produce bondage to prakṛti. Therefore, abandon all attachment to the results of actions, performing them purely for the sake of dharma, as a devotional offering of oneself to God. Thereby actions not only cease to produce bondage, but actually become instruments of liberation.

## Liberation Through Knowledge

Since this nonattached or selfless action is not in conflict with knowledge, Krishna can praise the way of knowledge even while he extols the value of selfless action, for this kind of action itself is said to culminate in knowledge. As it developed in the Upaniṣads, the way of knowledge reflected the assumption that the essential Self is ultimately pure consciousness. Consequently, knowledge of the essential Self was seen as the key to release from the limitations and bondage of embodied existence. Actions, since they obscure the nature of the essential Self and generate effects that strengthen the bonds of embodiment, were to be gradually abandoned. The Jainas, as we have seen in the example of Śāntisāgara (p. 108), developed this teaching to its limit, encouraging the eventual abandonment of all actions, including the physiological actions of bodily functions, looking for ultimate release in the holy death fast. It is true that the sages of the Upaniṣads and the Jainas emphasized ethical action, but this was only a preliminary means of purification; only knowledge could bring liberation.

What this liberating knowledge is thought to be changes according to the metaphysics accepted. For the Upaniṣads, it is knowledge of the supreme Brahman or Ātman, utterly different from every kind of manifested existence. For Sāṁkhya it is knowledge of the absolute separateness of puruṣa and prakṛti. In the Gītā, Krishna tells us that it is God that must be known.

How this liberating knowledge can be acquired also shifts according to the view of the self adopted. Meditative insight is stressed in the Upaniṣads and in Jainism, whereas Sāṁkhya emphasizes illuminating discrimination. In addition to insight and discrimination, the Gītā recognizes both knowing through faith in the teachings of others that are rooted in direct experience and insight and the knowledge that comes through disciplined action or yoga. But in the Gītā these different objects and means of knowledge are not taken to be exclusive of each other. They simply reflect differing approaches to the ultimate. Just as the city of Rome can be seen in many ways and approached by different roads, so can the supreme reality be viewed in many ways and approached by different means.

Meditative insight, discrimination, selfless action and faith in scripture are all means of liberating knowledge, according to the Gītā.

> Some see the Self in the self by meditation,
> Some see It by disciplined discrimination,
> And some see It by disciplined action.
>
> But others, not having this knowledge,
> On hearing It from others cherish It.
> They too cross beyond death through
> Devotion to the holy revelation which they hear.
> (13.24–25)

In a similar way, the Gītā recognizes that liberating knowledge may be thought of in different ways. For example, it may be thought to consist in seeing the divine nature of all beings while recognizing that they do not exhaust God's being.

> He who sees the supreme Lord
> Abiding equally in all beings,
> Not perishing when they perish,
> He [truly] sees.
> (13.27)

Or it may be thought to consist in seeing the difference between puruṣa and prakṛti while recognizing puruṣa to be the real Self.

> He who sees that all actions are
> Performed only by prakṛti

> Who sees also that Self is not the doer,
> He [truly] sees.
>
> (13.29)

A third view of liberating knowledge takes it to consist in seeing Brahman as the ground and transcendental unity of all existence.

> When he sees the various states of being
> Grounded in the One and
> Extending out from it,
> Then he attains Brahman.
>
> (13.30)

The importance of the knowledge of the differentiation between prakṛti and puruṣa for liberation could hardly be stated more emphatically than in the last verse of Chapter Thirteen:

> They who know, by the eye of knowledge,
> The difference between the field [prakṛti] and the
> knower of the field [puruṣa]
> And the liberation of beings from prakṛti,
> They attain the Supreme.
>
> (13.34)

Other verses also extol the virtues of knowledge. For example, Krishna tells Arjuna, "Even if you were the worst of all sinners, simply by the boat of knowledge you would be able to cross over [the ocean of] all evil" (4.36). And

> The man of faith, restraining his senses,
> Intent only on it, obtains knowledge.
> Having obtained knowledge he quickly
> Attains the highest peace.
>
> (4.39)

## Bhakti: The Way of Devotion

Although Krishna finds a place for knowledge and action as legitimate and valuable means of salvation, the way of *bhakti*, or loving devotion to God, is his favorite way. And despite the claims of distinguished interpreters who find the central message to be either that of knowledge or that of action, it seems clear that the central teaching of the Gītā is that of selfless action and knowledge *through devotional love of and self-surrender to the Supreme Lord,* who is identified with the highest reality and with the Self that dwells within all beings.

This should come as no surprise, for after all Krishna, the divine teacher of the Gītā, is an incarnation of the supreme God from whom this whole existence issued and to whom it will eventually return.

Further, Krishna is so concerned about the well-being of the world that he incarnates himself whenever there is need of him in manifest form. Knowledge and action are completed in loving surrender to God, who is the essence of knowledge and the source and goal of all action.

In Chapter Nine, having explained the way of knowledge and the way of unattached action, Krishna tells Arjuna that both of these ways are actually forms of devoted worship of God. Those who revere knowledge and seek to know the Imperishable source of beings worship God in their own way.

> The great-souled, O Arjuna,
> Abiding in the divine nature,
> Knowing Me as the Imperishable source of beings
> Worship Me with an unswerving mind.
>
> (9.13)

But those engaged in action, having disciplined their action so that it is free from attachment, also worship God.

> Always glorifying Me,
> Striving with firm resolve, and
> Honoring Me with devotion,
> They, constantly disciplined, worship Me.
>
> (9.14)

But even more, knowledge and action can be seen as actual forms of devotion or bhakti, finding their culmination in loving surrender to God when they are offered to Him in the spirit of yajña:

> Others too, offering the yajña of knowledge,
> Worship Me as the One,
> In my unique and manifold forms
> Variously facing in all directions.
>
> (9.15)

Even those who follow the way of Vedic ritual are depicted as worshipping the Lord with devotion, for as Krishna says,

> I am the ritual action, I am the yajña.
> I am the ancestoral offering, I am the medicinal herb.
> I am the sacred verse and I am also the melted butter.
> I am the fire and I am the offering.
>
> (9.16)

Those who worship other Gods and do not recognize Krishna as the supreme God incarnate are also worshipping Him, even though they do not realize it:

> Even those who are devotees of other Gods,
> And, full of faith, worship them,

They worship only Me, O Arjuna,
Though not according to the prescribed rules.
(9.23)

Anyone who worships God in any form, as Shiva, Rāma, or Devī (or Yahweh or Allah), is regarded as worshipping the supreme God, and any form of worship is accepted as true worship if it is offered to God in the appropriate spirit of self-surrender.

Whoever offers, with devotion,
A leaf, a flower, a fruit or water—
That offering of devotion
From the pure in heart I accept.
(9.26)

Worshipping God with loving devotion overcomes all obstacles, for by offering oneself to God in love the divine power comes to direct one's life. Even wickedness is overcome by devotion to God:

Even a man of the most wicked conduct who
Worships Me with single-minded devotion
Must be regarded as righteous,
For he has resolved rightly.
(9.30)

However, bhakti is not put forth as an easier but inferior way intended only for those unqualified for the ways of knowledge and action. It is for the high born and wise as well. If bhakti can save even śūdras,

How much more, then, holy brāhmaṇas,
And devout royal sages!
Having come into this impermanent world of suffering,
Offer yourself in devotion to Me.

Fix your mind on Me, devote yourself to Me;
Worship Me, do homage to Me.
Having thus disciplined yourself, with Me as your goal,
You shall come to Me.
(9.33–34)

Indeed, in its usual spirit of accommodation, the Gītā suggests that even as action and knowledge can be seen as forms of devotion, so devotion can be seen as a means to knowledge and selfless action. Referring to those following the path of action, Krishna says, "To those constantly disciplined ones who worship Me in love, I grant the discipline of mind whereby they come to Me." In the next verse, Krishna says that He brings knowledge to those devoted to Him: "Out of compassion for these [persons devoted to me] I, while remaining in My own self-nature, dispel their darkness, born of ignorance, by the shining light of knowledge" (10.10–11).

## God

To understand how the three ways of knowledge, action, and devotion are accommodated and reconciled in the Gītā, we must turn to its vision of ultimate reality, in this case, the nature of God. As we have seen, Krishna sometimes praises action, sometimes knowledge, and sometimes devotion as the best way. And although he sees devotion as a means to knowledge and action, he also sees knowledge and action as means to devotion, and action and knowledge as means to each other. So which way is really the best?

Actually, there are three answers, all mutually compatible, and with none forcing us to make an exclusive choice from among these three ways of salvation. Distinguishing between different types of persons on the basis of birth (heredity) and circumstance (environment), the first answer says that the best way for a given person is the one best suited to his or her own nature and inclinations. According to the Sāṁkhya theory of the guṇa composition of existence, everyone is a combination of sattva, rājas, and tamas. But in some persons sattva predominates, while in others there is a preponderance of tamas or rājas. Since the guṇas constitute the forces of bondage, it makes sense for a person to follow a way that will be particularly helpful in overcoming the bondage of the dominant guṇa. Knowledge is particularly effective in destroying the bondage of sattva, and so is appropriate for the person in whom this guṇa predominates. On the other hand, for a person of action like Arjuna, in whom rājas predominates, the way of self-less action is especially appropriate. But both these types of person, as well as those persons in whom tamas predominates, can also be saved through loving devotion to God. Finally, since everyone is in bondage to all three guṇas, it becomes necessary to combine all three ways, even while giving emphasis to one or the other according to the preponderance of a particular guṇa.

The second answer is that, regardless of which is chosen as the predominant way, the other two ways become means or aids by which to follow the chosen way. We have seen that knowledge is regarded as a necessary means to self-less action, for knowing the separation of puruṣa and prakṛti provides motivation for abandoning attachment to the results of action. Nonattachment has always been regarded as a means of purifying the self and preparing the way for insight and mystic knowledge. Both knowledge and action are means to devotion, whereas devotion is also a means to action and knowledge.

The third answer is that each of these three ways actually incorporates the others, being at bottom only a different dimension or aspect of the same way. This answer, in effect abolishing the hard distinctions among love, knowledge, and action, says that there is only *one* way, the higher way, which consists in a unity of knowledge, action, and devotion.

Unlike the second answer, which maintains that these three ways are related to each other as means and ends, this answer says that action and knowledge are actually forms of love, that love and action are actually forms of knowledge, and that love and knowledge are actually forms of action.

One way of seeing this higher way that incorporates knowledge, love, and action is suggested by the Gītā itself: Knowing the difference between Self and prakṛti, desire is renounced, and a perfect equanimity or selflessness in all action is achieved through offering oneself as doer or agent to God who is the supreme in-dwelling Self, even though not yet realized as such. In this way, not only desire for the results of action, but even one's identification with the doer of action, is abandoned. Now, in offering to the Lord all of one's actions and knowledge in love and adoration, one's whole being is surrendered to God. Through this surrender one comes to share fully in the Divine Love, Action, and Knowledge constituting the true Self.

This higher reality in which the Self finds the divine life, in which love, action, and knowledge are united, is God. The God with whom Krishna identifies himself, though transcending the world, is also its source, ruler, power, and in-dwelling unity. In Chapter Seven, Krishna tells Arjuna to know him as the ultimate reality, a knowledge so difficult that not even one in a thousand acquires it. Here Krishna identifies himself with prakṛti and puruṣa, regarding the former as his lower nature and the latter as his higher nature. By regarding prakṛti and puruṣa as two aspects of his own nature, Krishna shows how the dualism of Sāṁkhya is transcended by the higher unity of the Divine Being.

Krishna tells Arjuna that as God He is present in all things and that all things are present in Him:

> All beings emerge from it [My nature].
> Know that of all of them,
> And of the whole world,
> I am the origin and the dissolution.
>
> Nothing higher than Me exists
> O Arjuna.
> On Me this [whole universe] is strung
> Like pearls on a string.
>
> (7.6–7)

But this vision is definitely not pantheistic, for God's Being and Divinity are by no means identical to Its presence in things. Pointing to His transcendence of the divinity present in the world, Krishna says, "Whatever being has glory, majesty or power, know that in every case it has originated from a fraction of My glory," and "I support this whole world with a single fraction [of Myself]" (10.41–42). Furthermore, although the world's existence depends on God, God's being is independent of the world, for as Krishna says, "My Self is the source of all beings and sustains all beings but does not rest in them" (9.4–5).

God's uniqueness and transcendence is indicated by calling Him not simply puruṣa, but the Supreme puruṣa; He is not simply Ātman, but the Supreme Ātman. All other realities are encompassed by His being, but as God He goes beyond them. In Chapter Fifteen, Krishna reveals how God, as the Supreme Person, goes beyond not only prakṛti, but even beyond Ātman.

> There are two persons in the world,
> The perishable and the imperishable.
> The perishable is all beings [prakṛti].
> The Imperishable is called the unchanging [Self].
>
> But there is another, the Supreme Person,
> Called the Highest Self [Parāmatman],
> Which as the Imperishable Lord
> Enters and sustains the three worlds.
>
> (15.16–17)

Being distinct, however, does not mean being separate. The Gītā clearly sees this supreme God as dwelling within all things and persons, even though their reality is not commensurate with His. In other words, though transcending the world, God is its Source, Power, Ruler, and indwelling Unity.

But the fullness of God's being is beyond human understanding. The whole of Chapter Eleven is an eloquent testament to the Hindu conviction that the ultimate reality cannot be comprehended by human beings. Only by God's grace is Arjuna granted a vision of this supreme reality, and even then he must be given a divine eye, for ordinary means of knowledge are totally inadequate to receive such knowledge. As one blind man perceived the elephant as a wall, so some of us perceive the ultimate as nirguṇa Brahman. And like another blind man, perceiving the elephant as a rope, some of us perceive the ultimate as a combination of Being, Knowledge, and Bliss. Another blind man perceived the elephant as a tree trunk, even as some of us perceive the ultimate as a divine personal being. For with respect to the ultimate we, with our limited means of knowledge, are like blind people; we are incapable of encompassing the whole of reality with our limited means.

The form in which the ultimate appears to us is not the true and complete form; that we are incapable of recognizing. As Krishna says, "I know all beings, past, present and yet to come. But no one knows Me" (7.26). Not even the Gods and the seers know the ultimate as it is in itself: "Neither the hosts of Gods nor the great seers know my Origin, for in every respect I am their source." "Neither the Gods nor the Demons know Thy manifestation," acknowledges Arjuna, for, "Only Thou knowest Thyself by Thyself, O Highest Spirit, Source of beings, Lord of beings, God of Gods, Lord of the world!" (10.14–15).

But if no one can comprehend the ultimate as it is in itself, then there is no basis for claiming that understanding the ultimate as a personal God is erroneous. Nor is there a basis for claiming that some other understanding, for example, the Upanishadic understanding of the ultimate as nirguṇa Brahman, is superior. For no one doubts that the ultimate *is* something; those who insist on nirguṇa Brahman only claim that whatever it is cannot be said.

The conclusion drawn by the author of the Gītā, and by the Hindu tradition generally, from the recognition that no human conception of the ultimate can fully capture its essence, is that a multitude of partial and fragmentary conceptions, representations, and images awaken us to more of the glory, splendor, and power of the Divine than either total silence or a single representation.

This is obvious not only in the Gītā, but in music and poetry, and in temple art and architecture, which dazzle us with their profusion of form and richness of detail.

The poetry of Chapter 11, rising to the occasion of Krishna's revelation of his divine form to Arjuna, reveals this Indian fondness for profuse description and imagery as a means of directing us to the highest reality.

Chapter 11 opens with Arjuna's request for a vision of the Divine Reality: "O Lord, reveal to me fully your glorious Form. If it is possible, if I can stand the sight, then make Yourself visible. Show me Your very Self, Eternal God!"

Krishna agrees to grant the vision, but tells Arjuna that, since no human eyes could perceive it, special divine eyes will be granted him with which to perceive the divine mystery and splendor. "I give you divine perception. Use these eyes, a new light," says Krishna. "Now look! See My glory, revealed to mortal sight!" Having said this, Arjuna's chariot driver, the supreme Krishna, stood up, and revealed His full glory, "displaying

> Innumerable mouths and eyes,
> Innumerable marvelous aspects,
> Innumerable Divine ornaments,
> Innumerable wonderful weapons held high.
>
> Wearing heavenly garlands and garments,
> With Divine perfumes and ointments,
> Infinite and full of wonders,
> His face was present everywhere.
>
> If in the sky a thousand suns
> Suddenly burst forth,
> That light would hint at
> The light of that exalted being.

## Summary

The Upaniṣads, especially the later ones such as the Śvetāśvatara and the Īśa, contain the insight that, although Brahman, the ultimate reality, goes beyond all possible attempts at description and definition, it can also be thought of in personal terms. This insight, that Brahman can be seen as the supreme Person, embodying infinite power, knowledge, and joy, comes to fruition in the Bhagavad Gītā. Here Krishna, an embodiment of the supreme God in human form, presents himself to Arjuna as encompassing every image and conception of the ultimate reality. He is nirguṇa and saguṇa Brahman, the supreme Ātman, the highest puruṣa, the totality of prakṛti, the essence of all the Gods. But in His own nature God goes beyond all of these.

The various conceptions of the ultimate are regarded as reflections of different approaches to the ultimate and are therefore seen as complementary rather than as excluding each other. But all of them together reflect only a small fraction of God's own being, which is revealed more fully only through God's grace—as when He grants Arjuna a divine eye and reveals his manifold glorious and awesome forms in Chapter 11.

Even though God utterly transcends this world and all our conceptions of the ultimate, He is still present everywhere as the source, ground, and power of all existence. Here the second great insight of the Gītā comes into play, for if this world is grounded in the Divine existence, then this world—and action in it—should not be regarded as evil or abandoned in the name of liberation. What are evil and to be abandoned are desire and selfishness, for they set human beings apart from God and the world through the divisiveness of ego. This insight enables the Gītā to present the three classic ways of salvation—knowledge, action, and devotion—not as conflicting with each other, but as complementary, and as partial aspects of a higher way that incorporates all three.

Action, says the Gītā, should be undertaken as an offering of self to God, without regard for results. In this way the energies of desire and grasping that create bondage to the ego are nullified and destroyed, making action a vehicle of liberation rather than bondage. But this selfless action incorporates an initial knowledge of the distinction between the higher self of Ātman or puruṣa and the lower self of prakṛti, bringing about a higher knowledge of the self through infusion of the Divine Self in the self-offering of action and knowledge. Thus, both the way of action and the way of knowledge are seen not only as acceptable ways of salvation in themselves, but also as parts of a higher way that incorporates them, along with the way of worship, into a way of loving devotion to God.

Since these three ways are not seen to exclude each other, the Gītā offers a choice of ways of salvation. For those dominated by rājas and inclined to action, the way of self-less action is especially appropriate, while for those dominated by sattva and inclined to knowledge and contemplation, the way of knowledge is more appropriate. Others, dominated by tamas, find the way of worship especially attractive. But all three ways, when performed in the spirit of self-offering and loving devotion to God, are transformed into a higher way, which, through God's Grace, allows the Divine Life to fill one's being with the Divine Action, Knowledge, and Love of God.

## Suggestions for Further Reading

*The Bhagavad Gītā*, translated, with introduction and critical essays, by Eliot Deutsch (New York: Holt, Rinehart and Winston, 1968), contains an extremely readable translation of the entire Gītā and a useful brief introduction that succinctly explains the basic concepts. The thirty pages of interpretation following the translation serve to emphasize the central teachings in a clear and concise way.

Franklin Edgerton's translation and interpretation of the Gītā—*The Bhagavad Gītā* (New York: Harper Torchbooks, 1964)—is an extremely literal translation—line for line—of great accuracy. His ninety-page interpretive essay is a masterful job. It explains the conceptual background and context of the *Gītā* as well as interpreting its main teachings in a clear and decisive way. The translation by J. A. B. Van Buitenen in a bilingual edition, *The Bhagavad Gītā* (Chicago: University of Chicago Press, 1981), is also excellent.

The only poetic translation in English that comes close to capturing the feeling of the Sanskrit is that by Sir Edwin Arnold. Originally published by David McKay Company under the title *The Song Celestial* (New York, 1934), it is now available from various sources in paperback editions.

The translation by Sarvapalli Radhakrishnan in *A Source Book in Indian Philosophy*, ed. C. A. Moore and S. Radhakrishnan (Princeton, N.J.: Princeton University Press, paperback, 1957), is reliable but is reprinted without interpretation or commentary. (The same translation with Radhakrishnan's excellent neo-Vedāntic interpretation is available from Allen & Unwin, Winchester, Mass.)

I should mention that not only have I benefited from books listed, but I have also relied on commentaries by Śankara, Rāmānuja, Gandhi, and Aurobindo within the Indian tradition and have profited from the provocative study of the Gītā by Antonio de Nicolas, in *Avatāra: The Humanization of Philosophy Through the Bhagavad Gītā* (Stony Brook, N.Y.: Nicolas Hays, 1976). Swami Nikhilananda's translation of the Gītā published by the Vedānta Press has been my constant companion for many years. But my understanding of the Gītā is derived in good part from that of my own teacher, the late S. K. Saksena. His seminars and private personal discussions have influenced me here, as in other areas of Indian philosophy—probably much more than I could specify.

# 10

# Devotional Hinduism: God as Joy, Love, and Beauty

In the previous chapter we saw how the ultimate reality manifested and revealed itself to Arjuna in personal form, inviting him—and humankind—to come to God in loving devotion, this being the surest and easiest way to salvation. How did India respond to this invitation? How was the ultimate conceived and imaged? What ideas and attitudes directed the development of devotional Hinduism? These are the basic questions this and the following chapter attempt to answer to see the place of God in Hinduism.

## Background

It is no easy task to show how the Hindu religious response to the ultimate reality manifested itself in devotional practice directed toward the Supreme Person in His or Her various manifestations. First, this response was tremendously varied, taking different forms at different times and in different places. Second, a great number of personal manifestations of the ultimate were recognized, human and nonhuman, male and female. Third, devotional practice itself has varied tremendously, depending not only upon the nature and quality of religious response and the ways in which the ultimate was conceived and imagined, but also upon sociopolitical and environmental conditions. The fact that the Indian consciousness has regarded chronological sequence as relatively unimportant further complicates matters, for it makes an historical approach almost impossible.

The historical origins of Hindu devotionalism cannot be located. While the recognition of Brahman with personal characteristics as the Lord of the Universe in the Śvetāśvatra and Īśa Upaniṣads shows that devotion to God was clearly compatible with recognition of the ultimate reality as the transcendent, quality-less ground of all existence, it does not establish the beginnings of devotionalism. It is also clear that in important ways the Gītā has provided the foundation of religious devotionalism for the last twenty-two hundred years. But, again, this does not establish the beginnings of devotionalism.

Perhaps these beginnings are to be found in Vedic religion. Although the Vedic emphasis is on sacrificial celebration rather than worship, and although the deities of the Ṛg Veda tend to be seen as something less than the ultimate reality, still a worshipful attitude is often shown them.

But then again, perhaps the origins of devotionalism are to be found in even earlier practice. Artifacts from the Indus civilization and the character of many of the major deities of the Hindu pantheon suggest a direct linkage from pre-Āryan religious practice in India to Hinduism in its classical form. After all, the art of Indus civilization reveals a proto-Shiva seated in yogic position, poised, calm, and perfectly controlled, but with penis erect, suggesting his function as Lord and controller of the universe and as its source or generative principle—both here combined as different aspects of the one reality from which all this proceeds. And Indus Goddess figures suggest that life, fertility, and reproduction were venerated as sacred, making possible a direct line of descent to later Goddesses of the Hindu tradition. So it may well be that devotionalism was integral to religious practice prior to the Āryan influence. The Gītā may simply represent the most important step in the accommodation of these non-Āryan traditions into the great Sanskritic tradition.

Lacking accurate historical information, however, we cannot be sure either that this is what happened, or if it did, how and why it happened. Two major problems confront the historical approach. First, aside from a few artifacts, there is no record of the ideas and beliefs of Indus or other early cultures on the subcontinent. Second, practically all literary documents belong to the Sanskrit literature of the Āryan traditions. This means that only those ideas that were accepted and assimilated by the authors of the Vedic tradition came to form part of the tradition that we usually associate with Hinduism and to which the Gītā belongs. Thus, prior to and during the period of the Upaniṣads and Buddhism there may have been widespread practices of devotional approaches to Gods and Goddesses that the Gītā accommodated in part and that, after this door was opened, came to be admitted in greater part in the Pūraṇas and other popular literature. That is, although the literary record suggests that the foundations of theism and devotional practice are found primarily in the Gītā (though suggested already by some of the Upaniṣads), this may not reflect what actually occurred. Perhaps a continuous development of indigenous religious devotionalism, directed toward one or the other of the various Gods or Goddesses, eventually came to be taken over and adopted by the Vedic tradition.

After all, it would be entirely unreasonable to suppose that the cultures existing in India before the ascendancy of the Āryans would have simply disappeared. Especially in light of the Āryan system of social classification, which allowed non-Āryans to be recognized as a part of the social order, it seems likely that earlier religious ideas and practice would have survived. Recall that only the first three varnas were recognized as twice born, as full participants in the high culture. The śūdras, constituting a large percentage of the population, were not allowed to participate in Vedic religion. Most likely they carried on earlier religious traditions that were not accepted as part of Vedic orthodoxy. Perhaps here, among the lower classes of society, Āryan and non-Āryan cultures began to influence and accommodate each other.

However likely the hypothesis that devotional Hinduism developed out of the mutual accommodation of quite different earlier religious traditions, the fact remains that we are woefully ignorant of the specific ingredients contributed by the various earlier traditions and know neither the chronology nor the chemistry of their combination.

Still, it seems clear that at least from the time of the Gītā on, there appears to be an increasing emphasis on the devotional approach. Adoration and love of the Divine conceived in personal terms as Krishna, Durgā, Rāma, Shiva, and so on, partially replace both the elaborate ritualism of yajña and the ascetic emphasis on knowledge that characterized not only the Upaniṣads but Jainism and early Buddhism as well. Even Buddhism, in its Mahāyāna form, despite the fact that the Buddha's own teachings neither presupposed nor recommended devotion to or worship of Gods and Goddesses, developed a way of bhakti directed toward the Bodhisattvas—Buddhism's version of Divine Beings who so love us and the world that they work unceasingly for our well-being and liberation from duḥkha. So strong was the devotional influence that eventually Mahāyāna developed the doctrine that it is sufficient simply to recite the name of the Buddha or a Bodhisattva with loving devotion to effect the transfer of His (or Her) merit to the devotee and thereby gain nirvāṇa. Images of the Buddha also came to be revered, bathed, and annointed, and offered food, flowers, and water, much as images of the Gods and Goddesses of the Hindus are treated in worship.

Despite the problems confronting an historical approach to the development of devotionalism, we can be optimistic about our chances to understand this aspect of Hinduism, for it dominates Hinduism today even as it has for approximately the last two thousand years. In the contemporary Hindu practices of worship that offer a freshly killed goat to Kālī at her temple in Calcutta; that awaken, bathe, annoint, dress, and honor the image of Krishna; that bring offerings of food and drink to Vishnu; that garland the linga of Shiva with flowers or anoint it with fragrant balm; that participate in a dramatic enactment of the wonderful feats of Rāma and Sītā; that pour forth joyous melodies of heartfelt praise to all the Goddesses and Gods in song; that parade the image of a favorite God or Goddess through village lanes or city streets on a special holiday—in all these we see the embodiment of the past.

By working backward from contemporary religious practice, we can hope to gain a good understanding of the underlying ideas and attitudes, for, despite constant change in peripheral matters and in details, the central features of Hinduism have changed little from two thousand years ago. Then, as now, the ultimate reality was conceived as something sacred, as a holy power that went beyond all conceivable characteristics but still could be effectively imagined in personal terms, as the Supreme Person who creates, sustains, and destroys the world.

As we saw in the last chapter, Indian consciousness is aware that the ultimate reality can in no way be circumscribed by human knowledge. Apprehended in diverse ways by persons with different qualifications, backgrounds, and approaches, the ultimate transcends all attempts to capture its ultimacy. But because the ultimate is somehow recognized, though dimly and feebly, to be the source and ground of human existence, it is impossible to resist the urge to know, feel, and relate to this reality. Its power is recognized everywhere, in the waters, in the sky, in plants, in animals, in humans, and in superhuman beings.

There is no limit to the number of forms that the ultimate takes, and therefore no limit to the number of forms that can be recognized as divine. When a Hindu says that there are 330 million Gods, no claim is being made that there are that many supreme beings, but only that the divine reality is present in as many forms as existence takes. The whole universe is sacred. Nothing is so humble that it does not possess the divine, and no event or action is so insignificant that it is not holy. This attitude renders the whole of life and the entire universe sacred for the Hindu. Everydayness is special; it is as sacred, though not as spectacular, as the special events in life or heavenly existence. The distinction between secular and religious reality falls away when this vision of reality is accepted.

Although stones, plants, and animals are all recognized as sacred forms of the divine reality, personal forms of the divine are generally recognized as higher forms. These anthropocentric forms of the divine as personal Gods and Goddesses tend to be the focus of Hindu religious life, for here a rich personal relationship is possible. Even though the Divine Family of Hinduism is wonderfully large and varied, three deities have had special importance in the development of Hinduism and are extremely popular in contemporary Hinduism. These are Kālī, God in Her terrifying and destructive manifestation; Krishna of Vṛndāvana, a manifestation of the beauty, joy, and playfulness of God; and Shiva, the great God who combines characteristics and features of all the deities and whose divine symbol, the linga, transcends all polarities.

Although it would require volumes to account for all the Hindu deities and the complexities of devotional activities, a good idea of the Hindu attitude toward the God and Goddesses and their main functions can be gleaned from a relatively brief glimpse of the Krishna, Kālī, and Shiva manifestations of the ultimate reality. Each of these Gods in a way embodies all the other deities, representing all their various characteristics.

For those readers who are interested at the outset in knowing whether Hinduism is polytheistic, monotheistic, or monistic, I can only say that none of these categories quite catches the truth, for actually Hinduism is all three simultaneously. But if these categories are taken to be exclusive of each other, that is impossible, and so perhaps then we should say that it is none of these! If we combine these two claims, that in some sense Hinduism is simultaneously polytheistic, monotheistic, and monistic and that in some sense it is none of these, we shall probably be close to the truth. But perhaps we should examine the Hindu attitude first without trying to pigeonhole it.

## Krishna

We begin with Krishna, for no other God is so beloved by Hindus as Krishna, embodiment of divine beauty, joy, and love. By doting on the beauty and playfulness of the divine child, and through the enchantment of stories glorifying the divine youth's tender love, Krishna's devotees are drawn into the loving embrace of the supreme God and taste the ecstasy of divine bliss through loving surrender to him.

The Krishna we met in the Gītā, who reveals the ultimate reality in personal form and invites the devotee to come to him in devoted love, is unquestionably important to the devotees of Krishna. But this God, the Supreme Lord, is scarcely approachable by his humble servants, who tremble before his august and fearful presence. Indeed, so terrifying is the awesome splendor and power revealed to Arjuna that this great warrior confesses that it is too much for him to bear and begs Him to resume His human form. The distance between human and this God is far too great to be bridged in a union of mutual love. Surrender may be possible, but love requires a mutuality that the relationship between lord and servant renders impossible.

So it is not surprising, then, that the Krishna who becomes the favorite deity of Hinduism is a much more approachable and ordinary person. In terms of Krishna's biography, it is not the Krishna as adult God, conquering hero, wise counsel, or Divine Lord, who appeals most to the Hindu imagination, but Krishna as an adorable little child, playful young boy, and beautiful, amorous youth. Furthermore, it is in the simple pastoral setting of Vṛndāvana that Krishna, as a humble cowherd boy, reveals the divine beauty, joy, and love of the ultimate reality. Here his childhood and youth express the divine nature as carefree, exuberant, playful, and exquisitely beautiful.

This Krishna, not even mentioned in the Mahābhārata or the Gītā, is the chief object of the purāṇic stories and of the great devotional poetry glorifying the divine child and the divine lover.

According to popular legend, Krishna was conceived when Vishnu, God of Gods, entered the womb of the beautiful and noble Devakī to be born in human form. Mother Earth had come to Vishnu complaining that she was being overrun by demons and that unless he could help her she would be destroyed. Vishnu assured her he would come to her assistance, ensuring that the forces of good would prevail. Thus, he arranged to take on human form as Devakī's son so that he could again defeat the demon leader Kalanemi, who had now taken human form as Kaṁsa.

To escape the curse of death placed upon all Devakī's children by the wicked Kaṁsa, Vishnu arranged that, upon birth, the baby Krishna would be given to the cowherd couple Yaśodha and Nanda in exchange for their own infant. Yaśodha, of course, assumed that this new-born baby, dark as the lovely blue lotus petal, was her own infant. Gazing at his incomparable beauty, she was beside herself with joy. Knowing nothing of his divine origin, she gave him all her motherly love, doting on him as the most precious baby in the world. In turn, he accepted her as his mother, filling her with wonderful happiness by his beauty, play, laughter, and love for her.

Here, in the simple cowherd village and pastures and forests of Vṛndāvana, Krishna spent his childhood and youth in play, without a care or concern in the world. The innocent and spontaneous playfulness of the little child turned into the frolicking, boisterous play of the young boy, which, in turn, was replaced by the amorous play of the youth. Work and worry were as foreign to him as dirt to a lotus petal. His life consisted only in play, joyous and free, springing spontaneously from the sheer exuberance of his existence.

Although it is Krishna's childhood and youth in Vṛndāvana that is of primary importance to the devotees of Krishna, the legends tell us that, after introducing the cowherd women of Vṛndāvana to the ecstasy of divine love through his wonderful love-play, he left the forest to take up the hero's task of destroying the forces of evil embodied in Kaṁsa. Going to Madhupurī, he is portrayed as a great warrior, destroying his enemies, the forces of evil, and as a wise advisor to the king and his cousins, the Pāṇḍu brothers. As we have seen, it was in his role as advisor to the Pāṇḍus that he revealed himself to Arjuna as the Supreme Lord, explaining how God could be reached by the paths of selfless action and loving devotion. Although he eventually kills the wicked Kaṁsa, as well as many other wicked men and demons, this part of his biography is relatively unimportant to Krishna devotees—as is the story of his later marriage to Rukminī and then to sixteen thousand other women!

Eventually he is accidentally shot in the foot (his Achillles heel) by a hunter and dies. As though to symbolize his return to Vishnu and complete transcendence, legend says that his whole clan is destroyed (in a drunken family brawl) and his beloved city of Dvārakā completely flooded by the ocean, so that nothing at all remains of Krishna and his earthly world.

How do his devotees relate to these three Krishnas (actually three episodes in Krishna's earthly life)? The epic hero who rescues the earth from destruction by demonic forces receives the least attention, while the baby, child, and youth of Vṛndāvana receive tireless and unending devotion. This is clearly the essential Krishna, the God to whom devotees come in adoration and loving devotion, surrendering themselves to his divine love.

## THE DIVINE CHILD

Poets and storytellers alike joyously proclaim this Krishna's unsurpassable beauty, grace, and charm, his unending playfulness, and his tender lovingness. As an adorable little child his mischief is precious, endearing him to everyone in the village. Crawling around the yard he tries to catch his shadow with his hands, laughing gleefully as it eludes the grasp of his chubby baby hands. To the watching adults his musical laughter, shining white teeth, and glowing dark beauty seem to be of another world, and when he comes to his mother to nurse, his contentment brings peace to the whole village.

But the playful child is entirely human. Innocent and obedient in his mother's presence, he misses no opportunity for mischief when her back is turned, according to her friends. This darling little boy unties the village calves and pulls their tails, mocks and laughs at his elders, teases little babies until they cry, and steals butter and sweets—often breaking the jars to get at their contents. Yaśodha's friends also complain that he sneaks into freshly scrubbed houses to urinate on the floors. But his mother, looking into Krishna's frightened eyes and beautiful face, doesn't have the heart to scold him. To her friends' dismay, she just laughs at his playful mischief.

Apparently neither Nanda nor Yaśodha was able to control the little Krishna or his brother, Balarāma. According to one of the early biographies these two played their games and perpetrated their mischief wherever and whenever they pleased. In an entirely approving tone, the author describes their play: "Like the sun and moon in the sky possessed by each other's rays, these two appeared. With their serpent-like arms they looked like two proud young elephants, going wherever they pleased. Sometimes, walking on hands and knees, they would enter the cattle sheds and play there until their hair and bodies were covered with cow manure. Sometimes they would delight their father with laughter over the tricks played on the village residents. . . . But Nanda had no control over them!" (Harivaṁśa, 62.3–12).

As Krishna grew up he retained all the playfulness of the little child, but now his play was rougher and more boisterous and his mischief was on a grander scale. He is never depicted as concerned about anything or seriously performing any work. Instead, as a young adolescent, he is shown leading a wild bunch of cowherd boys in fun and games. No longer under the watchful eyes of parents and elders, they create their own world in playful imitation of animals and birds, mimicking their sounds and actions. Jiva Gośvamin says that they raced with the shadows of birds, climbed the trees with the young monkeys, and leaped into the river with the frogs. At other times they wrestled and competed with each other at various sports, trying to outrun, outjump, or overpower each other. Another author tells us that "After going to the forest, some of the young cowherds, like young elephants freed from their chains, began to dance, sing, laugh, and do acrobatic feats, while others expressed their happiness by simply rolling on the ground. Some of the boys joked, and others indulged in sports of various kinds" (Kṛṣṇadāsa Kavirāja, *Govinda Līlāmṛta*, Sarga 6).[1]

Authors dwell on the mischievous play of Krishna and his brother. They make no apology for their naughtiness; rather, they glorify it as an expression of the divine freedom. Not restrained by social conventions and moral rules, Krishna acts spontaneously out of the fullness of his own being. Totally unconditioned and free, full of life and joy, there is no need either to work or to restrict his activity. The divine does not work; it only plays. Even the creation of the world is not work for the Creator, but a form of divine play (*līlā*), the manifestation of His own exuberance and joy, even as the world created by children in play is the manifestation of their own exuberance and joy.

This Hindu emphasis on God in the form of a child is rooted in the recognition—shared by most religiously oriented cultures—that in their beauty, joy, and spontaneous play, children are Godlike. A small child exhibits the joy and freedom, as well as the spontaneity and playfulness, of the divine existence. Not only does God as child speak to us out of our experience of childhood, both our own childhood and that of others, but in this form He is irresistably approachable. Who can resist the beauty, charm, and playfulness of a child? No rules bind, and no excuses for unconventional behavior are needed. The sheer exuberance of existence that issues in spontaneous play and shouting laughter symbolize the divine presence in existence to all who have eyes, ears, and a heart.

But the lack of design or purpose in a child's play by no means makes it meaningless or insignificant; indeed, it is the most significant and meaningful activity in which a person can engage. Most of us would trade all of our wise designs, clever purposes, and hard work in a minute for the wild, exuberant, creative, and spontaneous play of the child. Whatever creativeness and joyful exuberance we experience as adults, our lives seem hardly a shadow of the fullness of life expressed in the play of an innocent child.

Recognizing God as a free and playful child emphasizes the impor-

[1]In David R. Kingsley, *The Sword and the Flute* (Berkeley: University of California Press, 1977), p. 16.

tance of play, freedom, and joy in human life. Life is not merely to be endured and suffered through; it is to be celebrated and enjoyed. Krishna, the divine child, announces to the world that the essence of God is love and joy, expressed in the freedom of spontaneity of play. Within the larger Indian preoccupation with suffering and death and the heavy emphasis on the duties and obligations of life, this recognition of the childlike qualities of the ultimate reality appears as a breath of fresh air, sweet and intoxicating. Krishna does not take upon himself the burden of maintaining society or the world; he simply fulfills his own being through carefree and joyous play, inviting us to join him in this divine activity.

Even Krishna's combat with the forces of evil is a form of play. When Kāliya, the many-headed serpent, poisons the river, causing terrible destruction of life and threatening the whole village, Krishna comes to the rescue. Playfully he dives into the river, swimming around directly over the serpent's lair, roiling the water with his powerful strokes, and disturbing Kāliya's sleep. When Kāliya rises to do battle with this trespasser, Krishna toys with him, allowing himself to be encircled by the serpent's powerful coils. Then, breaking free, Krishna begins circling until the serpent becomes tired and dizzy, allowing his heads to droop. At this point the young God leaps out of the water and begins to dance on Kāliya's many heads, beating out a rhythm that eventually forces him into submission. But Krishna, never vengeful, does not kill him. Hearing Kāliya's offer of surrender and the pitiful pleas of the serpent-king's wives, Krishna mercifully grants him his life. None of this is work for Krishna; whatever he does he does only as play. Through play the world was created; through play all beings are fulfilled.

What a contrast with the austere invitation of the Upaniṣadic sages to practice asceticism and the hard discipline of yoga to transcend this manifested existence and return to the original unmanifested and quality-less source and power of all existence! In Krishnaism, the invitation is to come to God through laughter, play, and love, not to transcend these human feelings and emotions. As Kinsley points out, Krishna, the divine child is eminently approachable. "He is to be doted upon and coddled. He is to be approached with the intimacy with which a parent approaches a child. God, revealing himself as an infant, invites man to dispense with formality and undue respect and come to him openly, delighting in him intimately" (p. 18).

## THE AMOROUS YOUTH

As Krishna grows older, the boisterous and combative play of young boys is left behind. He now turns to games of love, much to the delight of the cowherd girls, who approach him with coy glances and sly remarks, hoping to get his attention and receive his favors. And he does not disappoint them. All who come to him, attracted by his exquisite beauty, symbolized by the haunting sweetness of his flute, are received in the warm embrace of divine love. Enticed into loving surrender to Krishna by his beauty, charm, and amorous playfulness, the women of Vṛndāvana are led into a wild and wonderful world of frenzied ecstasy. Tasting the nectar of divine love, they leave behind not only the cares, sorrows, and limitations of the world, but even its ordinary joys and pleasures.

Here bhakti, the way of salvation through loving devotion to the Divine Person, finds its full development. Already in the Gītā, bhakti was presented as an alternative way, complementing the Upaniṣadic emphasis on knowing the quality-less Brahman and the self-discipline practiced by yogins. But there it is presented in sober and dignified theological language, and the Lord is so majestic and awesome that he is hardly approachable in ordinary ways by ordinary persons. But in Krishnaism, this changes, and one's ordinary feelings and actions are regarded as adequate instruments for establishing a relationship with God.

The model of surrender to God in loving devotion is that of human love, where the lover achieves the ecstatic fulfillment of the deepest human longings in the embrace of the beloved. This model is developed in the story of Vṛndāvana where Krishna the cowherd becomes the lover of all the cowherd women—even the wives of the staid and conservative brāhmaṇas. The Lord can satisfy anyone who comes to him in loving devotion. When he dances the circular dance of love with the multitude of cowherd women, he becomes present in enough forms to satisfy every lover.

But to see and feel the intensity of the personal loving relationship, attention is focused on the relationship between Krishna and one cowherdess in particular, the beautiful Rādhā, his favorite. The poets never tire of describing the wonderful love-play between these two, dwelling on their erotic play, on their lover's quarrels, on the pain and longing of separation, and on the joy of reunion. This love-play is not simply a means to salvation; it is the highest life. Through surrender in love one is saved and the unending activity of love-play is the play of the saved, not of the seeking. There is no higher vision of heaven than the eternal love play of Rādhā and Krishna, both of them divine in their beauty, grace, and joy (Figure 4).

Perhaps something should be said here about the symbolism of the love between Krishna and Rādhā. Much of the poetry describing this love may at first strike the reader as erotic, glorying in the sexual details of human love. Indeed, the religious strength of this poetry is rooted in its appeal to human feelings. But the subject of the poems is never mere sexual activity. In the first place, we know that the lover is God, the Supreme Lord. This knowledge gives symbolic power to the vivid sensuousness of the poetic images. Evoking ordinary human feelings, the poetic images transform these sensuous feelings into a kind of spiritual life. Love, after all, is the fullest and most joyous expression of life that

**Figure 4.** Krishna Dancing with Rādhā. Early 18th century. (Courtesy, Philadelphia Museum of Art: Given by Mr. and Mrs. Lessing-J. Rosenwald.)

human beings can experience. And God's love is the perfect symbol of human love.

Love, of course, is many things. It is a child's love for parents, parents' love for a child, friends' love for each other. It is giving, receiving, sharing. It can be affectionate or detached, tender or strong. Sometimes it is all these together. But for most human beings, the deepest and fullest love is experienced when two people, who care deeply for each other and share each other's thoughts, hopes, joys, and sufferings, give themselves to each other in sexual embrace. In the fullness of shared love there is a sense of participating in a deeper reality that transcends the usual boundaries of the self.

From the Hindu perspective, this is a kind of divine activity, far transcending mere sexual pleasure. It is only through experience of deep human love in which the felt separateness of ordinary life is overcome that the divine love can be felt. This is why the love-play between Krishna and Rādhā is never merely physical; it involves sharing their entire beings with each other and, through this sharing, participation in the divine reality. This is the second reason why the sensuousness of this poetry is spiritual rather than merely erotic.

When we understand this, the poetry appears in a new light. It now evokes and symbolizes the deepest feelings and expressions of which we are capable, forming a bridge to the divine reality.

Before turning to textual descriptions of Krishna as divine lover we need to pause and look at the meaning of Vṛndāvana, scene of this wonderful drama. Vṛndāvana is a humble pastoral setting, the home of low-caste peasants who do not know or recite Vedic scriptures or practice yoga. Barred from Vedic scripture and ritual by caste, they are the most ordinary of humans beings, special only in that they respond to the divine beauty in existence, surrendering themselves to the beauty and joy of the divine Krishna. The emphasis on knowledge and self-less action in the Gītā is not found in Vṛndāvana. Play is what counts, the exuberant rapturous play of young Krishna, opening the eyes of everyone to the divine beauty and joy of existence. It is the ordinary world and commonplace everyday experience—not some remote God or ground of being—that is recognized and celebrated as sacred in Vṛndāvana.

Vṛndāvana symbolizes God's approachability. Krishna is an ordinary cowherd child, playing with the other cowherd children and making love to the cowherd girls. Here people do not approach him as a servant approaches a master; rather, they join him in play and love as an equal. At the same time lovely Vṛndāvana symbolizes the difference between the beauty, joy, and carefree play of life grounded in God's love and the drab suffering of ordinary existence caught up in worry and work. Conventional society and religion are not condemned in Vṛndāvana; they are just ignored as irrelevant to the fulfillment of life that comes through loving surrender to God.

Much of the charm and attractiveness of Vṛndāvana is that here conventional norms and activities of society are suspended and replaced by the extraordinary joy and beauty of divine play. As the locus of Krishna's divine love-play, it is like lovers' retreats the world over: hidden, serene, beautiful, and joyous—a world apart from the traffic of ordinary life. And even within Vṛndāvana it is not the village but the beautiful forest bowers and cool refreshing streams that Krishna and the cowherd women choose as a site for their games of love.

Enticed and intoxicated by Krishna's exquisite beauty, the cowherd girls follow him to the refuge of the forest. Cows are left half milked, hearths unswept, food left to burn on unattended fires, and husbands deserted when the women of Vṛndāvana hear Krishna's melodious song or the irresistibly sweet music of his flute. When he is silent and beyond their vision, they still find him, for so fragrant is his odor that they are attracted to him as bees to the fragrance of flowers.

No characteristic of Krishna's escapes loving description by the poets and storytellers. His large lotuslike eyes, curly black hair, shining white teeth, glowing dark complexion, and exquisite blue body constitute the quintessence of beauty and are described over and over, using a wide variety of similes and metaphors. Even his fingernails and toenails are worthy of description:

> And the white nails in the hands of the Lord are also like so many moons. As the Lord blows His flute there, little moons dance upon the holes of the flute. They appear as if the tune proceeds not from the flute but from the beautiful nails of the Lord.
>
> And the nails of His feet are also like moons. They also seem to dance as the Lord walks and the tinkling sounds proceeding from the *nupur* [ornaments adorning the feet] appear to be songs sung by the moon-like-nails.
>
> (Jiva Gośvamin, in *Gopala Campu*, quoted by Kinsley, p. 24)

This unsurpassable beauty is an essential part of God's nature, not a mere adornment. Its irresistible appeal brings the devotee not to a flowery and pretty heaven, but directly into the embrace of God Himself in his divine nature. Kinsley quotes a passage from the sixteenth-century poetess Mīrābāī, a devotee of Krishna, whom she declared to be her lover and husband:

> As in summer blooms a garden so my spirit buds and blooms; and of every flower the name is always Krishna. As a butterfly in sunshine filled with light in blue air hovers, thus I dance. In the golden halls of Brindaban I dance before my Krishna on whose brow gleams the Tilakam. Holy Krishna. From my lips I tear concealment and my willing breasts reveal; love inflamed, I dance into the Light of the Blessed Krishna!
>
> (p. 25)

Mīrābāī here captures perfectly the mood of passion and ecstasy that transports Krishna's lovers in Vṛndāvana beyond the conventions of social propriety and feelings of shame or embarrassment.

Surrounded by hundreds of cowherd women in the Vṛndāvana forest, Krishna initiates them into the joys of divine love, teaching them the carefree play of love as an expression of their own divinity, awakened by surrender to Krishna's embrace. The Pūraṇas describe this love-play in great detail, telling how one girl would seize the flute from his hands, while another would snatch away his clothes, teasing him before returning them. While some garlanded him with flowers, others delighted him with moonlike faces, delicate waists, and full breasts. Some danced for him; others forced him to dance with them. Krishna, of course, the initiator of this play, joins fully in the fun, dancing now with one girl, now with another, sometimes stealing a woman's clothes or loosening the knot of her undergarments. As the play goes on passions increase. Kissing and caressing become so intense and lovely that even the Gods are said to assemble and watch this exhibition of divine joy. Finally, transformed by passionate longing, they consummate their love. With Krishna's assuming a separate form for each lover, they completely surrender themselves to each other in the total ecstasy of divine love.[2]

Krishna's love-play with the multitude of cowherd women shows that all who come to him in loving surrender are embraced and fulfilled by the divine love. No one is too humble or unworthy of his love. But human love is too intimate and revealing to be shared with a multitude; it flowers into full beauty only in the closest of personal relationships, ordinarily between a man and a woman who live only for each other. Recognizing this, the stories of Krishna the divine lover focus especially on the love between Krishna and Rādhā, the cowherd girl who becomes his favorite and special partner, eventually to be honored as a Goddess herself. The Brahmavaivarta tells a charming story about their love that depicts their divinity as well as they humanness.

Once when Krishna was a little boy and his father was grazing his cattle in the Vṛndāvana pastures, the child, by superhuman powers, caused a huge storm to come up suddenly. While Nanda worried about how to save himself and his herd, the little boy began to cry out of fear of the storm and the flooding waters. Just then the beautiful Rādhā appeared. She is described as having a gait that shamed even the swans, a face that robbed the harvest moon of its splendor, and eyes that stole the beauty of lotuses blooming in the autumn afternoon. Her shining black hair was fragrant with jasmine blossoms and her beautiful body annointed with musk. Her earrings were brighter than the summer sun at midday and her lips rounder and redder than ripe bimba berries. When she smiled her pearllike teeth surpassed the whiteness of freshly opened water lily buds and her cheeks were perfectly round. On her breasts, firm as bilva fruits, lay necklaces of sapphires and other precious jewels.

When Nanda saw her heavenly beauty, lighting up the skies with a brilliance greater than a million moons, he knew that she was the divine consort of the divine child sitting on his lap. Giving her the child, he asked for a special favor: "Grant me love for the feet of you and Krishna; grant it to us both, O Goddess, mother of the worlds." Rādhā, holding the divine child in her arms, complies willingly. "I shall grant you unsurpassed devotion and love. Day and night you [and your wife] shall both have the rare memory of our lotus feet, by which your hearts

[2]See Brahmavaivarta Pūraṇa, Chapter 5, and Vishnu Pūraṇa, Chapter 5, for typical descriptions.

will flower. By this favor you will be freed from illusion and when you have abandoned your human bodies here you will come to us."

Taking the beautiful child deep into the forest, Rādhā finds him transformed into a handsome dark youth, fragrant with sandalwood and aglow with the graces of a million love gods. Dazed by his beauty, she lovingly drinks the moonlight of his face with her moonbeam eyes, her love-stricken body quivering with anticipation of union. Krishna, seeing her lotus face glowing with love, speaks to his Rādhikā: "You are dearer to me than my life, beautiful Rādhā. As I am, so are you; there is no difference between us. As there is whiteness in milk, heat in fire, and fragrance in earth, so am I in you always. A potter cannot make a pot without clay and a goldsmith cannot make an earring without gold. Likewise, I cannot create without you, for you are the soil of creation and I am the seed. Come and lie with me, good woman, take me to your breast. You are my beauty, adorning me as an ornament adorns the body. People call me Krishna when I am separate from you, but Śri-Krishna when I am united with you. You are the Goddess Śri, the foundation of success and prosperity. You are woman, I am man, Rādhā; so it is set forth in the Vedas" (Brahmavaivarta, 4.16).

The text goes on to describe their wedding and the beautiful play of their love, telling how they annointed and dressed each other and exchanged food and drink, taking it from each other's lips. In love-play they undressed each other, touching and kissing each other in all of the known ways, embracing in every position. When the battle of love was over, Krishna rebraided Rādhā's hair and dressed her body with consummate skill before resuming his childlike form again and allowing Rādhā to take him home to his parents. But every night he resumed his youthful form and Rādhā made beautiful love with him in Vṛndāvana.

The love between Rādhā and Krishna is the subject of the Gītāgovinda, Jayadeva's Love Song of the Dark Lord, one of the most beautiful love poems in the world. Composed in the twelfth century, it gained increasing popularity in succeeding centuries, inspiring temple architecture, song, dance, worship, and poetry throughout India. These songs, along with many others based on this classic work, are still sung today by many devout Hindus.

Like St. John of the Cross, Jayadeva interweaves the sensuous mood and color of human feelings with divine love through skillful poetic use of sound, rhythm, and imagery that never departs from the concrete and sensual level of human love and longing. Yet the divine, and one might say, transcendent, dimensions of God's reality are clearly and forcefully evoked. These verses leave no doubt that, for all its sensuousness, the love between Krishna and Rādhā is an unending cosmic event depicting the eternal divine love.

The opening verse, expressing the subject of the poem, typifies the poet's skillful use of explicitly sensual imagery to evoke an awareness of the divine.

Sky is thickened by clouds,
Forest darkened by Tāmala trees.
Krishna is frightened by the night.
Take him home, Rādhā, says Nanda.
At his request they leave,
Passing thickets of trees along the way,
Until Rādhā's and Mādhava's secret love
Triumphs on the bank of the Jumna.

The flute is the symbol of both Krishna's beauty and his sexuality (Figure 5). Its sweet and penetrating melodies enter the ears and hearts of the cowherd women, summoning them to rendezvous with the young lord under the full moon of an autumn night. In his eleventh song the poet sings to Rādhā of the beautiful Krishna, longing for her love, as he calls to her on his magical flute.

He plays your name on his sweet flute to call you,
Cherishing wind-carried pollen that caressed your delicate body.
On the wind-swept Jumna bank, in a grove of trees,
Garlanded by wild flowers, Krishna waits.

The call of Krishna's flute is absolutely irresistible. Sounding the sweet music of divine love, it summons humankind to a life beyond the chores, cares, and duties of conventional life. Animals and even plants are freed from the restraints of their ordinary existence when they hear Krishna's flute. Chandidāsa describes the power of the flute in the following verse.

How can I describe his relentless flute,
which pulls virtuous women from their homes
and drags them by their hair to Shyam
as thirst and hunger pull the doe to the snare?

Chaste ladies forget their lords,
wise men forget their wisdom,
and clinging vines shake loose from their trees,
hearing that music.
Then how shall a simple dairymaid withstand its call?
(Kinsley, p. 37)

Krishna even enchants and intoxicates himself with his wonderful flute. In a succinct and expressive description of this marvelous symbol of Krishna's incredible beauty and irresistable call, Kinsley says,

By means of his flute, Kṛṣṇa fills himself and the universe with bliss. He distracts everyone and everything from normal activity and enchants them to revel in ecstasy. His flute sends shudders of delight to the very foundations of the world. Natural laws fall away as rocks and trees respond to his call and stars wander from their courses. . . .

**Figure 5.** Krishna playing the flute: Gopas and cows, water with expanded rose, lotuses. 17th century. (Courtesy, Museum of Fine Arts, Boston. Ross Coomaraswamy Collection.)

> His music explodes upon the world and society insisting that all be forgotten. It is time, it proclaims, to join his symphony of joy, to frolic in the forest, to scamper in play, to realize every dream that one has ever dreamed in his world of infinite possibility. Kṛṣṇa's flute incites the world to dance, to lose itself in superfluous rhythms. It invites man to return to that carefree, playful world of his youth. It asks nothing but surrender to its frenzied tune and enthusiastic participation in its magic world.
>
> (pp. 40–41)

When Rādhā and Krishna follow the sound of the flute and surrender themselves to each others' love in answer to the flute's call, their ordinary existence is left far behind. The idyllic bowers of the Vṛndāvana forest where they play at love symbolize the extraordinariness of the world to which love transports them. In the twenty-first song, Jayadeva invites and encourages Rādhā to enter Krishna's intimate world of love, describing his forest hideaway with words of sensuous praise. "Come," he says, "Revel in wild luxury on the sweet thicket floor, in a thick bed of rose petals plucked as an offering, in a shimmering retreat piled with flowers, in the fragrant breeze of blowing sandal-forest winds. There swarming bees, drunk on honey, hum soft sounds. There flocks of cuckoos cry sweet sounds, in tangles of creeping vines growing new shoots."

Reminding Rādhā that her beauty fulfills itself in attracting her lover and enriching their lives through joyful union, her friend urges her to fulfill her ardent desire and satisfy her passionate yearning for Krishna by receiving him in loving embrace: His need of you is as great as yours of him; he is your willing slave. Do not be afraid that you will get hurt. Open your heart to him in love. Referring to Rādhā as Śrī (the name of Vishnu's divine consort), she says,

> Carrying you in his heart
> Inflamed with love so long, has drained him.
> He longs to drink the nectar of your sweet berry lips.
> Adorn his body with your own.
> Like a slave captured by Śrī's darting eyes
> He worships your lotus feet.
> Why are you afraid?
>
> (Song 21, verse 9)

And of course, Rādhā comes to Krishna to consecrate their joyful union in loving embrace, for the union of lover and beloved is the point of the entire cycle of poems and songs that Jayadeva sings and recites.

But only in the twelfth and last part of this lyrical drama do the lovers consummate their love. Symbolic of the divine love whereby human beings are reunited with God, the love between Rādhā and Krishna cannot be consummated until the forces that separate them are overcome. The intense longing for each other, the fear of surrendering themselves to each other, and the feelings of pride and shame that separate them symbolize the human relationship with the divine reality. Much as we long for reunion with the ultimate reality from which we issued and of which we are a part, the pride, stubborness, and fear that spring from the ego hold us back. But once having tasted the nectar of divine love, separation is painful and the soul becomes desolate. Jayadeva shows us this initial taste of love as Krishna and Rādhā spend a night of love together. But then the young cowherd abandons her to play with the other cowherd girls. Now Rādhā becomes, by turns, jealous, lovesick, desolate, and hopeful. Throughout all but the first and last parts, she is a separated lover, longing for reunion.

Despite her yearning, a combination of pride and shame keep her from going to him, while her imagination torments her with pictures of him making love to another. Anger and jealousy harden her heart to his entreaties.

> The teethmarks she left on your lip causes anguish in my heart;
> Why does it now recall the union of your body with mine?
> Damn you, Mādhava! Go Keśava, leave me!
> Do not bring your lies to me!
> Go to her, Krishna,
> Let her ease your despair.
>
> (Song 17, verse 6)

Turned away by sullen jealousy and locked out of her heart, the proud Krishna suffers as much as Rādhā, for he is held captive by the unbreakable cord of her longing. The thought of her lover's suffering eventually overcomes Rādhā's jealousy and pride, and tormented by their mutual hurt she listens to her friends' advice:

> Why create a despondent burden in your heart?
> Listen to me tell how he regrets betraying you.
> Don't turn your wounded pride against Mādhava.
> He too is proud, despairing Rādhā.
>
> Let Hari come! Let him speak sweet words!
> Why condemn your heart to loneliness?
>
> (Song 18, verse 8)

Coming to his secret place, her useless modesty and shame left behind, she listens to his pleas to revive his life with her offering of love. Intoxicated by his beauty and overcome by passionate love, she surrenders herself completely to him, and the play of divine love begins. The song that the poet Vidyāpati puts in Rādhā's mouth expresses the total joy and fulfillment found in the embrace of divine love:

> The moon has shone upon me,
> the face of my beloved.
> O night of joy!
>
> Joy permeates all things.
> My life: joy,
> my youth fulfillment.

> Today my house is again
> home,
>   today my body is
> my body.
> . . .
> for now my body has meaning
> in the presence of my beloved.
> (Kinsley, pp. 51–52)

Come to me in loving devotion; surrender yourself to me and you will be saved, so says Krishna to Arjuna in the Gītā, sounding the central theme of devotional Hinduism. But it is Krishna as the child and youth of Vṛndāvana that shows the way, lighting up the world with the joy and delightful play of the child and transporting human life into another world through the self-surrender and pure ecstasy of total loving.

As child and lover, God's joyful presence is warm and approachable, irresistably appealing. No wonder that Krishna, embodiment of divine beauty, joy, and love, is beloved by Hindus as no other God. Play and beauty are sacred. They express the fullness of the divine reality. Showing the way, Krishna invites humankind to come to him in play. Through play—including singing, dancing, music, and love making—says Krishna, we discover and fulfill our own true nature, reaching the highest bliss.

## Summary

Devotional Hinduism seeks a relationship with ultimate reality in its personal manifestation as the Supreme Person or God. But God takes many forms, male and female, human and nonhuman; everything that exists embodies the divine reality and is, therefore, sacred and recognizable as a God or Goddess. Out of a potentially infinite number of forms, more than a dozen have assumed great importance. However, of all the deities, none has been so beloved as Krishna.

He embodies the divine beauty, grace, and joy of the ultimate reality. An incarnation of Vishnu in the Gītā, he comes to be seen as the essential form of God by his devotees. Although they recognize that he is the supreme Vishnu who reveals himself to Arjuna in the Gītā and that he is the cosmic creator and champion warrior against injustice, the Krishna they come to in loving devotion is primarily the child and youth of Vṛndāvana. In the wonderfully creative, spontaneous play of the child and the warm loving embrace of the amorous youth, his devotees feel the beauty and playfulness of the divine reality resonating in their deepest being, calling them to surrender to God's greatness.

As an adorable little child, Krishna exudes joy. His play is wonderfully free and spontaneous, and his beauty is enchanting. His devotees can be as intimate with him as with any little child, allowing them to feel the joy and beauty of ultimate reality in their personal relationships with Krishna.

As a youthful lover, Krishna symbolizes the truth that through deep personal love, human separateness, and loneliness can be transcended. The love between Krishna and Rādhā tells his devotees that, in the fullness of love, a deeper level of reality is attained, the level of divine existence.

Through his manifestations as playful child and youthful lover, Krishna reveals that God is pure love, beauty, joy, and freedom. Come to God through play and love, Krishna tells his devotees.

## Suggestions for Further Reading

*The Sword and the Flute*, by David R. Kinsley (Berkeley: University of California Press, 1977), is a brief but compelling study of Krishna and Kālī that, more than any other book I know, brings these deities to life. There is no better place to begin one's journey into the Hindu devotional mind than with this small paperback book. It is exciting reading and contains a good bibliography.

*Love Song of the Dark Lord: Jayadeva's Gītagovinda*, ed. and trans. by Barbara Stoler Miller (New York: Columbia University Press, 1977), offers one of the most influential devotional poem-song cycles in an excellent translation. The sixty-page introduction to this paperback is enormously helpful without being pedantic. The poem itself ranks with the finest devotional love poetry in the world.

*The Divine Hierarchy: Popular Hinduism in Central India*, by Lawrence A. Babb (New York: Columbia University Press, 1975), will give the reader a good idea of what the practice of Hinduism is like in this part of India—a practice that is representative of practice throughout most of India—and provides some analysis of the underlying motifs and functions of devotional Hinduism. He may exaggerate the importance of purity and pollution, but these concerns do play a significant role in Hindu practice.

*Krishna: Myths, Rites and Attitudes*, ed. Milton Singer (Honolulu: East-West Center Press, 1966), is an interdisciplinary study of Krishnaism by eight outstanding scholars. Not always easy going, it is rewarding reading for anyone interested in Krishna and the role of Krishnaism within the broader Hindu context. Another collection of essays, *Hinduism: New Essays in the History of Religion*, ed. Bardwell L. Smith (Leiden: E. J. Brill, 1976), focuses on Hindu devotionalism. But it also contains an extremely interesting structural analysis of the myth of the Churning of the Ocean of Milk by J. Bruce Long.

*Classical Hindu Mythology*, ed. and trans. by Cornelia Dimmitt and J. A. B. van Buitenen (Philadelphia: Temple University Press, 1978), and *Hindu Myths*, trans. and intro. by Wendy Doniger O'Flaherty (New York: Penguin Books, 1975), are both excellent collections of stories about the divine beings of Hinduism. The former selects only from the purāṇas, whereas *Hindu Myths* draws upon other sources as well.

# 11

# Devotional Hinduism: Kālī and Shiva

## Kālī

In many respects Kālī is just the opposite of Krishna. In her are manifested all the terrifying and hideous dimensions of reality. Whereas Krishna's beauty and playfulness invite us to discover ourselves in the joy and beauty of play, Kālī's hideous and terrifying presence reminds us of suffering, violence, and death and our need to come to terms with these aspects of existence. She is the very personification of death and destruction.

But she is also the Divine Mother, for God in her feminine manifestations takes many forms. She is Mata, the loving mother; Lakshmi, source of success and happiness; Durgā, destroyer of evil; Saraswati, power of knowledge; Śrī, the embodiment of beauty; and Pārvatī, the embodiment of the peace of virtue and love; as well as Kālī, the fearsome. Dozens of other manifestations and names appear in the literature, revealing that no single manifestation is the total undivided ultimate reality and attesting to the fluidity of metamorphosis that reveals God's power to assume any form at will.

Kālī's origins within Hindu mythology are by no means clear. Most likely she combines various features of earlier deities, perhaps accommodating features of different Āryan, Indus, and tribal Goddesses. In the Caṇḍi portion of the Markandeya Purāṇa, she is sometimes seen as a form of Durgā, "the Goddess," thereby associating her with an earlier Goddess whose position in the pantheon was secure at this time. This is a common device, and most new Gods and Goddesses that enter the

Hindu pantheon do so by an initial identification with an already established deity. Eventually, as they become accepted and established in their own right, these earlier identifications fade into the background. But in the "great Goddess" portion of the Purāṇa, Kālī already has many of the characteristics that the more recent tradition associates with her.

According to the purāṇic account, Kālī is manifested in her fearsome form to defeat the demons and rescue the Gods. The Gods, conquered by the demon armies, have petitioned Durgā to help them. Assuring them that she will defeat the enemy and set them free, she prepares for battle against the demon armies led by Caṇḍa and Muṇḍa. When the first demon warriors approach her with drawn bows and unsheathed swords, Durgā becomes furious. Her face turns black as ink and from between her brows emerges the terrible Kālī, brandishing a sword and carrying a noose. She is described as wearing a garland of human heads, carrying a skull-topped staff, and covered by a tiger skin. Her mouth gapes open, her long tongue protrudes, thirsty for blood, and her sunken eyes are red with anger as she fills the four quarters of space with her howling. With her shriveled skin and protruding fangs, she is a gruesome sight indeed. Kālī does not simply attack and defeat the demons; she completely destroys them. The story tells how, with one hand, she seized elephants with riders, drivers, warriors, and bells and hurled them down her throat. In the same way she devoured warriors with their horses, and chariots with their drivers, grinding them up horribly with teeth. Those that she did not devour she trampled to death, slayed with the sword, bashed with her skull-topped club, or crushed between her jaws.

When Caṇḍa and Muṇḍa saw their whole army being destroyed in this way, they rushed at the horrible Goddess. Caṇḍa showered her with arrows while Muṇḍa hurled thousands of discuses. But all these weapons she caught in her mouth, where they shone like a multitude of suns entering the belly of the clouds. Then, howling horribly and laughing wickedly, her mouth gaping wide and fangs glittering, Kālī mounted her huge lion and, in a terrible rage, cut off Caṇḍa's head and ran her sword through Muṇḍa. The deed done, she grabbed the heads of the two demons and, shrieking with fierce wicked laughter, presented them to Durgā as a sacrificial offering. Other images of the black Goddess are even more gruesome and horrifying.

As death personified, Kālī is widely known as the Goddess of the Cremation Ground. There she feeds the corpses to which she first gave life and from which she then sucked the warm lifeblood in their hour of death.

She is also known as the Goddess of the Ocean of Blood and is depicted standing in a boat floating on an ocean of blood. Dipping her skull bowl into the warm red blood, she thirstily drinks the lifeblood of the children of the world that she is continually creating, sustaining, and consuming.

An early eighteenth-century Kāngrā painting shows her dancing on her husband's corpse. Surrounded by skulls and bones and jackals and vultures, the terrible Kālī, black as death and garlanded with severed heads, does her eternal dance of destruction. But another aspect of Kālī is also revealed in this painting, for, although in her right hands she brandishes a sword and a scissors, symbolizing her power to destroy and cut the cord of life, her left hands display a bowl, the symbol of nourishment, and a lotus, the symbol of life and purity. And there are two bodies beneath her dancing feet. The lower Shiva, a bearded naked ascetic, completely out of touch with her nourishing energy is totally lifeless. But the upper Shiva, beautiful and youthful, is stirring into life as a result of contact with her divine energy.

The highly stylized Bengali painting shown here (Figure 6) is less gruesome, but also reveals Kālī as the source of both life and death. Here, too, the lower Shiva ("Shava") is totally lifeless while the upper Shiva, gaze fixed on "The Mother," is stirring to life.

This painting reminds me of a story—and its inevitable moral—told by one of the attendants at the Kālī temple in Calcutta (Kalighat) during my first visit to India in 1964. According to this story, Kālī was summoned by all the other Gods and Goddesses to destroy a wicked monster who seemed invincible because from every drop of blood he shed there sprang forth a thousand new demons fully grown and ready to do battle for him. But he and his hordes were no match for the blood-thirsty Goddess, who leaped and whirled among them, cutting them down by

**Figure 6.** Kālī dancing on Shiva-shava. (Courtesy, Victoria and Albert Museum.)

**Figure 7.** Kālī, the devourer. (Courtesy, Victoria and Albert Museum.)

the thousands with her sword. Before their drops of blood could reproduce their existence she lapped them up, drinking all the blood they shed. Finally, she swallowed the blood seed monster himself.

Then, beginning her victory dance she became more and more frenzied, forgetting what she was doing. She was time gone crazy and out of control, threatening all creation. As the earth trembled and quaked, and destruction of the universe appeared imminent, the Gods came to her husband, Shiva, and begged that he intercede and stop this wild dance of destruction. But she paid no heed even to him. Finally, in desperation he threw himself at her feet. Still she paid no attention and began dancing on his body. Eventually, realizing what she was doing, she stopped her frenzy, saving the universe from the ravages of time's mad dance. As the storyteller commented, Kālī's terrible dance of destruction is ultimately the destruction of evil. But all those who come to her for refuge, throwing themselves at her feet, she rescues, destroying evil for them just as she did for the Gods and Goddesses when Shiva threw himself at her feet.

To encounter Kālī in any of her horrible manifestations is to recognize and feel the instability and disorder of the world and its ever-present dangers. Heinrich Zimmer refers to a wood-carving from Nepal that shows her as the terrible all-consuming power of life. (See Figure 7.) She looks like death itself, with her fierce hollowed faced, sunken stomach, and skeletal limbs. Squatting on a corpse she feeds herself on her victim's intestines with one hand, while the other cups one of her breasts, suggesting her life-giving power even while she is consuming the life she gives.[1]

## DESTROYER OF DEATH AND FEAR

Why these horrible and gruesome images of Kālī? The answer is twofold. First, they help to awaken us to the reality of suffering and death and of fear and despair. Her presence in the graveyard confronts us with our own death and loneliness, the pain and suffering of all creatures, the violence and spitefulness of human beings, and the piteous condition of all created existence. All the things that we are conditioned in a thousand ways to suppress and ignore, but that continue to feed our deepest fears and anxieties, confront us in the images of Kālī. Hurt and suffering are so integral a part of human life that they cannot successfully be ignored or denied. To attempt to do either is simply to drive our fears of them deeper into the unconscious, where they manifest themselves as a deep disquieting anxiety and disaffection with life itself. Second, not until they are faced can these fears be conquered. Kālī represents an embodiment of the fearful aspects of existence that helps us to face and conquer our fears of hurt, disorder, destruction, loneliness, and death.

The aim of Kālī is not to terrorize, but to remind us of reality and to force us to confront it realistically exactly as it is—beauty, joy, and life

[1]See Heinrich Zimmer, *Myths and Symbols in Indian Art and Civilization* (New York: Harper Torchbooks, 1962), p. 213.

mixed with ugliness, sorrow, and death. Every devotee knows that, no matter how terrible her manifestations, if the Goddess is approached correctly she will be totally helpful, the Divine Mother who loves and protects her children. Vivekananda, Ramakrishna's foremost disciple, put it nicely:

> The heart must become a
> burial ground
> Pride, selfishness, and desire all
> broken into dust,
> Then and then alone will the Mother
> dance there!
> (Kinsley, p. 145)

But as Kinsley points out, "Kālī is Mother to her devotees not because she protects them from the way things really are but because she reveals to them their mortality and thus releases them to act fully and freely, releases them from the incredible binding web of 'adult' pretense, practicality and rationality" (p. 146).

Although Kālī may be "the mother" to her devotees, her association with death is inescapable. Her very name is the feminine form of Kāla, or time, the destroyer of all beings. Her mighty exploits occur on the battlefield, a field of death; her home is the cemetery or cremation ground; and her food is the blood and bowels of killed offerings. On special days of Kālī worship, her image is set up in the cremation ground and the bloody devotional offerings made there.

The point of this preoccupation with death and the Goddess with whom it is associated is profound. Kālī, as time and death personified, represents not merely death but the conquest of death. By Death will death be defeated. The author of the following Bengali lyric understood well this function of the Divine Mother in her form as Kālī.

> My Mind, why so fretful, like a motherless child? Coming into the world you sit brooding, shivering the dread of death. Yet there is a Death that conquers death, the Mightiest Death, which lies beneath the Mother's feet. You, a serpent, fearing frogs! How amazing! What terror of death is this in you, the child of the Mother-Heart of all? What folly is this, what utter madness? Child of that Mother-Heart, what will you dread? Wherefore brood in vain sorrow?
>
> (Kinsley, p. 141)

To her devotees Kālī gives the courage and strength to conquer fear of time and death, making possible the joyous freedom to accept the full richness of life and to participate wholeheartedly in its total expression in every moment of existence. For them life is not a curse, but a wonderful blessing.

This brings us to the second part of the answer to why Kālī is imaged in such horrible and gruesome ways. She is the personification of the total energy and process of existence—as well as the embodiment of time in which the eternal energy manifests itself. Existence confronts us with two faces. The first is its mere presence or being, which the Indian mind tends to personify as masculine. The second is its power or energy, which is usually personified in feminine form. From this divine energy or Shakti, all the creative processes issue—this is why the various Goddesses are frequently called simply Shakti.

But creation has its destructive side as well, for as the seers of the Upaniṣads had already noted, living beings are food for each other; through the death and destruction of one being, another lives. As Kinsley notes, "She [Kālī] is not only the creative source of life but also the dimension of life that untiringly insists on sustenance, satisfaction, satiation. Her lolling tongue, her blood-smeared lips and body, and her bloodied cleaver represent the irreducible truth that life sustains itself on life, that the throb of life—the pulsing beat of rushing blood, the insistent flow of sap—demands an unending stream of life energy to go on, that death and decay form the only fertile ground for the hungry pulse of life" (p. 156). The creative Goddess in her terrible and destructive form forces this realization upon us and allows us to face the repressed fears of death and destruction that, in the final analysis, prevent us from experiencing the beauty and joy present in existence.

Although the gruesome appearance of Kālī and her wild, blood-thirsty caprice is a long way from the middle path of the Buddha, she embodies a kind of parallel to the four noble truths of Buddhism. Through her, Hindus realize the depth and pervasiveness of duḥkha and also the truth that its causes can be recognized and overcome. Through the worship and devotion that is part of the Kālī devotee's spiritual discipline, duḥkha is confronted and conquered, enabling one to see her as the joyous loving mother. Hindus recognize that beneath her frightening appearance is the truth that life, though fraught with suffering and terminated in death, is ultimately rooted in joy. But to realize this joy, suffering and death must be faced. Only by conquering them through recognizing them for what they are, thereby reconciling one's hopes and expectations with them, can peace and joy be found.

This is why Kālī reveals death and hurt for what they are, in all their horrible and frightening characteristics. The aim is never to destroy the devotee but, rather, to set him or her free from the deep-seated fears of these ever-present forces of existence. Paradoxically, it is her fearsome appearance that enables the devotee to see her as the joyous and loving mother and to appreciate fully the joy and beauty of existence. Freedom comes in facing the objects of one's fear and conquering them, not in running away from them in fear. Duḥkha cannot be overcome by trying to withdraw from the world; only by confronting it, can it be conquered.

## THE DIVINE MOTHER

Kālī, the fearsome destroyer, is the Death that destroys death and the Fearsome that destroys fear. But she is also the Divine Mother, the creator and sustainer of life. It may at first seem paradoxical that the personification of death and destruction should be seen as a loving mother, but the inner truth of this paradox is that, when death and terror are faced and accepted in a spirit of love, they lose their hold over us. There is no way to conquer death except by accepting it. To accept it is to embrace it. What a difficult thing to do! But how easy to embrace one's mother! When death is the mother it can be embraced through love for the mother and thereby overcome. Here, in loving devotion one conquers time, death, and fear.

This function of the Goddess has inspired Tantra, where the underlying aim is to become aware that all of the dimensions and powers of existence are actually manifestations of the divine energy, or Shakti. Because this is exceedingly difficult to accomplish with the horrifying and repulsive aspects of life, they become the special focus of Tantric practice, for unless even these aspects are recognized as part of the divine reality, insecurity, anxiety, and fear cannot be overcome. That is why Tantric practices sometimes include eating meat, drinking liquor, and having sexual intercourse outside of marriage, practices that are regarded as extremely polluting and sinful outside of Tantrism. The rationale of using them as spiritual aids is that the sinful and polluting, too, must be faced and accepted as part of life to get free from its bondage.

It should be pointed out that, contrary to popular opinion, Tantric practice does not encourage the degradation of life or promote licentiousness. Its aim is the spiritual transformation of life by conquering those aspects of it that by their very repulsiveness are particularly destructive and binding. Tantric metaphysics can be summed up in the observation that, if you are going to accept any part of existence as sacred, you must accept the whole bloody mess as sacred. Its central methodology is encapsuled in the axiom that poison is to be fought with poison.

Ramakrishna, a nineteenth-century saint and Kālī devotee, expresses this attitude very well in describing his own Tantric practice. Noting that under the Tantric influence the distinction between the sacred and the ordinary and the pure and the polluting was overcome, he describes how he sometimes even rode a dog and shared his food with him—both especially degrading and polluting experiences from a non-Tantric Hindu perspective. "Sometimes I rode on a dog and fed him with luchi, also eating part of the bread myself. I realized that the whole world was filled with God alone," he says.[2]

In his early life Ramakrishna was filled with a deep sense of loneliness and separation from the Divine Mother. Frantically, and almost desperately, he attempted to reach her and overcome this separation through ecstatic mystic visions. As he developed his psychic energies and achieved greater control of their powers, he came to see the divine presence in everything around him. No matter where he was or what he

[2]Swami Nikhilananda, trans., *The Gospel of Sri Ramakrishna* (New York: Ramakrishna-Vivekanada Center, 1952), p. 544.

was doing, there was the Divine Mother, as close as every thought and feeling. Even a dirty dog was the Divine Mother for Ramakrishna now, because he had overcome the fear of the horrible and polluting destructive forces of the world by realizing their innate divinity within the total sacredness of all existence.

Ramakrishna's aim was to become as childlike as possible, for he recognized the innocence and fearlessness of a child as issuing from the total acceptance of everything and everyone as good and pure. The child does not regard anything as innately evil, destructive, or polluting. These attitudes and the accompanying fears are only learned gradually, as a child grows up and makes all the "appropriate" distinctions between the sacred and the profane, the pure and the polluting, life and death, peace and violence, and so on. But to overcome fear and sin one must unlearn all this and retain the childlike state of innocent delight in all aspects of existence. Of course, one cannot become a little child again, and the knowledge of evil, fear, and destruction cannot easily be unlearned. This is precisely why the difficult practices of Tantra must be taken up and evil faced and conquered directly on its own terms. Only then will the underlying sacredness of all existence be realized, allowing a person to delight in the totality of existence without fear or insecurity. And Kālī is the supreme helper in this difficult task.

There is another important aspect of childlike existence that Ramakrishna emphasized. A child creates his world in play, even as the Divine Mother creates this world in play. To appreciate the sacred play of the Divine Mother, one must be like a little child and join in this play. Ramakrishna says that in mystic vision he saw that the divine energy of existence that expresses itself in the creation and destruction of the world, when personified as the Mother, is like a child at play. Her playground is the universe and all existence her playthings. Here Kālī is obviously much more than personified fear and destruction; she is the ultimate reality in personal form.

Indeed, when Ramakrishna considers the question of Kālī's relation to Brahman, the absolute reality, he states unequivocally,

> Thus Brahman and Shakti are identical. If you accept the one, you must accept the other. It is like fire and its power to burn. . . .
>
> Thus one cannot think of Brahman without Shakti, or of Shakti without Brahman. One cannot thing of the Absolute without the Relative, or of the Relative without the Absolute.
>
> The Primordial Power is ever at play. She is creating, preserving, and destroying in play, as it were. This Power is called Kālī. Kālī is verily Brahman, and Brahman is verily Kālī. It is one and the same Reality.
>
> (Nikhilananda, p. 136)

This is a very clear expression of the traditional understanding that the Goddess in her various forms embodies the dynamism of the world, both in its creative and destructive forms. Like a human mother, the Divine Goddess generates existence out of her own being, sharing her life with the newly created existence. But the other side of creation is destruction, and the Divine Mother is also represented in her destructive capacity. In truth, the Goddess has two faces, one smiling with grace and love, the other scowling blackly, fearful and horrifying. By accepting her in her darkness her devotees are able to conquer their fears and come to realize her joyful and loving nature.

The feminine form of God appeals especially to those who find the mother-child relationship and symbol more satisfying as a revelation of the divine reality and of a possible human relationship to that reality than the father-child relationship. While Krishna provides the model of a loving relationship between lovers, the Divine Mother provides the model for a loving relationship between mother and child, a relationship that begins with the sharing of the mother's life in the child's embryonic beginnings, nurture, and refuge within her body, a sharing that continues as she cradles the infant in her arms and nurses it from her breasts.

The mother makes no demands on the infant and small child, freely showering on the child the same love through which he or she was conceived and given life in the womb. In return, the child can trust the mother completely and openly, without feelings of guilt and obligation. Total trust, security, and love characterize the ideal mother-child relationship. A mother's love does not have to be earned by the child; it is freely given, even though already before birth the infant has ruined the mother's digestion, disturbed her sleep, and kicked her from inside the womb. As the child grows, all the mother demands is its love and trust. When the child gives its mother its complete trust and love, all actions, no matter how mischievous or naughty, can be overlooked—or at least forgiven—in the mother's love. In the same way, Kālī's devotees are secure in her love and protection—no matter how fearsome her appearance. She is the Divine Mother, as Ramakrishna emphasized over and over.

## Shiva

Although Krishna and Kālī both embody the main characteristics of the other Gods and Goddesses, thereby allowing each of them to represent the totality of the divine, the fact remains that Krishna's primary identification is with the beautiful and joyous aspects of the divine, whereas Kālī's primary identification is with its ugly and fearsome aspects. Shiva, on the other hand, has no primary identification with any particular aspect of reality, for he represents the underlying unity of existence in which all opposites are reconciled.

In him are embodied the dualities of death and life, ascetic withdrawal and passionate involvement, creativity and destruction, love and anger. He is the great ascetic, dressed in a blackened animal skin and smeared with the ashes that signify his death to this world. Yet he is also the beautiful Lord of the Dance, dancing out the creative rhythms of all existence. In Shiva these dualities do not cancel each other out but complement and enrich each other. They are not something added to existence; *they are existence*. Even male and female are united in Shiva, both in his own person as half male, half female and in his marriage to Shakti, the eternal female.

By combining these dualities in his own being, Shiva shows the complementariness of these opposites and their fundamental unity. Liberation does not take place in the absence of bondage, and joy does not occur except in the presence of sorrow. Unless these opposites can be reconciled in a higher unity, it is impossible to reach the unending peace and freedom of mokṣa. Shiva's linga, his fundamental symbol, is not only the axis of the universe, but extends infinitely beyond, suggesting that even the polarity between the temporal and the eternal, and the polarity between manifested existence and the unmanifested Brahman, are overcome in his being.

One of the ways of emphasizing Shiva's transcendence is to refuse to give him a fully developed personality and connected life story in the religious literature. Stories abound in the mythology of Shiva, but they reveal now one aspect of his existence, now another, never giving primary significance to any one aspect and never connecting them all together in a single life history. Of course, Shiva's transcendence does not exclude his immanence in all existence, for he is omnipresent in this manifested world that he creates. Therefore these stories are important in conveying different aspects of the divine existence as it is present in the ordinary world of human experience.

## MYTHS AND NAMES

One old and well-known story about Shiva's incredible power is told in the Mahābhārata. The demons, in their eternal mischief and war with the Gods, had succeeded in achieving a kind of immortality by immersion in a magic lake that restored the dead to life. Now, totally without fear of destruction by the Gods, they were ravaging the world and destroying civilization. The multitude of Gods, knowing themselves powerless against the demons with their potent magic, came to Shiva for help. The text says that though they had imagined many splendid forms of this great God, when they saw that he contained all of them in his manifested form while infinitely exceeding them in his unmanifested being, they prostrated themselves before him in awe and honor. Refusing his offer of a portion of his power because they knew it was too great for them, they surrendered half of their power to him, requesting that he use it to destroy their enemies, thus clearly acknowledging that among the Gods he was the Great God. Summoning his mighty energies that dwell within all of the cosmic powers and that energize every form of existence, he concentrated mightily on the three cities where the demons lived. So great was his concentration that the three cities became one, making it easy for him to destroy the demons and burn their city with a single arrow from his majestic bow (12.274).

Another story recalls how long ago a great sage by the name of Mankanaka had achieved such great success in his yogic efforts to become one with all of existence that when he cut his finger he bled plant sap. Overjoyed by his success, he began to dance with such energy and power that the whole universe forgot its business and began to dance with him. Alarmed, the Gods asked Shiva to stop him, for their sake and that of the whole universe.

"Do you think it such a great thing to go beyond the limitations of human and animal life and merge with the greatness of the primordial life-sap?" Shiva asked. "Look at this." So saying, he cut his own thumb with the tip of his finger. When the sage saw the snow-white ashes pouring forth, demonstrating Shiva's identity with that greatness which goes beyond even life and death, he was restored to a more modest and appropriate perspective and ceased his proud dance (Vāmana Purāṇa, 17).

Still another story illustrates the tension between the ascetic and the erotic that has resulted in an interesting cultural ambivalence toward these two opposite attitudes toward sex. Shiva's semen is the potent seed from which this whole universe arises. Yet he is the supreme ascetic, refusing to spend his seed. He is sexually attracted to the beautiful Pārvatī, daughter of the mountains, and has no peace until he takes her in marriage. But once married, he refuses her the love that she needs and practices asceticism. Although father of all creation, he refuses to impregnate his own wife. Pārvatī's children are of curious origins. Her son Ganesha (or Ganapati), an extremely popular deity in contemporary Hinduism, was born from the dirt she removed from her own body while bathing and became both her companion and her guard. The story of how Ganesha came to be elephant headed illustrates Shiva's quick temper and outrageous behavior.

Once when Ganesha was guarding the bath house, Shiva arrived and attempted to enter. Not recognizing the lord, Ganesha beat him with his staff. But even after Shiva explained that he was Pārvatī's husband, young Ganesha refused to let him enter. Now Shiva was sorely perplexed: "If I back down, people will say that I am afraid of my wife," he mused. "But if I fight her guardian, I am fighting with her. It is not easy to know what to do." As his rage mounted, he began to fume: "How can a woman be so stubborn, especially toward her own husband? This is all her fault! So let her reap the fruits of her action." So saying, he directed his armies to wage all-out war against Ganesha and his forces. Furious with rage because the battle was not going well, Shiva, watching for an opportunity, cut off Ganesha's head with a mighty blow—without ever discovering that he was his wife's son!

Now, the story continues, Pārvatī's rage threatened to destroy the world. A million Gods were destroyed by her mighty power before Shiva agreed to restore the youth's life. "Go north, he told his entourage, and cut off the head of whomever you first meet and give it to the slain youth." As it turned out, the first living thing they met was a one-tusked elephant. Following instructions, they severed its head and placed it on Ganesha's body, thereby restoring him to life as the elephant-headed one.

Interestingly, Ganesha is in many respects Shiva's opposite. He is happy and sociable, a grantor of boons and prosperity, commonly worshipped as the Lord of Success and Prosperity.

Of course, just because Shiva is the great destroyer does not mean that he does not create, sustain, and nourish existence as well. In numerous stories he is shown using his mighty powers to sustain and protect life on earth. One of the better known of these stories tells how he made possible the descent of the heavenly Gangā (Ganges River) to earth. Once there was a drought so bad that the saintly King Bhagīratha could not even find enough water to make the required ancestoral offerings. Through enormous ascetic powers generated by a thousand years of the severest penances, he was able to persuade Brahmā to let the waters of the heavenly river descend to earth. But because the heavenly Gangā was so enormous that the force of its water's pouring directly onto the earth would split and shatter the planet, Brahmā advised King Bhagīratha to continue his austerities until the great Shiva would notice and come to his aid. Sure enough, after an additional year of the most intense concentration imaginable, Shiva noticed and agreed to help. Placing his mighty head in the path of the descending stream, he cushioned the river's descent with his long matted hair, allowing it to spread gently down over the Himalayas and into the hot and dusty Indian plains below.

Another story illustrating concern for and protection of existence tells how he drank up the poisonous venom that threatened the whole universe. The Gods and the demons were churning the great ocean of milk to obtain from it the nectar of immortality. Using the divine serpent Vāsuki as the churning rope and the great Mt. Mandara as the churning rod, they churned furiously for a thousand years. Suddenly a terrible poisonous venom began gushing from the serpent's thousand mouths, threatening the very existence of humans, Gods, and demons. Moved by the request of the great Vishnu, Shiva agreed to receive the poison as a gift of the first fruits of the churning, swallowing the poison as if it were the nectar of immortality, thereby saving existence from extermination. Although Shiva's great powers prevented the poison from harming him, the venom left his throat a dark blue color, a characteristic frequently depicted in artistic representations, and the source of one of his epithets, Nīlakaṇṭha, or Blue-Throat.

Blue-Throat is only one of the many names of Shiva, most of them derived from his various Godly exploits. All together he has 1,008 names, a number suggesting that ultimately he is unnamable. Most frequently he is called simply Shiva, which means "auspicious." But he is also known as Hara, the Great Remover, who destroys and sweeps away everything that gets in his way. Although at one time this name probably signified his function as God of destruction and source of fire and fever, when he came to be recognized as Lord of the Gods (Maheshvara), this title was sometimes interpreted to mean that he is the destroyer even of destruction. In a similar way, as Mahākāla, or Great Time, he is the master of time, consuming all beings in the rushing stream of time, but simultaneously the bringer of eternal life, for he devours time itself. He performs a similar function as Lord of the Sleep, for when existence becomes weary and run down, it enters into the deep sleep of Shiva who revitalizes and re-creates it. In contemporary imagery, we might think of the Lord of Sleep as the great recycling agent who devours the old, spent, and worn out existence, only to create it again in new forms.

Other names of Shiva reveal his protective and beneficent nature. Shaṅkara (Giver of Joy) and Shambhu (Abode of Joy) signify his role as the final resting place of all beings, for only in the Great Lord is eternal bliss found. As Pashupati, Lord of the Beasts, he is the divine herdsman. All created beings are his herd, and he is their protector and keeper, for although the destroyer, he is also the refuge of all beings. He is also called the Great Yogin, for he transcends even his own creative and destructive powers by the techniques of yoga, through which the unmanifest source of manifest existence is realized. In the sectarian literature, the titles Great Lord (Maheshvara) and Great God (Mahadeva) are used frequently, suggesting his superiority over other Gods.

Although the myths of Shiva provide some insight into this great God, his iconographic images are much more revealing. The linga is the primary symbol of his transcendence, regarded by tradition as the only "Immovable" symbol. The popular portrayal as Lord of the Dance is a wonderful revelation of his divine energy and his power to unify polar opposites.

## ICONOGRAPHIC IMAGES

It is as Lord of the Dance that Shiva's simultaneous functions as destroyer and creator are most vividly portrayed. (See Figure 8.) Here, embodying the primordial creative energies of the universe, he transforms the beat of his dance into the rhythms of life and the forms of his energetic movements into the teeming multitudes of life-forms. This whole universe is nothing other than the effects of Shiva's eternal dance, which both creates and destroys the world in a never-ending process.

In his upper right hand Shiva holds the drum that furnishes the rhythm for his dance. It symbolizes the eternal sound vibrating in the ether of space to create the first forms of existence and the first stirrings of revelation and truth. Opposite, held in the palm of the upper left hand, is a tongue of flame, representing the forces of destruction. These two polar forces—creativity embodied in sound and destruction embodied in fire—keep each other in check. In their balance they constitute the continuous creation and destruction that mark all manifested existence.

But there is nothing to be feared in this frenzied dance of creation and destruction, as signified by the lower right hand, which is displayed in a "fear-not" gesture. The lower left hand, held in a pose imitating that of an elephant's "hand" (trunk), points to the upraised left foot, which, when worshipped, provides refuge and salvation for Shiva's devotees.

**Figure 8.** Naṭarāja: Shiva as Lord of the dance. Chola period, 12th century. (Courtesy, The Asia Society: Mr. and Mrs. John D. Rockefeller 3rd Collection.)

The right foot is shown dancing on the demon of ignorance, which must be stamped out to attain the pure wisdom that will release one from bondage to the unceasing creative-destructive forces of the world.

Thus, the dancing Shiva embodies all five activities of the primordial energy commonly worshipped as his five great manifestations: creation, maintenance, destruction, concealment, and divine favor. The hand with the drum signifies the creative power and rhythm, the hand with the flame signifies destruction, and the "fear-not" gesture symbolizes maintenance. The right foot dances on the embodiment of the concealing ignorance that hides the true nature of reality, causing us to mistake the play of opposites for the ultimate. The uplifted left foot signifies the favor of acceptance and revelation that the Lord grants those who come to him in devotion and worship.

But the incessant energetic gyrations of the cosmic dancer do not exhaust the nature of the great Lord. Look at his face! It is wonderfully calm, entirely removed from the frenzied actions of the dancing Lord. Symbolizing the transcendence of time and space and the frenzied play of opposites that they contain, the balanced, immobile head and the wonderfully calm face reveal that ultimately saṁsāra can be conquered. The beautiful inward smile reflects the bliss of absorption into that deeper reality where sound and silence, time and eternity, motion and rest are reconciled in a greater unity and divine peace.

The whole of the dance takes place within the sacred ring of fire, symbolizing simultaneously the sacredness of existence and the destruction of ignorance and delusion that marks final release from saṁsāra.

The face of the dancer is also the face of the ascetic. The ascetic embodies the peace and tranquility of self-fulfillment that transcends the dualities of the world. But at the same time the dancer is the total manifested energy of existence in all its polarities. Both are combined in one and the same reality, proclaiming the ultimate unity of the transcendent and the immanent, of the manifested and the unmanifested, of power and being.

The transcendent unity of ultimate reality is best symbolized by the linga, generally acknowledged to be the most perfect symbol of Shiva. It emphasizes his transcendence even while visually proclaiming his immanent power and virility. It is seen most often in the form of a dark, polished, cylindrical stone with a rounded top. Often it is displayed in association with the yoni, a phallic symbol of the female creative energy of the universe, frequently with the yoni forming a receptacle for the base of the linga. Quite often, the yoni is represented by a circle of small stones placed around the cylindrical linga, thus portraying the fundamental unity of the eternal male and female generative forces of existence.

Although clearly a male phallic symbol, the linga does not represent erotica. On the contrary, it symbolizes the male creative energy of Shiva as it is contained and controlled, prior to being spent in the creative process. The Elephanta Caves near Bombay are rich in Shivaite art and symbolism, with the whole complex of cave temples designed to house and honor the linga in the central cave temple; there it stands at the very center of existence, creating the universe and drawing it back into its unmanifest fullness.

There is a wonderful white granite sculpture, probably 1400 years old, that was discovered this century during some road construction at Parel, near Bombay. Standing about four meters high, it visually proclaims the transcendent unity of the great God while at the same time affirming his dynamic, multidimensional immanence. (See Figure 9.)

Commenting on the Parel linga's symbolism, the late Heinrich Zimmer, whose profound understanding of Indian art and ideas is almost universally praised by Indian scholars, said, "In the Hindu spirit, as in this wonderful, granite masterpiece from Parel, there is an ultimate, marvelous balance between the dynamism of manifestation—process—constant evolution, and the serene, static repose of eternal being. This monument is meant to teach the total union and coincidence of all kinds of opposites in the one, transcendent source. From it they pour and into it they again subside" (Zimmer, p. 136).

The overall design of the sculpture, according to Zimmer, is that of a transcendent Shiva linga, but with the internal dynamism revealed through a series of Gods growing out of the top and sides of the central Shiva figure—all of which can be seen by the effect of a cut-away technique allowing us to see inside the linga. The central figure of Shiva is standing firmly on both feet, with the right hand holding a rosary, reaching out in a teaching gesture. To show the power of Shiva, a second deity, another Shiva, is shown growing out of the first, and then a third growing out of the second. The second Shiva carries the water pot of the wandering ascetic in his left hand while holding the right in a gesture of meditation. The third Shiva, extending ten arms in a semicircle, displays a combination of objects and gestures that symbolize simultaneously the heroic, evil-conquering powers and the meditative spiritual powers of the Great God.

The dynamism of the linga is further revealed by the other Shiva-like figures bursting forth from both the right and left sides of the central axis of the triple Shiva. Each figure throbs with life, and the whole conveys a sense of primordial energy-matter exploding into form. Zimmer comments, "The giant granite slab seems to be expanding, both vertically and sidewise, with the life-force of the athletic organisms that throb and heave across its surface" (p. 134). Indeed, like some primordial life-form at the root of all evolved life-forms, it is charged with an energy that expresses itself in a never-ending process of growth through self-duplication, suggesting that ultimately all forms of life and growth are only expressions of Shiva's cosmic self-duplicating energy.

The three central figures can be seen as the Great Lord in his triune form as Brahmā the Creator, Vishnu the Sustainer, and Shiva the Destroyer, the three functions characterizing and making possible existence. But these three functions and deities are ultimately only different

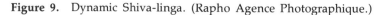

**Figure 9.** Dynamic Shiva-linga. (Rapho Agence Photographique.)

aspects of the same primordial energy-being here identified with Shiva. Consequently, all the beings emanating from the basic Shiva look like duplicates of this original. What a beautiful and powerful way of saying that the whole world, both in its dynamic, multiformed manifestation and in its sublime, unmanifested source, is nothing other than the Lord in His manifested and unmanifested forms!

## Perspectives

Now, having examined three quite different Hindu images of the personal form of ultimate reality, we need to step back and get a broader perspective, deepening our understanding of devotional Hinduism. For this purpose it will be helpful to answer three important questions: What is the place of devotionalism within the whole of Hinduism? What is the underlying aim and rationale of theistic Hinduism? and, Is Hinduism ultimately polytheistic, monotheistic, or monistic?

Turning to the first question, it must be noted that despite its importance devotionalism by no means exhausts the Hindu approach to religious transformation. Although devotion to a personal God became increasingly prominent in Hinduism after the fifth century, its development did not exclude other means of salvation. Yoga and various forms of asceticism continued to be important, as did various kinds of yajña. The great events in life continued to be celebrated with sacramental rituals, frequently using Vedic formulas. And although devotionalism tended to transcend class and caste, and somewhat de-emphasized the duties of class and life stage, the norms of class and caste and the normative ideal of the life stages have continued to provide the basic structure of Hinduism right up to the present time. Popular as devotional hymns and poems to a favorite God or Goddess became for the worshipper, the sacrifical formulas of the Vedas and the wisdom of the Upaniṣads continued to inspire and guide Hindu life. Mokṣa, the goal of complete freedom that promises to remove all forms of suffering and all kinds of limits from human existence, continued to be the fundamental aim of life for all Hindus, regardless of the approach taken and the means used.

The development of the devotional way was not seen as incompatible with other ways of salvation, but as complementary, and therefore was added to the treasurehouse of ideas and practices called Hinduism. It is here like it is with all the ideas and practices that have been encountered and adopted on the subcontinent. Nothing is ever rejected or discarded; the new is simply added to the old. Even the old that falls into relative disuse and unimportance is remembered as part of the continuing tradition out of which everything new emerges or to which it must be accommodated.

The fundmental aim of theistic Hinduism—like that of all other forms of Hinduism—is to achieve complete freedom, an aim that can be achieved only by removing every limitation of human existence. This preoccupation with the limitlessness of perfect existence permeates Indian thought and action. It is reflected in the vastness of the cosmological scale; the endless serpent of time; the never-ending details of art, architecture, and sculpture; the long and unending musical compositions and performances. Even life in heaven, no matter how great and wonderful, is poor and limited in comparison with the goal of complete limitlessness and freedom that mokṣa represents. From the perspective of created, manifested existence, time is unending. But there is no perfection and freedom within time. The cycles go on and on, endlessly repeating the processes of creation and dissolution. Ultimately only what is beyond the ravages of time can be saved from its consumption. Time, devourer of all beings, must itself be consumed to achieve complete freedom.

Time is not the only limit that must be transcended in the name of freedom and perfection. Space, too, limits all beings. The cosmology of Hindu myth stretches the boundaries of space as far as the imagination allows, postulating countless millions of universes, each containing countless millions of planetary bodies, each greater than this solar system—which includes millions more bodies than just this earth. But vast as space is, freedom requires going beyond its boundaries, and thus the immortal Self and the supreme God are both conceived as going beyond space and time. Space and time are eternally contained in the body of Vishnu or Brahmā, or the lingam of Shiva, from which they emerge and into which they are reabsorbed periodically (every so many billion years). But like the worlds that emerge and are reabsorbed, they too are grounded in the eternal and spaceless (infinite) reality that in its own being transcends space, time, and manifested existence.

Through identification of the inner essence of human beings with Ātman-Brahman—the eternal and infinite ground of being—a theoretical basis for liberation from the bondage of space and time was established. By seeing this eternal and infinite ground of being in personal terms, as God, it became possible to establish a personal relationship with the fundamental powers of existence. Through devotion to a personal God or Goddess, Hindus found that they could transcend the limitations inherent in the lesser modes of reality ordinarily mistaken for the true self and ultimate reality.

We now turn to that important question sidestepped at the beginning of this chapter, namely, "Is Hinduism polytheistic, monotheistic, or monistic?" By now it is probably obvious that this question does not fit Hindu thought or practice. The question presupposes that polytheism, monotheism, and monism are exclusive alternatives, whereas Hindus would regard them as partial, but complementary, visions, each true from its own perspective. Short of rejecting the question outright, the Hindu response can only be that, in a way, Hinduism is simultaneously polytheistic, monotheistic, and monistic.

Hinduism appears to be polytheistic, for all of reality is deemed sacred, with different aspects of this sacred existence seen and worshipped as different deities. Krishna, Kālī, Shiva, and dozens of other Gods and Goddesses seem to proclaim the polytheism of Hinduism.

But this is a curious kind of polytheism, for as we have seen, each of these deities is regarded by its devotees as the supreme God or Goddess, with the other deities seen as simply aspects or dimensions of this one supreme deity. Thus, since Shiva is the Supreme Lord and the embodiment of all the other Gods and Goddesses, it is clear that there is no God but Shiva. And the same can be said of Kālī, or Krishna. So quite clearly, Hinduism is monotheistic!

Yet, the understanding that any one God or Goddess embodies all the others reaches beyond the personal form of the ultimate reality to a unitary unmanifested reality that is the very source and ground of all existence—even that of the Gods. It is therefore obvious that Hinduism is monistic as well!

The insight underlying polytheism is that the divine is present in all things and persons. Logically developed, this view goes well beyond the recognition of the sacredness of the creative, redemptive, and sustaining powers of reality embodied in a single God or Goddess. Rivers, trees, animals, speech, love, hearing, vision, courage, military power, and so on are all recognized as sacred and venerated as deities in India. Thus, when Yājñavalkya was asked how many Gods there are, he first said 3,003, but he then kept reducing this number until finally there were none, for the sacredness represented by all the different deities is at bottom the same ultimate divine power. And this ultimate power is, in itself, beyond human conception. This is why even the conception of the ultimate as God, the Supreme Person, is eventually transcended in a spiritual monism that transcends all limitations. But the polytheistic approach preserves the sacredness of each particular form of life and power important to everyday life. It expands the domain of the sacred into every aspect of life and into every corner of the world, while monotheism unifies this sacred power, approaching it as one supreme person.

As we saw in the previous chapter, the Hindu feels no great compulsion to eliminate one approach to the sacredness of existence in favor of another. Because no one conception of the ultimate can ever totally capture its essence, no particular approach yielding access to, and developing relationships with, the ultimate should be rejected. Instead, all these different approaches should be allowed to co-exist, for they are complementary and mutually enriching. Their complementarity follows from the intuition that what is sacred and divine is somehow not divided in itself and that, therefore, the many realities into which it is apparently divided by human approaches to it represent only differences in approach rather than ultimate differences in the sacred reality.

If we insist that our understanding of reality must be ruled by an exclusive logic carving reality into neat little pieces that can be stacked in neat little piles and labeled "Either this, or this, but not both," then Hindu recognition of ultimate reality as simultaneously polytheistic, monotheistic, and monistic may appear self-contradictory, the result of confusion and poor logic. But if we see reality as far surpassing the reach of logic and conceptual thinking, then it seems small-minded and arbitrary to rule out and ignore all those dimensions and aspects of reality that cannot be caught within the logical net. In its own sphere, logic is valuable and its rules must be respected. But the soul knows more than the mind can understand, and it would be a tragic mistake to kill the soul with the tools of the mind.

## Summary

As we saw in Chapter 10, where we focused on Krishna, Hindus have sought a personal relationship with ultimate reality through the Gods and Goddesses symbolizing the divine power of the ultimate. In this chapter we have focused on Kālī and Shiva as personal manifestations of ultimate reality.

Kālī embodies the horrible and destructive aspects of reality. In her gruesome images as a blood-thirsty monster, killing and drinking the blood of her victims, feasting in the graveyards and cremation grounds, and dancing on her husband's body, she forces us to recognize and come to terms with our fear of suffering, loneliness, and death. To her devotees Kālī's terrible and fearsome images suggest kindness and love. The Divine Mother reveals the ugliness of hurting and dying so that we can conquer our fear of them and attain the freedom to experience the peace and joy that is also present in existence. Ultimately, she is the destroyer of suffering, fear, and death, and therefore her devotees come to worship at the loving mother's feet, bringing the bloody offerings she demands.

Shiva represents the complementariness and fundamental unity of all polarities. In him are reconciled the dualities of male and female, life and death, creation and destruction, asceticism and passionate involvement. Although given a personality—actually a series of personalities—and numerous life stories—actually fragments of many life stories—Shiva's most perfect and fundamental symbol is the linga. As a phallic symbol it suggests the creative energy of ultimate reality in its pure, controlled, and potent form prior to being spent in the creative urge of world-creation. As axis of the universe it extends infinitely beyond the manifested worlds, suggesting that even the polarity of the temporal and the eternal and that of manifested existence and the unmanifested Brahman are overcome in Shiva's being. The linga embodies the truth that the opposition existing between bondage and liberation, or between suffering and joy, can be reconciled in a higher unity that makes possible the unending peace and freedom of mokṣa.

Resisting the pressure of an exclusive logic to force it to choose among polytheism, monotheism, and monism, Hinduism can be seen as embracing all three options simultaneously, proclaiming the truth of each. The truth of monism does not prevent the manifestation of the ultimate in personal forms, recognized as different Gods and Goddesses, thereby affirming the sacredness of every form of existence. But in affirming the underlying unity of all the different Gods and Goddesses as different embodiments of the same supreme personal form of the ultimate, Hindus are monotheistic. The mind may see a contradiction here, but the soul recognizes a great truth.

## Suggestions for Further Reading

*Myths and Symbols in Indian Art and Civilization*, by Heinrich Zimmer (New York: Harper Torchbooks, 1962), is a fine integration of visual and conceptual understanding of basic themes in Indian thought. The seventy plates are well chosen and integral to the text. Many Freudian and Jungian insights shine through this little gem. For the reader seriously interested in Indian art, Zimmer's two-volume work (edited and completed by Joseph Campbell), entitled *The Art of Indian Asia*, 2nd ed. (Princeton, N.J.: Princeton University Press, 1968), is a must. It contains over five hundred plates, all carefully described, offering a fascinating and enjoyable opportunity to approach the Indian mind and heart through truly great art.

*The Art of India*, by Calambur Sivaramamurti (New York: Harry N. Abrams, Inc., 1974), is a six-hundred-page visual feast. Its 1,175 illustrations include 180 in color, and the accompanying text is one of the best essays on Indian art available. Sivaramamurti is the former director of the National Museum in New Delhi, and this magnificent volume is a generous sharing of the results of his life-long immersion in Indian art.

*The Presence of Śiva*, by Stella Kramrisch (Princeton: Princeton University Press, 1981), is clearly the best book on Shiva to appear so far. Must reading for anyone seriously interested in Hinduism.

*The Dance of Shiva and Other Tales from India*, by Oroon Ghosh (New York: Signet Classics, 1965), is wonderful little collection of some of India's most popular stories, charmingly translated.

*Hindu Polytheism*, by Alain Danielou (New York: Bollingen Foundation, 1964; distributed by Pantheon Books), describes and explains the more important Hindu deities, drawing upon the major myths and classical art. The introductory essay on the nature of polytheism and its relation to ultimate reality conceived monistically is especially well liked by some of my Indian friends. The plates are beautiful and the descriptions of iconographic rules informative.

*The Hindu Religious Tradition: A Philosophical Approach*, by Pratima Bowes (Boston and London: Routledge and Kegan Paul, 1977), is a good introduction to almost the entire spectrum of Hinduism, displaying sympathetic insight while remaining objective and critical. *The Hindu Religious Tradition*, by Thomas J. Hopkins (Encino, Calif.: Dickenson Publishing Co., 1971), is a useful introductory survey.

# 12

# Systematic Philosophy: Bondage, Liberation, and Causality

## Characteristics of Systematic Indian Philosophy

The preceding chapters make clear the deep and pervasive Indian concern with achieving liberaton from the suffering and limitations of life—a concern underlying and providing motivation for India's systematic philosophies and distinguishing them from most Greek and European philosophies. In one respect the fundamental problems of Indian philosophy are the same as they are in the West: What is reality? What is the self? What is knowledge? What is the nature of causality? and How can the highest good be achieved? But in another respect there is a considerable difference, for in India answering these questions is important primarily not as a means of satisfying human curiosity about the world, but as a means of overcoming bondage. Whereas Aristotle observed that philosophy is born of wonder, Indian philosophers maintain that philosophy arises out of the effort to overcome suffering.

What causes bondage? and How can liberation be achieved? are the practical questions that lead Indian philosophers into the theoretical and universal questions about the nature of self, reality, causality, and knowledge. Speculation on these fundamental questions, in turn, is expected to provide an improved basis for the practical efforts to attain liberation. Our studies of Jainism, Buddhism, and Yoga have all shown this practical dimension of Indian thought, which is demonstrated with great clarity in the four noble truths enunciated by the Buddha in his first sermon at Banaras. The first truth, that there is duḥkha, establishes that the human condition is one of bondage to duḥkha; the second truth announces that this bondage is caused; the third, that ignorance and grasping are the fundamental causes; the fourth, that liberation is possible by following the noble eightfold path. All the questions of Buddhist philosophy arise out of the attempt to understand and defend these four insights of the Buddha.

An excellent example of the practical orientation of Indian philosophy is provided by a bit of dialogue in *A Thousand Verses of Teaching*, by Shaṅkara, one of India's greatest philosophers. Although the work is filled with rational analysis and argument, it is clear that these philosophical arguments and theories are regarded as important only to the extent that they remove ignorance about the conditions of bondage and the means of liberation, thereby preparing one for the awakening of the liberating knowledge of Brahman. In this dialogue a student approaches a teacher established in Brahman knowledge and asks,

> "Your Holiness, how can I be released from saṁsāra? I am aware of the body, the senses and their objects. I experience suffering in the waking state and I experience it in the dreaming state—after getting relief again and again by entering into the state of deep sleep again and again. Is this suffering indeed my own nature? Or does it result from some cause, my own nature being different? If it is my own nature, there is no hope for me to attain liberation, for one cannot avoid one's own nature. If it is due to some cause, then final liberation is possible after the cause has been removed."
>
> The teacher replied, "Listen, my child, this is not your own nature, but results from a cause."
>
> When he was told this, the pupil asked, "What is the cause? And what will remove it? And what is my own nature? When the cause is removed the effect due to the cause does not exist. Then I will attain to my own nature—like a sick person [recovers his health] when the cause of his disease has been removed."
>
> The teacher replied, "The cause is ignorance. It is removed by knowledge. When ignorance has been removed you will be released from saṁsāra—which is characterized by birth and death—since its cause will be gone and you will not experience suffering in the dreaming and waking states."
>
> "What is that ignorance?" asked the pupil. "What is its object? and what is knowledge, remover of ignorance, by which I can realize my own nature?"
>
> (Prose part, Chap. 2, paragraphs 45–49)[1]

The fundamental questions of Advaita philosophy—and most other Indian philosophies as well—are raised in this brief dialogue: (1) How is release from suffering possible? (2) Is suffering natural to human beings and therefore inevitable? (3) Or is it caused by something extraneous to human nature? (4) What is the nature of the self? (5) What is the cause of suffering? (6) If the cause of suffering is said to be ignorance, how is it removed? (7) What is ignorance? (8) How is ignorance related to knowledge? (9) How can the self, which is said to be of the nature of knowledge, be ignorant? (10) But if ignorance does not belong to the self, then how can it cause the self to suffer and transmigrate?

Indian philosophies also differ from Greek and European philosophy by their emphasis on insight, personal experience, and scriptural authority—rather than ordinary perception or reason—as the fundamental sources of

[1]In Sengaku Mayeda, *A Thousand Teachings* (Tokyo: University of Tokyo Press, 1979), p. 234 with modifications.

truth. Perception and reason are regarded as both indispensable means of clarifying and defending one's own philosophical vision and of destroying the opponent's views. But they are too limited to provide access to the deepest truths of reality.

However, one should not be misled by the practical character of Indian philosophy and its tendency to rely on suprarational means of knowledge. The teachings of the Vedas or Upaniṣads, or of the Buddha or Mahāvīra, may be taken to embody the highest truth and reveal the surest way to liberation, but they must be interpreted, clarified, and defended against attacks from every quarter. Both skeptics and believers posed challenging questions: Is liberation possible? If so, how is it possible? Appeals to faith and reiteration of a teacher's pronouncements or scriptural testament do not provide adequate answers to these questions. Careful analysis and rational justification are demanded, giving rise to India's long and rich tradition of philosophical debate.

Those who think that in India the fundamental questions concerning the nature of reality, self, knowledge, and causality were settled by intuition, faith, scripture, or dogma are sorely mistaken. They obviously know nothing of the sharp and lively debate among the philosophers. They have not encountered the Shaṅkara who, in the course of systematizing and justifying the teachings of the Upaniṣads takes a sidewise glance at the philosophies of rival systems and says, "There is some danger of men of inferior intelligence looking upon the Sāṁkhya and similar systems as requisite for perfect knowledge, because those systems have a weighty appearance, have been adopted by authoritative persons, and profess to lead to perfect knowledge. Such people might therefore think that those systems with their abstruse arguments were propounded by omniscient sages and might on that account have faith in them. For this reason *we must endeavor to demonstrate their intrinsic worthlessness*."[2] This statement is followed by a searching criticism of the Sāṁkhya claims and a logical refutation of their arguments that typifies the lively philosophical exchanges that have occurred between adherents of the different systems from ancient times right up to the present.

To defend one's own views and to attack those of the opponents, it is necessary to develop techniques of analysis and methods of argument that are convincing on the basis of their appeal to human reason. Appeals to faith or metaphysical vision are useless for this purpose, because differences over the contents of their faith and visions divide the philosophers in the first place. But the principles of logic underlying rational analysis and argument are universally valid.

Even the Jainas were forced to admit the validity of the principles of noncontradiction and excluded middle. If statement A is accepted as true, then its contradictory, not-A, must be rejected as false. And if not-A in-

[2]Commentary on Vedānta Sūtras, 1.2.1; quoted in *A Source Book of Advaita Vedānta*, by Eliot Deutsch and J. A. B. van Buitenen (Honolulu: University Press of Hawaii, 1971), p. 81.

cludes everything other than A, then either A or not-A must be false. The Jainas, of course, insisted that we can never know either A or not-A completely and therefore can never oppose them completely, but only in a certain respect. This allows for the possibility that in some other respect either they are not opposed or there is some alternative other than their being opposed to each other. But to make and defend their case, they too rely on the rational principles of noncontradiction and excluded middle.

The principles and techniques of logic developed by the Nyāya philosophers were used by all of India's philosophers with great enthusiasm and rigor to support their positions and destroy those of their opponents. This point is sometimes overlooked by people who focus on the spiritual and practical nature of Indian thought and on the appeal to suprarational means of attaining insight and truth. For while it is true that reason was usually regarded as less than fully adequate to comprehend the true nature of reality, it is also true that there was never any doubt among Indian philosophers that reason was a criterion against which all views had to be tested. To show that a view was logically inconsistent or self-contradictory was to effectively destroy it. Although reason might not be the final arbiter of truth, nothing that failed the test of rational coherence and consistency could be accepted as true. And since the primary task of philosophy in India was to provide a basis of understanding and truth for practice leading to liberation, consistency and coherence became the necessary conditions of successful philosophy in India—just as they did everywhere else.

There is, of course, a big difference between regarding reason as a sufficient condition of truth and regarding it only as a necessary condition. As noted earlier, most Indian philosophers assumed that reality transcends the limitations of reason and therefore saw reason as a necessary, but not a sufficient, condition of truth. In practice, this frequently meant that they used rational analysis and argument to refute the views and arguments of their opponents and to clear away objections from their own positions. But the positions they were defending were frequently accepted ultimately on the basis of personal experience or the authority of another person or scripture. Nevertheless, rational analysis had much to do with how personal experience or authoritative teachings were interpreted and understood. For example, the Vedāntic nondualism of Shaṅkara and the Vedāntic dualism of Madhva are quite different systems of philosophy. However, both are presented as the true teachings of the Upaniṣads and the Brahmā Sūtras!

## Philosophical Problems and Systems

In the process of clarifying, interpreting, and defending traditional insights and views, a number of philosophical systems developed, more or less side by side, contending with each other over such fundamental issues as the causes of bondage, the means of liberation, the nature of reality and the self, and the means of valid knowledge. Although our approach will focus on these issues—rather than on the development of the different systems—it will be helpful to first briefly describe the major philosophical systems.

Indian tradition recognizes nine different major and enduring philosophical systems. Six of these, Nyāya, Vaiśeṣika, Sāṁkhya, Yoga, Mīmāmsā, and Vedānta, are called orthodox because they accept the truth of the essential Vedic and Upaniṣadic teachings. The Materialist (Cārvāka or Lokāyata), Buddist, and Jaina systems are regarded as unorthodox because they reject these scriptures as primary revelations of truth.

These philosophical systems have their origins in ancient times, most likely sometime between the sixth and second centuries B.C., even though most of the texts that survive are all much more recent. That the texts are more recent than the philosophies themselves is not surprising for not only do manuscripts decay quickly in the Indian climate, but the Indian tradition has been primarily oral. A written text, even today, suggests a deficiency in the sage and teacher, who is expected to memorize everything of importance.

Most of the basic texts that do survive from early times are collections of the briefest of aphorisms, called *sūtras* or "threads." On these threads are woven the entire teaching, including elaborate analyses and arguments that are provided orally by the teacher. Without a teacher or a teacher's commentary, these aphoristic threads are almost unintelligible. A single aphorism of four words, such as the yoga aphorism, *yoga citta vṛtti nirodha*, might be the condensation of thousands of words of doctrine, analysis, and argument. Each sūtra author strives to eliminate every possible word and every possible syllable without breaking the thread. The witticism that a sūtra author takes greater delight in saving a single vowel than in the birth of a son may not be true, but it certainly makes an important point! Fortunately, many commentaries have survived, and from these, along with the criticisms by philosophers of one system against the positions and arguments of those of rival systems, it is possible to get a fairly clear idea of the central teachings of each system and often of individual philosophers.

We have already examined both the Yoga vision of the causes of bondage and the means of liberation, and the associated Sāṁkhya dualism that emphasizes the distinction between prakṛti, the source of the entire psychophysical world and puruṣa, the pure spiritual self.

Mīmāmsā philosophy takes its stand on the ritual or injunctive portion of the Veda, holding that ritual action constitutes the primary effective means of liberation. The chief concern of Mīmāmsā philosophers is to work out a theory of knowledge that will accommodate scriptural testimony as a valid means of knowledge and, on this basis, to provide a theory of scriptural interpretation that will explain the meaning and truth of the Vedas.

Vedānta philosophers take their stand on the Upaniṣads ("end of the Veda," or "Vedānta"), emphasizing knowledge as the means of liberation. Brahman is the ultimate reality, and the Self is ultimately the same as Brahman. But when the question of Brahman's nature and relation to the world comes up, Vedāntists disagree: the Advaita, Dvaita, and Viśiṣtādivata schools of Vedānta all give different answers. Yet they all agree that knowledge rather than ritual is of primary importance for liberation, though the latter two schools place more emphasis on devotion as a means of knowing and relating to Brahman.

Nyāya is concerned primarily with questions of logic and valid knowledge, and the philosophers of this school worked out a system of logic and argument and a theory of knowledge that most of the other systems have adopted, though occasionally with modifications. Nyāya views of self and reality are taken over from its sister system, Vaiśeṣika. Since Vaiśeṣika philosophers reciprocate by adopting the Nyāya logic and epistemology, it is customary to treat these two systems together as Nyāya-Vaiśeṣika.

Vaiśeṣika metaphysics can best be described as pluralistic realism. There are a number of fundamentally different kinds of reality, which in their subtle atomic forms combine in practically unlimited ways to constitute the incredibly diverse universe we experience, and which can be known through perception and reasoning. Of all the systems Vaiśeṣika is closest to common sense.

The Jaina vision, as we saw earlier, sees reality as constituted by two fundamentally different kinds of beings, spiritual beings, which are living, and nonspiritual beings, which are not. Bondage of the spiritual self is caused by material particles that are attracted by the self's energy when it is polluted by ignorance and passion. All actions, it will be recalled, generate bondage. But knowledge, achieved through a kind of extrasensory insight or awakening, reveals the pure, unbound nature of the self and provides incentive for the ascetic destruction of previously accumulated karmas.

Buddhists take a more radical position, rejecting the commonsense view that regards reality as constituted by a variety of fundamentally different things with an even greater variety of changing qualities. Instead, they view existence as process, as continuously changing states of events. There is no one thing that causes something else to come into being or to change. Each successive state of an event is determined by all the preceding states. Things are only intellectual abstractions from the concrete processes that everywhere make up existence. Bondage and suffering are caused by the ignorance through which the self assumes a kind of permanent identity, grasping for permanence in a world where there is only change.

Ordinary perceptual and conceptual knowledge distort reality by cutting continuous process up into discrete events and construing these events as things. But a genuine kind of knowledge that sees immediately and directly into the process of existence is possible through a combination of understanding, moral perfection, and meditation. This knowledge enables one to see through the illusion of death and removes the conditions of suffering, thereby bringing the joyous peace of nirvāṇa.

But Buddhists defended these views in a variety of ways, and thus different philosophical systems arose within Buddhism. The Vaibhāṣika-Sautrāntika schools take the momentary events constituting existence to be psychophysical, whereas the Yogacāras take them to be essentially mental. Buddhist logicians tend to accept the reality of the processes experienced, but see them as the conglomeration of logical moments, whereas Nāgārjuna presents the Mādhyamika positions as midway between the view that the mental alone is real and the view that the material alone is real. His claim is that reality is beyond all attempts to characterize it and therefore "empty" of the "reality" imputed to it by the various philosophical views. It cannot be grasped by any ordinary kinds of knowledge. Only direct insight and experience can penetrate this reality.

The remaining system is that of the Materialists. Although denigrated by philosophers from all of the other systems, they made extremely important contributions to Indian civilization and philosophy. Their trenchant criticism of the assumptions and arguments found in the various philosophical systems challenged other philosophers to develop rationally coherent and defensible philosophies. In addition, their "this-worldly" philosophy led to great advances in the various sciences and medicine and in the arts of politics, social administration, and economic production. Unfortunately, their philosophical texts have not been preserved—with the exception of a few fragments—and our understanding of their views and arguments is drawn mainly from summaries by their critics.

These summaries and criticisms suggest that the Materialists held a variety of philosophical views, having in common only that they rejected the possibility of mokṣa or nirvāṇa. This means, of course, that the opposition between Materialists and the other eight systems is more basic than is that between those accepting and those rejecting the Vedas, for Jainas and Buddhists agree with the orthodox philosophers that achieving liberation from bondage is the fundamental problem of life.

Serious challenges to the view that liberation from bondage is possible go back at least to the fifth century B.C. Jainas and Buddhists, who themselves had rejected the authority of the Vedas and Upaniṣads, were greatly concerned about the teachings of people like Kesakambala, Gośala, and Sañjaya, teachings that apparently were quite popular during the lifetimes of the Buddha and Mahāvīra.

Kesakambala was a thoroughgoing materialist who believed in neither an imperishable self nor an extrasensory reality. He taught that mokṣa is impossible; it is only a fool's dream. The only way to live is to minimize suffering and maximize happiness here and now.

Gośala, teacher of the extremely popular Ājīvika sect, was a complete determinist. His position was that, even if mokṣa is possible, there is nothing a person can do to achieve it because everything is predetermined by fate. Human beings have no freedom to act.

Sañjaya was a complete skeptic who denied the possibility of any genuine knowledge. Even if there is a transcendent reality and a way of reaching this reality, knowledge of such a reality and way is impossible, and therefore nobody can possibly know what to do to achieve liberation.

These so-called Materialist teachings clearly attack the central presuppositions of all the other systems. To meet these attacks, it became necessary to show that there is a higher order of reality that is the ground of freedom and perfection; to show that, although bondage is causally determined, liberation is possible; and to show that knowledge of reality and of the means of liberation is possible. Without developing rationally defensible theories of reality, causality, and knowledge, the various systems could not meet the materialist, determinist, and skeptical challenges.

This is why it is preferable to approach Indian philosophy topically, rather than system by system. What theories of knowledge, reality, and causality do the different systems develop to show how bondage is caused and how liberation is attainable? Approaching Indian philosophy in terms of these fundamental questions, we get a sense of the shared life of debate and argument that the different systems enjoyed over the centuries as they competed and cooperated with each other in working out, clarifying, and justifying their philosophical visions.

Although our approach is not historical, it is important to understand that most of the systems have had a continuous history of more than two thousand years, existing side by side, with now one in ascendancy and now another. But none of these systems was ever regarded as having been decisively refuted and therefore to be abandoned. They are still alive and have their defenders and advocates, even though in some cases the most inspirational philosophers of the system may have lived more than a thousand years ago. Dasgupta's magnificent five-volume *History of Indian Philosophy* reveals many fascinating and important developments in Indian philosophy over the last twenty-five hundred years, as philosophers from the different systems criticized each others' views and developed their own views to meet the criticism of opponents.

We will obviously have to forego such a detailed analysis—both for reasons of space and because our purpose is to get an overall understanding of Indian philosophy's central aim and the ways in which it tried to achieve this aim. For our purposes it is preferable to focus on the causal chains of bondage and the means of liberation that constitute the *raison d'etre* of every system except the Materialist and to examine the theories of causality, reality, and knowledge that were developed to defend the fundamental visions of bondage and liberation.

## Chains of Bondage and Paths to Freedom

We have already examined the Jaina, Buddhist, and Yoga views of the causes of bondage and the means to liberation. As seen earlier, Jainas hold that bondage is caused by the karmic matter attracted to an essentially pure and free self by actions rooted in ignorance and motivated by passion and the will to hurt others. To overcome the bondage of karma, a fourteen-stage path of purification and knowledge is laid out. By following this path, insight into the pure nature of the self is awakened, passion is purged, and the will to hurt others is overcome. Finally, through extreme asceticism and the eventual cessation of all actions whatsoever, the previously accumulated karmic bondage is exhausted and the self is freed.

The Buddha's insight into the causes of duḥkha is depicted by the wheel of becoming, which represents the twelve-linked chain of causation. Ignorance and grasping are the crucial links in this causal chain, which can be broken by following the eightfold noble path of right action, wisdom, and meditation.

According to Yoga, the causal chain of bondage begins with ignorance of the true nature of the self as puruṣa. This ignorance results in the mistaken identification of the self with prakṛti, which leads inevitably to a desperate attempt to create an ego self out of prakṛtic existence. This attempt leads, in turn, to insatiable grasping for whatever pleases the prakṛtic self as well as aversion to whatever threatens it. Now the will to live forever in the modalities of prakṛti becomes the driving energy of life, binding the self to the limitations and suffering of prakṛtic existence. To eliminate these causes of bondage, Yoga prescribes a set of eight techniques of self-discipline and meditation that are roughly comparable to the Buddhist eightfold path.

Mīmāmsā philosophers see the cause of fear, suffering, and death in the failure to participate ritually in the fundamental processes of creation and sustenance through yajña. The path to freedom from suffering and death is through full participation in yajña, the ritual acts whereby life is continuously renewed and fulfilled.

Nyāya-Vaiśeṣika philosophers see wrong identification of the self with the body as the root cause of fear, suffering, and death. Each person has a unique self that is independent of, and separable from, the body and the mind. Liberation is achieved through knowledge of this unique self and its differentiation from all other objects of knowledge. Although rational knowledge is emphasized in these two systems, the truth of scripture and the insights of meditation are also regarded as necessary means of knowledge.

Vedānta philosophers, following the teachings of the Upaniṣads, emphasize Brahman as the source and ground of all reality. Through mistaken identification of the self with lower levels of reality, an ego existence is created that experiences fear, suffering, and countless limiting bonds. Advaita Vedāntists, such as Shaṅkara, insist that Brahman is the sole reality and that the self is ultimately completely identical with Brahman. They regard knowledge of this identity as the essential means to freedom. Dvaita Vedāntists, such as Madhva, see the self as essentially different from Brahman in which it is grounded. They also stress knowledge, but they give much greater scope to devotional practices as a way of returning to the source and perfection of existence. The same is true for Viśiṣṭadvaitins who, like Rāmānuja, hold that bondage is rooted in the ignorance that prevents us from realizing that we are part of Brahman. Both Rāmānuja and Madhva emphasize the personal nature of Brahman as God, whereas Shaṅkara emphasizes the impersonal, quality-less character of Brahman. But, of course, the personal and impersonal conceptions of Brahman are not really exclusive of each other; each is true in its own way.

These brief sketches of the causal chains of bondage and the paths to freedom are intended to help us see how the questions of causality, reality, and knowledge arise in the different systems. The fundamental problem is the conflict between freedom and determinism. Each system assumes that certain actions—knowledge, ritual, morality, devotion—will necessarily lead to freedom. Unless, for example, taking the actions that constitute the noble eightfold path can be counted on to bring about the liberated condition known as nirvāṇa, there is no point in following the path. Indeed, unless it leads somewhere, there is no path. It is assumed that each way of liberation has the power to determine the intended effect of liberation. Unless a person seeking liberation has reason to think that the efforts made have the causal power to effect that liberation, there is no point in making the effort. Efforts that have no effects or whose effects are random or unknowable are worthless as means of liberation. Thus, every path to freedom assumes a causally determined chain that can bring about the intended effect of liberation.

Each chain of bondage also assumes that bondage is an effect, causally determined by certain preceding factors or conditions—ignorance, passion, grasping, inaction. If bondage is not causally determined, but happens only by chance, then it will be impossible to understand the conditions and factors on which it depends. But without this understanding, it is impossible to chart a path to freedom by eliminating the causes of bondage. Only because the Buddha recognized that duḥkha is caused, and that the critical causes were ignorance and grasping, could he chart a path to freedom that would eliminate these causes and thereby eliminate duḥkha, their effect. Thus, some kind of causal efficacy or determinism is necessarily assumed both for the chain of bondage and for the way of liberation accepted by each system.

But while assuming causality, each system must also assume that the individual is free to choose and follow a path to freedom. Unless both freedom and causality are assumed, it becomes impossible to show how certain kinds of practices can lead from this ocean of suffering to the far shore of nirvāṇa or mokṣa. How can this assumption of freedom be reconciled with the assumption of causal determinism? It is this problem that led the philosophers to investigate the nature of causality. What is the nature of the relationship between cause and effect? Every answer to this question must posit a relationship strong enough to account for the conditioned nature of bondage and to guarantee the effectiveness of the path to liberation. But the causal relationship must not be so strong that it becomes impossible to choose and follow a path to freedom.

## Causality

There are two fundamentally different theories of causality, a strong theory and a weak theory. According to the strong theory (*asatkāryavāda*), the effect is a new reality, brought into existence by the causal power of a previously existing reality. This view is held by philosophers of the Nyāya-Vaiśeṣika and Prabhākara Mīmāmsā systems and supports their pluralistic metaphysics.

The weak theory (*satkāryavāda*) maintains that the effect already pre-exists in the cause prior to its appearance as a separate existence. The new effect is not a totally new reality but, rather, a transformation of the thing that existed previously. Sāṁkhya-yoga and Vedānta philosophers adopt this weak causal theory, enabling them to explain how this whole world is simply a transformation of the primordial prakṛti (Sāṁkhya) or the manifestation of Brahman (Vedānta).

Both theories are attempts to account for the relation between cause and effect that is responsible for change. What happens, for example, when milk sours and becomes curd or when an acorn germinates and becomes an oak tree? Is the tree a new reality caused by the acorn? Or is it just a different form of the acorn? Is the curd a new reality separate from the milk? Or is it just a different form of milk? Weak causality theories insist that no new reality comes into existence; that oak trees and curds are just acorns and milk transformed. But strong causality theories maintain that these effects are new realities, separate from their causes.

We will first look at how the strong and weak theories were formulated, criticized, and defended by the philosophers of the various systems. Then we will look at the Jaina theory of causality, which accepts both strong and weak causality, and the Buddhist theory of dependent origination, which, in a way, rejects both.

### STRONG CAUSALITY

The strong theory of causality, which is somewhat akin to our commonsense views of causality, is formulated most clearly by Nyāya-Vaiśeṣika philosophers. They attempt to show that cause and effect are two different and separate realities to ensure that freedom can be attained without destroying either the self or the world. To do this they must show that cause and effect are related to each other *as* cause and effect by a third reality, which is precisely the causal relation. For example, oil is produced when seeds are pressed but not when stones are pressed because the causal relation holds between the first pair but not the second. Unless the causal relation were something distinct from the mere collocation of two entities, then whenever any two entities are brought together one would be a cause of the other. But this is clearly not the case, argue the Nyāya philosophers, showing that the causal power inhering in the relation must be something other than mere co-presence of two entities and that it cannot be identified with either of the two entities brought together in a causal relation.

It is important to show that the causal relation is separate from either of the realities involved in a causal relationship because if either the self or the world were held to be the cause of suffering, freedom could be attained only by destroying one or the other of these realities. But by maintaining that causality is something separate from either the world or the self, that it is a special kind of relation between them, the Nyāya-Vaiśeṣika philosopher can argue that only the causal relation—and not the world or the self—must be destroyed to break the causal chain of bondage.

Although it enables its advocates to set out a way of liberation that does not require repudiation or destruction of either the world or the self, the Nyāya-Vaiśeṣika theory is not without its problems—as philosophers from the other systems were quick to point out. By looking at some criticisms of this strong theory of causality, and Nyāya-Vaiśeṣika responses to these criticisms, we will get a better idea of its strengths and weaknesses.

A popular criticism, advanced by Sāṁkhya and other weak causality theorists, is that, unless the effect is already pre-existent in the cause, any cause should be able to produce any effect. The reason that oil can be gotten from seeds but not from stones, they argue, is that oil pre-exists in seeds but not in the stones. But if oil pre-exists in neither seeds nor stones, then why cannot stones as well as seeds cause oil? There are two questions here. First, if the effect does not pre-exist in the cause, then how can it be produced by the cause? Second, if the effect does not pre-exist in the cause, then why can a given cause produce only certain effects and not others?

Nyāya-Vaiśeṣika philosophers respond that, although causality is a universal relation, it actually obtains only between those things and events that are immediately and inseparably joined together as cause and effect. Thus, certain causes are potent with respect to certain effects but not with respect to others, and a cause can effect only that for which it has the causal potency. Since seeds are potent with respect to oil but stones are not, it follows that stones are not the cause of oil, but seeds are.

This response is difficult to maintain, however, for as critics are quick to point out, the notion of potency is simply a way of smuggling in the notion of pre-existence, as the potency is said to reside in the cause prior to the effect's being produced. But this is just another way of saying that, in some sense at least, the effect pre-exists in the cause, and is not a totally new reality. What the Nyāya-Vaiśeṣika philosopher must show is that causality is a unique kind of reality, distinct from both the effect and the cause, which functions to relate cause and effect in just those cases where something new comes into existence. Their efforts to do this, however, come under fire from another direction.

Both Jainas and Buddhists attack the notion that causality is a real force inhering in a special relation between cause and effect. If this inherent force is the causal power that connects things to each other then, they argue, it must either be eternally present or else it must come into being at some particular time. But if it comes into being at some particular time, then it must itself be caused, for nothing comes into being that is not caused. If it is caused to come into being by something else, then obviously this special relation postulated by Nyāya philosophers cannot be the principle of causal efficacy. On the other hand, if it exists eternally, then it holds all causes and effects together eternally, making it impossible to break the causal chain that produces suffering. In that case liberation becomes impossible.

"Not so," reply the Nyāya-Vaiśeṣika philosophers. "You mistake causality for a particular thing, when actually it is a universal. This particular pot must be caused by something else for it to come into being. And if it were eternal, it could never be destroyed. But 'potness,' the universal, does not have to be caused by another, for it exists everywhere at all times. And it continues to exist even when particular pots are destroyed. In the same way, a particular cause may be destroyed without thereby destroying the universal causal relation itself."

This view of causality as a universal relation is attacked by the Buddhists who argue that, if causality is a relation, then it can exist only when there are two (or more) things to be related. Suppose that causality inheres in the threads producing the effect of cloth. If the threads are destroyed, then where does the cause reside? It cannot inhere in the threads, for they do not exist. Nor can it inhere in the cloth, for that does not exist either. But if there is no place for the causal relation to inhere, it makes no sense to claim that this inherence exists.

This argument is similar to the Sāṁkhya argument that begins with the following principle: if there are no things to be related, then there can be no relation between them. But if an effect is a new reality, separate from the cause, then before it is caused it cannot exist. Similarly, before the effect is produced there is no cause, for a cause is a cause only of its effects. But if there is nothing in which the causal relation can inhere before the effect is produced, then obviously it cannot account for the coming-to-be of the effect.

To defend themselves against the charge that, unless both cause and effect exist before the effect is produced, no relation between them is possible, and therefore that the causal relation cannot produce new effects, Nyāya-Vaiśeṣika philosophers argue that the universal causal relation always exists between every potential cause and effect. But it exists as a potential relation that is actualized only in those cases where an effect is produced. If this were not the case, they argue, it would be impossible for anything that is not now a cause ever to become a cause in the future. But then no new effects would ever be produced, which would mean no change whatsoever. But since change is an obvious fact of experience, it must be the case that a causal relation that exists potentially between two things is actualized on precisely those occasions when an effect is produced. What is potential in the cause is not the effect itself, but the *power* to produce the effect.

This line of defense opens the Nyāya position to yet another attack. If some causes are only potential causes at one time and actual causes at a later time, then some change must have occurred in the causal relation itself to account for what was merely potential becoming actual. What caused the potential cause to become an actual cause? Since this does not happen all the time, but only on those occasions when an effect is caused, it, too, must be an effect of some previous cause. But the same can be said of that previous cause, and the cause previous to that cause, and so on to infinity.

Shaṅkara presents this argument in a classical form that is adopted by many philosophers. Beginning with the Nyāya-Vaiśeṣika claim that causality is a reality distinct from the things it relates, he argues that for any two things, A and B, to be causally related, a third thing, C, is required. But C must itself be related to both A and B. For C to be related to A, another reality, D, must be assumed. And for C to be related to D, still another reality, E, must be assumed, and so on *ad infinitum*. But then no things whatsoever could be related, for unless the series had a beginning there would be no causal relation now between any cause and effect.

The Nyāya-Vaiśeṣika response is that no other relation is necessary to relate causality to the entities that it relates, for it is the nature of causality to relate things to each other without itself requiring a relation to relate it to what it relates. This presupposes that a relation of any kind, be it that between cause and effect, that between whole and part, or some other kind, is a different kind of reality from the realities it relates.

This, of course, leaves unanswered the question of precisely what status causal relations have. But it is precisely this extremely difficult problem of specifying exactly what kind of thing a causal relation is that has made causality a perennial philosophical problem, both in India and elsewhere.

## WEAK CAUSALITY

Let us turn now to the weak theory of causality. By insisting that the effect already pre-exists in the cause before it appears in the form recognized as effect, its advocates avoid the problem of trying to relate something that does not exist to something else which is said to be its cause. On this account all effects have pre-existed from eternity.

One obvious difficulty these philosophers face is to account for new beings and new events coming into existence. How can something that is caused today but that did not exist yesterday, have already existed yesterday? Obviously it cannot be said to have existed yesterday *in the same way* that it exists today, for that would rule out all change whatsoever. So weak causality philosophers must argue that, while today's effect already existed yesterday, it now exists in a different form. The curd already existed yesterday in the milk that was sweet though not in the form of curd. But today it is in the form of curd, for sweet milk and curds are the same thing, except in different forms.

The major problem for philosophers holding the weak causality view is to account for the transformation that the cause undergoes. Granted that the cause and the effect, milk and curds, for example, are the same reality, but in a different form, what causes the transformation of milk into curds? Either some additional reality must be postulated as a cause, or else it must be argued that the transformation is only an appearance, that the apparent transformation of reality is a kind of illusion. This latter view, advocated by Shaṅkara, comes close to denying causality altogether, for it denies that change is ultimately real. But even here it is necessary to account for the novelty of the appearance of change.

Before examining Shaṅkara's theory we will look at the Sāṁkhya view of pre-existent effects, which, in the classic formulation of Īśvarakṛṣṇa, takes the transformation of the cause to be a real change in the world. In the light of the general difficulties facing such a view, why do Sāṁkhya philosophers hold this theory of pre-existent effect? In the earliest available formulation of the Sāṁkhya vision, Īśvarakṛṣṇa gives five reasons: "The effect pre-exists because (1) what is non-existent in a cause cannot be produced from it; (2) because there is a definite connection between effect and cause; (3) because not everything is possible; (4) because a cause transforms only that which it has the capacity to transform; and (5) because the effect is of the same nature as the cause" (Sāṁkhya Karika, 9).

The first argument is relatively simple. It says, in effect, that you cannot get out of a cause what was never there. Curds are not caused by water because they do not pre-exist in water in any way. The reason why some causes can produce some effects but not others is precisely that the effects it can produce pre-exist in it, whereas the effects it cannot produce do not pre-exist in it. This is the "definite connection" referred to in the second argument.

The third argument develops the corollary of the second, namely, that unless there were a definite relation between the cause and effect any cause could produce any effect whatever. But since a given cause cannot produce everything, there must be a definite connection between it and its possible effect.

The fourth argument goes on to claim that the instrumental cause can operate on a material cause to produce its effects only if that definite relation between cause and effect exists. For example, bringing threads together with a loom will produce cloth, but bringing grains of sand together will not. Pressing seeds will produce oil, but pressing stones will not.

The fifth argument claims that this definite relation is one of pre-existence, because, for example, cloth is of the same nature as threads and oil is of the same nature of seeds. The reason why cause and effect are of the same nature is that the cause is really a pre-existent form of the effect.

Nyāya-Vaiśeṣika philosophers attack this view in several ways. Their first argument is that, if the effect is essentially the same as the cause, it should be possible to know the effect prior to its being caused just by knowing the cause. But this is clearly impossible: effects cannot be known before they are produced, since before they are produced there are no effects to be known. Nyāya philosophers claim this shows that the effect is a new reality, different from its constituent parts. No matter how many jars of milk one knows, one does not thereby know curds, for curds are a different reality from milk, even though caused by milk.

The Sāṁkhya reply to this argument is that its major assumption, that a reality is different from its constituent parts, makes no sense. Varying the example, they respond that the reality of a piece of cloth is not different from the reality of a number of threads arranged in a certain way. If the cloth were different from the threads, then it would be possible to see the cloth without seeing the threads. But this is clearly impossible; seeing the cloth is simply seeing the threads interwoven together.

They also attack the Nyāya claim that cause and effect are different realities because they are perceived as different. This, they say, is only to beg the question, which is whether the effect is different from the cause or simply the cause transformed. Since this claim begs the question, the subsequent Nyāya claim, "therefore seeing a new reality," can be dismissed without further argument.

Strong causality proponents also attack the pre-existent effect theory by challenging Sāṁkhya philosophers to explain why an agent or instrument of change is needed if the cause already pre-exists. For what already exists no agent or instrument is needed, and if an agent or instrument is needed to produce the effect, this can only mean that it did not exist prior to being caused. Sāṁkhya meets this objection by agreeing with it in part, admitting that the effect did not exist in this same form prior to being caused and that an agent or instrument is required to transform the cause in such a way that the pre-existent effect appears. This reply amounts to turning the argument aside by claiming that the agent or instrument simply manifests and makes explicit what was previously implicit and unmanifest, and does not create something new. Examples adduced to support this reply include the lump of gold that can become an earring or a coin without ever becoming anything other than gold and the tortoise contracted in its shell or spread out, both being different forms of the same thing.

The other part of the Sāṁkhya reply is to point out that, on *any* theory of causality, some explanation will have to be given for why some effects appear out of a cause and not others. Since a new form is something new, even though not a totally new reality, the role of instrumental cause in the weak causality theory is no more problematic than in the strong causality theory. Indeed, it is less problematic, for, by claiming that the effect pre-exists, Sāṁkhya philosophers do not face the difficulty of claiming, as Nyāya philosophers do, that the instrument operates on nothing.

The most serious objection to the Sāṁkhya theory of causality, however, is that if all effects pre-exist in their causes eternally, and if bondage is an effect, then bondage must exist eternally. If the theory maintains that no reality is produced as an effect, it must also maintain that no reality is destroyed as cause. But that means that if bondage is an effect—as Yoga philosophers claim—then it is an eternally existing effect, and liberation is impossible. Or, from the other side, if liberation is an effect of knowledge and action, it either always existed or else is impossible to achieve. How, in other words, if effects always pre-existed, can the coming-to-be of either bondage or liberation be accounted for?

This is an extremely difficult problem for weak causality theorists. Sāṁkhya philosophers attempt to solve it with a dualistic metaphysics. They claim that the real self, the puruṣa, never is bound, and that the world of change is eternally bound or determined. What happens, they say, is that the reflection of the free self is caught up in the processes of the changing world of mind and matter (prakṛti) leading to the mistaken conviction that the self is bound to these processes. But actually puruṣa is always free. What has to be destroyed is neither self nor world, but only the ignorance whereby world is mistaken for self. Once this ignorance is destroyed, the self's eternally existent freedom is realized.

But the critics are not ready to accept this metaphysical response without a challenge. What causes the original stuff of the world to become transformed in such a way that it can be mistaken for the Self? Is the transformation of prakṛti and the mistaken identification of self with this manifested prakṛti caused by prakṛti or by puruṣa? Since, Sāṁkhya philosophers avoid being forced to admit the Self's eternal bondage by insisting that puruṣa is an entirely different kind of reality from prakṛti, and eternally free, they cannot admit that there is a real causal relationship between self and the world.

Īśvarakṛṣṇa now resorts to analogies to suggest how puruṣa and prakṛti can affect each other without really being related. Prakṛti evolves because of the mere presence of puruṣa, he says, just as a dancer dances simply because of the presence of an audience, without there being a direct causal relation. In a similar way, once the audience has experienced the enjoyment of the dance the dancer stops, even as once ignorance is overcome and the self enjoys its freedom, the play of the world no longer engages its interest.

This and similar analogies are not totally convincing, however. The problem is that the Sāṁkhya philosophers cannot establish a causal relation between Self and the world. By itself, their assumption that Self and world are totally different kinds of realities does not convince critics that bondage is actually caused and that liberation is an effect, attainable by the causes of knowledge and action.

Faced with these difficulties, some proponents of weak causality, like Rāmānuja or Madhva, adopt a theistic position that allows them to postulate God as the cause of bondage and liberation. But they face the difficulty not only of proving God's existence, but also of showing how, if God is the source of both bondage and liberation, the self has any freedom whatsoever.

Others, like Shaṅkara, avoid these theological difficulties by rejecting the dualistic metaphysics and arguing that the self is ultimately identical with Brahman and is eternally free. To succeed in this approach, Shaṅkara and other nondualists must explain the appearance of the world and suffering as a transformation of Brahman while maintaining that Brahman never changes! The key element in the explanation is a revised theory of how pre-existent effects are transformed.

Unlike the Sāṁkhya account, which holds that the cause is actually transformed into its effect, becoming something different in the process, Shaṅkara insists that the cause remains essentially the same. He agrees with the Sāṁkhya argument that the effect cannot be a new reality; if it were, one would be faced with the impossible task of explaining how existence can come from non-existence or how a causal relation can exist between the existent and the non-existent. Since it makes no sense to say that something comes out of nothing or that something is related to nothing, Shaṅkara rejects the Nyāya-Vaiśeṣika theory that the effect is a new reality.

But the same argument renders the Sāṁkhya theory of causality as the actual transformation of a pre-existent reality equally unacceptable. Although the Sāṁkhya theory maintains that the material nature of the effect pre-existed, it claims that the form of the effect is something new. But the point of the Sāṁkhya philosopher's objections to strong causality was precisely that this theory could not account for the coming into being of something new! Since the problem is the same, whether it is new matter or a new form that is claimed to come into being, the very arguments used to disprove his opponent's theory undermine the position of the Sāṁkhya philosopher, as Shaṅkara enjoys pointing out.

Shaṅkara's solution to this problem is to show that a change in form is not a change in reality because form has no independent reality. Form, he argues, exists only in formed matter. There is no form of a pot except in the form of clay (or other matter). If a change in form were a change in reality, then a person sitting down would be a different person from the same person standing up. But obviously this is not the case, showing that a change in form is not a creation of a new reality, Shaṅkara claims.

However, to claim that neither matter nor form really comes into being is to deny the reality of change itself. This radical position is accepted by Shaṅkara, who maintains that Brahman alone is ultimately real and that what is ultimately real never changes. But he does not deny the existence of the world and of selves in bondage, a denial that would make the entire enterprise of liberation meaningless. Instead, he argues that the existence of the world and bound selves is at a lower level of reality than the existence of Brahman. It is only at this lower level of reality that bondage and liberation appear as the effects of causal chains.

This proposal to see bound selves and the world as lower levels of the same reality that, at a deeper level, is totally free and changeless, faces its own challenge. It requires making sense of a doctrine of distinct levels of reality, while at the same time providing for sufficient relationship between the levels to at least allow the bound self to achieve freedom. How can the ignorant self, living at the lowest levels, achieve knowledge of the highest level? We will see how Shaṅkara responded to this challenge in the next chapter, when we look at the metaphysical views complementing the different theories of causality.

The two remaining theories of causality, the Jaina and the Buddhist, are, respectively, an acceptance of both weak and strong theories as complementary and a rejection of the presuppositions of both theories.

## MAYBE BOTH STRONG AND WEAK CAUSALITY

Jainas fall back on their principle of the many-sidedness of existence, arguing that their opponents view strong and weak causality as mutually exclusive because they fail to see that each theory is true only from a certain perspective, which, unfortunately, is taken to be absolute rather than relative to other perspectives. If reality is seen in terms of substances in which various qualities come into being and cease to be, then one is correct in saying that the effect pre-existed in its cause, the substance in which the new quality came to be. The self in whom ignorance and bondage come into being as qualities is the same self in which the essential quality of freedom is realized when bondage and ignorance are destroyed. However, when qualities are related to each other, they cannot be said to pre-exist, for qualities pre-exist only in substances, not in each other. The quality of bondage excludes that of freedom; freedom is a quality that appears only when the previous quality of bondage is eliminated.

That may be fine on the assumption that reality consists of unchanging substances characterized by changing qualities, say the Buddhists, but what if reality is of the nature of process, where it makes no sense to distinguish between substances and qualities? The Jaina again turns to the principle of the many-sidedness of existence, arguing that it is only from a certain perspective that reality appears in the substance-quality mode. From another perspective it appears as process, a continuous flow of events. And from this perspective neither weak nor strong theories of causality are adequate, for all events are interdependent. To take one event as independent and call it cause and to take another event and call it dependent upon the first as an effect is to overlook the mutual interdependence of events. On the other hand, to emphasize this mutuality to the exclusion of dependence is to run the risk of overlooking the possibility of achieving liberation by removing the conditions upon which bondage depends.

Although the Jainas avoid some of the problems of the other two theories of causality by combining them as different perspectives on the same reality, they generate other problems for themselves. First, to the extent that they accept strong causality as a valid perspective on change, they must face all the objections confronting this theory, and also confront the objections to weak causality, which they also accept as a valid perspective. Second, they must be able to show that their doctrine of the many-sidedness of existence is a valid perspective. Indeed they must go further, for if they are to refute the other positions as being only partial and limited perspectives, they must argue that many-sidedness is true because that is the way things really are. But this very principle of many-sidedness forces them to admit that many-sidedness may itself be only a partial and limited truth!

Finally there is Shaṅkara's argument that, by occupying this middle position of indeterminateness from which every view is maybe true and maybe false, Jainas render action aimed at liberation impossible. To take action one must take a stand, accepting certain things as true and certain actions as effective in bringing about certain desired conditions. If all one can say is "maybe," the conviction required by action is ruled out. But then there is no room for a path to liberation. To the Jaina response that for the sake of effective action certain views be accepted provisionally as true, Shaṅkara replies that, in effect, this is what all the other theories also do!

## PROCESS VIEWS

We turn finally to the Buddhist view of causality, which, as we saw earlier, is a theory of complete interdependence of events called "dependent origination." By rejecting the entire substance view of reality which maintains that reality consists of interacting substances whose qualities undergo constant change or modification, Buddhists avoid the difficulties plaguing those who posit inherent causal relationships as well as the problems facing those who claim that effects pre-exist in their causes. The Buddhist view is that reality consists not of things, but of ongoing, interrelated, processes. From an analytical point of view, it consists of momentary and fleeting events with no substance or duration. Reality is simply energy in motion. Therefore, there is no need to posit any special thing, force, or relationship to account for causal connections among *things*.

As a theory of the connections between certain events and their necessary conditions, dependent origination postulates that change is the result of mutually influencing factors continuously imparting energy and movement to each other, giving rise to a constant stream of new becoming. But these constantly arising new forms of existence are not independent of the originating conditions. Only when all the necessary conditions obtain does a particular process arise, for example, the process of a burning candle. The flame is admittedly a process; it does not remain the same, even for an instant, and there is no one thing that can be said to be the cause of a particular moment in the burning process. But if all necessary conditions are present (e.g., heat for ignition, wax for fuel, wick for connecting fuel and ignition heat), then a candle burns continuously. If any one or more of the necessary conditions is absent (e.g., ignition heat), then the process stops.

Fire can also be used to illustrate the Buddhist view that permanence is only an illusion. Not only does the fire appear to be continuous and self-identical over a period of time—even though we know quite well that it is continuously changing—but if one takes a candle or torch and whirls it overhead in a circular motion it will appear to the observer that there is a ring or circle of fire above his head. In reality the circle is just an appearance caused by a continuously moving torch. Similarly, the continuous movement of processes gives the appearance of enduring things, when in fact these supposed "things" are nothing but continuously changing processes.

Still, the Buddhist must account for the connections between moments or events in the processes called existence. What brings events together to cause suffering? And what can remove those events that constitute the conditions of suffering? Unless these questions can be answered, the eightfold noble path to nirvāṇa cannot be shown to be effective.

Actually three different Buddhist answers can be distinguished. Vaibhāṣika and Sautrāntika philosophers hold that the continuous processes constituting existence are made up of logically discrete moments. These atomic moments come together in sequence to form continuous events, with the patterns of their coming together giving each event its specific characteristics. These moments are taken to be logically prior to the events constituted by them and are therefore regarded as having a kind of independence of the processes themselves, allowing these Buddhists to regard the fundamental moments as the causes of the processes. It is, they say, the patterns formed by these atomic moments that cause the processes to change; that make the difference between the processes of duḥkha and nirvāṇa.

The Yogācāra analysis is similar, except they take the fundamental moments of process to be mental units, with physical moments being simply the external correlates of knowledge. There are two important reasons for this move. On the one hand, it seems clear enough that whatever we know of the external world we know through the images and concepts of our knowledge. The external world is known through the mind, making all knowledge of physical reality dependent on ideas in the mind. This gives mental reality an important kind of priority, for physical reality is dependent on the mind, at least so far as knowledge is concerned. On the other hand, if the fundamental units of process are mental, then it is possible to see how knowledge can become a condition of liberation, for the new understanding gained in meditative insight represents new patterns in the process constituting what we call self. These new patterns represent the breaking of the chain of bondage by eliminating the old patterns of ignorance and grasping.

The most serious objections to both of these Buddhist positions comes from the third Buddhist position, represented by Nāgārjuna's "middle way" philosophy. Both of them, he suggests, have betrayed the Buddha's central insight that everything is completely interdependent. In their zeal to provide a conceptual basis for liberation from duḥkha they, like the advocates of other causal theories, argue for the independence of certain conditions on which other conditions, the conditions of duḥkha and liberation, are dependent. That the Sautrāntikas, to emphasize the conditionedness of duḥkha, take physical reality to be independent whereas the Yogācārins, to emphasize the possibility of liberation through knowledge, regard ideas as independent, does not matter. What does matter is that they overlook the fact that both the bondage-producing ignorance and the nirvāṇa-producing knowledge require mutually dependent subjects and objects. If the objective is given independence, then liberation becomes unintelligible. But if the subjective is given independence, then bondage becomes unintelligible.

To emphasize this complete interdependence of everything, Nāgārjuna insists that things and events have no nature or reality of their own. Their existence is nothing more, and nothing less, than the mutual interaction of a great multitude of factors—indeed, ultimately the mutual interaction of all the factors of the entire universe. This lack of independence or self-sufficiency Nāgārjuna calls *śūnyatā* or emptiness. All beings are empty of self-nature because they are completely dependent on the multitude of interrelated processes that constitute the particular stream of becoming usually mistaken for an independent and enduring self or thing.

Causality is essentially a way of accounting for change by showing how something coming to be is dependent upon something else, called a cause. Since the cause is taken to be independent, it is usually assumed that an event has been explained satisfactorily if it has been shown to be the effect of a cause. Consequently, Nāgārjuna's refusal to admit that anything is independent in relation to anything else leads him to reject every causal theory as inadequate.

But he does not thereby reject the fact of bondage, the possibility of liberation, and the Buddha's path leading to liberation. Instead, he rejects the notion that a conceptual understanding of these things is possible in the final analysis. Human reason works by cutting up and separating what insight reveals to be united in its interdependence. When these cut-up pieces are mistaken for independent realities, the irresolvable problem of trying to relate them as cause and effect arises. But if the truth of dependent origination is recognized, no theory of causality is needed: there are no separate and independent things to be related as cause and effect.

Although Nāgārjuna's analysis may direct one away from useless conceptual games and toward the practices of morality and meditation that Buddhists view as generative of insight and freedom, it will not satisfy anyone who wants a philosophical theory giving a rational account of the nature and causes of bondage and of liberation. Indeed, by rejecting the adequacy of causal explanation in general, Nāgārjuna has ruled out the possibility of defending his position by recourse to such a theory.

## Summary

At the heart of Indian philosophy lies the perception of human bondage and suffering and the recognition that liberation from these conditions is possible. By following a path of self-transformation involving knowledge and action, freedom from the causes and conditions of bondage can be attained. To show how and why a prescribed path of liberation can succeed, philosophical explanations of the nature of self, reality, and causality were developed. In addition, it was necessary to explain how knowledge of reality and causality is possible to meet the challenge of those skeptics who insisted that it is impossible to know either the causes of bondage or the means to liberation.

Because theories of causality, reality, and knowledge are all interlinked, it turned out that different visions of the causes of bondage and the means of liberation resulted in different philosophies, giving rise to the nine major philosophical systems that have dominated Indian speculative thought over the last two thousand years.

In this chapter we have examined the various theories of causality and have shown some of the philosophical debate characterizing traditional efforts to support a favored theory. Since our discussion itself has been a summary of the classical positions and arguments, no further summary will be attempted here. But the reader may wish to look ahead to the summary of the next chapter, where a brief overview of the philosophies of causality in relation to the various metaphysical views characterizing the different systems is presented.

## Suggestions for Further Reading

S. Chatterjee and D. Datta, *An Introduction to Indian Philosophy*, 6th ed. (Calcutta: Calcutta University Press, 1960), is an excellent introduction to the nine major Indian philosophical systems, with a separate chapter devoted to each. This is a standard textbook that has gone through numerous editions and continues to be widely used, both in India and the United States.

M. Hiriyana's *Outlines of Indian Philosophy* (New York: George Allen & Unwin, 1932) is also very good, although it is somewhat more difficult going than Chatterjee and Datta. This has recently become available in the United States in a paperback edition.

My earlier book, *Oriental Philosophies* (New York: Charles Scribners' Sons, 1970), contains a fifty-page introduction to the six Hindu systems and two chapters on Buddhist views of self and reality. Written for students with no previous acquaintance with Asian philosophies, it continues to be a popular book for introductory courses in Eastern philosophy.

Karl Potter's *Presuppositions of India's Philosophies* (Englewood Cliffs, N.J.: Prentice-Hall, Inc., 1963) examines the various philosophical views from the perspective of their visions of the means to freedom and the causes of bondage. Metaphysical and epistemological issues are discussed in relation to the central issue of causality. This is a rewarding book for those with a serious interest in philosophy and some prior knowledge of Indian thought.

# 13

# Systematic Philosophy: Knowledge and Reality

The reason that causality is so important in Indian philosophy is because it explains the connection between bondage and its conditions and between freedom and its conditions. But how this connection is explained depends also on the metaphysical views of reality that both support and are supported by these different theories of causality.

## Reality

Every theory of reality—except the Materialist—has three fundamental objectives. First, it must simultaneously account for the tremendous diversity that we experience and unify this diversity into a coherent whole. The starting point of metaphysics is the commonsense view that accepts the differences in our perceptions and experiences as a sign of the different kinds of existence making up reality. This tells us that reality is made up of fundamentally different kinds of processes and things. There are physical processes and mental processes, spiritual things and material things, actions and knowledge, emotions and appetites, space and time, and so on. But many of these different kinds of things and processes are obviously related to each other. What is the basis of these relationships?

Every attempt to know or to understand the universe assumes some kind of underlying unity as a basis for comprehending the universe as a whole. If there were no relations at all between any of the processes and things constituting reality, there would only be chaos instead of a universe. Since we experience reality not as chaos, but as an ordered and unified whole, the critical question is, What is the basis of the underlying unity of existence?

To assume that this unity results from all these different processes and things being simply different aspects or functions of some original and unitary being, for example, God or Brahman, is to run the risk of denying the plurality of existence that we experience. On the other hand, to insist on the plurality of different kinds of existence is to run the risk of not being able to unify our experience. As we shall see, the pluralists—Nyāya, Vaiśeṣika, and Mīmāmsā—prefer the latter risk, while the dualists and monists—Sāṁkhya, Yoga, and Vedānta—prefer the former.

The second basic objective of Indian metaphysics is to establish a basis for liberation by showing that there is a level or kind of reality that is free from the limitations of ordinary existence. Whether it is called God, Brahman, Self, Puruṣa, or Śūnyatā is not important. What is important is that this higher reality is free from the limitations associated with bondage and suffering. Also there must be some connection between ordinary existence and that greater reality such that human life can be transformed into the perfect and unlimited existence characteristic of the highest level of reality.

The fundamental challenge to this objective is to maintain the reality of ordinary existence while still making room for liberation by showing that there is a higher order of reality. It is this challenge that pushes many philosophers into a dualism between material and spiritual existence. But the dualistic position faces the difficulty of showing how two fundamentally different kinds of reality can be related to and interact with each other to produce bondage and make liberation possible.

The third metaphysical objective is to account simultaneously for change and stability. Our experience suggests both that something remains identical over an extended period of time and that change is the common rule for everything that exists. Each one of us thinks that in an important sense we are the same person born twenty or forty years ago. Yet we know that all our cells, as well as our knowledge and feelings, have been changing constantly since the day we were born. How can we remain the same while we are constantly changing? Because of the Indian preoccupation with achieving liberation, this question has a special urgency. Whether or not it is possible to explain a change from an original perfection to the state of suffering and bondage that we find ourselves in, it must be possible to explain how the change from bondage to liberation occurs. This is obviously the most important change that can occur to anyone, and every way of liberation must have some way of accounting for *how* it can occur.

The challenge of accounting for both change and permanence produces the dichotomy between process philosophers and substance philosophers. Process philosophers—the Buddhists—say that reality is essentially of the nature of process; there are no beings, there is only becoming. They try to account for permanence and self-identity in relation to the continuous stream of becoming which is taken to be fundamental. Substance philosophers, on the other hand, say that reality is essentially of the nature of permanent things that undergo various changes. They try to account for becoming in terms of the permanence and self-identity of beings. All except the Buddhists maintain a substance view of reality.

As we examine the different views of reality, we will see how well they meet these three objectives. Since the pluralistic substance view is closest to common sense, we will begin with the view of the Vaiśeṣika philosophers, a view that is accepted, for the most part, by Nyāya and Mīmāmsā also.

## PLURALISM

The Vaiśeṣika view of reality begins as a kind of philosophical common sense. It assumes that the fundamental categories of thought—substance, quality, action, generality, particularity, and inherence—are also the fundamental kinds of reality, an assumption that easily follows our ordinary view that the characteristics of our knowledge are also the characteristics of the world. Substances or things are constituted by combinations of nine fundamental kinds of indivisible elements or atoms, which are of the nature of earth, water, fire, air, ether, time, space, self, or mind. These combinations of atoms support the various qualities making up the vast differences among the various things of the world.

Assuming that the effect is a new creation, differing fundamentally from its cause, Vaiśeṣika thinkers claim that this whole creation begins when the primordial atoms combine with each other, first in pairs, then triplets, and so on, progressively evolving into the complexities that we recognize all around us. Eventually these combinations will dissolve and the whole world will be destroyed, as it is returned to its original conditions of separate atoms. Out of that condition, creation will again take place by a repetition of the original process, giving rise to great cycles of evolution and destruction of the universe.

To account for the fact of bondage and the possibility of liberation, the self is taken to be a special kind of being, a nonmaterial being, that, although associated with material existence through its bodily incarnation, is capable of existing independently of other substances and their qualities. Indeed, it is precisely this independence that constitutes liberation.

The chief problem this view faces is to explain how all these different kinds of things can be related so that they constitute a single universe, and how, in particular, the self, as a separate and independent kind of being, can be related to other kinds of reality in such a way that its bondage is intelligible and its liberation possible. As we have seen, these philosophers rely on causality as the essential relation bringing all these different kinds of realities together. But their difficulties in maintaining a consistent and coherent theory of causality affects their metaphysical views adversely. Indeed, many Nyāya and Vaiśeṣika philosophers bring in the additional assumption of God as creator of the world to unify the claimed plurality of existence.

God is assumed to be an intelligent agent operating on pre-existent matter to give it the intelligible order and unity required to explain our knowledge of the universe. In addition, this intelligent agent ensures the operations of karma, according to which each person will receive precisely the rewards or punishments warranted by his or her actions, including eventual liberation when it is deserved.

This view of God's place in the scheme of things has its own problems. First, how can the existence of such a being be proved? Second, even if God does exist, to view Him (or Her) as an agent is to reduce Him to the level of a person, for an agent acts to achieve something that he or she lacks, usually because of some desire or passion. But God can lack nothing and is not driven by desires and passions.

Furthermore, the agency of God in creating the world cannot be maintained without showing what relationship exists between the unevolved elements and the Lord. But since both God and the primordial elements are claimed to be eternal and independent of each other, there is no possibility of showing a relationship without subordinating one to the other—a violation of the original assumption of two eternal and independent realities, one the material cause and the other the agent cause. But if no relationship between them can be shown, it is impossible to maintain that God is the cause of the evolution of the original elements of the universe or the keeper of cosmic justice.

For these reasons some Nyāya and Vaiśeṣika philosophers, and practically all Mīmāmsā philosophers, reject this introduction of God as a special kind of reality to unify and order the material universe. But they are hard pressed to explain how the intelligible order of the universe can proceed from nonintelligent material elements without assuming an intelligent being or principle.

## DUALISM

This is also an acute problem for the Jaina view of non-living existence and for the Sāṁkhya theory of prakṛti. Let us recall for a moment the dualistic Sāṁkhya account of bondage and liberation. The Sāṁkhya way of making room metaphysically for liberation and bondage is to claim two fundamentally different kinds of reality. There is the Self (puruṣa), of the nature of pure consciousness, unbound and unsuffering, and there is prakṛti, the basis and nature of everything that is not puruṣa. As prakṛti evolves from its primordial unmanifested state into this incredibly diverse universe, the independent and pure self is reflected in the evolutes of prakṛti. It is this prakṛtic reflection of puruṣa, mistaking itself for the true self, that experiences bondage and that seeks liberation. In reality, the true self never is bound and never requires liberation. Liberation consists simply in removing the ignorance wherein prakṛtic existence is mistaken for the self.

To account both for the transformation of the primordial prakṛti into this wonderfully rich and diversified universe, and to explain the process by which bondage arises through ignorance of the pristine nature of the self, Sāṁkhya postulates an evolutionary transformation. When the initial equilibrium of its three constituent threads or modes (guṇas) is upset, their mutual interactions cause the evolution of the world to begin. In the initial evolutionary step, the dominant guṇa, sattva, characterized by luminosity, picks up and traps the reflected image of puruṣa. As evolution continues, this image is tied ever more tightly to the various modes of material existence, constituting its bondage.

But what causes the initial equilibrium of prakṛti to be upset? Opponents point out that, since only prakṛti and puruṣa are ultimately real, it must be either one or the other. Since puruṣa is claimed to be of an entirely different order of reality and totally separate from prakṛti, it cannot be the cause, for there is no causal interaction between these two totally different kinds of being. But there is no other external agent of change that could possibly have upset the original equilibrium. Sāṁkhya must show either that, despite its seeming impossibility, puruṣa actually does interact with prakṛti and cause its evolution or else that prakṛti is self-caused.

Since Sāṁkhya thinkers deny that puruṣa and prakṛti actually interact, they are forced to defend the view that evolution is self-caused. But this view is open to serious criticism. Unless there were some intelligence directing the evolution of prakṛti, the experienced order of the universe—including the sequence of knowledge and action leading to liberation—would be impossible. By definition, however, prakṛti is devoid of intelligent consciousness.

The chief problem with dualism is the reverse side of its main attractiveness. If the self is separate from the non-self it is clear that the non-self cannot really hold it in bondage. But the price paid for weakening or destroying the non-self's power over the self in this way is very high. This very dualism stands in the way of explaining how the self and non-self can be related to each other at all. And unless self and non-self are related in some way, it does not make any sense to say that the self's relation to the non-self causes or constitutes its bondage. If there is no relation between them, then nothing the non-self does can possibly have any impact on the self, and vice versa. But then how can the ignorant and bound self do anything at all to effect its liberation?

To avoid the conclusion that the self is inevitably doomed to bondage, Sāṁkhya thinkers seize the other horn of the dilemma and claim that the self is eternally free. In the last analysis, they say, bondage is an illusion produced by the ignorance of the self's eternal purity and freedom and of the total separateness of the self and non-self (puruṣa and prakṛti). The activities of yoga and knowledge aim not at achieving a separation between self and non-self but, rather, at destroying the ignorance generating the *illusion* that they are joined together and therefore that they need to be separated. Liberating wisdom is the insight into this eternal separateness of puruṣa and prakṛti that destroys the illusion of bondage.

## MONISM

Shaṅkara and other monists go even further. The hypothesis of a non-self that is not at all related to the self and that has nothing to do with bondage is totally irrelevant and unnecessary according to them. Shaṅkara's view is that ultimately there is only one absolute and independent reality. This is the unchanging, quality-less Brahman, intuited by the sages of the Upaniṣads as the ground of all existence. Although the basis of all empirical existence, this ultimate ground goes beyond all the limitations of empirical existence—both personal and impersonal.

The self, in its ultimate nature, is Ātman, identical with Brahman, transcending all the limitations of psychophysical existence just as Brahman transcends all the limitations of nonpersonal existence. The only difference between Brahman and Ātman is the perspective from which the ultimate is approached. Approached as the ground of the self, it is called Ātman; approached as the ground of nonpersonal existence, it is called Brahman. But these are only different names for the same reality—even as Morning Star and Evening Star are different names for the same reality (Venus), according to whether it is seen in the morning or the evening.

Since the self as Ātman-Brahman is an ultimately pure, unlimited, conscious being, it cannot be subjected to bondage by anything else, for everything else that exists is derived from Brahman and is secondary to it. This vision guarantees liberation by making bondage illusory while avoiding the Sāṁkhya problems of trying to relate the two incommensurable realities of prakṛti and puruṣa. And since Brahman alone is ultimately real, the underlying unity of experienced diversity is also ensured, for the experienced differences are only different appearances of Brahman.

However, when it comes to explaining change, Shaṅkara's vision of reality faces serious difficulties. Since Brahman, the sole reality at the ultimate level, is completely changeless, it follows that, at least at the ultimate level, reality itself must be said to be changeless. But if change is denied, it makes no sense to talk about the self's becoming bound or attaining liberation. This is why Advaitins are forced to say that the Self, which is nothing but Brahman, is never really bound. It always exists in a pure and unlimited way.

Here serious problems arise, however, for even though the self may always be liberated in some ultimate sense, it is obvious that bondage and suffering do exist at this ordinary, empirical, level and that the attainment of liberation is the highest goal of life. How can this existence of bondage be reconciled with the pure and unlimited nature of the Self? And how can the multiplicity and change experienced at the empirical level be reconciled with the insight that ultimately the unchanging Brahman is the sole reality?

Shaṅkara's answer is to distinguish between different levels of reality. At one extreme are those things that cannot exist at all (e.g., sons of barren women and square circles) because they are logically impossible. Then, at the first and lowest level of reality, are those things that exist in dreams and illusory experiences. It cannot be denied that the snake perceived when a rope in the dark is mistaken for a snake, or the bill collector heard ringing the doorbell in a dream, exist in some sense. But when the light is good and the rope is seen for what it is, or when one awakens and becomes aware that the bill collector appeared only as part of a dream, then the snake and the bill collector are known to be unreal because their existence is negated and repudiated by the greater reality encountered in the waking experience.

This world of waking experiences is the second level of reality. Although from an empirical perspective it appears as the highest level of reality, the experience of Brahman reveals it to be ultimately unreal, even as waking experience shows the objects experienced in dreams to be unreal. It is only from the perspective of this third and highest level of reality that the change and multiplicity experienced at the second, empirical, level are said to be unreal.

Although his critics accuse Shaṅkara of rejecting the empirical world as altogether unreal, as totally illusory, this seems to be a distortion of his distinction between levels of reality. That the world exists is no more denied than is the existence of objects in dreams. The question is not whether or not dream objects and objects of waking experiences exist—Shaṅkara clearly asserts that they do. But what is the status of these objects? Unless one awakens from a dream, there is no way of knowing that the objects experienced in the dream are ultimately unreal. Within the dream, they are accepted as real, and the dream self experiences terror or joy because of them. In a similar way, this empirical world of ordinary veridical waking experiences is accepted as real from the perspective of this level of reality. Only when a person awakens to a greater reality—the reality of Brahman—can the existence of the empirical world and self be recognized as ultimately unreal.

Thus, Shaṅkara does not deny the existence of the world or devalue its experience from the empirical perspective. But he suggests that there is another level of reality, that of Brahman, which is of ultimate value and which cannot be negated or repudiated by anything else. Only in relation to this reality is ordinary existence unreal. Even as the dream experience must be taken as real until one awakens from the dream, so empirical waking experience must be taken as real until one awakens to the higher reality of Brahman. Only then is it possible to understand that, although the world of ordinary experience *exists*, it is ultimately *unreal*.

While this theory of different levels of reality avoids many of the problems of dualism, it faces its own serious problems. How can the distinctness of these different levels be maintained while at the same time showing that they are all related to each other and all grounded in Brahman, the ultimate reality?

The Advaitin compares the relation between the ordinary world of suffering and bondage and the ultimate reality of Brahman with that between the illusory snake perceived in poor light and the rope perceived in good light. In the last analysis, the rope alone is real. But not knowing that what is perceived is really a rope, a person superimposes the characteristics of a snake on this elongated and twisted darkish colored patch. Convinced now that there really is a snake, a person becomes frightened and tries to scare the snake away—or runs away from it.

Although the snake is unreal—as the person realizes when it becomes known that there is only a piece of rope lying in the road—the fear engendered by the mistaken impression is real. But because this fear is rooted in ignorance, only knowledge that what exists is not a snake, but simply a rope, can alleviate this fear.

In a similar way, the ultimate unchanging reality of Brahman is mistaken for this changing world of suffering and bondage. Because of ignorance of Brahman and the resulting superimposition of the characteristics of change and limited existence on this unchanging and unlimited reality, it is mistaken for the frightening world of saṁsāra. Not knowing better, a person accepts this appearance of saṁsāra as real and seeks a way out of bondage—just as person who thinks the rope is a snake seeks to escape its threatening presence. But because this appearance is generated by ignorance, it can be overcome only by knowledge.

Because bondage is caused by ignorance and because only knowledge can eliminate ignorance, Shaṅkara, like many of the sages of the Upaniṣads, insists that, in the final analysis, knowledge alone leads to liberation: "Only knowledge can destroy ignorance; action cannot, for it is incommensurate with ignorance. Unless ignorance is destroyed, passion and aversion will not be destroyed" (Upadeśasāharsī, 1.1.6).

What about morality, ritual, and devotion? Do not they also constitute effective means of liberation? In the final analysis, the answer is clearly "No." At best they can be recommended only as means to prepare one for, and dispose one toward, reception of the liberating knowledge. Shaṅkara cannot recommend any kind of action as the means of liberation because of his view that bondage is caused by ignorance, not action. Action does not cause bondage because the true nature of the self is not that of agent but that of pure consciousness or knowledge. His rejection of the view that the self is an agent is stated quite explicitly:

The view that Self is an agent is false, for it arises from the belief that the body is

Self. The belief, "I do not do anything," is true and arises from the right means of knowledge. The view that Self is an agent is due to factors of action, whereas the idea that it is not an agent is due to its own nature. It has been fully ascertained that the understanding, "I am an experiencer," is false."... I am always changeless, motionless, pure, free from old age, liberated and non-dual."

(*Ibid.*, 1.12.16–19)

Moral and religious actions are recommended, but only as preliminary means. For a person deluded into identification of himself with the body and mistaking the agent self for the real self, action is inevitable. For such a person the rule is to act in accord with dharma, in such a way that one will be prepared for the way of knowledge. But only through knowledge can the bondage born of ignorance be destroyed.

The implicit rejection of the moral and devotional means of liberation entailed by Shaṅkara's philosophical view ran counter to a strong medieval emphasis on the personal nature of Brahman as Lord and to an accompanying emphasis on developing personal relationships with the Lord as a primary way of achieving liberation. Consequently, many other thinkers, who also took their stand in the teachings of the Upaniṣads, Gītā, and Brahmā Sūtras, insisted that there was no incompatibility between Brahman as Lord and Brahman as beyond all characteristics. Since conceiving of the ultimate in personal terms emphasized the creative, active dimension of reality—the Lord is the Supreme Agent—room was found here to accommodate both the view that the self is an agent and the view that the self is pure consciousness.

Rāmānuja, for example, also wished to avoid the metaphysical problems of Sāṁkhya dualism. He, like Shaṅkara, claimed that Brahman alone is real. But unlike Shaṅkara, he admitted differentiations within Brahman as a basis for the reality of the world and self as agent. Using the analogy of self and body, he regarded selves and the world as the body of Brahman, which though different from, is still one with, the self of Brahman. This enabled Rāmānuja to explain how this complex world of manifested existence comes to be, for it is directed and controlled by the inner self of Brahman, seen as the Supreme Lord. Thus, the world comes to be through God's design and purpose and is real because it is created by the Lord out of Himself.

By viewing the ultimate in personal terms as God, and seeing the world and self as God's personal creations out of His own Body, it would appear that Rāmānuja makes room for a human self whose actions can be effective in securing liberation. But, in fact, this is not the case. If Brahman is the ultimate agent, then the individual self is totally at God's mercy, for the whole universe is designed and directed by God. Strictly speaking, the individual can do nothing to gain liberation. All that can be done is to prepare oneself to accept God's grace, for only through God's grace can a person be liberated.

The strength of this position is that, as the ultimate reality, God can secure liberation for all those who come to Him in loving adoration and surrender themselves to His love and power. But the price paid for this guarantee of liberation is that the individual's own efforts must now be seen as inadequate to secure his or her own liberation. Liberation is, so to speak, entirely in God's hands.

Furthermore, since this position removes the basis for self-determination, not only with respect to liberation, but also with respect to bondage, it makes God the cause of bondage as well as the source of freedom. This raises an extremely difficult question. Why did God create bondage in the first place? This is the Indian counterpart to the Judaic, Christian, and Islamic problem of why a good and loving God should have created or permitted sin and evil in the world.

Both the Indian and the Mideastern theistic positions provide for salvation. If the individual submits to God and follows His will, he will be saved through God's almighty power. But neither position can explain why evil should exist in the first place. Surely, an omniscient and omnipotent God could have created a world without evil.

The same logic that allows God to be praised as the savior of humankind also allows Him to be blamed for creating or permitting the conditions of suffering and bondage from which we wish to be saved or liberated. No theist wants to accept this position, of course, so while God usually gets the credit for goodness, humans and demons must shoulder the blame for evil. But this is a difficult position to maintain philosophically.

## PROCESS VIEWS

Buddhist views of reality face a different set of problems entirely. While the various substance views have difficulty explaining how unchanging substances can become bound and liberated, process views have difficulty explaining how, if everything is constantly changing, the same person who suffers bondage can attain liberation. Since no one ever remains the same from one moment to the next, what is the basis for saying that the Siddhārtha who attained nirvāṇa through meditative insight and moral practice was the same person who previously suffered? Unless a person endures continuously over time—from the time of suffering to the time of liberation—it makes no sense to say that this person can achieve liberation by following the noble eightfold path.

Buddhists are agreed that there are no permanent things or substances. The three axioms of Buddhist metaphysics are (1) duḥkha—there is suffering; (2) anitya—there are no permanent things of any kind; and (3) anātman—there is no permanent self. By coming to realize that reality is constituted entirely of interrelated processes, a person overcomes fear of change and stops grasping for permanence, thereby eliminating duḥkha.

But who realizes the truth of anitya and anātman? And what is the connection between this person and the person who eliminates duḥkha? If in practicing right speech and action today, I am a different person than I will be tomorrow, then how can today's practice possibly contribute to *my* liberation tomorrow? On a substance view of reality, "I" and "my" refer to the unchanging substantial self, which, despite changes in various qualities, remains identical with itself over time. But since Buddhists deny the existence of a substantial self, "I" and "my" clearly cannot refer to such an unchanging self. Then to what do these terms refer?

They refer to a continuously changing stream of becoming in which the immediately preceding moments determine the succeeding moments, thereby providing for continuity without unchanging identity. On this all Buddhists agree, for this is the heart of the Buddha's teaching of dependent origination. But they do not agree on what the nature of the moments constituting the stream of becoming are or on how they are connected to each other.

The Vaibhāṣikas claim that the moments of process are made up of elemental forces that exist exactly as they are experienced in our interaction with the external world. Because these elemental forces are held to be real independently of experience, this view is described as realism. And because many different elemental forces are claimed, it is called pluralistic.

The Sautrāntikas hold a somewhat similar position, but they object to the Vaibhāṣikas' claim that the elemental features of experience can constitute the ultimate elements of process. Experience is conditioned, they say, not only by the reality experienced, but also by the experiencer. To take the fundamental elements of experience to be the ultimate moments of process upon which everything else is dependent violates the fundamental principle that everything is interdependent, that there are no ultimate and independent realities. Indeed, it comes dangerously close to asserting a substance view in disguised form.

The Mādhyamika philosophers take the Sautrāntika argument even further. If whatever exists, exists in dependence upon something else, then it makes no sense to search for, or to postulate, ultimate elemental forces upon which individual streams of becoming depend and by which they are determined. The quest for ultimate elements of process, real in themselves, they say, is a misguided search for substances, betraying the principle of complete interdependence of all existence.

According to the Mādhyamikas, all moments or elements of existence are devoid of self-identity and independence. This is the meaning of Nāgārjuna's claim that all elements of existence are empty of reality. The theory of emptiness does not proclaim a metaphysics of total nonexistence or nihilism. It proclaims the mutual interdependence of all processes and attacks the view that some beings or elements exist independently by their own natures.

The Yogācārins worried that, by giving up the quest for ultimates altogether, the Mādhyamikas left no room for the truth of the Buddha's teaching and no basis for the noble eightfold path as an effective means of overcoming duḥkha. Unless there is some independent reality, they argued, it is not possible to interrupt and stop the chain of becoming that constitutes duḥkha. Since it is through right knowledge and right intention that ignorance and grasping are eliminated as causes of duḥkha, the fundamental forces of consciousness must have a kind of independent existence, the Yogācārins argue. If consciousness exists independently, and if everything else depends on consciousness, then a transformation of consciousness can lead one from duḥkha to nirvāṇa.

From the Mādhyamika perspective, however, the Yogācārins were also flirting with a substance view of reality. But unlike the Vaibhāṣikas, who took the elements of external reality to have an independent reality, the Yogācārins took the elements of consciousness to have independent reality and made external processes ultimately dependent upon consciousness, winding up with a kind of idealism.

Neither the Yogācāra idealism nor the Vaibhāṣika realism accepts the total interdependence of all processes of existence. The Vaibhāṣikas accepted the independence of external processes to account for the causal chain of duḥkha, and the Yogācārins accepted the independence of internal processes of consciousness to provide a basis for the elimination of duḥkha. As their critics were quick to point out, the Vaibhāṣikas and Sautrāntikas have trouble accounting for the effectiveness of a path of liberation, while the Yogācārins have trouble accounting for the causal chain of bondage.

Nāgārjuna, on the other hand, by refusing to accept anything as independent, seems to deprive himself of a basis for a causal theory that will account for either bondage or liberation. His move is to point out the overwhelming problems confronting the views of all the other philosophers, both Buddhist and non-Buddhist, arguing vigorously that none of them provide a conceptually satisfactory account of the causes of suffering or the means to liberation. Rather than advocating a philosophical theory of his own, he suggests that we need to distinguish between the reality we construct with our concepts or theories and reality itself.

Reality itself is beyond all concepts, theories, and views. It is prior even to the division into subject and object that makes conceptual knowledge possible. Only through direct insight and complete openness to the full richness of its movements can reality be experienced in enlightenment.

When we approach this organic, interrelated reality with the logical constructs of concepts and theories, we cut it up into isolated pieces—which are then mistaken for reality itself. It is like taking a still picture of a playful child. The photo cannot possibly capture the enthusiasm, joy, life, and fullness of the child's life. And if the photo is mistaken for the reality, the result is almost a complete distortion of the life photographed. Just as the camera "freezes" the full rush of life into a still frame, so do our logical constructions "freeze" the flow of existence into static concepts and theories.

Nāgārjuna's point is not that concepts are somehow evil in themselves or intrinsically bad. Not at all. Like photos, concepts can be both delightful and useful. And like good photos, concepts can capture a good deal of the life that they represent. But a concept necessarily isolates its object, severing it from its living context and its rich interrelations with everything around it. Of course, when concepts are related to each other in theories, an attempt is made to exhibit the relations between the different parts or features of reality represented by the various concepts. But the fact remains that concepts and theories are abstract and static entities, whereas the reality they refer to is a dynamic organic reality, undivided in its wholeness. And when the logical constructions of concepts and theories are mistaken for reality itself, a person comes to live in an unreal world, separated from the rest of reality by his or her own mental constructs.

This, of course, is what happens to most of us most of the time, say the Buddhists. What we fear is not death itself, but our idea of death. The self whose loneliness we wish to avoid is the self constructed in our own minds. When our idea of self as a permanent unchanging reality is mistaken for the living reality of our existence, we do everything possible to protect and preserve this ideal self, putting all our passions and vitality at its disposal. This is duḥkha, the estrangement, anxiety, and suffering caused by ignorance of reality, and the consequent grasping for the unreality of a constructed world and self. The way to nirvāṇa is to remove this ignorance and the consequent grasping for its objects.

But the knowledge that will remove this ignorance cannot, according to Nāgārjuna's own position, be any kind of conceptual or philosophical knowledge. Philosophical views are part of the constructed world, and from within this world it is not possible to say whether or not a particular theory represents reality as it is in itself. Indeed, the very distinction between the constructed world of ideas or theories and reality itself is itself only another idea—unless it too is grounded in direct insight into, and participation in, reality itself.

Philosophical analysis can show the essential relativity of the logically abstract world constructed by the mind, the nonultimacy of philosophical views of this world, and the conditioned and dependent nature of its contents. But while this paves the way for going beyond the constructed world of ideas to an immediate and direct realization of reality in its full richness, it does not itself bring about such a realization. A leap out of the trap of this world is required, a leap that Buddhists say is possible by practicing the eightfold noble path. The completely interdependent nature of the processes constituting reality can be realized only by direct intuitive insight and a spontaneous compassion for and identification with all other life-forms. Ordinary knowledge of causes of bondage, means to liberation, and nature of reality must be transcended to attain liberation from duḥkha.

The chief philosophical objection to this view is that it subordinates philosophy itself to nonrational or suprarational insight and experience. In claiming that by illuminating the causes of suffering and becoming aware of its own limitations philosophy has served its essential task and now must make room for a "higher" practice, Mādhyamika may be loyal to the demands of religious life, but this loyalty subordinates philosophy to religious experience. Once again we encounter the Indian tendency to regard the highest truths as beyond the ken of rational thought. There words and ideas do not reach; only the insight and knowledge that goes beyond the bifurcation of reality into subject and object modes can bring one face to face with the highest reality.

## Knowledge

As we have seen, despite their differences with each other, most Indian philosophers find the root cause of bondage to lie in ignorance or wrong knowledge. Liberation depends upon the removal of ignorance. But what constitutes right knowledge? And how can what is claimed to be knowledge be shown to be true? Pushed by skeptics, like Sañjaya, who denied that knowledge of the causes of bondage or means of liberation is possible, it became necessary to develop a theory of knowledge to maintain one's vision of reality and one's claims about the causes of bondage and means of liberation.

Although most Indian philosophers agree that in the last analysis extraordinary means are required to know the highest reality, they do not therefore dismiss ordinary means of knowledge as worthless. On the contrary, they emphasize the importance of ordinary knowledge not only for conducting one's practical affairs in the world, but also for coming to see the need for, and the place of, the higher knowledge that results from meditation and direct insight.

The central question is, What are the valid means of knowing? Nyāya philosophers have always taken the question of how reality can be known as their special concern, and since most of the other systems have adopted much of their analysis, we will concentrate on their theories of perception and inference, the first two means of knowledge they identify. The third means of valid knowledge they recognize is comparison. However, most other philosophers regard comparison not as a separate means of knowledge but, rather, as a combination of perception and inference. On the grounds that it is logically reducible to perception and inference, we will not treat comparison or analogy as a separate means of knowledge—even though Nyāya philosophers argue vigorously that it is separate from all the other means. The fourth means, testimony, is important for everyone who accepts the testimony of sacred scripture or holy persons as a valid source of knowledge. Since the Mīmāmsā philosophers have developed the most elaborate and influential theory of testimony as a valid means of knowledge, we will follow their account of this means rather than the less influential Nyāya account.

## PERCEPTION

Perception is defined in the Nyāya texts as "the true and determinate knowledge arising from the contact of the senses with their proper objects." The stipulation that it be *determinate* perception is intended to rule out cases where something is perceived, but what that something is, is not known. For example, if a sound is heard, but it is not known whether it is the sound of a bird or a flute, the perception is indeterminate and therefore does not constitute a case of perceptual knowledge.

Indeterminate perception is simply the awareness of the presence of something or other by the sense in question. Because there is no judgment of any kind, there is no possibility of error. But by the same reasoning, there is also no possibility of perceptual knowledge. Determinate awareness, on the other hand, is capable of yielding genuine knowledge, for here the object causing the sensation constituting the determinate perception is known to be a definite something, or to stand in a definite relation to something else. A definite judgment, capable of being true or false, is made in this case.

This distinction between determinate and indeterminate perception also makes possible an important distinction between error and ignorance. Ignorance may be due to a lack of either the immediate sensory experience or a determinate perception. Error, on the other hand, always results from mistaking what is given in immediate sensory experience for something other than what it actually is. To take a stock example, when a rope is erroneously perceived as a snake, the immediate sensory experience correctly reveals an elongated, twisted, darkish colored patch. In the erroneous determinate perception, this colored patch, the object of a valid sensory experience, is mistaken for a snake. But the ignorance involved in this mistaken knowledge claim is quite different from the ignorance of a person who lacked even the indeterminate perception of the color patch. Thus, indeterminate perception is a necessary condition for perceptual knowledge, but it should not be confused with perceptual knowledge itself.

Since erroneous perceptual claims obviously do not constitute knowledge, Nyāya insists that only determinate perceptual claims *that are true* can count as knowledge. This stipulation, of course, raises the difficult question of how to determine whether a particular perceptual claim is erroneous or true. How can the truth of a knowledge claim be tested? Like most other philosophers, Nyāya thinkers insist that a claim is true if and only if what is claimed to be the case actually is the case. But how can this correspondence be known? It is impossible to test the correspondence between the claim and reality directly, for the perceived reality obviously cannot be known independently of perception. To compare the claim with reality, reality must be known. But this means that the knowledge claim being tested is not being compared with an independent reality, but only with another knowledge claim. This means that at best the claim being tested can be corroborated by the claim resulting from a second or third perception. But such corroboration clearly cannot constitute a proof of the correctness of the original claim, for the questions raised about it could also be raised about the second perceptual claim, and so on. Although the collective weight of many corroborating perceptual claims gives us confidence in the correctness of the original claim, no number of such corroborating claims *absolutely* proves the original to be true.

Recognizing this dilemma, Nyāyakas suggest that the ultimate test of the correspondence between reality and a perceptual claim is practice. If practice based on the assumed truth of the claim in question is successful, then it has passed the crucial test and is entitled to be called true. The ultimate test is whether or not practice based on claimed knowledge of the causes of bondage and the means of liberation actually leads to liberation. But there are other tests, easier to apply. For example, varying a classic illustration, you do not know whether the granulated white stuff in the cup is sugar or salt. If putting some in your coffee succeeds in sweetening it, you know that the claim, "this is sugar," is true. If it does not sweeten the coffee, you know that the claim is false.

While practice is undoubtedly an important test of truth, it poses some difficult theoretical problems. In the example given, the truth of the claim, "This is sugar," depends on, among other things, whether or not the practice of using it to sweeten coffee succeeds. But whether or not it succeeds in sweetening coffee depends upon perception. How do we know that our perception of sweetness is valid? Whatever kinds of reasons there are for doubting the truth of the original knowledge claim based on perception—that sensations are intrinsically misleading or that the sense organ is defective, for example—would apply equally to claims about the success of practice that are based on perception. If the criterion of practice constitutes the test of perceptual knowledge claims, and if this test itself depends upon perception, then the test is vitiated by an obvious circularity. In other words, if perception itself cannot be trusted, then our perception of the results of the pragmatic test cannot be trusted either. This renders practice useless as a test of perceptual truth claims.

This is an extremely serious matter, for since all other means of knowledge—inference, testimony, and comparison—presuppose the truth of perceptual knowledge, we cannot be sure of any knowledge unless we can be sure of perceptual knowledge claims. Mīmāmsā philosophers push this consideration to the limit, arguing that the truth of perception must ultimately be accepted as self-evident. Its truth is assured by the very conditions that give rise to perceptual knowledge in the first place. Unless the light is poor, the eye diseased, and so on, there can be no grounds for doubting the truth of a perceptual knowledge claim. The grounds for any such doubt would themselves assume the self-evident truth of other perceptual knowledge. Even the most thoroughgoing skeptic must trust and accept the testimony of the senses some of the time. Otherwise he would have no reason for his skepticism!

Since even doubts about the truth of perceptual knowledge claims presuppose the validity of perception as a means of knowledge, the Mīmāmsās argue that it makes no sense to doubt the intrinsic truth of perception. The real challenge to a theory of knowledge is not to prove the truth of knowledge in general but to show how *particular* claims can be shown to be false and how error can be removed or avoided.

When do we have reason to doubt the truth of a particular knowledge claim? Only when it conflicts with another claim, they say. And in such a case we must check both the conditions of perception and the reasoning behind the claim that there is a conflict. Is the sense organ in question healthy? Are the conditions for seeing, hearing, and smelling, for example, good? And is the conclusion that one or the other of the claims in question is false itself based on a valid chain of reasoning? Applying these tests thoroughly will enable us to resolve conflicts that arise among knowledge claims, entitling us to confidence in our knowledge, argue the Mīmāmsās.

## INFERENCE

The process of comparing knowledge claims that conflict with each other as a basis for concluding that at least one of them must be false is an instance of inferential knowledge. Although inference assumes the truth of prior knowledge, it goes beyond this prior knowledge in the conclusions it reaches, thus constituting a separate means of knowledge. Nyāya developed an extremely elaborate philosophy of inference over the course of some two thousand years—a philosophy that we can only briefly summarize here.

Inference enables us to know something that has not been perceived—an inferential claim—by a process of connecting this inferential claim with another claim, known by perception. A third claim, the reason validating the inference, connects the perceptual and inferential claims. For example, in the inference, "There is fire on the hill, because there is smoke on the hill, and wherever there is smoke there is fire," the third claim, that smoke is invariably associated with fire, is the reason enabling one to move from the perceptual claim, "There is smoke on the hill," to the new inferential claim, "There is fire on the hill."

This example, a stock illustration of Nyāya texts, is set out in full as follows:

1. Yonder hill has fire.
2. Because it has smoke.
3. Whatever has smoke has fire (e.g., a stove).
4. Yonder hill has smoke such as is always accompanied by fire.
5. Therefore yonder hill has fire.

When reasoning to convince oneself, it is not necessary to set out all five steps as shown. Either the first or last two propositions can be eliminated. But if the inference is intended to convince someone else, then Nyāya insists that all five propositions be set down formally, as shown. But clearly the essential process involved in the inference is coming to know that there is fire on the hill on the basis of perceived smoke and knowledge of the invariable connection between smoke and fire.

Thus, in the example, "1" is the new knowledge claim, "2" gives the perceptual grounds for this new knowledge claim, "3" gives the reason for going from a claim about smoke to a claim about fire, "4" asserts that the reason applies in this case, and "5" repeats the original claim, now not as a matter for testing, but as a valid knowledge claim, established by the reasons given.

The critical step in this chain of reasoning is going from the claim that there is smoke to the new claim that, therefore, there is fire. That there is smoke is established by perception, but that there is fire is not. Its truth depends on the truth of both the claim that there is smoke and the reason connecting smoke with fire. The truth of the reason, "whatever has smoke has fire," is crucial, for it entitles one to infer what has not been perceived, in this case that there is fire on yonder hill. But how is the truth of the reason established? The reason claims that smoke is *invariably* connected with fire; how is this connection known to be invariable?

Nyāya philosophers regard the enumeration of individual cases of connection as an important part of the process of establishing invariable connections. But enumeration of individual cases is clearly not enough. If smoke is known to be associated with fire in each of ten cases tested, there is some likelihood that the eleventh case will be the same. But there is certainly no guarantee, and even if a million cases in which smoke is found to be connected with fire are examined, there is no guarantee that the very next case will not be different. And if, no matter how many cases support the claim that there is an invariable connection between smoke and fire, it is still possible that in other cases smoke is not connected with fire, then obviously enumeration of cases where there is a connection does not guarantee the truth of the crucial claim in the inference.

Well aware of this problem, Nyāya philosophers, despite placing much emphasis upon enumeration as an indication of invariable connection, argue that the basis of invariance is ultimately not that many positive instances have been enumerated but, rather, that the connection is *causal*. It is because smoke is *caused* by fire that it is known to be invariably associated with it. There is nothing about the nature of crows that causes them to be black, and therefore, although the first million examined might be black, the next one might be an albino. If whiteness were caused by crowness, as smoke is caused by fire, then the connection would be invariable and exceptions impossible.

However, even if some connections are causal, how would that be known? Unless there is some basis for *knowing* that a connection claimed to be invariable is causal, there is no guarantee of its truth, and its use as the reason for inferring a new knowledge claim is still suspect.

Since this problem arises with respect to inference itself, it would be circular to argue that the invariable connection is known to be of the causal variety on the basis of inference. The only way in which the connection can be known to be causal is through perception. But how can it be known by perceptual means that smoke is caused by fire? The smoke is perceived, and so is the fire. But how is the causal connection perceived?

Nyāya philosophers argue that by a kind of extraordinary perception the very nature of something is perceived. For example, when we perceive a certain individual, Rāma, we perceive not only his individual characteristics, but also that he has a certain nature; that he is a certain *kind of thing* rather than another. In addition to perceiving two arms, two legs, curly black hair, and so on, we perceive that he is a man rather than, say, a tree. And knowing his nature as a man, we know also that those characteristics *caused* by his nature will invariably be associated with him. For example, we know that he will be capable of rational activity, of moral perception, risibility, and so on.

Only in those cases where the invariance of the connection is known to be caused by the nature of the thing in question is the truth of the new inferential claim guaranteed by the truth of the perceptual claim and the reason connecting it with the claim about what has not been perceived. These cases occur either when the unperceived effect is inferred from the perceived cause or when the unperceived cause is inferred from the perceived effect. All other inferences, since they are not guaranteed by a necessary causal connection, are only probably true.

Despite the difficulty of showing that the cause can actually be perceived (e.g., that in perceiving fire it is also perceived that it causes smoke), Nyāya philosophers are satisfied that they have established a secure basis for valid inferential knowledge. But they are aware that inference can go wrong in many ways. Consequently, they catalog a long list of kinds of wrong reasonings that must be guarded against at all times. Although important, much of this discussion is technical and may be left for consideration at another time.

## TESTIMONY

The third independent means of knowledge recognized as valid by most Indian philosophers is testimony (*śabda*). Literally, testimony is the word of a person, and it refers to the knowledge attained by being told something by a reliable person. If testimony is to qualify as knowledge, it must be distinguished from opinion. Hearing another person's opinions does not count as a valid source of knowledge because mere opinions are frequently erroneous. Only when true knowledge claims of another person are heard and understood does that person's word count as a source of knowledge. To guard against confusing mere opinion with reliable testimony, three basic criteria are insisted on: (1) the speaker must be absolutely honest and reliable with respect to that about which he or she is speaking; (2) the speaker must actually know that which is being communicated; and (3) the hearer must hear and understand exactly what is being said.

Mīmāmsās go beyond this generally accepted view of testimony as a valid means of knowledge. They claim that there are certain eternal sounds, constituting the very essence of reality, which reveal the highest eternal reality. This position is rooted in the Vedic emphasis on hearing as the primary means of knowledge and the corresponding view that ultimately all things are created out of the eternal sound of the primordial reality. According to this view, the primary reality and ground of being is neither God nor Brahman, but AUṀ, the Eternal Sound that is the basis of all sounds and all reality.

Because the great Vedic sages felt the power and movement of this Eternal Sound in their hearts and gave voice to it in their chants, the verses of the Veda vibrate with the creative energies of existence. Their melodious and rhythmic vibrations resonate with the reverberations of the world-creating energies of the Eternal Sound. Through participation in this creative activity and sensitivity to its sounds, the sages were able to find words, melodies, and rhythms with the power to open the human heart, mind, and feelings to these same vibrant world-creating energies. Through the liturgical chants of sacrificial celebration (yajña), all humans are enabled to hear these creative sounds and join in the eternal process of cosmic creation, particularly self-creation and the creation of community. Although the particular tones, melodies, and rhythms of the chants were shaped by the great sages who first gave voice to them, the sound to which they gave shape was not their own creation but the Eternal Sound of the Primordial Reality.

According to the Mīmāmsās, to know the ultimate reality, we too, must hear the Eternal Sound in our hearts as we participate in the world- and self-creative process. Since it is precisely this participation that yajña aims at making possible for all human beings, the liturgical chants of ritual creation are regarded by the Mīmāmsās as the highest and most profound kind of knowledge. Its truth is guaranteed by the transformation of existence achieved through such participation.

## YOGIC KNOWLEDGE

This brings us to the last and most important means of valid knowledge generally accepted within the Indian tradition. Ordinary perception, inference, and testimony yield knowledge only of ordinary or conventional existence. To achieve the knowledge that can overcome bondage, a direct and immediate realization of the highest reality is required. Ritual knowledge, emphasized by the Mīmāmsās, is one important means to this knowledge. The other is the knowledge attained through meditation or yogic insight.

All the systems except the Materialist and Mīmāmsā agree that, ultimately, the self is of the nature of knowledge. The ordinary means of knowledge appropriate to the embodied self by no means exhaust the self's capacity to know. Indeed, since the self is of the very nature of knowledge and of the same nature as, or identical with, the highest reality, the highest knowledge can be achieved simply by knowing oneself.

To do this, of course, all the obstructions of the embodying matter must be overcome. As we saw in our examination of yoga, all the affections of embodied consciousness must be destroyed, and its movements stilled, so that the self's own luminous nature can stand revealed in its shining brilliance. Except for Mīmāmsā, which stresses ritual participation in the ultimate processes of reality, and Materialism, which does not believe in liberation, all the systems stress the importance of achieving the direct insight of self-revelation through some form of yogic purification and concentration as the key to overcoming bondage.

## Summary

In this chapter we have examined the relationships between theories of causality and theories of reality. We have noted how those philosophers who saw effects as new creations, separate from their causes, tended to advocate a pluralistic metaphysics and a realistic theory of knowledge. Nyāya, Vaiśeṣika, and Mīmāmsā are good examples of this tendency. On the other hand, those philosophers who saw effects as pre-existing in their causes attempted to account for the unity of existence by postulating a single reality that, through a series of transformations, acquired all the characteristics of the empirical world and selves by which we are surrounded. Those who saw the fundamental reality as actually transformed by change tended to be dualistic, like the Jainas and Sāṁkhya philosophers. Thinkers of these two systems held both that there is a single fundamental nonspiritual reality that is actually transformed into the world and empirical selves by an evolutionary process and that there is also an eternally pure and changeless spiritual reality that must be realized as the eternal, unchanging self to achieve liberation.

Other thinkers, like Shaṅkara, were monistic, rejecting the view that the ultimate reality was actually transformed into something else. They had no need of the postulate of an ultimate nonspiritual reality. For them, Brahman-Ātman is the sole reality, eternally unchanging in its essential nature. Its manifested powers produce the appearance of change, which, when mistaken for reality, produces bondage. Since the true Self is never really changed from its eternally free condition to one of bondage, it follows that liberation is not a matter of actually changing from a condition of bondage to freedom. Rather, it is a matter of realizing that bondage is simply the lived ignorance of the true unchanging spiritual nature of the self. When there is lived realization that Ātman is the true self, there is neither bondage nor suffering.

Buddhists approach the entire question of causality from a different perspective. Instead of assuming that reality consists of relatively permanent things that impact on other things, causing changes in their characteristics even though their underlying nature remains essentially unchanged, Buddhists see change or process itself as the essence of reality. Process is real and things are only abstractions from the continuous stream of becoming. Self-identity and permanence are characteristics attributed to these abstractions by the mind.

The crucial problem for Buddhists is not that of explaining how the self can change from bondage to liberation but, rather, that of explaining how the processes constituting the stream of becoming are connected in such a way that the same person who was bound is now free. The proposed solution is the theory of dependent origination, according to which the moments or factors of a given process are intrinsically linked together in their arising and ceasing in such a way that continuity from moment to moment is provided despite the lack of self-identity over time.

These various systematic views of causality and reality are supported by accompanying theories of knowledge. These theories attempt to account for the validity of ordinary perceptual and inferential means of knowledge as well as extraordinary means whereby reality can be penetrated by direct and immediate insight. The different systems tend to share a common view of perception and inference that is most elaborately worked out by Nyāya, even though each system introduces various modifications to accommodate their particular views of self and reality. They also tend to share a common view of yogic knowledge, which through concentration and meditation removes the obstructions to knowledge, permitting direct insight into the true nature of reality without the mediation of ideas.

## Suggestions for Further Reading

In addition to the books recommended in the previous chapter, more ambitious readers may want to consult S. Dasgupta's *History of Indian Philosophy*, 5 vols. (Cambridge: Cambridge University Press, paperback, 1975), or S. Radhakrishnan's *Indian Philosophy*, 2 vols. (London: George Allen & Unwin, 1962). Despite all the knowledge gained in the fifty years since these two works were first published, they continue to be the standard references in the field.

Eliot Duetsch's *Advaita Vedānta: A Philosophical Reconstruction* (Honolulu: East-West Center Press, 1969) is the best introduction to this important system. It gives the reader a great deal of help in understanding Shaṅkara's philosophy. *A Source Book in Advaita Vedānta*, by Eliot

Deutsch and J. A. B. van Buitenen, (Honolulu: University of Hawaii Press, 1971), provides excellent translations of the important texts as well as a useful introduction to the philosophical context in which Advaita philosophers worked. Karl Potter's *Indian Metaphysics and Epistemology* (Princeton, N.J.: Princeton University Press, 1977) is the most comprehensive and best work available on Indian logic and Nyāya theory of knowledge. It is only for the advanced student, however.

*A Source Book in Indian Philosophy*, ed. Charles A. Moore and S. Radhakrishan (Princeton, N.J.: Princeton University Press, paperback, 1957), contains many basic philosophical texts in English translation. It is a must for every serious student, even though the nineteenth-century English of some of the translations may appear quaint.

Finally, mention should be made of two journals. *Philosophy East and West*, edited by Eliot Deutsch and published by the University of Hawaii Press, contains many excellent articles on Indian philosophy. For example, Robert Thurman's article comparing Wittgenstein and Candrakīrti, Vol. 30, no. 3 (July 1980), gives the reader a good idea of the high-level and logically sophisticated treatment of key epistemological issues by Indian (Buddhist) thinkers. *Indian Philosophy*, edited by Bimal K. Matilal and published by D. Reidel, is devoted exclusively to Indian philosophy and stresses its technical and analytic side.

# 14

# Islam in India

Although the subcontinent of India was not divided into the separate nations of India, Pakistan, and Bangladesh until the twentieth century, this partition was prefigured already in the eleventh century when Islamic civilization found a permanent home in India. Both Islam and Hinduism were deeply conservative and each represented a highly developed culture—cultures that were worlds apart. The ideological differences between them were exaggerated by the fact that the ruling Muslims regarded Hindus as inferior to themselves and Hindus considered Muslims to be sources of spiritual pollution. Although Hindu and Sufi saints were able to inspire and influence each other, for the orthodox on both sides, the relationship was primarily one of confrontation. Each side felt forced to conserve its own traditions and to resist yielding to "foreign" influence.

Faith dominated Islam, and the orthodoxy of belief discouraged philosophical speculation. As a result, very little Islamic philosophy developed on Indian soil, and there was not much interaction between Hindu and Muslim philosophers. Religious thought, on the other hand, found many challenges in the meeting of these two quite different religious ways. The strict monotheism of Islam was attractive to many Hindu thinkers, while the monism implicit in much of Hinduism led some Muslim thinkers to place greater emphasis on God's transcendence. Devotionalism and saint traditions in both religions provided a great deal of common ground.

A number of sects, notably those initiated by Kabīr and Dādū, arose out of an attempt to combine the strengths of both Hinduism and Islam.

Indeed, one sect, the Sikhs, inspired by Gurū Nānak, was so successful in its attempt to go beyond both Hinduism and Islam that it developed into a world religion with some fourteen million adherents today—including more than one million in the United States and Canada.

Sikhism will be discussed in the next chapter. Here we focus on the following questions: How did Islam establish itself in India? What is the way of Islam? and How did Islam and Hinduism interact with and influence each other?

## The Advent of Islam

Islam swept across the Middle East, western Asia, northern Africa, and Spain like a huge tidal wave during the seventh, eighth, and ninth centuries, finding its way to India within eighty years of Muhammad's death in 632. It came peacefully to the southern coast via Arab traders. But to the Northwest it came with the conqueror's sword, as Muhammad Ibn Qasim, in pursuit of the robbers who had pirated an Arab ship, led his army of six thousand to victory over the much larger army of Dahar, king of Sind, in a battle at Debul (near modern Karachi) in 711. Within three years Dahar's army was destroyed and Arab Muslim rule soon extended over most of what is today Pakistan. Additional conquests followed, soon bringing Muslim rule to much of the subcontinent.

Islam brought to India not only a succession of foreign rulers who were to govern much of India for nearly a thousand years, but a new religious philosophy and way of life as well. Not since the coming of the Āryans, two thousand years earlier, had a foreign civilization been able to exert as much influence on the Indian people as Islam would over the next thousand years.

For almost three centuries following Ibn Qasim's conquest of the northwest, this portion of the subcontinent was ruled by Arab Muslims. But by 1030, at the end of Mahmud of Ghazni's reign, the Turkish Muslims, operating largely from the Afghan base of Ghazni, had conquered most of the northern portions of the subcontinent, creating the Ghaznavid empire. Al-Biruni, the great Muslim historian and Mahmud's contemporary, described Mahmud's raids on Hindu temples and palaces and his military violence as totally ruining the prosperity of the country, killing and dispersing Hindus in all directions, while creating in the survivors the most inveterate hatred of all Muslims.

Despite their dislike of the Muslims, Indian armies were no match for the well-disciplined and brilliantly led Turkish Muslim armies and were forced to choose between submission or flight. In 1192 the Muslims, under the brilliant general Muhammad Ghuri, defeated the powerful Rajput armies of Prithvi Raj at Tarain, giving the Muslims control of Lahore and Delhi. Unlike his predecessors, Muhammad was more interested in political control than in victories or wealth and used his military victories to consolidate political power. On his death in 1206, his freed slave, Aibak, ruled from Delhi, establishing the Delhi sultanate that ruled over most of India, as far east as Bengal, and stretching south into central India.

The limited foreign rule by Muslim generals initiated with Qasim's first conquest in 712 became, nearly five hundred years later, a reign of almost total political control over Indian affairs of state by a firmly entrenched power representing an almost totally different culture. For the next four hundred and fifty years, the Delhi sultans and the Mughal emperors were to rule almost all of the subcontinent, bringing Islamic civilization to new heights and spreading its influence all the way from the Arabian Sea to the Bay of Bengal and deep into the Deccan.

The establishment of Muslim rule in India by generals and conquerors guaranteed a refuge and a home for the millions of Muslims who were forced to flee the ravages of the Chinghis Khan as he and his Mongol hordes ruthlessly destroyed the heart of the Muslim civilized world. The early Arab and Turkish conquerors had come to India primarily for glory and plunder, establishing their rule only to control the captured wealth and to announce their glory to the world. Under them Indian culture was practically undisturbed. But beginning in 1220, the Chinghis Khan destroyed the Muslim centers of learning and culture in Samarqand, Balkh, Ghaznin, and other major cities. When Baghdad itself was sacked, the scholars, poets, and other bearers of a rich and proud civilization incorporating much of the best of Persian and Greek culture were either killed or forced to flee. Many came to India, and both the Delhi sultanate and the Mughal courts were distinguished by the scholars, poets, artists, historians, and scientists that they attracted. From this time on Islam in India was not merely a "foreign" rule. It was now also a foreign culture at home on Indian soil.

Two points about this émigré culture are especially important. First, for the first time since the coming of the Āryans, India was the home of two quite different civilizations, existing side by side. Second, Islam is naturally conservative, looking back to the life and example of the Prophet for inspiration and guidelines for action. This natural conservatism was accentuated by the fact that initially Muslim civilization in India was essentially a cultural colony in refuge, trying to preserve itself while its home was being destroyed by enemies. When Baghdad was destroyed in 1258 and the Abbasid Caliph killed by Mongol forces led by Hulagu, Chinghis Khan's grandson, Muslim civilization itself was threatened with extinction. It is only natural that these immigrants sought to preserve the past and re-establish the old ways rather than attempt to embrace a new civilization and adopt a foreign culture. And we should remember that these immigrants must have felt extremely insecure, for not only were they in a strange land, but they felt themselves threatened from every side. They were surrounded by Hindus, even while the Mongols were threatening to follow them across the Indus and destroy their newly found refuge.

Of course, Indian civilization was itself conservative, looking to the past for its own basic norms. Furthermore, Hindus in the northern part of India had found themselves attacked and their temples looted and destroyed ever since Ibn Qasim's conquests in Sind. So they also felt the need to preserve and strengthen the old ways in the face of attack from the invading and ruling foreigners. The consequence was that these two great civilizations, both of them naturally conservative, each fearing for its survival and guarding itself against encroachment and erosion by the other, came to exist side by side on Indian soil. Like polite strangers, they were careful and guarded in their interaction because of a deep distrust and suspicion of each other. Small wonder that there was to be so little mutual influence and interaction for the next seven hundred years. Indeed, what is surprising is that there was as much influence and interaction as there actually was. Although Muslim influence on painting, architecture, and poetry is considerable, dance, music, philosophy, religion, and the entire range of moral and social values that characterize Hindu society were virtually untouched by seven centuries of Muslim rule.

Indeed, the main impact of Islam on India may have been to foster an attitude of extreme conservatism. It is natural enough for a people subjected to foreign rule and the threat of an alien religious culture to resist by conserving and strengthening the ideas and practices that have already been developed in their own tradition. But this conservative attitude works against, rather than facilitates, the energetic forces of great persons and cultural cross-fertilization to create new forms, ideas, and practices. While it would be too great an exaggeration to say that Hinduism has been in a holding pattern for almost a thousand years, this image does suggest the attitude of reaction and conservation that has dominated the Indian mind for the last thousand years.

But culture, religion, and philosophy do not continue to exist anywhere without changing, and India is no exception. The greatest change in India, of course, was the fact that India was now ruled by Muslims rather than by Hindus. The impact of this change can be seen most dramatically simply by noticing that millions, indeed, tens of millions of Hindus (and many Buddhists) converted to Islam. By far the great majority of Muslims at the time of partition in 1947 were the offspring not of conquerors or immigrants, but of converts—more than 100 million in all.

Among the different reasons for conversion to Islam, four stand out, two essentially sociopolitical and two essentially religious. First, conversion opened up job opportunities within the Muslim administration and army. Second, outcast and low-caste persons found the egalitarianism of Islam very attractive, promising them improved social positions and opportunities. Third, the pious example of Sufi saints and mystics attracted many devout Hindus and most of the remaining Buddhists. Fourth, the simple and well-defined Muslim way was attractive, for the sacred law, grounded in the Qu'rān and interpreted by the community, left little doubt about what a person should do to live well in society and to gain salvation.

But there were other changes as well. Hindu devotionalism and the emphasis on holy persons or saints inspired the Sufis in India, who, in turn, inspired later generations of devout Hindus—to the extent of converting many of them to Sufic Islam. Many Indian Muslims, of course, combined their newly found Islam with their traditional religious practices and attitudes, creating, in effect, a new religious way. In addition, great thinkers like Kabīr and Gurū Nānak attempted to combine the best features of both religions in a new and purer religious way. Under Akbar, the imperial court itself encouraged religious ecumenism. But, for the most part, these two great civilizations practiced a kind of cultural and religious separatism. Long before political partition of the subcontinent in 1947, there were two separate civilizations existing side by side, with the Muslims particularly dominant in the northwest, now Pakistan, and in East Bengal, now Bangladesh.

The other religious groups, the Parsis in Bombay, the Jews and Christians in the south, and the relatively small Jaina communities in the west and south, continued to exist as small and separate communities, but their cultural influence was relatively minor. After the decline of Buddhism, almost simultaneously with the advent of Islam, India was to all extents and purposes either Hindu or Muslim. Sometimes these two cultures warred and sometimes they interacted peacefully. The overriding tendency, however, was to try to conserve tradition in face of the threat of encounter with, and influence by, the adjoining, but alien, culture. Thus, the tendency was to become more staunchly Muslim or Hindu rather than to experiment, compromise, or adapt foreign ideas and practices.

To understand both the clash between the Indian and the Islamic ways and the reasons for the relative lack of mutual influence, as well as to understand the nature of the mutual influence that did occur, we must first see what Islam is in its fundamentals, as a way of life based on obedience to God and service to humanity.

## The Meaning of Islam

Islam, the way of submission to God, claims to begin with the first revelation of God to Adam, the very first human being. As God's revelations continued, the great religions of Judaism and Christianity developed around the teachings of the prophets, who gave voice to the messages of God to His people. But these revelations, contained in the Bible, were received by Moses, Jesus, and God's other messengers according to their own capacities and limitations, resulting in an incomplete revelation, according to Muslims. In addition, sometimes their misunderstandings (e.g., Jesus' claim to be one with God) led them to unintentional distortions of God's truth.

But for Muslims, all this changed in the seventh century: for in the fullness of time, God presented humankind with a full and perfect revelation through His Messenger, Muhammad, who lived in Arabia, from 570–632. Although recognizing that God's revelation to humankind began with the first human beings and that the fullness of His revelation to Muhammad covered a period of many years, Muslims recognize Muhammad's emigration to Medina in 622 as the historical beginning of their religion and even begin their calendar with this date. By Muhammad's death in 632 this new religious community had become a powerful state. Within a few more decades it became an empire—an empire that within a single century threatened to conquer and control not only the Middle East, central and southern Asia, and Africa, but Europe as well. Except for Charles's victory at the Battle of Tours in France in 732, Europe and the Americas may well have become part of the "house of Islam."

## BASIC TEACHINGS

According to its believers, Islam is the religion that brings peace to the faithful who commit themselves to God's way and submit to His will. The world "Islam" comes from the root *slm*, meaning "peace," and means "peace through submission." To a Muslim, one who submits to God's will and finds peace by following His way, there is no god but God (Allah) and no religion but Islam. God sent His Messengers to all the corners of the earth to make known His message of life and salvation. By the time of Muhammad, humankind was ready for the full and final revelation from God, and therefore Muhammad is known as the seal of the prophets and Islam as the complete and perfect religion. This conviction that their God is the only true God and that their religion is the only full and true religion underlies the Muslim zeal for propagation of the Faith.

To understand Islam we must ask what a Muslim is expected to believe, do, and realize, for faith, action, and spiritual realization define the way a Muslim is committed to God and submits to His will.

**Faith.** The foundation of Islam is Faith. Through Faith a Muslim believes that

1. God alone is real. Everything else is His creation and exists in dependence upon Him.
2. All creation exists as a manifestation of God's power and glory, and its purpose is to reflect the power and glory of God. Therefore, the proper relationship of a human being to God is that of a servant to his Lord. To serve God is the fundamental purpose of life for a Muslim. We are all God's servants.
3. The way to serve God is revealed in God's message transmitted through the prophets, especially Muhammad, for he is the seal of the prophets.

4. Muhammad is the final and most perfect Messenger of God. This entails belief in the Qur'ān as the word of God in its fullest and most complete form, and in Muhammad as the most perfect example of human relationship to God. Muhammad is the ideal servant, and his life as embodied in his saying and practice (Ḥadīth or Sunnah), constitutes a norm of faith and action for all Muslims, providing guidance for life and the most important clues to the meaning of the Qur'ān.

**Action.** The action by which a Muslim is defined includes

1. *Prayer*, five times a day, to recall human dependence on God and to sustain and nourish life in service to God.
2. *Fasting*, for one month each year, to realize inner spirituality and develop a closer relationship with God. Eating, drinking, smoking, and sexual intercourse are forbidden from dawn till sunset every day during the month of Ramaḍān, and every effort is made to avoid all evil thoughts, actions, and words during this time.
3. *Charity*, requiring that all people donate a percentage of their income and savings every year, to help the needy. The underlying assumption is that everything belongs to God and that all wealth is held in trusteeship for the well-being of all God's creatures. Everyone is entitled to share in the community's wealth according to their need, and everyone is expected to gladly share with those who are less fortunate.
4. *Pilgrimage*, to Mecca, symbolizing the unity of the Muslim community, the equality of all persons, and the oneness of humankind. Here one effectively suspends all worldly activities in order to foster the realization that the essential concern of life is that of developing the right relationship between the soul and God.

**Spiritual Realization.** These four requirements of action plus the requirement of faith in God, the Qur'ān, and Muhammad constitute the five pillars of Islam, defining the essential duties of every Muslim. According to the holy Qur'ān, each person is free to submit to God's will and to live the life of righteousness delineated in the Qur'ān and in the tradition based on the life and sayings of Muhammad. Or one may choose to live in ignorance or defiance of the way ordained by God. But life does not end with death, and all will face the judgment of God on the Day of Judgment. The righteous, who have submitted to His way, will reap God's blessings in Heaven, but those who do not submit will go to Hell to suffer eternal punishment.

Although every Muslim is motivated by the promise of heaven and the threat of hell, a deeper motivation is provided by love of God. Out of love for God a true Muslim strives to make his or her will an instrument of the Divine Will, bringing it into harmony with God's will. The divine spark within each person that constitutes the likeness of God enables one to enter into a spiritual relationship with God, bringing the human will into harmony with the Divine Will, thereby making one a perfect instrument of the Creator. This spiritual realization of the right relationship between God and the individual sanctifies all of life. It also becomes the basis of righteous action, guiding and directing one's life in the holy way of submission to God (Islam).

The whole world, material and spiritual, body and soul, is created by God, and every sphere of human action has a moral and spiritual dimension. The secular cannot be separated from the religious within Islam; everything is ultimately religious, because everything proceeds from God and belongs to Him. This means that Muslim Holy Law (*Sharī'ah*) extends to every sphere of human action, individual and collective, social, political, and economic. The modern inclination to separate state and religion is entirely foreign to Islamic tradition. A Muslim cannot say, "Give to Caesar what is Caesar's and to God what is God's," because everything is God's. Life is an integrated whole and all of it must be lived as an act of service to God.

## MISSION OF ISLAM

Muslims are convinced that there is not God but Allah and that part of their sacred duty lies in bringing others to this realization. They are also convinced that righteousness consists in submitting to God's will and living according to the way ordained in the Qur'ān and exemplified in the life and teachings of His Messenger, Muhammad. These convictions underlie the Muslim obligation to strive (*jihād*) to promote the way of Islam through words and action. Commitment to God and His way requires that one devote as much of one's time, effort, and money as are required to realizing the spread and practice of Islam throughout the world. Because it is God's will, no effort or sacrifice in spreading the teachings and practice of Islam is too great. Even one's life must be given if necessary, and tradition maintains that Heaven awaits all those who give their life for their faith. It is this conviction that provided the motivation and energy for the spread of Islam in the early centuries.

A word should be said here about the relation between Islam and other religions, for the conviction outlined in the preceding paragraph suggests the possibility of religious intolerance. And although history does record Muslim intolerance for people of other religions, as "conversion by the sword" is by no means unknown, the teaching of the Qur'ān is that God has sent His messengers to all the corners of the earth, implying that there is some of God's truth in every religion. Since Islam accepts the scriptures of Judaism and Christianity as the genuine—though incomplete—message of God, Jews and Christians have generally been accorded special status as "people of the book," and their religious practices and institutions respected. But Islam is the only true religion; only through Muhammad was the complete and final message of God revealed. Even Christianity and Judaism, grounded in

God's truth as they are, are only partially true. Not only is their revelation incomplete, but the truth of that revelation has also been obscured by human inventions and wrong interpretations.

Other religions were frequently regarded as false and their adherents denounced as infidels—despite the Qur'ānic declaration that God has sent His messengers to all the peoples on the earth. The religions of India fared much better than did many of the religions of Africa, for example, because Muhammad ibn Qasim, leader of the first Arab conquest of the Indus Valley, treated Hindus and Buddhists as "people of the book," according them the same status and protection as Jews and Christians. As Muslim law became codified in the next several centuries, all but Jews and Christians were officially designated as idol worshippers and infidels. But the precedent of treating Hindus as protected unbelievers continued to be observed, for the most part, even under the Ghurids and Mughals who conquered and ruled India in the succeeding centuries.

Part of the reason for according Hindus special status may have been due to the great respect India's brilliant scientists and mathematicians earned at Baghdad, then capital of the Muslim world. It was during these early days of the Muslim empire that the Indian base ten numerical system and the decimal system were adopted by the Arabs—henceforth to be called the "Arabic number system"—and that the Indian sciences of astronomy and medicine were incorporated into Arab learning.

Some of the Muslim rulers, like Akbar, also had great respect for the piety and sincerity of the Hindus and appreciated the profundity and subtlety of Indian metaphysics. That Indians were not always regarded as a people to be protected, that many monks and holy men were killed, and that most Hindu temples were looted and destroyed cannot be denied. But these atrocious acts did not constitute the norm of Muslim rule in India.

## SUNNI AND SHĪ'AH

A word about the way in which God's message to His people through Muhammad was perpetuated and interpreted is also in order, for a difference of opinion on this issue caused a deep split in Islam, resulting in the Shī'ah and Sunni sects. Even though most Indian Muslims were of the Sunni persuasion, it is important to understand the difference between these two sects. Shī'ahs insist that the living continuity of the faith is furnished by direct renewal of the original "light of Muhammad" through the Īmāms of each generation. The Īmām stands in direct lineal descent from Muhammad, and his authenticity is guaranteed by the previous Īmām, all the way back to Muhammad. He is therefore regarded as participating in Muhammad's Messengership, mediating in this final message of God to His people. This is why the Īmām constitutes the final authority in all matters of truth in the eyes of the Shī'ah faithful.

Sunni Islam, on the other hand, looks to no one person as the current mediator of the final revelation or as the living authority on truth. Here the whole community, led by the Ulamā, renews the Faith through its adherence to the holy law. The holy law, of course, is rooted in the Qur'ān and the tradition of Muhammad. The Ulamā, though guardians and interpreters of the law, have no special authority.

Important as this theological difference over the continuity and authority of the Faith is, it does not explain the persistent bitterness between Shī'ahs and Sunnis. The ill will that Shī'ahs hold for Sunnis goes back to the death of Ali's two sons at the hands of the Sunnis within fifty years of Muhammad's death.

Ali, Muhammad's cousin and son-in-law, felt that he should have succeeded as Caliph upon his father-in-law's death. When first Abu Bakr, then 'Umar, and finally Uthman, were all named Caliph ahead of Ali, his followers became extremely resentful and challenged the Caliphate. As a result of this challenge, when Ali finally became Caliph in 656, in compromised circumstances, his rule was not accepted by many Muslims of good standing and power.

After Ali's murder in 661 his followers struggled, rather unsuccessfully, against the authority of the first Umayyad Caliph at Damascus. But when Yazid, the next Umayyad Caliph, assumed the Caliphate, he was challenged by Husain, younger son of Ali. The challenge failed, and when Husain refused to submit, even though his forces were totally surrounded, he and his entire force were massacred.

This horrible act, when coupled with the murder of Husain's elder brother eleven years earlier, robbed the house of Ali of the only grandsons of the Prophet. It evoked an intense hatred for the perpetrators and fostered the growth of a strong bond of allegiance among Ali's followers. Ali himself was remembered as an extremely saintly and generous person, and this memory, along with the tragic suffering of his widow and family, became a rallying point for the new Shī'ah sect. That the blood of the grandsons and successors of Muhammad had been spilt by usurping orthodox Muslims was never to be forgotten or forgiven. This is the basis for bitterness and hatred between Sunnis and Shī'ahs to this day.

## Religious Thought and the Sufi Way

Within Muslim India, which was almost totally Sunni, the main tension was between the orthodox Sunni and the Sufi ways. Since the attempt to reconcile these tensions in a creative way gave rise to yet a third response, we can distinguish between three different attitudes toward religion among Indian Muslims.

The first attitude, characterizing what is frequently called orthodox Islam, stresses the embodiment of Islam in combined religious and public law (sharī'ah). Orthodox Islam stresses the accumulated tradition of the Muslim community in interpretation of the Qu'rān and promulgation of religiously based social rules dominates.

The second attitude stresses the spiritual experience and fulfillment of the individual, seeing the community and tradition as a natural derivation of intense personal experience of the reality of God and the truth of His revelation. This is the Sufi attitude that modifies the rigidity of the accumulated tradition by the personal experiences and needs of the individual, just as the orthodox attitude modifies the sometimes whimsical and idiosyncratic impulses of the individual by stressing the more normal experiences and needs of the entire community. There is an almost continuous tension between these two attitudes within the history of Islam, a tension that for the most part has been healthy, promoting both stability and personal spiritual growth.

The third attitude arises from this tension between the previous two tendencies and attitudes. It emphasizes the need to coordinate personal experience and belief with the laws and practices of the larger community. This attitude resulted in the movement of thought that helped to transform the inherent tensions between the orthodox (Sunni) and Sufi ways into a healthy and mutually enriching complementarity. In a way, this third attitude amounted to a continuous reformation of Islam that helped to keep the tradition and the law from becoming sterile or dead and that restricted the extravagances of the personal mystic way. The religious thinkers who embodied this attitude went beyond the letter of the Holy Law to the spirit on which it was based. For the Sunni majority, Islam was simply submission to the Holy Law as interpreted and enforced by the political system that the leaders of the community accepted more or less blindly and insisted upon dogmatically. For the religious thinker, it was necessary to go beyond this blind and dogmatic attitude to the spirit of personal religious life that underlies the law. The Holy Law had to be interpreted and applied to particular circumstances in a creative way according to this underlying spirit.

## AL-GHAZĀLĪ

Perhaps of all the thinkers who experienced this tension and tried to accommodate both dimensions of Islam the greatest was Al-Ghazālī. His work gave respectability to Sufism while curbing its excesses. He also gave orthodoxy a lasting theology, framing its spiritual basis and insights in doctrinal formulations consistent with scripture and tradition, yet defensible by reason.

Al-Ghazālī (1059–1111) grew up in an environment dominated by Sufism. But deeply interested in philosophy, theology, and jurisprudence, he began a serious study of these subjects in his late teens. Still in his twenties, he was recognized for his brilliance and was appointed to the most famous university in Baghdad, the center of Islamic scholarship at the time. However, despite his fame as the unequaled authority of

Muslim theology and law, he felt his scholarship destroying his Faith and his life.

At the edge of despair because of the terrible emptiness in his heart preventing him from studying and teaching, Al-Ghazālī finally turned again to the Sufi way that he had known as a youngster. Here he found the inner peace he was seeking and discovered that, wonderful as reason is, it cannot reach into the depths of the heart, illuminating the divine likeness that abides there. On the contrary, reason, taking itself as the ultimate criterion of truth, can reduce itself to absurdity, destroying faith and life in the process. Reason, he concluded, is a fine servant and tool. But when mistaken for a master and seen as an end in itself, it can be destructive beyond compare.

Convinced of the priority of faith and intuition over reason, and of the need to employ reason in its proper sphere of clarifying, interpreting, and defending the insights of faith and the knowledge of the heart, he wrote his masterpiece, *Revival of Religious Sciences*, through which he gave Islam a lasting theology. Quickly embraced by almost the whole Islamic community, it has served both Sunnis and Sufis well over the intervening centuries, providing a commonality sufficient to keep them within the same House of Faith—even though in separate rooms.

The *Revival of Religious Sciences* maintains that ultimately God is the only real object of knowledge and that God can be known only through Faith. It responds to a challenge constituted by the philosophers' emphasis on reason. Inspired by translated works of Plato, Aristotle, and the Neo-Platonists, Arab philosophers developed philosophical systems that took reason—rather than the Qu'rān—as the ultimate criterion of truth. Ibn Sina (Avicenna), for example, taught that the world was uncreated, existing eternally, because although the scriptures taught that the world was created by God out of nothing, reason can make no sense out of something being created out of nothing. Therefore, he concluded that creation was really a transformation of something existing previously. Even though it might be a radical transformation, it was not creation out of nothing.

In a similar way, Ibn Sina argued that, since all knowledge is of universal intelligible forms rather than of concrete existence, it follows that God's knowledge, too, is not of particular things in their concreteness but only of universals. This conclusion, however, runs contrary to the scriptural teaching that God knows all things in every detail.

In a corollary argument he claimed that, since the soul is the knowing part of a person, and since knowledge is only of forms, therefore, the soul itself is a form. If the nature of the soul were different from that of knowledge, knowledge would be impossible, Ibn Sina argued. But if the soul is a form, then it is universal and indestructible. The body, on the other hand, is naturally destructible. Although from this it follows that the soul is indestructible, it also follows that there can be no eternal resurrection of the body—a conclusion that flies in the face of the Qu'rānic teaching of the eternal resurrection of the body after the Last

Judgment. It thus repudiates the teaching that the resurrected person will either suffer eternal punishment in Hell or enjoy eternal rewards in Heaven.

In light of such contradictions between philosophical conclusions and the teachings of scripture, it is easy enough to understand why the orthodox believers felt threatened by the philosophers who, like Ibn Sina, relied on reason rather than God's word as the criterion of truth. No wonder Al-Ghazālī's *The Nonsense of Philosophers*, in which he showed that reason could be used to defeat the arguments and conclusions of reason just as easily as it could be used to defeat the doctrines of faith, was, to put it mildly, so warmly received by the orthodox and enshrined, along with his positive theology (*Revival of Religious Sciences*), as "official" teaching. Although Al-Ghazālī's attack on philosophy was subjected to a brilliant criticism by Ibn Rushd (Averroes) in a book aptly titled *The Nonsense of Nonsense*, Al-Ghazālī had already convinced the orthodox that reason by itself was an unreliable and dangerous tool.

It is interesting to speculate that, if Al-Ghazālī had not won the day and convinced Muslim orthodoxy that rational thought was a great danger to the Faith, modern science might have developed in the medieval Muslim world rather than in modern Europe. The Arab philosophers were acquainted with Greek logic and science. They recognized causal connections between all natural things, connections that could be known through a combination of experimentation and reason. Their sense of the capability of reason and the value they placed on knowing God through rational knowledge of His creation might well have inspired Muslim thinkers to have developed something akin to what we call the scientific attitude and method. But like St. Thomas in Europe, Al-Ghazālī insisted that the proper employment of reason is not in speculation about the natural world but, rather, in defense of scripture and orthodox theology. And just as St. Thomas gave enduring shape to Christian theology, so Al-Ghazālī provided the theological foundation for Islam—both in its orthodox (Sunni) form and in its mystical form (Sufism).

## LOVE AS THE BASIS

Although Ibn Sina's natural theology was rejected because it clashed with the Qu'rān, his metaphysics of Divine Love fared much better, becoming the philosophical basis for the Sufi way of devotion to God through love. Starting from the philosophies of Plato and Aristotle, Ibn Sina gave reason an honored and highly respected place, regarding it as the last word in matters of science and logic and as the ultimate criterion of truth for our knowledge of nature. But religious experience told him that the human heart has a more direct and immediate access to the ultimate truth. Through the soul's intuition, the light of God is reflected in the mirror of the human soul, illuminating the entire universe in the process.

God, the ultimate reality is eternal beauty, according to Ibn Sina, as demonstrated by the beauty of nature. It is the very nature of beauty to be self-expressive, he says, and nature is simply the self-expression of God. In God, this self-expression, not different from His Being, is the supreme love, for love is nothing other than the expression and appreciation of perfect beauty. In other words, beauty is the ultimate being of the universe while love is its ultimate energy, causing all beings to seek their original perfection. But being and energy are simply different aspects of the same reality. It is through love, therefore, that a person can turn away from imperfection and return to full perfection in the eternal beauty that is God. This is possible because God is love and humans are created in His image, having a spark of the Divine Love in their own souls, a spark that can ignite the whole being and reveal the eternal oneness with God.

Although the underlying metaphysics is abstract, Sufi life is not, and the supreme love for God experienced in the Sufi's heart is manifested typically through sharing the concerns and sorrows of others and is frequently given literary expression through the images of human love. Sufis usually lived extremely simple, sometimes ascetic, lives. Indeed, Sufism began as an ascetic movement to prepare the way for direct personal experience of human relationship to God.

Although asceticism continued to be a Sufi hallmark, the increasing emphasis on personal experience led to the development of devotional practices aimed at facilitating spiritual experience. Love for God and adoration of His name and presence ruled Sufi life. But Sufis rarely became hermits. The bonds of God's love for them and their love for Him reached out to embrace their fellow humans. Most Sufis understood that one of their urgent purposes in life was to provide spiritual guidance for the people. This meant guidance in worldly affairs as well as spiritual affairs, for in Islam these are not really separate.

To provide this guidance it was necessary for Sufis to discover the innermost heart of those who came, and to open their own hearts, sharing the heart's most intimate secrets. This "discovery and sharing" require keeping in close touch with the daily lives of the people. It also meant staying out of the political fray because political involvement would hinder the Sufis' personal quest for a deeper spiritual relationship with God and get in the way of their efforts to comfort the troubled hearts of their fellow human beings. Only by staying out of politics and government could they come to know and share the trouble in the hearts of those who came to them in need of solace. As an old Sufi saying has it, "though there are as many paths to God as there are particles in the universe, none is shorter than that of bringing comfort to troubled hearts."

Sufi disdain of administrative service and professional work was based on the conviction that such work required allegiance to a ruler or professional goals rather than to God, resulting in ego gratification rather than spiritual fulfillment of one's relation to God and humanity.

The typical Sufi attitude toward government or professional activity is exhibited in a story about a young man who had just finished his studies and had approached Shaikh Nizamuddin, presumably to ask for his guidance. In reply to the shaikh's question about what he intended to do with his life, the young man declared that he was hoping to get a government position. The shaikh remained silent until the young man had gone. He then observed that a good verse is something fine, but when people compose odes of praise and take them to all sorts of people, it becomes quite disgusting. In the same way, he suggested, knowledge itself is something noble. But when it is made a profession and pedalled from door to door it loses all dignity.

Perhaps the best definition of the Sufi ideal is given by Shaikh Fariduddin in advice to his disciples about how to live. Men of God, he advised them, are like this: "First, anxiety as to what they shall eat and what they shall wear does not enter their heart. . . . Secondly, in private and in public they remain absorbed in God: that is the essence of all spiritual striving. Thirdly, they never utter anything with the idea of pleasing people and attracting them toward themselves."[1]

Sufis who were able to put this advice to practice were distinguished by their serenity and holiness. Their spiritual greatness prompted many stories about their extraordinary powers. For example, once the opponent of a blind saint came to him hoping to cast doubt upon his saintliness. Thinking that the external flaw of blindness was certainly mirrored in an internal spiritual flaw, the opponent, hoping to trip up the saint in some way, asked him, "What is the sign of a saint?" While asking the question a fly settled on the opponent's nose. Though he brushed it away, the fly returned. Again he brushed it away, but when the fly landed a third time the blind saint said, "One of the signs of a saint is that no fly lands on his nose!"[2]

Another wonderful story tells how a very old spiritual master, Badr-ud-Din, would get up and dance with great joy whenever he heard a devotional song. Music and dance were forbidden in orthodox Islam, but they became important means of inspiration and attainment in Sufism. Sufis, of course, regarded music and dance not as profane, human creations but, rather, as expressions of the Divine Love to which the human soul responded through its body. Even when very old and scarcely able to move, Badr-ud-Din would become so filled with ecstasy by the sound of a devotional song that he would get up and dance like a young man. When asked, "Shaikh, how can you dance like this when you cannot even walk?" he replied, "Where is the Shaikh? It is only Love that dances!"

This Love, of course, is the Divine Reality. Though transcending all created existence, it is nonetheless present everywhere in all existence. According to the Sufi theory of the oneness of existence worked out by

[1]Quoted in M. Mujeeb, *The Indian Muslims* (London: George Allen & Unwin, 1967), p. 146.

[2]*Ibid.*, p. 123.

Ibn Arabi (1165–1240), transcendence and immanence are simply two different aspects of the same reality. God is both transcendent and immanent, for in Him, being and existence are one and inseparable. Although it is impossibe to *become* God, since He is the Creator and we are the created, it is possible for the mystic to realize that his existence is eternally contained in God's existence—even as a drop of water in the ocean is contained in the ocean—for God's creation is part of His existence.

This philosophy, though by no means identical to yoga, is certainly compatible with it, and the Sufi stages of preparation for this realization often resemble the eightfold path of Buddhism and the eight aids to yoga enunciated by Patañjali. Indeed, many Sufis studied and practiced yoga to aid their efforts at realizing their existence in God.

## THE SUFI PATH

The spiritual preparation required to achieve this realization constitutes the very heart of Sufism. It is the path to God, a path marked by a series of stages. These stages are often described in different ways, but the following is a typical description.

1. *Repentance*. An awakening to the heedlessness and sinfulness of life accompanied by a repentant attitude and the resolve to live virtuously, according to God's law.
2. *Abstinence*. Possessions and enjoyments are abandoned in recognition of the truth that nothing belongs to oneself; everything belongs to God, and only God is to be sought.
3. *Renunciation*. Not only must pleasures and possessions be abandoned, but even the desire for them must be renounced.
4. *Poverty*. Everything that can distract the mind from God must be rejected so that it cannot stand between the soul and God. Although poverty begins with nonownership, it requires abandoning not merely property, but wishes and thoughts that separate the soul from God.
5. *Patience*. Any misfortune must be accepted as part of God's way, and one must be willing to follow His way even when human inclinations run in a contrary direction.
6. *Trust in God*. Complete confidence in God's grace is required to overcome all obstacles on the path, including the traveler's sinfulness.
7. *Satisfaction*. At this stage nothing satisfies the pilgrim except following God's will. But accepting and following the Divine Decree is completely satisfying.

These seven stages are achieved primarily by the individual's own efforts. To progess farther along the path requires Divine help. Indeed, even as the pilgrim makes his way along the first stages of the path, God gives him (1) the power to meditate, (2) the sense of closeness to

Him, (3) love for Him, (4) fear of separation, (5) hope and longing for the Divine embrace, (6) intimacy with Him, (7) inner peace, (8) ability to contemplate the Divine, and (9) confidence in salvation through God's help.

These divine gifts, in conjunction with the achievements of self-effort, prepare the traveler on the path to receive the Divine Light from God Himself. Through this Divine Light the likeness of the soul to God is recognized and all passions, desires, and conscious thoughts are utterly extinguished. The individual soul is now like a drop of water in the great ocean that is God's Being. Subsisting in this wonderful condition allows the Truth to be seen and the soul to be reunited with God.

Although some of the Sufis, speaking from the ecstatic rapture of their vision, declared themselves identical to God, the more sober, like Al-Ghazālī, recognized that the experience was beyond the limitations of thought and language and refrained from misleading statements that might confuse the religious seeker and scandalize the orthodox. Since the instruments of power were always in the hands of the orthodox, Sufic excesses could prove dangerous. In 922 Al-Ḥallāj was executed for heresy in Baghdad. His "crime" was to give expression to his rapturous experience of the Divine Reality by declaring that God was incarnate within him. But for the most part the Sufis built upon the foundations of orthodoxy rather than attempting to destroy those foundations. In the spirit of Jesus, a thousand years earlier, they saw their work as fulfilling the holy law rather than destroying it.

## Interaction

Although the Muslim ruling class in India was almost exclusively Sunni, the Sufis exerted the most influence on Hindus. They also received the most from Hindu culture, for these sincere spiritual seekers interacted freely with spiritual persons whatever their background or allegiance.

The Sufis were concerned almost exclusively with realizing a personal inner relationship with God. Striving to find the living presence of Allah in their personal experience, they abandoned the wealth, luxury, and material distractions of urban civilization in favor of an ascetic and rural existence. Because nothing mattered so much as spiritual experience, and because the very restrictions of Muslim orthodoxy were rejected, the Sufis were open to spiritual practices and ideas wherever they found them. They were influenced by Christianity, Buddhism, and Hinduism and inspired by the ideas of the Upaniṣads and Plotinus as well as by the scriptures and traditions of Islam. The basis of Sufi thought and practice remained Islam, of course, but there was considerable borrowing, adapting, and adopting in the encounter of mystic Islam and Hinduism.

Although undoubtedly there was considerable interaction between Muslims and Hindus—for millions of Hindus converted to Islam and a new religion, the Sikh, was born of this encounter—scholars are in considerable disagreement over the precise nature and extent of this interaction. The reason for this disagreement is that there are very few records of religious life and religious movements from the tenth to the nineteenth centuries. Sometimes, as in the case of devotional mysticism, it may be that Hinduism influenced Islamic Sufism, which in turn influenced Hindu devotionalism. But the record is by no means clear.

What is clear is that millions of Hindus converted to Islam, with many converts coming from Hindus influenced by the saintly examples of the Sufis, whose piety and religious devotion were extremely attractive to people whose culture had prepared them to venerate saints—indeed often to honor them as incarnations of Gods or Goddesses. If Islam could produce saints of the holiness and stature of the great Sufis who wandered into the provinces and villages where the powerful arm of government hardly ever reached, then surely it must be a worthy way that could be safely followed in the quest for liberation and perfection by any sincere spiritual seeker.

## POETS AND SAINTS

Even among those Hindus who did not convert to Islam, the piety and devotion of the Sufis had an impact, and among the many devotional sects and movements that flourished in the fifteenth and sixteenth centuries there can be traced a Muslim influence. The great Hindu devotional poet from Maratha, Nāmadeva (Namdev), for example, blended Islamic worship of God with Upaniṣadic monism in his verses. Using many Persian and Arabic words, he showed great respect for the one, omnipotent God.

His compatriot Tukārām, who lived perhaps a hundred years later and is one of the greatest devotional poets of medieval India, was also deeply influenced by Islam. In a typical verse he says,

> First among the great names is Allah, never forget to repeat it.
> *Allah* is verily one, the prophet is verily one.
> There Thou art one, there Thou art one, there Thou art one, O! friend.
> There is neither I nor Thou.[3]

No hostility toward Islam is found in the poems and songs of Nāmadeva, Tukārām, and other devotional poets of the time. They sing the praises of Allah along with those of the Hindu deities, seeing all as manifestations of the Supreme unmanifest reality uniting and pervading all existence.

Sometimes hostility did exist, of course, as in the case of Shivaji, one

[3]Quoted in Tara Chand, *The Influence of Islam on Indian Culture* (Allahabad: The Indian Press, 1954), p. 228.

of the fiercest enemies with whom the Muslim rulers had to contend in India, who expressed his hostility in political opposition. But even in this case we detect an earlier feeling of respect and goodwill, for Shivaji's father, Shaji, was named after the great Sufi saint, Shah Sharif of Ahmadnagar, suggesting that Shivaji's grandfather was a great admirer of this saintly Muslim.

Of course, many of these influential Muslim saints went very far in the direction of admitting the validity of Hinduism, urging their followers to follow what was best in both of these great religions, encouraging them to see what they had in common at their spiritual core rather than emphasizing their differences and antagonisms at the periphery. Three of the most notable examples of this tendency are Kabīr, Dādū, and Gurū Nānak.

Kabīr, born near the beginning of the fifteenth century, was a disciple of both the Sufi Shaikh Taqi and Rāmānanda, the great Hindu bhakta (devotee) who was instrumental in spreading devotional Hinduism across northern India. Although he is frequently claimed by Hindus as a Hindu mystic and reformer, it is almost certain that Kabīr was born into a Muslim family and that he never renounced Islam. But he certainly denounced both the narrowness of Islam and the rigid sectarianism of Hinduism.

His Hindu guru, Rāmānanda, may also have been influenced by Islam, though this is not certain. In any event, Rāmānanda himself protested against the caste system, admitting all persons equally into his following. But since the best of the Hindu devotional leaders emphasized that true devotion and spiritual realization surmounted the distinctions of sect and caste, the fact that Rāmānanda accepted people of all castes, as well as outcasts and even Muslims, certainly does not prove Islamic influence.There is no doubt, however, that Kabīr accepted both Islamic and Hindu ideas and practices, attempting to reconcile these two religions on the basis of what he recognized as a deeper unity. His most trenchant criticisms of Islam are directed at the rigid formalism and the exclusive absolutism that refuse to recognize as true or spiritual any idea or practice that is not so defined and accepted by previous Islamic authority. He saw formalism and absolutism suffocating spiritual life under the external wrappings of required beliefs, observances, practices, and laws.

On the other hand, he was unsparing in his denunciation of Hindu caste, polytheism, and idolatry. No one, he said, should be denied a full measure of both human dignity and access to spiritual practice simply because of birth into a low caste or outcast family. Idolatry he condemned for directing the energies of devotees away from what is truly spiritual, while polytheism was seen to detract from devotion and service to the Supreme.

Kabīr was embraced by later Hindus as a great saint and reformer and was given a thoroughly Hindu biography. That he was actually a Muslim reformer did not initially matter to Hindus nearly as much as his spiritual message, which offered hope to millions of poor and oppressed persons. Hinduism has always been able to accommodate radicals and reformers, enfolding them into its lifestream even as it has absorbed Āryans, Ājīvakas, Buddhists, and countless other religious movements and persons over the ages. But the formalism of Islam, against which Kabīr militated so vigorously, was too rigid to allow him to be accepted as a Muslim saint, except by a handful of admirers.

Gurū Nānak (1469–1539), founder of the Sikh religion, was in the same spiritual tradition as Kabīr. He may also have been a Muslim, although both Hindu and Sikh traditions regarded him as Hindu. Like Kabīr, he sought to transcend the differences between Islam and Hinduism, uniting Hindus and Muslims on the basis of the great underlying spiritual truths that these two religions held in common. He also denounced the idolatry and polytheism of Hinduism, insisting on the pervasive Will of a single omnipotent and omnisicient God. But his insistence on the uniqueness and absoluteness of God was based not on the Islamic tendency to exclude from God what was not of His own nature but, rather, on the ancient Indian tendency to include all things in a greater unity, thereby admitting opposites as corollaries and complementarities.

As Gurū Nānak traveled around the countryside, often in the presence of one or both of his steady companions, one a Muslim, the other a Hindu, he attracted a large following, which soon became the basis for the new Sikh religion. Because of its continuing importance, the entire next chapter will be devoted to the Sikh religion. There we will see that Sikhism's intense military opposition to Islam, and the resultant militant nature of the Sikh religion, are due entirely to political circumstances in the seventeenth century.

Dādū (1544–1603) was another Muslim reformer whose combination of Muslim and Hindu ideas influenced many Hindus. The inspiration for his reform efforts was found in the teachings of of Kabīr, for he was a member of a Kabīr sect. But as they did with other great saints, later Hindus gave Dādū a Hindu biography and accepted him as a strictly Hindu saint.

It is, of course, part of the traditional Indian way to accept as saints great spiritual persons whose ideas are worthy of belief and whose practice is worthy of emulation. Most of the religions and sects that developed on Indian soil began as small groups of followers of a holy person. If the following grew sufficiently, it became a separate sect or even, as in the case of Buddhism and Jainism, an independent religion. In other cases, the following was small or did not endure sufficiently long to achieve independent or semi-independent status. But in any particular time in history, including contemporary India, what we call Hinduism is made up of many sects, distinguished on the basis of different deities, different saint leaders, or differences in practice and belief—sometimes despite common deities or a common saint leader.

The truth about Hinduism is that no person or institution has ever existed to define Hindu orthodoxy, and no exclusive doctrine or practice has ever become the basis for orthodoxy. And in the absence of orthodoxy, unorthodoxy is undefinable and heresy quite impossible. Hinduism is rather like a large family of practices and beliefs in which there is no central authority or head. As long as all members live under one roof or on the same soil, they accept each other as members of the same family, despite considerable differences among them. When Muslims on Indian soil were perceived as true spiritual seekers and genuinely devout, holy persons, they were accepted as part of the religious family, to be honored as saints.

Later, in the seventeenth and eighteenth centuries, when opposition between Hindus and Muslims grew intense—primarily for political reasons—Hindus often conveniently forgot the Muslim ancestry of some of these saints and in some cases, almost certainly in that of Dādū, deliberately falsified the historical record to blot out Muslim origins. But the saint was not forgotten or pushed into oblivion, for sainthood essentially has nothing to do with politics or nationality or religious sect; it is simply a matter of holiness and spiritual realization.

Of course, the movement of religious influence was not only from Muslim to Hindu, but also from Hindu to Muslim. Because of the rigid structure and formalism of Islam, however, there was little perceptible change in orthodox Islam. Nevertheless, there was considerable Hindu influence on the lives of individual Sufis and—through them—on the lives of many Indians whom the Sufis converted to Islam.

Indeed, Hinduized Muslims had their own caste system and observed Hindu sacraments and holy days along with their observance of the five pillars of Islam. Although it shocked Muslim orthodoxy, many Hindu converts to Islam, influenced by the cultural inclusive attitude, saw no inconsistency between being a Muslim and observing Hindu practices. It is as though they recognized that the ultimate reality and the ultimate religious practice both go beyond all names and forms, beyond all rules and conventions, beyond proclamations of doctrine and definitions of orthodoxy.

## RELIGION AND POLITICS

This urge toward religious unification was felt even by one of India's greatest rulers, and religious interaction promised to develop at the very center of the Imperial Court during Akbar's reign (1556–1605). Out of deep personal interest in religion and dissatisfaction with the narrowness of Islam and the continuous theological and juridical haggling of his two chief religious advisors, Akbar invited Hindu pandits, Jaina sādhus, Parsi mobeds, and Jesuit priests to religious discussions in the Imperial Court.

Although scholars disagree over whether Akbar actually promulgated a new religion, the *Dīn-i Ilahi*, there is no doubt that he encouraged religious dialogue and openness among people of different faiths and sects. It is also clear that he accepted disciples and that as emperor of India he saw himself responsible for the well-being of all the people, Hindus, Jainas, and Parsis as well as Muslims. In this concern he promulgated decrees against involuntary cremation of widows, child marriages, and the taking of multiple spouses.

But the promise of interaction and unification at the imperial level was unfulfilled because historical forces were against the attempt. Although Akbar's spirit of tolerance and sense of fairness in allowing all classes and creeds to participate in the Mughal administration became a regular part of the Mughal policy—and, by any measure, a great success in political integration and tolerance—the same cannot be said about his efforts to secure religious tolerance and integration.

Part of the reason is that a great Hindu religious revival, initiated by Chaitanya, among others, spread across India and became strongly established at Mathura, almost within earshot of the Mughal court. This had two important effects. On the one hand, it alarmed the orthodox Muslims, for it threatened both their religion and their security and drove them to repudiate the tolerance that they felt had encouraged this revival of Hinduism. This reaction of the conservative Muslims at court touched off a wave of protectionism and intolerance that threatened to destroy the existing basis for cooperation and mutual toleration between Hindus and Muslims. On the other hand, this strong revival of Hinduism led to a greater pride in Hinduism and a defiance of the felt need to submit to rulers of a foreign faith who falsely regarded themselves as the only truly religious people.

Half a century after Akbar's death, his grandson, Aurangzeb, began his fifty-year rule as emperor of India. Aurangzeb's reign began in 1658 when he imprisoned his father, Shah Jahan, builder of the beautiful Taj Mahal, and ended with his death in 1707. Aurangzeb's religious policy was almost directly opposite to that of his great-grandfather's. In place of Akbar's emphasis on equality of religions and toleration of all creeds and practices, Aurangzeb insisted that his kingdom was Muslim and that it be governed and administered strictly according to Muslim law. Orders were given to collect the military support tax from non-Muslims, to destroy non-Muslim places of worship, and to prohibit the teachings and practices of the "infidels." He also greatly decreased the scope of service for non-Muslims in his administration.

It is hard to judge to what extent these orders and their subsequent enactment flamed the fires of Hindu political rebellion and encouraged the ongoing Hindu religious revival. But they certainly added to the deepening rift between Muslim and Hindu communities that was to eventually make it impossible for them to cooperate to defeat the British and that later would lead to the carving of the subcontinent into the two separate Muslim states of Pakistan and Bangladesh and the secular, but Hindu-dominated, state of India.

Aurangzeb's reactionary religious policies seem to follow the lines indicated by Shaikh Ahmad's open letters to the Muslim court. Shaikh

Ahmad (1564–1624) was a disciple of Khwaja Baqi Billah, who established the Naqshbandi movement in India to exert religious influence on the political rulers. Up to this time the various Islamic spiritual orders in India had not gotten directly involved in purely political affairs. Shaikh Ahmad, following his teacher, felt that everything that involved the well-being and welfare of Muslims was a religious concern. No activity was excluded, of course and political activity, because of its far-reaching effects, became a central area of religious concern and a target for religious influence. Unlike Akbar, Ahmad regarded India as a Muslim state. He complained that "non-Muslims carried out aggressively the ordinances of their own religion in a Muslim state and the Muslims were powerless to carry out the ordinances of Islam; if they carried them out, they were executed." Although Ahmad may be referring to only scattered incidents, his observations are rooted in facts that were upsetting to many other orthodox Muslims as well. He complained in other letters that Hindus destroyed Muslim mosques and tombs to replace them with temples. He made it clear that he felt that Akbar's imperial policy had weakened the positions of Muslims and had strengthened the position of Hindus. He lamented that "during the sacred month of Ramaḍān, they [Hindus] openly prepare and sell food, but owing to the weakness of Islam, nobody can interfere. Alas, the ruler of the country is one of us, but we are so badly off!"[4]

Aurangzeb did attempt to institute Muslim reforms that would strengthen the position of Islam and curb the power and practices of non-Muslims. But the fact that many new temples were contructed in Bengal in the seventeenth and eighteenth centuries, that Krishna and Kālī worship flourished, and that many Hindus were powerful enough to refuse to pay the *jizya* (military support tax) or to negotiate a lower rate suggests that, although Muslims ruled India, they by no means controlled the people. And this is understandable, considering the Muslim political principle that, so long as non-Muslim communities paid their taxes and did not interfere with the practice of Islam, they should be allowed to manage their own affairs. This meant that throughout most of India, caste organizations and village panchyats were the real governing powers, almost totally immune from Muslim rule.

The near immunity from the influence of political rule helps to explain how, despite a generally conservative attitude, exciting developments in Indian logic, yoga, metaphysics, and religion occurred under Muslim rule. The religious and philosophical activities described in the four previous chapters by no means came to an end with the advent of Islam. Lively and imaginative debates and careful study marked the continuing development of philosophy—study and debate practically untouched by Muslim ideas. Any strictly historical account of Indian thought would have to devote many volumes to Hindu religious and

[4]All quotations from Ahmad are from S. M. Ikram, *Muslim Civilization in India* (New York: Columbia University Press, 1964), pp. 171–172.

philosophical thought occurring from the twelfth to the nineteenth centuries (though, of course, the framework for most of these developments had been worked out centuries earlier).

## Summary

For nearly a thousand years, from shortly after Qasim's conquests in Sind in the early eighth century almost until the official imposition of British Crown Rule in 1858, most of the subcontinent was under Muslim rule. The Muslims brought with them an entirely foreign civilization, rooted in Islam, a religion that was in many ways antagonistic toward Hinduism.

Faith dominated Islam, and the orthodoxy of belief discouraged philosophical speculation, with the consequence that practically no Islamic philosophy developed on Indian soil. Religious thought, on the other hand, found many challenges in the meeting of these two quite different religious ways. The Sufis were especially influential and active in the encounter between Hinduism and Islam, for they were concerned more with developing a personal and immediate spiritual relationship with God than with maintaining the orthodox beliefs and practices for their own sake. Between Sufi practices of devotion to Allah and Hindu practices of devotion to Vishnu, Rāma, or Krishna there was much common ground, providing impetus for great spiritual persons and thinkers to seek a deeper spiritual basis that would accommodate both Hinduism and Islam.

Kabīr, Nanāk, and Dādū are among the outstanding medieval thinkers who discovered a kind of transcendental unity of religions. In Nānak's case, a whole new religion, Sikhism, emerged in the response to what was felt as his original and inspirational insight into the essential unity of God. In other cases, such insight provided for a reconciliation in the heart and mind of a given individual or in the lives of a whole sect, but without becoming a separate religon.

On the whole, however, there was remarkably little mutual interaction and influence. Radically different and deeply conservative, these two great civilizations went their own ways, concerned, for the most part, to retain their distinctively Hindu or Muslim ideas and attitudes. The political separation of the subcontinent in the twentieth century was prefigured centuries earlier in the religious and cultural apartheid between Muslim and Hindu India.

## Suggestions for Further Reading

*The House of Islam*, by Kenneth Cragg (Belmont Calif.: Dickenson Publishing Co., 1969), is an excellent introduction to the meaning and message of Islam. It combines an emphasis on fundamental ideas and practices with a good sense of historical development. A slightly more advanced introduction is provided by *Islam: Its Meaning and Message*, ed. Khurskid Ahmad (London: The Islamic Foundation, 1976). In addition to an excellent twenty-five-page introduction to the way of Islam, this volume contains short articles by twelve leading Islamic scholars on topics ranging from Muhammad's life and the role of women in Islam to Islam's place in the modern world.

S. M. Ikram, *Muslim Civilization in India*, ed. A. Embree (New York: Columbia University Press, 1964), is a very good general survey of Indian Muslim life, emphasizing the broad cultural and religious dimensions of Islam in India. *The Indian Muslims*, by M. Mujeeb (London: George Allen & Unwin, 1967), is a comprehensive statement of the life of Islam in India. It is divided into three parts, dealing with early middle, and late Muslim periods. The chapters on orthodoxy and religious thought are particularly helpful. Many of the writings of Aziz Ahmad are also helpful. *Studies in Islamic Culture in the Indian Environment* (Oxford, 1964) is especially useful.

*Kabīr*, by Charlotte Vaudeville (London; Oxford University Press, 1974), is a comprehensive and reliable work on the life and ideas of this great apostle of Hindu-Muslim unity.

*Sufis of Bijapur, 1300–1700: Social Roles of Sufis in Medieval India*, by Richard Maxwell Eaton (Princeton, N.J.: Princeton University Press, 1978), is the best available analysis of Indian Sufism and its place in the functioning of Indian society. He emphasizes the great variety of ideas, attitudes, and practices that characterized Sufi relationships with orthodox Islam (the *Ulamā*) and with the Hindus, giving us a rich picture of Sufi life and influence in India.

S. A. A. Rizvi is one of the truly outstanding scholars of Islam in India. Any of his writings will guide the more advanced reader in pursuing both the questions of Islamic development in India and Muslim-Hindu interaction. I am eagerly awaiting his new book on Sufism.

# 15

# The Faith of the Sikhs

One of the most impressive results of the Hindu-Muslim religious interaction noted in the last chapter is the Sikh religion. Originating with Gurū Nānak (1469–1539), the Sikh religion not only withstood concerted Muslim efforts to suppress it, but developed into a world religion that today has some fourteen million adherents. Although most Sikhs, nearly twelve million, live in India, there are Sikh communities around the world, notably in Australia, Southeast Asia, Africa, Canada, Britain, and the United States. There are probably a million Sikhs in the United States and Canada, with perhaps half that many living in England. In the United States, Sikhism has received considerable publicity through the work of Yogi Bhajan (Harbhajan Singh Puri) with his "Healthy, Happy, Holy Organization," known popularly as 3HO. Through his efforts thousands of Americans have converted to Sikhism.

In this chapter we will be concerned primarily with Sikh religious and philosophical thought. After a brief overview of Sikh beliefs, we will examine the foundations of Sikhism in the life and teachings of its founder, Gurū Nānak, and his successors. Then, following a review of the main religious and philosophical influences that shaped Gurū Nānak's vision, we will focus on his ideas of God, human nature, and the way of salvation.

## Basic Vision

The way of Sikhism is to find salvation through union with God by realizing, through love, the in-dwelling Person of God. Union with God is the ultimate goal. Apart from God, life has no meaning. As Gurū Nānak says, "What terrible separation it is to be separated from God and what blissful union to be united with him!"[1]

Separation from God causes the suffering experienced as the usual human condition. Although human beings and the world are created by God, human perversity and pride, stemming from self-centeredness, lead to attachment to the pleasures and concerns of this world. According to Sikhism, this attachment separates us from God, resulting in all forms of human suffering, including the seemingly endless round of deaths and re-births.

It is God, one without a second, formless and eternal, who created all existence, and it is God who sustains all forms of existence by dwelling within them. Through His will we are sustained, and through His grace God reveals Himself to us through His creation. This divine revelation calls forth recognition of our separateness and sparks the response that can bring salvation through union with Him in love, according to Gurū Nānak.

Only when God's voice is heard within the human heart and the heart responds is salvation possible. Worship of images and asceticism are pointless, as are yoga and ritual actions. Only through love for the Person of God can the bliss of union be achieved. As Divine Guru, God declares His message directly to the heart of those who will hear. In the message of Gurū Nānak and the other gurus, as recorded in the scripture called Ādi Granth (or Gurū Granth Sāhib), is to be heard the message of God, the Original Guru.

## Gurū Nānak and the Sikh Community

The essential ideas of Sikhism, as outlined above, are found in the teachings of Gurū Nānak. They continue to be the basis of Sikhism today, even as they were five hundred years ago. Before examining these basic ideas further, however, it may be helpful to say something about Gurū Nānak himself, and about the origins of the Sikh community.

### LIFE OF GURŪ NĀNAK

Although reliable information about Gurū Nānak's life is hard to come by, it appears that he was born into a Hindu family of the kṣatriya class living in the village of Talwandi. His father was a revenue officer for the Muslim owner of Talwandi and sufficiently affluent to provide Nānak with a good education. According to the traditional biographies, not always factually reliable, Nānak became dissatisfied with Hinduism al-

[1]AG, 1; McLeod, 148. AG, 1 means Ādi Granth, page 1. Unless indicated otherwise, all quotations from the Adi Granth are McLeod's translations, taken from W. H. McLeod, *Gurū Nānak and the Sikh Religion*. (New York: Oxford University Press, 1968). McLeod, 148 means that the quotation is found on page 148 of *Gurū Nānak and the Sikh Religion*.

ready as a teenager. Living in a heavily Muslim area, he explored Islam as an alternative to Hinduism but found this equally unsatisfactory. These biographies also emphasize his eagerness to meet and talk with yogis and holy persons of any sect or religious persuasion.

Only after a personal experience of enlightenment did Nānak find what he was looking for. Once while bathing in the river he disappeared and was presumed dead. Upon his return, he explained that in the three days he was mysteriously absent from his village he had been taken to God's court. There he was given a cup of nectar (*amrit*) and told

> This is the cup of the adoration of God's name. Drink it. I am with you. I bless you and raise you up. Whoever remembers you will enjoy my favor. Go, rejoice in my name and teach others to do so also. I have given you the gift of My Name. Let this be your calling.[2]

This direct experience of God apparently settled the matter of whether Hinduism or Islam had greater claim to being the true religion, for tradition tells us that Nānak's first words after the enlightenment experience were, "There is neither Hindu nor Muslim, so whose path shall I follow? I will follow God's path. God is neither Hindu nor Muslim, and the path I follow is God's."[3]

Gurū Nānak now turned to meditation on God by listening to His word in the deep stillness of his own heart and by joyfully singing God's praises. As his spiritual life deepened, he attracted an increasing number of followers wishing to share in his experience and discipline. According to tradition, Gurū Nānak settled his family in Kartapur in about 1521, establishing the first exclusively Sikh community. The rest of his life was devoted to serving the community that had been formed on the basis of loyalty to him and his teaching.

Shortly before he died Gurū Nānak named Lehna, a former Hindu devotee of the Goddess Durgā, but now an unusually humble and devoted member of the community, to succeed him as head of the Sikh community. Renaming him Gurū Aṅgad (meaning "part of me"), Gurū Nānak declared that Aṅgad did, indeed, possess Nānak's own spirit and being and was qualified to lead the community. Thus was born the succession of guruships that continued unbroken until Guru Gobind Singh, the tenth guru, installed the Scripture itself as guru, thereby ending the tradition of human gurus as leaders of the Sikh community.

## THE SIKH COMMUNITY

The origins of Sikhism as a corporate religion are found in the small group of followers who gathered round Gurū Nānak to hear his words

[2]See W. Owen Cole and Piara Singh Sambhi, *The Sikhs* (Boston: Routledge and Kegan Paul, 1978), p. 10.

[3]*Purātam Janam Sākhi*, ed. Vīr Singh (Amritsar, 1959), p. 16.

of wisdom in the last twenty years or so of his life. They accepted him as *guru*, teacher of spiritual truth, capable of awakening within them the wisdom that leads to salvation.

The place of the guru is central in Sikhism, but one must distinguish carefully between human guru and Divine Guru. Nānak was accepted as their guru by his followers because they understood him to be giving voice to the word of God. God alone is truly Guru, for all revelations of divine wisdom come only from Him. Gurū Nānak and the nine other human gurus who succeeded him as heads of the Sikh community were gurus only because God spoke through them. It was the divine message they expressed, not their persons, that made them gurus, and this was really God's message expressed through them.

This is why, when the third guru, Amar Dās, made the first collection of scriptures he included, along with his own hymns, not only the hymns of Gurū Nānak and Gurū Aṅgad, but also those of non-Sikhs regarded as transmitting the voice of God. Only because it was regarded as the voice of God did this collection, along with the additions of the fifth gurū, Gurū Arjan and the hymns of his father, Gurū Ram Das, became the primary scripture, indeed, the Guru of the Sikh community. Known initially as the "Original Collection" or Ādi Granth, it eventually came to be called Gurū Granth Sāhib (Collection of Sacred Wisdom).

Near the end of his life Gurū Gobind Singh, tenth and last of the Sikh gurus, declared that with his death the line of personal gurus would end. From then on the scripture itself, the Gurū Granth Sāhib, would be the guru of the community. But since God speaks directly to people whose hearts are pure and devoted to him, the Gurū Granth Sāhib shared this central place with the corporate Sikh community. Thus, today when Sikhs meet in the presence of the Gurū Granth Sāhib to make decisions, the Divine Guru is considered to be present, giving voice to His message through the living community as well as through the Gurū Granth Sāhib.

Although the institution of the scripture and the corporate community as guru marks a significant development in Sikhism, there is no radical break with the earlier tradition. God had always been recognized as the True Guru and His message, heard within the deepest recesses of the heart, had always been understood to be the true message of revelation.

Gurū Gobind Singh instituted other changes that were more radical, transforming the Sikh community into a powerful force capable of fighting fiercely for the sake of peace and righteousness. During this guru's leadership (1675–1708), the Sikh community was under heavy assault by Aurangzeb, the Muslim ruler of India. Later, between 1757 and 1769, Ahmad Shah Abdali of Afghanistan would launch no fewer than nine invasions of the Punjab in a "holy war" against the Sikh "infidels." Clearly, great strength was needed if Sikhism was to survive.

According to a well-known account, Gurū Gobind addressed an assembly of Sikhs gathered to celebrate New Year's Day (April 13, 1699). He stressed that the times were perilous and the danger to the community great. Weakness would have to be replaced with strength and unity. Loyalty to the guru would have to come before any personal considerations. To demonstrate his seriousness, he drew his sword and asked men to come forward, and out of inner conviction and loyalty, offer their heads to him. With uplifted sword, he awaited their approach. At first no one came. Then, breaking the fearful silence, one Sikh stepped forward, and was led into the guru's tent. When the guru came out alone, his sword bloodied, four more brave men stepped forward and were escorted into the tent. The hushed crowd waited for the guru to come out alone a second time, with fresh blood dripping from his sword. But to their surprise, he emerged from the tent together with all five Sikhs. Mixing nectar (*amrit*) with a two-edged sword, he now initiated the "beloved five," as they are usually called, into the Pure Order (*Khālsā*).

After receiving his own initiation into the Pure Order by the five original initiates, Gurū Gobind proclaimed a code of discipline for all Sikhs. Tobacco, eating meat of animals slaughtered according to Muslim ritual, and sex with Muslims were forbidden. Furthermore, from now on, as a sign of their loyalty to the Pure Order, all men were to wear the five K's: (1) uncut hair (*keś*), (2) the comb (*kangha*), (3) sword or dagger (*kirpan*), (4) wrist guard (*kara*), and (5) short pants (*kach*).

The men admitted to the Pure Order all took the name Singh (lion) and the women took the name Kaur (princess). Thousands of men and women were initiated that day, and ever since, initiation into the Khālsā, accepting the prohibitions, and the five K's has been an integral part of Sikhism. It should also be mentioned that, although the Sikh community had always been open to men and women from every caste, the formal initiation by Gurū Gobind of śūdra men and women along with kṣatriays institutionalized the equality of castes and sexes within Sikhism.

## The Influence of Tradition on Gurū Nānak's Thought

Before turning to Gurū Nānak's thought, we need to say something about the ideas that influenced him. Without in any way disputing his originality and the uniqueness of Sikhism, it must be insisted that earlier traditions had considerable influence on his thought. The Hindu Sant tradition to which Nāmdev and Kabīr belonged was especially influential, and the Muslim Sufi traditions probably had some direct influence on Gurū Nānak as well as influencing the Sant tradition itself.

The small Punjabi village of Talwandi where Gurū Nānak was born lies about fifty-five miles west of Lahore, in an area that, although predominantly Hindu at the time, was experiencing a considerable Muslim influence. The Hindu worship of Rāma and Krishna—two very popular manifestations of Vishnu—predominated, but the influences of Tantric practices were also felt.

Buddhist Tantric practices, popular in this area hundreds of years earlier, had gradually come to influence Hindu practice as well, especially among the worshippers of Shiva. The followers of Shiva in this region venerated Him as the Great Yogi, following His way of yoga to achieve union with the Ultimate.

## THE SANTS

The tradition to which Gurū Nānak was directly heir, however, was that of the Sants. "Sant" means "holy person," and when we speak of the "Sant tradition" we are talking about a rather loose but historically continuous, federation of religious seekers who, though not a corporate entity, were united in their belief in a supreme, formless God. This distinguished them from the majority of Hindus who worshipped the form of God manifested in one of his incarnations, for example, Krishna or Rāma.

The Sant emphasis on control over the senses while living a pure and holy life also distinguished them from the Tantric yogins, who advocated the full use of the entire range of the potentialities of the senses and the body—including the ritual use of meat, alcohol, and sex.

While the Sants did not constitute a separate religious sect, individual Sants, like Kabīr, for example, had followers. Indeed, the Kabīr sect survives to this day. The fellowship constituting the Sant tradition was sustained by a common devotion to a formless God as the highest reality and recognition of the need to control the sense and mind in order to realize this Supreme Reality. Meditating on the Name of God, they said, was the way to experience the Divine Being. In this experience, a union with God was realized, a union that dissolved the ordinary sense of duality between self and God, and between one person and another. Since within their experience of wholeness, neither caste discrimination nor worship of images made any sense, the Sants rejected both.

Their strong sense of community prompted the Sants to express their religious experience in poems and songs so that others could share in their vision and joy. They used the vernacular language so that men and women of the lower castes, who were ignorant of Sanskrit, could learn and be inspired. Unlike most religious sects, their teaching was open to anyone, regardless of caste or sex. They did not regard themselves as gurus and claimed no human gurus of their own. God, they said, is the only Guru, communicating His own truth through His creation.

Gurū Nānak was clearly influenced greatly by the Sants and, through them, by the major ideas that had combined to shape the Sant tradition itself. The Sant tradition is deeply rooted in the devotionalism that swept across India in the seventh to ninth centuries, a devotionalism that expressed itself primarily in loving surrender to one's chosen deity, for example, Krishna. Although firmly rooted in the earlier Hindu devotional tradition, this devotionalism of loving surrender was probably strengthened by Muslim influence, particularly by the pious and devout Sufis. In the twelfth and thirteenth centuries, for example, three Sufis—Shaikh Ismail Bokhari, Data Ganj Baksh, and Shaikh Farid—converted many Hindus in the area around Lahore to Islam by their personal example of holiness and their teachings of the way of devotion to the One, True God. So great is Sikh respect for the teachings of Shaikh Farid, that 116 of his hymns are included in the Ādi Granth.

It may well be that the Muslim emphasis on the One True God reinforced the earlier Hindu emphasis on the quality-less nature of the ultimate reality (nirguṇa Brahman). In any event, the Sant tradition rejected the idea that Krishna, Rāma, and the other manifestations of God were truly God. They emphasized the One, True, Formless God and insisted that only devotion to Him could bring salvation.

The Sants were also influenced by a sect of Nāth yogis who combined veneration of Shiva with yoga practice and asceticism. The word *nāth* means "master," and the Nāths regarded themselves as followers of the original Master, the great Yogi, Shiva. They considered all scriptures, rituals, and ceremonies to be useless; yoga is the only means of attaining salvation. They also rejected the caste distinctions, pollution taboos, and moral norms of Hinduism as irrelevant.

## INFLUENTIAL SANTS

Of the individual Sants who seem to have made a considerable impression on Gurū Nānak, at least three must be mentioned. Lallā, a Kashmiri Shaivite, who lived in the early fourteenth century, emphasized in her hymns that there is a Supreme Being who is nameless, formless, and colorless and without lineage. Through realization that this Ultimate One already dwells within the heart, union with God is possible, she said. Bearing witness to the truth that God alone is truly Guru, she claimed no human guru.

Nāmdev (1270–1350), the Vaishnavite saint from Maharasthra, emphasized over and over that God is the only true Guru. Many of his hymns celebrate the greatness of the True Guru.

Kabīr was so influential that over five hundred of his hymns are included in the Gurū Granth Sāhib. His dates are not known precisely, but he probably lived from about 1440 to 1518. Several of the influences we have been discussing seem to have come to bear directly on Kabīr. He probably belonged to a Nāth family that had very recently been converted to Islam—though in a somewat superficial way, as indicated by Kabīr's own independence of Islam.

Although Sufic influence in Kabīr's work can be noted, and his emphasis on heartfelt devotion suggests strong devotional influence, the strongest influence in his work is probably that of the yoga emphasized by the Nāths. In Kabīr's emphasis on love as the way to God is found a combination of Hindu devotionalism and Sufic mysticism. In his rejection of rituals and ceremonies, scriptures and caste, and in his insistence on discipline is found the Nāth influence. God is the true Guru, Kabīr sings over and over. God, the One, Eternal, Formless, is the only God.

Although there is no reason to believe that Gurū Nānak was ever a disciple of Kabīr or that he even had met him, clearly the great influence of earlier ideas came to Gurū Nānak through the Sant tradition as embodied in Kabīr. Even while insisting on the importance of Gurū Nānak's personal experience of God and the authenticity of his enlightenment, Sikhs can admit that both the reception of these experiences and their expression in his teachings were shaped by Sant influence.

Turning to the question of Muslim influence on Gurū Nānak, the common assumption that Sikhism is essentially a blend of Muslim and Hindu ideas should probably be rejected. Although many Western scholars have suggested that Gurū Nānak's thought is heavily indebted to Islam, particularly Sufic Islam, McLeod argues convincingly that this is not the case. His conclusion is that "Muslim influence upon the thought of Gurū Nānak must accordingly be regarded as relatively slight."[4]

Of course, to the extent that the Sant tradition is influenced by Islam, this influence is also felt by Gurū Nānak. And undoubtedly the Muslims living in the Punjab must have had some influence upon Gurū Nānak when he was growing up and seeking a way to God.

## Teachings of Gurū Nānak

Granted both the influence of tradition and the inspiration of personal experience of God, what are the essential features of Gurū Nānak's vision? As indicated in the brief statement of the Sikh vision at the beginning of this chapter, the key concept is that of God. Strictly speaking, God is formless, so no conception is possible. God cannot be realized through ideas; only by direct revelation of His being within the human heart can God be known. Through God's grace and human effort, the self can join with God through love, a union ultimately inexpressible in thought or words. Despite the inexpressibility of the Ultimate, it is clear that Gūru Nānak conceived of God as the sole reality, the One, the Only One, or as sometimes said, "the One without a second." It is also clear that he experienced God as a personal being through love and adoration.

This whole existence is God's creation, that is to say, nothing but God's manifestation of Himself. All dwell in God and He in them. His emphasis on God's unity and transcendence sometimes makes Gurū

[4]McLeod, *op. cit.*, p. 160.

Nānak's God sound like Brahman, the ultimate monistic principle. But this is misleading, for Gurū Nānak's God is personal. His experience revealed God to be experienceable through love, a Supreme Being reaching into the human heart through His love for His creation.

The root mantra of the Ādi Granth, held to be his first poetic expression after his enlightenment experience at Sultanpur, voices Gurū Nānak's experience of God.

> There is one God,
> Eternal Truth is his Name,
> Creator of all things and the all-pervading Spirit.
> Fearless and without hatred,
> Timeless and Formless.
> Beyond birth and death,
> Self-enlightened.
> By the grace of the Guru He is Known.[5]

So important is the belief in one God that the symbol Ek Oankar ('There is one God') is always found on the canopy above the Ādi Granth. There has always been complete unanimity among the Sikhs that God is one (*Ek*) and that there is no other but God. In reference to the six orthodox systems of Hindu philosophy, Gurū Nānak declared that, although there are six visions of reality, six enlightened teachers, and six patterns of instruction, the Guru of these gurus is One, though His manifestations are many. But the oneness of God is not completely undifferentiated unitary reality; Gurū Nānak's divine unity is personal, speaking to us through our innermost existence.

Sikhism stresses the unity of all existence in God because it sees separation from God as the primary defectiveness underlying human suffering. Through ignorance, God and the world are seen as separate realities, forcing us to divert our attention away from the one true reality and to live a kind of false or divided existence. But this does not mean that the reality of the world must be denied. Far from it. In Nānak's mystical vision, the world is real. But as God's creation *it is not separate from Him*. The key is that the unity of God *includes* the world. From a different perspective, the world is to be seen, not as something existing in its own right, separate from God, but as part of God's existence. This perspective accounts for the feeling that Sikhism is the "most materialistic" of India's religions, for the material world is embraced as as part of the divine unity of existence. It is not the world that is rejected, but only its separateness from God. This is the ultimate meaning of God's unity.

This creation, far from being unreal, is a manifestation of God, providing a revelation of God's own being to humans. Nevertheless, from the human point of view, the world should not be mistaken for the totality of God's existence. The world *is* divine; it is an expression of God's own being. But the world does not exhaust God's being. His

[5]AG, 1; After Cole and Sambhi, *op. cit.*, p. 69.

transcendence is as important to the Sikhs as is His immanence. Indeed, the essence of the divine unity is beyond all thought and expression. But through God's grace, by following the path of devotion to God and hearing His message, this unity can be realized directly within the human heart.

McLeod summarizes the Sikh understanding of God as follows:

> The ultimate essence of God is beyond all human categories, far transcending all powers of human expression. Only in experience can He be truly known. Man must indeed seek to give human expression to this mystical experience, and Gurū Nānak's works are directed to this very end, but the human expression can communicate no more than a glimpse of the ultimate reality.[6](p. 165)

In God's unity not only is the plurality of the world embraced, but also the plurality of Hindu deities. Gurū Nānak refers to God by many names: God is Hari, Vishnu, Shiva, Rāma, or Allah. All these are regarded simply as manifestations of the Supreme One; they are His manifestations, even this world is His manifestation.

> He, the One, is Himself Brahmā, Viṣṇu and Śiva; and
> He Himself performs all.
>
> (AG, 908; McLeod, 165)

In terms of the traditional distinction between the quality-less Ultimate Reality (nirguṇa Brahman) and the Ultimate Reality with qualities (saguṇa Brahman), God is nirguṇa in Himself, but saguṇa by His own will, in order that humans might know Him and realize union with Him. As Gurū Nānak says,

> From His absolute condition He, the Pure One, became manifest;
> from *nirguṇa* He became *saguṇa*.
>
> (AG, 940; McLeod, 167)

This whole world is God's creation. But creation was not the end of God's relationship with the world, for having brought forth this world, He now cares for it, watching over it constantly. A striking passage illustrates this aspect of God's existence.

> True Creator, True Sustainer, and known as the True One! Self-existent, true, ineffable, immeasurable! Uniting both mill stones [i.e., heaven and earth], He separated them. Without the *Gurū* there is utter darkness. Having created the sun and moon, He directs their paths by day and night.
>
> (AG, 580; McLeod, 169)

The traditional functions attributed to the various Gods, creation, sustenance, and destruction are all attributed to God, but his transcendence is emphasized. God is the Unborn, the Eternal. Only through union with Him is immortality and perfect bliss found.

To find bliss and immortality, says Gurū Nānak, attachment to, and love for, the world must be renounced in favor of love for God. Only by transferring our love from the world to God can the eternal personal relationship with Him that brings unending bliss be achieved. And when this transfer is accomplished, the world itself is embraced in the embrace of divine love. To see why love of God is the true path of salvation for Gurū Nānak, we must examine the Sikh concept of humanity.

## Human Nature

Why, as God's creature, should man be separated from God? This is the central theological problem of Sikhism. The answer has to do with the human perversity and pride, stemming from self-centeredness, which takes one's own separate existence to be the ultimate reality.

Why are humans like this? The Sikh answer is tied up with a theory of the self, more particularly with what is called the *man* or soul. It means something more than mind in its usual sense of organ of consciousness, but something less than the traditional concept of Ātman. The soul is consciousness, self-image, senses, and will, as these function together creating a sense of individual existence capable of thinking and acting in the world. It is the soul that determines virtue or sinfulness; it is the soul that realizes truth or falsehood; it is the soul that is the instrument of meditation. The soul is also the source of human love and the receptacle of God's love.

But in the sense that the soul can transcend the influences of other people and the world, rising to the level of God's love and existence, it is independent of the world and society. In a way it is also independent of the body, for it is the soul that survives death and enjoys eternal union with God. As McLeod notes, the soul (*man*) "combines the functions of the mind, the emotions of the heart and the qualities of the soul." He goes on to say, "*Man* is mind, heart, and soul. It is the faculty with which one thinks, decides, and feels, the source of all human good and evil, and that one indestructible attribute which must be released from the body and merged in the being of God" (p. 180).

Because the soul is capable of evil as well as good, of hatred as well as love, it is the soul that must be purified and reformed if salvation is to be possible. The soul of a proud and egotistical person attaches itself to the world as something separate from and even opposed to God. However, it is not the intrinsic nature of the soul that causes sinfulness and separation; it is only an impure and unrestrained soul that does this. In its own nature the soul is capable of realizing God. It is the greatest of treasures. But like a wonderful gem, it needs to be cleaned and polished to realize its brilliance.

## SELF-CENTEREDNESS

The chief defect of the soul is self-centeredness. Pride and perversity are seen as results of self-centeredness (*haumai*). The concept of self-centeredness functions in Sikhism something like the concept of sinfulness does in Christianity. There is an inclination in human nature to sinfulness or self-centeredness, but neither sinfulness nor self-centeredness is inevitable. Yet, self-centeredness is the ultimate cause of human suffering, separating humans from God. The self-centered person is full of self-love—not love of God. Filled with self-love and self-will such a person does not hear the word of God, but clings to the self.

The self dominated by self-centeredness is motivated by the evil passions. The Ādi Granth describes such a person as follows:

> Day and night are the two seasons when he crops his land; lust and anger are his two fields. He waters them with greed, sows in them the seed of untruth, and worldly impulse, his ploughman, cultivates them. His [evil] thoughts are his plough and evil is the crop he reaps.
>
> (AG, 955; McLeod, 184)

Lust, greed, anger, attachment, and pride dominate the self-centered person, making it impossible for him or her to hear the voice of God. Yama, Lord of Death, uses these evil impulses to snare for himself the souls of those who fail to overcome their self-centeredness and transform themselves into God-centered persons.

## THE WORLD

For the self-centered person the attractions of the world become seductive, entrapping the self in a life that is ultimately a life of untruth and deceit, because separate from God. Having abandoned God for the world, a person can only be described as hating truth; compared with God the world is untruth. Wealth, sex, power, family, status and honor, comfort, food—these are the seductive attractions of the world, catching the self-centered person in their trap.

The problem is not the world, but the human response to the world. If the world is accepted as God's creation and seen as a means to God-realization, it is like a beautiful gem. But when it is mistaken for something separate from God, something existing in its own right to serve the purposes of the self-centered person, it becomes a fraud and an untruth. For the self-centered person, the world is a source of suffering and death, while for the God-centered person it is a source of joy and eternal life.

The curse of the self-centered person is separation from God. This isolation robs a person of wholeness and deprives him or her of eternal life. There is only fear, anxiety, and restlessness for one separated from God. And Yama, with his inescapable net, waits for those who become separated from God and lost in the world.

## Realization of God

Seeking self-fulfillment through attachment to external things, there is only suffering and death. But by turning inward to the light within the heart, the soul can find God, showing the way to joy and eternal life. God dwells in the hearts of all created beings. If they will but listen to His voice and respond to His love, they will find redemption in union with Him.

The doctrine of God speaking to us through the heart is crucial to Sikhism; it is the key to salvation. How does God do this? How does God communicate with human beings?

Sacred Word, Guru, Divine Name, Divine Norm, Truth, and Grace are important concepts pointing to the nature, content, and method of the divine communication to human beings. To understand how the divine message is made available to human beings so that it can be recognized, accepted, and followed, we need to examine each of these concepts.

**The Word.** The Word (*śabad*) is the sound of God reverberating through His creation; it is God's message. By meditating on this sound, union with Him can be achieved, for it is the revelation of God's own being, resounding in the deepest recesses of the human heart. When this revelation is heard and responded to, self-centeredness is destroyed, for the Word is the vehicle of God's saving message.

God's Word has a dual function: first, it is the means through which God can be known, and second, it reveals the path leading to union with God. It is, therefore, the essential means of salvation. McLeod sums up the role of the Word in Sikhism as follows: "By contemplation of the Word and by the total conforming of one's life to its dictates the *man* [self] is brought under control, self-centeredness is cast out, the individual grows ever nearer to God until, ultimately perfected in His likeness, he passes into a condition of union which transcends death and the cycle of transmigration" (193). As Gurū Nānak reminds himself, "Nānak, the Lord, the true Creator, is known by means of the Word!" (AG, 688; McLeod, 193).

The Word is not a singular sound or expression, but everything that reveals either God or the path to Him. It includes everything that is True, that expresses the nature of God, and that reveals the means of attaining Him. The word of God speaks through all creation, through the divine laws governing the universe as well as through personal mystical experience.

How can a person hear the Word of God? Initially, it is by God's grace or favor that He enables His message to enter a person's heart. But granted this initial favor, Sikhs say, there is present in the understanding of every person a sufficient capacity to hear and respond—at least to the extent of feeling a longing for God.

**God's Name.** As we have seen, the Word of God is the revelation of His Being. God's Name refers to His Personal Being, the dimension of

God that can be known and loved by humans. God's Name does not mean some arbitrary title affixed to God, but the very being of God. Gurū Nānak's teaching is that by focusing on His Name we enter into relation with the personal dimension of God, creating a personal relationship capable of transmitting God's love to us, and our love to Him.

The Name of God is used in two ways. It refers to the being of God, and it refers also to the means of God's communication with His creatures. But these uses are related, for just as all creation resounds with God's word, so is all creation the expression of God's being. As the scripture says, "Whatever He has made is an expression of His Name. There is no part of creation which is not such an expression" (AG, 4; McLeod, 196).

This tells us that the answer to the question, "Where do I look for the Word of God?" is "Everywhere!" We must simply look around us. He is present in, and speaks through, everything He has created. He is as near as one's own self; understand the self and God is heard.

McLeod sums up the role of the Name of God: "The Name is the total expression of all that God is and this is Truth. *Sati Nām*—His name is Truth. Meditate on this and you shall be saved" (p. 196).

**Guru.** An understanding of the meaning of "guru" is essential to understanding Sikhism, for it is the religion of the followers of the *Guru*. God is the Original Guru, Nānak is the first Sikh guru, and the scriptures, which are the very heart of Sikhism, are commonly referred to as the Gurū Granth Sāhib.

What does "guru" mean? In reference to Nānak and the other nine gurus, it means an illuminator of the truth that brings salvation. The ten gurus were persons who by their own perfection could illumine the inner truth of God's word, exemplifying in their own lives His Truth. After the death of Gurū Gobind Singh, the Sikh community viewed their combined personalities as merged into the scripture and the Sikh community.

But what is the source of these gurus' illumination, of their understanding of God's Truth? The answer is clear: God Himself is the Original Guru, revealing His Truth through His creation.

A guru is a spiritual teacher. So important was the guru in the devotional tradition prior to Nānak that it was common to venerate the guru as well as God. Indeed, the guru's voice was taken to be the voice of God. Gurū Nānak was heir to this tradition, but, like the Sants before him, transferred the veneration of the human guru to God as the only True Guru. Human gurus are simply the instruments of God's Word.

The transition is fairly simple in conceptual terms. Originally, in the devotional and yogic traditions, the human guru was seen as the mediator between the seeker and the truth of ultimate reality. The guru in Sikhism is still the mediator, but now the True Guru is seen to be God himself. As Gurū Arjan states explicitly, "The True *Guru* is *Nirañjan* [God]. Do not believe that He is in the form of a man" (AG, 895; McLeod, 198).

But as McLeod points out, the Original Guru is not purely and simply

God but, rather, His Voice. The Guru is God's word, the means by which He imparts Truth to humans. He quotes from Gurū Nānak's answer to the question, "Who is your guru, he of whom you are a disciple?"

> The Word is the *Gurū* and the mind [which is focused on it] continually is the disciple. By dwelling on the Ineffable one, on Him the eternal *Gurū-Gopāl* [unincarnated Illuminator], I remain detached. It is only through the Word that I dwell in Him and so through the *Gurū* the fire of *haumai* [self-centeredness] is extinguished.
>
> (AG, 943; McLeod, 199)

For Gurū Nānak, the Guru is God, the Voice of God, and God's Truth. These are seen as ultimately identical, for God is Truth, Truth is illumination, and God's Word is the illumination of His own Being.

This brings us to the question of how God's truth is to be apprehended by human beings. This question appears explicitly right at the beginning of the Ādi Granth "How is Truth to be attained, how the veil of falsehood torn aside?" (AG, 1; McLeod, 200). The answer is also explicit: "Nānak, thus it is written: Submit to the *Hukam* [Divine Norm], walk in its way" (AG, 1; McLeod, 200).

**The Divine Norm.** Hukam, the Divine Norm, is God's will as expressed in the orderly functioning of existence. Reminiscent of the Vedic concept of Ṛta, Divine Norm of the universe, it suggests a sacred pattern and regularity within existence. The Divine Norm regulates the fundamental order of reality in its constant processes of folding and unfolding. It manifests and illuminates the divine existence through the creative process. In accord with the Divine Norm, says the scripture, we are born and die, and everything, ahead and behind, is pervaded by it (AG, 151).

The Divine Norm is a kind of harmony and rhythm of existence. The lack of harmony normally experienced in human life is the result of being outside this rhythm. Departing from the Divine Norm obscures the Truth and mutes God's voice, keeping us from hearing His Word. Only through participation in the harmony of the Divine Norm is God's voice heard and his Truth understood. And only by hearing God's word and understanding His Truth can union with God and ultimate freedom be attained. As Gurū Nānak says, "Beloved, he who comprehends the divine Order of the Lord attains Truth and receives honour" (AG, 636; Mcleod, 202).

**Grace.** The Divine Norm expresses God's Truth through His creation. But how do humans discover this harmony? And how, through this harmony, do they hear the voice of God? Not purely by human effort. As Gurū Nānak says, "Salvation is not fashioned through one's own efforts. Nānak, such a claim would bring destruction" (AG, 1289; author). In the last analysis, it is God's grace or favor that enables humans to hear His voice. This is His gift to humankind.

Gurū Nānak notes that, while the determining forces of our own actions dictate our birth and station in life, it is God's grace that opens the door to salvation. "*Karma* determines the nature of our birth (lit. the cloth), but it is through grace that the door of salvation is found" (AG, 2; McLeod, 205).

The crucial question here is why some people remain ignorant of God. Why do some hear, while others remain deaf to God's word? Only through divine favor or grace is the heart opened to the divine sound of God's voice, says Gurū Nānak. Only by the gift of grace can a person's heart be opened to God's presence. If the divine favor is refused the heart remains closed. If it is accepted the heart opens to the Guru's voice. Of course, opening the heart to the divine voice of God is not automatically tantamount to salvation. This is only the beginning. Now comes the discipline required to follow the path to union with God.

## The Path to Salvation

The path to salvation is succinctly stated by Gurū Nānak:

> By meditating on God in my heart I shall become like Him. (My heart) is filled with evil, but in it there also dwell redeeming qualities. Without the True *Gurū* these are not perceived and until they are perceived one does not meditate on the Word.
>
> (AG, 936; McLeod, 207)

As Gurū Nānak emphasizes, the individual's effort can succeed only with God's grace, for without God's grace the redeeming qualities of the heart are unperceived. But the individual must make the necessary effort to purify the heart and meditate on God. There is no question that Sikh discipline, though outwardly manifested in the prohibitions and the five K's, is essentially an interior discipline aimed at opening the heart to God. Gurū Nānak emphasized the importance of inner purification with strong language:

> If anyone goes to bathe at a *tīrath* [sacred place] with an evil heart and the body of a thief, one part (the exterior) is cleansed by bathing, but the other (the heart) becomes even filthier. Outwardly he is washed like a faqir's gourd, but inside he is poison and impurity. A *sādhū* [holy person] possesses goodness even if he does not bathe and a thief, even if he bathes, remains a thief.
>
> (AG, 789; McLeod, 211)

Because true religion is inwardness, a preparation of the heart for meeting God, Gurū Nānak rejected the customary Hindu and Muslim rituals and scriptures. Because all are God's creatures, he rejected caste and sex discrimination. In declaring the importance of inner purity he said,

> If one gains anything from visiting places of pilgrimage (*tīrath*), from austerities, acts of mercy, and charity, it is of negligible value. He who has heard, believed, and

nurtured love in his heart has cleansed himself by bathing at the *tīrath* [sacred place] which is within.

(AG, 4; McLeod, 213)

The heart is the sacred place, for it is there that God dwells, there that His voice is heard, and there that His love is experienced. It is the heart that must turn to God in loving devotion, that must find union with God in love. As Gurū Nānak says, "He who worships the True One with adoring love, who thirsts for the supreme love, who cries out beseechingly, he finds peace, for in his heart is love" (AG, 505; McLeod, 213).

Because of God's greatness, the human heart beholds Him with awe and reverence, with holy fear. Reverent fear springs from acknowledgment of God's greatness and is seen as a dimension of true love for God. It also encourages complete surrender to Him in loving devotion.

How is love of God cultivated and expressed? Ideally, every act, thought, and feeling is both a cultivation and an expression of love for God. But in practice, the techniques for achieving this total kind of loving devotion that are most emphasized are singing God's praises (*kīrtan*) and meditating lovingly on His name. Singing God's praises is a much appreciated Sikh way of opening the heart to God; congregational Sikh worship without singing is practically unthinkable. Singing God's praises attunes the heart to God even while expressing the joy felt in His presence.

Meditation on the Divine Name, including heartfelt repetition, is central to the Sikh discipline. Gurū Nānak says, "This world is entangled in earthly affections and so in the immense suffering of death and rebirth. Flee to the True *Gurū's* shelter. There repeat the Name of God in your heart and so obtain salvation" (AG, 505; McLeod, 214). By "loving God's name" is meant more than merely loving a name; it means loving God's being as it can be experienced within the deepest recesses of the human heart. God's name is ultimately indistinguishable from His being. But since His full being transcends merely human capacity to experience, His Name is usually understood to refer to God's immanence, His being as dwelling within His creation. McLeod describes the Divine Name as "the revelation of God's being, the sum total of all His attributes, the aggregate of all that may be affirmed concerning Him" (p. 215).

One loves God's name by repeating it, not mechanically, but as a sacred mantra, where the sound of God's name pervades the devotee's whole being, filling it with the reverberating energy of the divine sound, calling every fiber of one's existence to witness God's greatness. One also loves God's name by calling to memory (*simarana*) everything the Divine Name stands for. Calling the fullness of God's Name to mind is a way of creating space for God within the heart so that God might truly become a living part of the self. Gurū Nānak says, "Repeating [the Name] of the True God means engrafting [Him] in the *man* [soul]" (AG, 936; McLeod, 216).

Thus we see that "loving the Name" is a way of meditating on God. Nothing is more important, for only by opening the heart to God can His love be experienced, and only through His love can Union be achieved. And, it must be recalled, only through union with God can the separation underlying all human suffering be overcome.

Meditating on God enables us to become aware of His constant presence; an awareness that shows the shallowness of everything separated from God. Both one's own self-centered existence and the supposed independence of the world are revealed to be creations of ignorance. Whatever exists, exists as part of God; there is nothing independent of, or separate from, God.

Meditation is a loving response to God's presence enabling the individual to grow in love toward God, until one's own being is merged into the divine being and all separateness overcome. Concerning merger into the divine being and the overcoming of separateness, Gurū Nānak says, "If God shows favor one meditates on Him. The *ātmā* [self] is dissolved and is absorbed (in God). (The individual's) *ātmā* [self] becomes one with the *paramātmā* [Supreme self] and inner duality dies within" (AG, 22; McLeod, 224).

But it is not easy to meditate on the True Name; it is a difficult discipline requiring great effort. Gurū Nānak says, "If I repeat the Name I live; if I forget it I die. Repeating the Name of the True One is hard, but if one hungers for it and partakes of it all sadness goes" (AG, 9, 349; McLeod, 218).

## STAGES ON THE PATH

On the path leading to union with God five distinct stages are referred to by Gurū Nānak. Each stage represents a fuller experience and a higher level of existence. The first stage is that of piety. Here a person realizes the interconnectedness of existence and the moral and religious significance of everything that is done. A will to act so as to maintain God's law and help others manifests itself at this stage.

The second stage is that of knowledge. Here a person becomes aware of the vastness of the universe and the deeply mysterious nature of existence. One also becomes aware of the greatness of other persons who have found God in the depths of their hearts. This knowledge helps a person to overcome self-centeredness and realize a sense of identity with the whole of God's creation.

The third stage is that of effort, where inner perception and understanding are fashioned. Here the soul becomes attuned to God, capable of hearing the Divine Word spoken through all creation.

The fourth stage is that of fulfillment. Here a person is filled with spiritual power, carrying one beyond error and death. Those who reach this stage are said to be beautiful beyond all description, for God dwells in their hearts. This is clearly a stage of God-realization, bringing peace and equanimity.

The fifth and final stage is that of Truth. Here one enters into union with God's own true, formless being. Although it can be experienced, this stage is beyond description, because the formless is indescribable. The Ādi Granth says, "In the Realm of Truth dwells the One without form. Having created, He watches over His creation. He looks upon His people with grace, and they are in bliss" (AG, 8; author).

This is the final goal of every Sikh.

## Summary

Sikhism is a religion of profound inwardness. Rituals, ceremonies, pilgrimage, and worship are all regarded as ineffectual means of realizing God. Only through purification of the heart and meditation on the Name of the Formless, Eternal, God can union with Him be attained.

Gurū Nānak, the founder of Sikhism, rejected both Islam and Hinduism because of their emphasis on the external features of religion. He announced that God was neither Hindu nor Muslim and that he would follow only God's way. The heart of this way is meditation on the fullness of God within one's own heart. By God's grace the heart is open to His Word, which resounds through His entire creation. Through discipline the heart can be purified and made an instrument of God's love. When the instrument is perfected, love can create a union between self and God. In Sikhism this union of love is the ultimate goal; it is the realm of indescribable joy and freedom, beyond the shadow of death.

What keeps humans from this perfection is their separateness from God. Gurū Nānak saw self-centeredness as the chief defect of human existence, the cause of all suffering. The self-centered person attempts to live separately from God and other persons. Filled with self-love and self-will, such a person does not hear the word of God. Desperately clinging to the self, the self-centered person is dominated by lust, greed, anger, attachment, and pride, constantly anxious and afraid. Only when love overcomes self-centeredness is the individual returned to his or her original wholeness, a wholeness that brings peace, joy, and freedom. Fillled with God, a person is one with the world, but filled only with self, one is constantly at odds with the world, continuously fighting a losing battle to find wholeness outside of God.

At the beginning of this chapter we noted that, although Gurū Nānak was highly original, advocating a way that transcended both Hinduism and Islam—rather than trying to synthesize them—he was greatly influenced by the earlier Sant tradition to which Nāmdev and Kabīr belonged. Through the Sants he was influenced by the Hindu devotional tradition of loving surrender, the practices of Tantric yoga, Sufi devotionalism, and the strict monotheism of orthodox Islam, in a way inheriting the best of numerous Indian traditions.

# Suggestions for Further Reading

*The Sikhs: Their Religious Beliefs and Practices*, by W. Owen Cole and Piara Singh Sambhi (Boston: Routledge and Kegan Paul, 1978), is probably the best place to begin. In only two hundred pages the authors present a tremendous amount of information in a clear and interesting style. The scholarship is sound, but unobtrusive. It is good on Sikh practice as well as on Sikh thought.

*Gurū Nānak and the Sikh Religion*, by W. H. McLeod (New York: Oxford University Press, 1968; Indian paperback edition, 1978), is the authoritative work on the traditional biographies of Gurū Nānak. I have relied heavily on Chapter 5, "The Teachings of Gurū Nānak," (pp. 148–227). This is must reading for anyone seriously interested in Gurū Nānak; indeed it is by far the best work on Gurū Nānak I know.

*Kabīr*, by Charlotte Vaudeville (New York: Oxford University Press, 1974), is outstanding on Kabīr and the entire Sant tradition.

Serious students will also want to consult Kushwant Singh's two-volume *History of the Sikhs* (New York: Oxford University Press, 1966).

# 16

# Renaissance in India

In the nineteenth and twentieth centuries the Indian way faced a challenge even greater than that of Islam. The establishment of British rule brought Western ideas of rationality, liberty, progress, individualism, nationalism, humanitarian ethics, and social reform. Would these ideas and values become the basis for a new Westernized India? Or would they be rejected by a majority of Indians, resulting in still another civilization on the subcontinent, alongside the Islamic and Indian in a curious three-way cultural apartheid? A third possibility was a creative synthesis, incorporating both traditional and Western ideas and values. The issue would be decided by the Indian response to Western presence and influence.

What would that response be? Would the Indians be as indifferent to Western civilization as they were to Islamic? Would they vigorously reject the West? Would they abandon their own traditions and adopt the ways of the West? Or would they critically examine both the Indian tradition and the new Western ideas, adopting what appeared to be the best of both worlds as a basis for a new India?

We know from the historical record that Indians responded in all these ways, some ignoring the West, others enthusiastically accepting the West as a replacement for the old India, and yet others rejecting everything Western. But the most influential response, by far, was that of criticism and reform, as the great leaders of India—Ram Mohan Roy, the Tagores, Dayananda, Tilak, Sen, Bose, Aurobindo, Gandhi, Nehru, and Radhakrishnan, to name a few of the outstanding ones—struggled to meet the challenge, not just of another great civilization thrust upon them, but of modernity itself. There was no single response, of course, for India has never spoken with one voice. But almost all these persons accepted the validity of at least some of the new ideas and values that came with British rule, and all recognized the need for major reforms in Indian society. Furthermore, they saw the Indian tradition as a rich source of ideas and values, capable of providing a basis for necessary reforms and modernization.

How each person responded to either the West or the Indian tradition, and how they envisioned the new India, varied tremendously, of course. Our main questions are, What was India's response to Western ideas and values? and How did this response shape the modern Indian way? Since the challenge of the West forced most Indian thinkers to confront and rediscover their own ancient ideas and values, we have titled this chapter "Renaissance in India." There was a rebirth of the ideas and visions that we have been examining in this book but that for a thousand years or more had been slowly receding into the background. First, however, we must answer the preliminary question, How did the Western presence that served as catalyst for this renaissance come to be established in India?

## The Western Presence

The attraction of India to the European powers was trade. At first it was primarily spices that India offered, but soon calico, silks, indigo, and saltpeter became important items of trade. Later, as industrial manufacture became important to England's economy, cotton and hemp from India kept the mills in Manchester and Birmingham humming. The Portuguese came first, establishing their empire at Goa in the early sixteenth century. The Dutch followed, and in the early 1600s it appeared that they were going to establish an East Indian trade monopoly. But events in Europe precluded that development and enabled the British and the French to gain a foothold in India. When the French established themselves at Pondicherry in 1674, it began to appear that India might become a colony of France. Indeed, had not the European Peace Treaty of 1749 restored Madras to the British, and had not Louis XV and Madame Pompadour refused to support him, it is likely that Dupleix, the French master politician, might have become the next emperor of India.

But that was not to be. The British learned much from Dupleix, and when, by 1757, Clive's leadership had secured British victory over the French and had defeated the Indian armies of Siraj-ud-Daula at the battle of Plassey, the position of the British in India was secure. Between then and the successful nationalist movement that procured India's independence in 1947, the only major challenge was the revolt and war of 1857, a futile attempt that tried, too late in the day and with insufficient cooperation, strength, and organization, to halt the sweep of British colonization. The British were so convinced of their right to rule and the strength of their rule that they referred to this unsuccessful revolution as simply a "mutiny." So it is no exaggeration to speak of two hundred years of British rule in India, even though the Crown did not officially assume rule until 1857.

Although the Western powers gained a foothold in India in the sixteenth and seventeenth centuries, their influence was rather insignificant until the eighteenth, and only in the nineteenth was British rule firmly established and a significant Indian response generated. The seventeenth century was truly a hundred years of Mughal glory. The imperial power and luxurious life of the century's great emperors, Jahangir, Shah Jahan, and Aurangzeb, were talked of throughout the world. The Agra Fort with its magnificent palaces and the beautiful Taj Mahal across the river stand as testaments to this century of Mughal glory—as does the now museumlike Red Fort in Delhi. It was only in the eighteenth century that a combination of civil wars, Afghan and Persian invasions in the northwest, imperial corruption and incompetence, and factional strife combined to undermine Mughal rule and make the subcontinent easy prey for the enterprising foreigners from Europe.

The British, like the other European colonial powers, had come to India for the sake of trade. But wars in Europe, America, and India convinced them that trade could be secured only through political control. Robert Clive may have been primarily an adventurer seeking fortune and glory, but Hastings sought political power. During his appointment as governor from 1772 to 1785, this scholarly man, who learned Urdu on the job and gave great impetus to the study of India, devised an effective administrative system that turned a profit for the East India Company and greatly extended its power on the subcontinent. But it was his successor, Cornwallis, governor and commander-in-chief of Bengal's army from 1785 to 1793, who, more than any other person, designed the rule that was to govern India for the next 150 years.

Completely convinced that the British were the most enlightened of all peoples and pre-eminently qualified to rule the world in the best interests of both rulers and the ruled, he designed the Cornwallis code as a basis for administration. This set of forty-eight wide-ranging regulations formed the basis for British rule throughout India, determining procedures and criteria for military and civil services, revenue collection, and the courts. These regulations were to endure practically unchanged until the end of British rule and, indeed, were, in large part, incorporated into the national Indian government after independence.

Included were provisions for reorganizing the military and civil services and for land ownership by the Zamindari tax collectors. Convinced of British superiority, Cornwallis reorganized the officer core of the Bengal army along traditional European lines, with the provision that all the high-ranking officers would be non-Indian. This went along with the reorganization of the civil service of the company restricting Indian officials to ranks receiving less than five hundred pounds a year, thereby assuring that all important positions would be filled by British officers.

The Zamindari Land Settlement Act of 1793 gave those responsible for tax collection ownership of the land from which they collected taxes. This was the first time that the land was really regarded as private property, for up to now it all belonged to the ruler and was temporarily "leased" to various persons in return for their services and favors to the ruler, with an implicit understanding that they held it in trust for the tillers and the whole community, a truly interdependent network. Cornwallis saw private ownership as the foundation of law and government and the engine of British supremacy and, therefore, surely good for India as well. In addition, private land ownership would greatly aid in tax collection, for now the new owners would clearly owe the tax, and there would be no question about how much to collect from whom. The disastrous consequences of this change for society, culture, and agricultural production itself could hardly have been foreseen by Cornwallis and his advisors, but they are still visible in India today.

Although questions of economic policies and political administration are outside the scope of this book, it is important to realize that the British felt themselves sufficiently enlightened and superior to attempt major reforms of Indian society. Unlike either traditional Hindu or Muslim government, both of which stressed local autonomy and interfered socially only to the minimum extent necessary for collecting revenues to support the government and to maintain the military establishment, British rule saw the promotion of citizen well-being at all levels as a government duty. Not only did they feel justified in ruling the ignorant heathen locals, but they felt a moral and political obligation to administer to their needs. This idea of a welfare state underlay the wide variety of social reforms initiated in the nineteenth century, reforms ranging from the abolition of widow burning and infanticide to the provision of schools and hospitals.

It was primarily this social involvement that brought the Western ideas of individualism, progress, property, rational ethics, and nationalism into the mainstream of Indian intellectual and political life. It is also important to note that the modern idea of separation of politics and religion was incorporated in British rule, making it much easier for Hindus to accept many of the new Western ideas on which British administration and sociopolitical policies were based. If the social reforms of Indian society attempted by the British had been perceived as religiously motivated, they probably would have been stiffly resisted, and everything Western would have been condemned and rejected along with such unwarranted religious interference. Indeed, officers of the East India Company had a keen sense of the importance of separating business and administration from religion, as is clearly seen by their vigorous attempts to keep Christian missionaries out of India.

The separation of religion from state and politics enabled many Indians to examine Western ideas without prejudice while rejecting the claimed superiority of Christianity. It also enabled them to work for the reform of their own society—either through renewal based on traditional ideas or through social change inspired by Western ideas—without giving up their Hinduism or admitting the superiority of a foreign religion. The legacy of these two ideas—the separation of religion and politics and public welfare as the business of government—is found in the contemporary, secular, welfare state of India.

## The Indian Response

We turn now to the story of the renewal of the Indian tradition under the influence of British rule and Western ideas. It is, of course, quite impossible in a single short chapter to do justice to the visions and actions of India's leading thinkers and agents of change. But by examining the thought of four extremely important modern Indian thinkers, each of whom reacted in a different way and each of whom had a great impact on the development of Indian thought in the last two centuries, we can at least convey a sense of both the variety and the pattern of India's response to the challenge of the West and modernity. For this purpose we have chosen Ram Mohan Roy, founder and leader of the Brahmo Society, the single most influential Indian organization of the nineteenth century; Dayananda Sarasvati, the brilliant reformer who looked almost exclusively to the past for inspiration and who established the Arya Society to reform Indian society in accord with Vedic ideas and values; Gandhi, the man of action, who brought everyone's attention to the poor and suffering by arguing that the conditions of poverty and suffering could be removed only through the practice of love and truthfulness; and Aurobindo, a revolutionary turned yogi who developed an ideal of evolutionary spiritual progress and an integral yoga as a means of realizing this ideal.

## Ram Mohan Roy and the Brahmo Society

Ram Mohan Roy is often called "The Father of Modern India" because he set the tone, and pointed the direction, for India's response to the West. Through the Brahmo Society, which he founded in 1828, nineteenth-century India evaluated the ideas and values of Western civilization, comparing them with those of the Indian tradition, borrowing, adapting, and reforming as necessary to have the best of both worlds. By their open-minded response to the challenge of the West, Ram Mohan and his successors in the Brahmo Society began the reshaping of the Indian mind that has made it simultaneously both traditional and modern today.

Ram Mohan was born into an orthodox Hindu brāhmaṇa family in

1772 and was just twenty-one years old when the Cornwallis code establishing the basis for English rule of India was adopted by the East India Company. He served as a revenue officer for the company as a young man, but due to considerable affluence was able to retire at the age of forty and devote the rest of his life to study and reform. He was well educated, knowing Arabic, Persian, Sanskrit, and English as well as his native Bengali and Hindi. His readings and personal contacts made him familiar with much of Western thought, including the Deist movement, which was extremely critical of even theism, to say nothing of polytheism, and which saw most religious ritual as idolatry. From the Deists and Unitarians he probably received much of the inspiration for his criticism of idolatry and polytheism in Hinduism. From the ethical ideas of Christianity and the moral and political philosophies of Europe, he received inspiration for his protests against live widow cremation, child marriages, and the practice of untouchability.

However, as he began to read India's own ancient texts on morality, society, and reality (Dharma Śāstras and Upaniṣads), he discovered that the corrupt practices of Hindu society were contrary not only to the ideals of the West, but to the ideals of India as well. Thus, he often argued that Hinduism had been corrupted because people had forgotten their ancient scriptures. By returning to them one could discover that the corrupt customs and beliefs disfiguring modern Hindu society were without sanction in the sacred texts.

In 1828 he established the Brahmo Society to enable like-minded Indians to meet for discussion of the great ideas of the day and to work together creating a modern India that would combine the best ideas and traditions of both India and the West. To this end, Brahmos, as society members were called, were vitally interested in the reform of Indian society. But first it was necessary to rediscover the basis of the Indian way established long ago. The Upaniṣads had to be rediscovered and reinterpreted to show that the basis of Indian tradition was secure in these sacred texts of wisdom.

At the same time it was necessary to examine the ideals of the West, especially of Christianity. To this end Ram Mohan's secular analysis of the New Testament in his *The Precepts of Jesus* is paradigmatic, for it strips the text of its doctrinal features, singling out Jesus' humanitarian ethics as the essence of the text. Once the ethics had been separated from the religious contents, there was no obstacle to adopting these moral principles as a basis for social reform; they were compatible with and strengthened the ethics discovered in the Upaniṣads.

Ram Mohan personally abandoned belief in reincarnation, rejected the use of idols in religious worship, adopted appeal to reason as the ultimate criterion of truth, and emphasized both individualism and a rational humanitarian ethics. All this set him aside from the current Hindu community, and the fact that these beliefs and attitudes characterized the Brahmo Society virtually guaranteed that it would stand as a sect or society quite outside the mainstream of Hinduism. The

Brahmos in fact never were regarded as being part of the stream of Hinduism. Although it had a tremendous impact on modern Hinduism, their society was never to fulfill its dream of becoming the center of the new Hinduism. It had made too many concessions to the West too quickly to be accepted by most Hindus. In fact, many of the Hindus who joined the Brahmo Society were kicked out of their families and rejected by their communities.

The three pillars of the Brahmo Society—rationalism, humanism, and social reform—are clearly derived from Ram Mohan's own thought, which was heavily influenced by Western ideas, especially as encountered in Unitarianism. Although he and other reformers took great pains to show that these ideals were consistent with the best in Indian tradition, the truth is that their inspiration flowed from Western influence. In Ram Mohan's case the influence of the Unitarians was extremely powerful, constituting the moving force behind his own work and ideas. The Brahmo Society itself was an outgrowth of the Calcutta Unitarian Committee that Ram Mohan helped to found in 1823.

Although never meeting them personally, Roy had considerable correspondence with, and was greatly influenced by, Joseph Tuckerman and William Ellery Channing, two leading American liberal Unitarians. Lant Carpenter, perhaps the leading Unitarian figure in the world at that time, made so great an impression that Roy went to England to meet with him. In fact, Roy died at Carpenter's home in 1833 and was buried in England.

The Unitarians were so named because of their insistence on the unity of God. In the name of God's unity they denied the doctrine of the Trinity, for the rationalism to which they were so deeply committed could make no sense of one God who was also simultaneously three distinct Gods. It is worthwhile to pause here briefly and consider the fundamental ideas of Unitarianism, for they are reflected clearly in the Brahmo Society and in a great deal of modern Indian thought.

The underlying principle, derived from the European Enlightenment, is that human reason is fully capable of understanding the universe and regulating human affairs. This means that faith as a source of understanding and authority as a source of rules for action were greatly deemphasized in Enlightenment thought generally and in Unitarian thought in particular.

Derived from this fundamental principle are three basic ideas that not only guided Unitarian thought but also contributed to the making of the modern social conscience, energizing the liberal reform movement. The first idea is that religious belief (faith) was to be based on reason, rather than on feeling, dogma, or myth. The second idea, that of social reform, is that all underprivileged members of society were to be uplifted through programs of social reform, including universal education and civil rights. Instead of the traditional assumption that the fulfillment of human life can occur only after death and that this life is to be endured as a trial by suffering to test one's qualifications for heavenly existence, the new attitude postulated that this life is important in its own right; religion should aim at the fullest possible life on earth. The third idea, that of salvation through service, combines the ideas of progress and humanitarian ethics. The perfectability of humankind can best be achieved by service to humanity incorporating social reform, for this is the way that God has designed for our spiritual progress.

The Unitarian influence on Ram Mohan and the other Brahmos was a fortunate coincidence for India, because, although it grew out of developments within Western civilization, Unitarianism was critical of many traditional Western assumptions—for example, that faith was separate from reason or service and that faith alone saved; that ritual and doctrine were the essence of religion; that faith was essentially nonrational; and that human perfection and salvation were essentially unaffected by service to humanity. All these widely accepted modern Christian ideas were challenged by the Unitarians.

The fact that Unitarianism was itself a religious reform movement made it much easier for Indian leaders like Ram Mohan to accept these ideas, for instead of simply responding to Western criticism and condemnation, here was an opportunity to collaborate with the advocates of these new ideas in the work of reforming religion and society worldwide, not just in India. With respect to religious and social reform, England, America, and India were all in the same boat. This recognition gave Indian leaders like Ram Mohan a sense of partnership in the movement and generated a great deal of confidence to deal both with the new Western influence and with Hindu reform.

Although the Unitarians did not reject God, the effect of their ideas was to replace God with humanity and to glorify reason and rational, humanitarian ethics as the noblest qualities of humanity. This transfer of the divine qualities of God to humanity made the meeting of Christianity and Hinduism a much easier event. Both Hindus and Christians could find a basis in human qualities for transcending the differences between these two great religions.

For example, the doctrine of God's incarnation in the person of Jesus was dealt with by seeing him in wholly human terms; he was a prophet and moral teacher of great persuasion, inspired by God. But the teaching that Jesus actually was God was denounced by the Unitarians as a superstitious belief. This understanding of Jesus is the basis for Ram Mohan's analysis of the teachings of Jesus as simply humanistic morality. This analysis, contained in *The Precepts of Jesus*, not only constitutes an important Unitarian tract, but its wide acceptance in India paved the way for the acceptance of some of the loftiest moral ideas of the Western world and provided a model for a modern ethical interpretation of the teachings of Krishna in the Gītā. Other reformers, following Ram Mohan's lead, began to separate the moral teachings of all important Hindu literature from the mythological and ritual aspects in order to show the moral profundity of the Indian tradition. Gandhi, for example, came to see the Gītā as primarily a moral testament, calling for action in the service of society.

The same rational, humanitarian perspective that led to emphasis on the human qualities of Jesus and on the moral content of his message manifested itself in the social gospel of Unitarianism. The reformers who dominated the Unitarian movement—and whose influence extended far beyond Unitarianism—saw the presence of poor, suffering, and underprivileged masses as a condemnation of Christian practice. They argued that Christianity, as advocated in the example and teachings of Jesus, was a message of salvation through service to humanity, a message that uplifted the poor and the underprivileged. The Brahmos accepted this social gospel as the first principle of religious practice, agreeing that God's will is that the conditions of humans on earth be improved through human effort, that service to God means service to humanity, and that piety demands that the poor and the suffering be helped.

We see here the beginnings of the social philosophy underlying the concept of the modern welfare state. From the recognition that service to humanity and social reform constitute both a moral and a religious duty and that they represent the noblest of human actions, it is a small step to the twin social principles of the Brahmo Society. These principles are that (1) every human being has a right to all the means of improvement that society can provide and (2) every society has an obligation to provide all the means to a full and human life possible. Food, clothing, shelter, health care, education, employment, civil liberties, and cultural opportunities for the citizenry are to be provided by the government to the full extent of its powers.

That Ram Mohan and his successors in the Brahmo Society were deeply influenced by the Unitarians should not be taken to mean that they succumbed to the persuasion of the Christian missionaries in India. Far from it, for most of the missionaries, concerned with "saving souls," believed in the Trinity, in the authority of the Church, and in faith and dogma rather than in reason. They tended to see the Unitarians as a threat to the faith, as atheists who had been led astray by a Godless philosophy. The Unitarians, of course, saw the missionary effort to save souls as misguided and unfortunate and attacked the reliance on dogma and superstition that supported the missionary efforts. Thus, it turned out that the Unitarian influence gave the Indian reformers the ideas and principles they needed not only to reform Hinduism but to attack the Christian missionaries as well.

For example, the insistence on the unity of God enabled the traditional Christian conception of God as Father, Son, and Holy Spirit to be seen as a form of polytheism. This, in turn, allowed Ram Mohan to see that, despite the basic teachings of monotheism in Christianity, Christians had in fact succumbed to polytheism, just as Hindus had forsaken the monotheism of the Upaniṣads.

Ram Mohan was not at all reluctant to use these ideas to counterattack the missionaries. Provoked by their abusive criticism and scornful attitude, he attacked their belief in Jesus as God. "I do not wonder," he said, "that our religious principles are compared with those of atheists by one whose ideas of the divine nature are so gross that he can consider God as having been born and circumcised, as having grown and been subject to parental authority, as eating and drinking, and even dying . . .".[1]

Clearly, Ram Mohan felt it necessary to repulse the missionary attack that regarded Hinduism as a heathen practice of idolatry and superstition. He pointed out that in practice Christianity was no better. But his real concern was to show that the original ideals of Hinduism are fully the equal of the ideas of Christianity and, therefore, that Hindus can look to their own traditions for inspiration and principles of reform. In the preface to his translation of the Īśa Upaniṣad (which was to become Gandhi's favorite Upaniṣad), he explains that the reason for undertaking this translation is that of ". . . producing on the minds of Hindoos in general, a conviction of the rationality of believing in and adoring the Supreme Being only; together with a complete perception and practice of that grand and comprehensive moral principle—*Do unto others as ye would be done by*."[2]

In the preface to his Bengali and Hindustani translations of an abridged version of the Vedānta Sūtras (of Bādarāyaṇa)—which he distributed free to as many people as he could—he says that the reason for this work is to vindicate his own faith, that of his early forefathers, and that of his Hindu friends, by showing the grand monotheism and the humanistic ethics of their own tradition. It was here, in the rediscovery of the Vedānta, that Ram Mohan and the Brahmos found both a vision of ultimate reality and the norms for conduct enabling them to remain loyal to their own traditions while at the same time undertaking the badly needed reforms of religion and society.

Indeed, when we look back at the accomplishments of the Brahmo Society—which includes the efforts of Ram Mohan's successors, especially the Tagores and Keshub Chunder Sen—the identification of the Vedānta as the scriptural source and foundation of Hinduism is among the most important. Of course, Brahmo encouragement of religious and social reforms, the development of a humanitarian ethics independent of sectarian prejudice, and the rational-symbolic interpretation of myths and ritual have also had far-reaching consequences. But their main contribution is less tangible. It is the Brahmo contributions to the creation of rational, critical, and humanitarian reforming attitudes that have enabled Indians over the last two centuries to meet the challenges of modernization without surrendering the best of their own traditions.

[1]*The Hindu Tradition*, ed. Ainslie T. Embree (New York: Random House, Inc., 1966), p. 286.

[2]*Ibid.*, p. 284.

## Dayananda Sarasvati

Unlike Ram Mohan Roy and the Brahmos, Dayananda Sarasvati (1824–1883) and the Aryas, members of the Arya Society that he founded, reacted to Western influence by consciously rejecting it and insisting on the superiority of the ancient Indian tradition. Dayananda was a truly remarkable man, brilliant, strong, and incredibly energetic. He is described by Jordens, author of the best book-length study of this great reformer, as "an individualist consumed by a passion for action, principled yet pragmatic; a man with great inner depth yet totally involved in the present and always working for a better future; a mind receptive to the rapidly changing world around him but never passively submitting to its pressures; a man consumed by the dream of a better life for all, a happiness not only religious, but also social and economic."[3]

Although Dayananda consciously rejected both modern Western traditions and modern Hinduism as models for the reformation of Indian society, he was influenced by both. His own missionary activity, on behalf of reformed Hinduism, and the missionlike organization of the Arya Society formed to carry out the reformations he envisioned, suggest Christian missionary influence. His early childhood experiences in a strongly theistic Shivaite family contributed much to the strict monotheistic attitude of his later life.

Dayananda grew up in Gujarat, in western India, where British cultural influence was practically nil. His disgust with modern Hinduism and his perception of the need for reform originated in his own spiritual longing and his recognition of the need to consider the fulfillment of a person's whole being, not just the so-called spiritual being.

A turning point came when he was fourteen, some nine years after he had been initiated by his father into Sanskrit studies and the worship of Shiva. As a part of the Shiva worship on a special day, Dayananda went with his father to a local temple to observe a night of fast and vigil before the symbol of Shiva. During the "Night of Shiva" temple ceremony all the devotees but Dayananda fell asleep. As he kept his vigil he saw mice running over the clay emblem of Shiva, eating the God's offering, and polluting the idol. Surely, he reflected to himself, the Great God Shiva cannot be identical with this polluted idol in front of me. He awakened his father to express this doubt and concern. And though his father explained that Shiva was indeed fully present in the image but, because of the darkness of the present Kālī age, could not be perceived by humans, the boy was not persuaded.

To conceal his growing doubts he tried to avoid religious activities by

[3]*Dayānanda Sarasvatī: His Life and Ideas*, by J. T. F. Jordens (Delhi: Oxford University Press, 1978), p. 295.

burying himself in his studies. But a few years later when his fourteen-year-old sister was killed by cholera, a deeply felt tragedy that was followed shortly by the death of a favorite and much beloved uncle, the young man was deeply impressed by the cruelness and shortness of life. He now began to think and talk about taking up a saṅnayāsin's life of asceticism and yogic practice.

To prevent this, the parents hastened to arrange his marriage, already overdue by contemporary standards. Persuaded by Dayananda to give him an opportunity to continue his education, however, they agreed to postpone the marriage. But when he turned twenty-one he knew he could not avoid the marriage if he stayed home, so one night he quietly slipped away and began his quest for mokṣa. His father caught up with him after a few months, abused him in public, stripped him of his orange robe, and resolved to take the captive home to bride and family. But Dayananda's resolve was fully the equal of his father's, and during the night he escaped, never again to return to his parent's home.

For fifteen years he practiced yoga and searched for mokṣa, seeking out all the holy places and holy persons he could. His experiences convinced him that the religious leaders of his day were either ignorant or corrupt or, in most cases, both. Finally, after fifteen years of desperate effort and great hardships, he decided that he needed to study the Vedic texts that he had encountered in his youth. For this, however, he would need a much better base in Sanskrit than he had received as a child. This led him to seek out and become a pupil of Virjananda, the widely recognized master of Sanskrit grammar.

Almost three years with Virjananda, this brilliant blind guru in Mathura, not only provided Dayananda with an opportunity to learn grammar by studying Pāṇini and Patañjali, but, more important, brought him to see that not just his personal life and salvation, but all of Hinduism, were at stake. The beginnings of Dayananda the social reformer, the activist, are found here. His teacher's insistence that the corruption of Hinduism was due to the neglect of the great teachings of the ancient seers and the rise of inferior sectarian scriptures provided great inspiration for Dayananda's study of the Vedas, encouraging him to use them as the basis for his evolving program of reform.

It is significant that, in place of the traditional gift of appreciation given by a student to his guru upon completion of studies, Virjananda asked for a promise that his pupil devote his life to propagating the teaching of the ancient seers. Dayananda agreed, thus beginning the study of the Vedas that produced his famous commentaries and that provided the basis for his social reform and his work in education.

As we turn to the ideas that provided directon for Dayananda's life and work, we are faced with the problem of choosing from a continuously evolving set of ideas. Emphasis will be placed on the later ideas, especially as found in the second *Satyarth Prakash*, on the assumption that these express his fullest and most mature thought. But it must be noted that almost parallel to personal changes that transformed a child worshipper of Shiva into a young ascetic yogin seeking the ultimate liberation and that transformed the yogin into an active reformer, came a change in ideas. His early adult life was dominated by the ideas of yoga and asceticism as the ultimate transforming and liberating powers. But as he began to read the classical texts he came to be greatly influenced by Vedānta, and a brief middle portion of his life was dominated by the Vedāntic ideal of Brahman-Ātman unity. As he matured, however, his growing sense of individualism and his theistic interpretation of Brahman combined to persuade him of the eternal distinctness of God and the individual. At the same time both his sense of the urgency of reform and the need to seek the total well-being of the individual in society led him to abandon his early idea of the individual as essentially a knower in favor of the idea that to be human is essentially to be active, to be a doer.

The ideas that the ultimate reality is a personal God, that the Veda contains God's revelation, that agency is the essence of human being, and that salvation is possible only through action became the guiding forces for Dayananda's mature life, as well as for the Arya Society that he created to aid in his efforts to regenerate Hinduism and reform Indian society. Before discussing each of these ideas, however, it must be pointed out that it was the ideal of a new golden age that energized the reform efforts of Dayananda and the Arya Society.

Convinced that neither the West nor modern India held the key to the creation of a new golden age of Hinduism, Dayananda turned to the golden age of the Vedas for ideas and inspiration. Unlike the Brahmos, who turned to the Upaniṣads and the Vedanta for inspiration, Dayananda found the grand vision of Hinduism in the Vedic hymns, especially the hymns of the Ṛg Veda. Here was a vision of a full and complete life on earth, a vision that praised intelligence, courage, and human effort; that elevated the family and social community to a position of primary importance and respect; that saw noble, courageous, and intelligent action on behalf of the well-being of the community as the key to salvation; and that, according to Dayananda at least, recognized service to the one true God as the highest religious effort. These ideas and values had created the golden age lived by the Āryans in Āryavārta thousands of years ago and now could become the basis for a new golden age of Hinduism in the future.

In the Vedas, Dayananda found none of the emphasis on suffering and rebirth that he saw as the key to the gradual degeneration of Hinduism over the millenia. There he found an affirmation of the full reality—and, indeed, the sacredness—of this ordinary life and this ordinary world. The later idea that the empirical world and embodied existence were only relatively real and of secondary value, an idea that supported the emphasis on liberation from this suffering existence, was entirely absent from the Vedic vision of life.

This Vedic ideal of energetic and organized effort on behalf of the community inspired the organization of the Arya Society, directing its political involvement in social reform and the nationalist movement. But the ancient idea that truth has the power to manifest itself in the transformation of the world also guided Dayananda's thought and work. Because the ideal of the golden age of Āryavārta is true, it will generate the necessary power to actualize itself if the people will but come to see its truth.

For this reason Dayananda placed great emphasis on education. As the Arya Society moved into the villages and towns, a network of schools and colleges was created to further the realization of the truth that would eventually reform society. This combination of the idea of the innate power of truth and the idea of the need to work actively for the welfare of the community enabled Dayananda to work extremely hard for social reform, yet not push so aggressively and impatiently that the people would become confused by or even antagonistic toward either the vision or the practical efforts to realize it. As a result Hindus did not react to the Arya Society with the hostility that characterized their initial reaction to the Brahmos.

Dayananda's view of the Vedas was different from that of the Brahmos in two important respects. First, as already noted, by Vedas he meant the ancient hymns of the Vedas, the Ṛg Veda in particular, not the Upaniṣads, which were composed somewhere between five hundred and a thousand years later than the earliest hymns and which reflect the intermixing of the Āryan and indigenous ideas and values. Second, the Brahmos tended to reject all claims to an exclusive revelation and were quite eclectic in choosing scriptures to support their positions. But Dayananda argued that the Vedas were revealed directly by God and that they constituted a revelation both earlier than, and superior to, the Bible. Indeed, he insisted that all other scriptures were written by humans and represented only human ideas and observations. The Vedas alone came directly from God and therefore are the only scriptures that are eternal and timeless, true in every respect. Furthermore, he claimed, the Vedas are entirely rational. This is guaranteed by their source in God, the very embodiment of rationality.

To support these rather remarkable claims about the Vedas, Dayananda undertook a thorough, painstaking exegesis and analysis. In his effort to "show up" the Bible and Qu'rān, he determined to demonstrate that (1) the truths of the Veda are in no way inconsistent with the truths of reason and science; (2) all truths discoverable by reason are somehow already contained in the Vedas; and (3) all the apparent historical and mythic references are really oblique injunctions to action or subtle spiritual truths. Although not even all of his followers were able to accept these fundamentalist teachings, even his critics benefited from his rediscovery of the ancient ideals and values of this great fount of Hinduism.

Dayananda's view of Āryan religion as scriptural, and of the Vedas as direct and full revelation to human beings of God's wisdom for living, depends, of course, on his view of God. His conception of a personal

God was undoubtedly derived initially from his childhood initiation into Shaivite practice, which stresses the non-anthropomorphic nature of the Supreme Deity. His initial distaste for the common Hindu anthropomorphic emphasis probably also stems from a Shaivite background, which undoubtedly exposed him to the typical sectarian bias against Vaishnavism because of its anthropocentric conception of God.

He may also have been influenced by the monotheism of Debendranath Tagore as set forth in the *Brahmo Dharma,* a tract that made a considerable impression on Dayananda when he went to Calcutta to meet with the Brahmos. Debendranath himself was influenced by Christianity, especially the Unitarian approach, so it is possible that Dayananda's conception of the personal unity and the distinctness of ultimate reality as God owes more to Christianity than he himself was aware. In any event, after his trip to Calcutta, Dayananda gave up his earlier Vedantic view of the identity of Ātman-Brahman as the ultimate reality in exchange for a view that emphasized the eternal distinction between God and humans.

The main difficulty he faced in conceiving of God as a person was that of showing how any person, even the Supreme Person, could be free from every taint of evil and from all the limitations experienced by ordinary persons. His faith was able to overcome this difficulty, but his reason struggled with it throughout his life. He was also convinced that the essential nature of this Supreme Person is to create, preserve, and save the world. But he was not able to rationally solve the philosophical problem of how God can be completely unlimited if He needs the world to express His essential nature.

Perhaps the major shortcoming of his rational theology was his failure to provide a theoretical basis for the love and devotion to a personal deity he cherished so dearly in his own life. Here both his abhorrence of myths and symbols, which he unfortunately always associated with idolatry and superstition, and his commitment to a narrow scientific rationality, prevented him from developing his understanding of the Supreme Reality through an aesthetic epistemology of symbolic manifestation and expression—as, for example, Rabindranath Tagore managed to do.

The other side of Dayananda's view of God, his view of the relationship between God and humans, faces its own difficulties. In the first *Satyarth Prakash* he claims that the human essence, the jīva, was created in time out of God's potentiality and that the end of time is reabsorbed back into the Godhead. But this does not provide for the strong kind of distinction between God and humans that Dayananda desired, and it compromises God's omnipotence by subjecting at least one aspect of His being to the limitations of human existence. Therefore, in the second *Satyarth Prakash* he turns to the theistic Sāṁkhya position, affirming that God, jīva, and cosmos are three co-eternal but distinct realities. The danger here is that, by making God and jīva co-eternal, the radical distinction between God and humans is threatened, inasmuch as the liberated jīva that has achieved mokṣa is hardly distinguishable from God.

Dayananda's proposed solution to this problem carries a high price. He claims that mokṣa, as permanent liberation, is impossible to achieve because the jīva is eternally linked with the cosmos, which is eternally distinct from god. But this means that perfect knowledge and the complete elimination of karma are impossible. At best mokṣa is a temporary freedom or respite from cosmic entanglement, an implicit repudiation of one of Hinduism's oldest and most cherished ideals.

To understand why Dayananda was willing to accept this radically revised view of the jīva and of mokṣa, we must look at the conception of humanity required by his view of human service and social reform, since his insistence on the eternal distinctness of God and humans is only half the story. The Vedic view of human existence, as noted earlier, regards the essence of human being to be agency. Ultimately we are doers, not knowers; knowledge is for the sake of action, which is fundamental to our being. Only through action is human fulfillment possible. Dayananda accepted this view; during a debate on the relative merits of action and renunciation, he once said, "A life full of action, that is real life. To perform the good works ordered by the Veda, that is the real way of renunciation. Those people are entitled to be called alive, who spend their life in works for the good of mankind."[4]

Dayananda's ideal is the person dedicated to action in the service of humanity, a service guided by moral principles derived from an understanding of the requisites of a full life for everyone. Salvation, mokṣa, does not come through yoga, asceticism or knowledge. It comes only through works performed to uplift humanity and reform society. If this view implies that mokṣa itself can only be temporary, so be it. Dayananda refused to compromise his view that to be human is essentially to be a doer, and that no salvation is possible except through actions undertaken to help humanity.

## Gandhi

Mohandas K. Gandhi (1890–1948) was of an entirely different temperament and background than Dayananda. He was educated in London, worked as a lawyer in South Africa, and became the most important leader of the Congress party during the 1920s. Primarily a man of action, he was open to ideas, whatever their source, that ennoble the human spirit and contribute to human dignity and social reform. The Sermon on the Mount, the Īśa Upaniṣad, the writings of Tolstoy, Ruskin, and the Bhagavad Gītā contributed significantly to his vision of reality and humanity.

[4]Quoted by Jordens, *op. cit.*, p. 64.

His life-long religious attitudes were shaped by the practices of devotion and self-surrender to Vishnu that constitute the essential Vaishnavite means to self-fulfillment. He was only a small child when his devout mother initiated him into these religious practices, inspiring him with her love of God.

Working as a lawyer to secure rights and opportunities for the Indians in South Africa gave Gandhi an opportunity to fully appreciate the evils of discrimination. Here he began his experiments with non-violent resistance that shaped his whole approach to social reform.

No one contributed more to the creation of a modern and independent India, and no reformer was more loved by the people than Gandhi. Others may have been more brilliant, better scholars or more consistent thinkers, but none were more sincere or better at identifying with the masses. Voluntarily taking on their burdens of poverty, he enabled the ordinary people to identify with the nationalist movement and with vital social reform movements. His emphasis on personal purity and simplicity, and his insistence on a strict morality grounded in love for others, found a ready response in the hearts of tens of millions of India's poor and illiterate people. At the same time he reminded India's other leaders to look for the real passions and feelings of India in her villages, her true temples. Despite their squalor and backwardness, the villages held India's real hope. Here were her true strengths as well as her unfortunate present circumstances.

It is important to note how Gandhi changed the image of India. Previously most affected Indians had tended to react to Western influence either by regarding the West as superior and imitating everything Western or else by regarding India as superior and stressing the grandeur of ancient Indian thought and society. In either case the rich, the powerful, and the glorious—whether of India's past or of the present West—were held up for inspection and advocated as ideals. Gandhi changed this. The truth, he said, is that we are poor, hungry, and in need of help.

Through an integration of words, personal example, and action, he proclaimed on behalf of all India's poor a stirring declaration: We may be poor, but we have a great capacity for hard work, a spiritual strength, and a moral will that will enable us to feed, clothe, and educate ourselves, to rule ourselves, and to provide the necessary conditions for a rich and fulfilling life—all without giving up the moral and spiritual traditions that have nourished the Indian soul over the millenia and that will safeguard our innermost humanity as we enter the modern age with its strong economic, material emphasis.

Gandhi dedicated his life to the realization of this truth in the lives of all of India's people. Because he was primarily a man of action, his thought and writings flowed from his experience in trying to change the world and to perfect himself. This experience was constantly changing, leading to expressions of thought that were unsystematic and frequently conflicted with each other. He had neither the leisure nor the inclination to sit down and fashion an elegantly consistent theory of humanity and society; the world called for action, and he responded with all his strength and passion. But the key ideas underlying his commitment to action and his dedication to helping others clearly shine through his personal life, his actions, and his writings.

His most fundamental ideas, that no power is greater than truth and that love is the highest dharma (requirement) of action, he learned as a child at his mother's side. His first impressive lesson in the power of truthfulness and love came when he was a teenager. So that he could join older boys in smoking cigarettes and eating meat, he stole a few coppers and a bit of gold. Soon after, feeling guilty and remorseful for disobeying his parents by engaging in these forbidden practices, he confessed the horrible deed to his father. Though quite prepared to accept the severest punishment his father might mete out, the young Gandhi was quite surprised and deeply moved by what happened. His father neither rebuked nor punished him, but with silent tears forgave him. Here, Gandhi later recalled, was his first real lesson in the power of truthfulness to arouse love and of love to reform the heart, for he never again was tempted to smoke or eat meat.

His applications of these two ideas of truth-power and love-force in the interests of freedom, justice, and social reform made him famous worldwide. Most people are familiar with his techniques for nonviolent resistance to British rule. His civil disobedience campaigns, passive resistance, and hunger strikes showed India and the world a powerful new humane weapon against evil. But the basis of these techniques, truthfastness (*satyāgraha*) and love (*ahiṁsā*), are frequently not well understood, even though all Gandhi's ideas and actions spring from these two principles. His emphasis on the individual and progress are rooted in these principles, which furnished the inspiration and energy for his actions.

Like Dayananda, Gandhi was inpsired by the ancient idea of the innate power of truth, the idea that finds inscription today on the Indian seal in the motto *Satyam Jayate* (Truth Conquers). The best description he could find for his life was "The Story of My Experiments with Truth," the title of his autobiography. In his early life he used to say, as a way of pointing to the greatness of truth, that God is Truth. But later his experiences convinced him that even this was inadequate, so he went further and said that Truth is God! By this he meant that it is Truth that should be sought and Truth that should be served. Only through the realization of the Truth that resides at the center of all existence can human life be fulfilled and salvation found; to realize Truth is to also realize God and fulfill the inner law of one's own being.

In the Īśa Upaniṣad, Gandhi found inspiration for his vision of the identity of God, Truth, and Being. Commenting on its first mantra, which declares, "All this, whatever moves and changes in this changing world is enveloped by the Lord," Gandhi observed, "All that there is in this universe, great or small, including the tiniest atom, is pervaded by

God, known as Creator or Lord. 'Isha' means the Ruler, and He who is the Creator naturally, by every right becomes the Ruler too."[5] The rule of this Divine Ruler is the Truth of all creation, the divine law of the universe, according to Gandhi. In this law all things move and have their being, and only when they are in accord with the Truth of this law are they fulfilled. Every individual, every group, and every society must find this truth, and live in accord with its rule, to find their fullness and perfection.

This understanding underlies Gandhi's claim that the first principle of action is to hold fast to the truth or "truthfastness." *Satyāgraha* is a compound expression consisting of *satya*, meaning "truth," and *agraha*, meaning "holding to." One should hold to the truth expressed in the divine law, according to which all things exist and move. Truthfastness means both being in accord with one's own nature and purpose and acting in accord with the nature and purpose of all other beings.

Gandhi believed that the Truth from which all existence issues, uniting all beings into one family, even while giving each individual being its inner rule and purpose, is eternally present. But he also recognized the need for vigorous action to realize this Truth in practice. Ignorance and vice obscure this Truth, confusing the individual. Therefore vigorous action must be undertaken to achieve the purity and self-knowledge required to realize this inner Truth, making it the principle of all thought and action.

How is this purity and self-knowledge to be achieved? Gandhi's answer is clear. Since Truth is the God that dwells in all beings and since to love God is to love the beings in whom God dwells, it is through love that the self is purified and the inner Truth is revealed. The word Gandhi used for love was *ahiṁsā*, which literally means non-hurting or non-violence, as it is usually translated. But this sense of the term is really too narrow: Gandhi used it in the broadest sense to refer to a pure and perfect love, proceeding from the very depths of one's being and expressing itself in kindness, compassion, and tireless service to others.

Violence was abhorrent to Gandhi because he saw it as an expression of fear, growing out of inner weakness. Non-violence, on the other hand, is an expression of love, growing out of the central truth of one's inner being and the unity of all existence. Because love is kindness, compassion, and helpfulness, there is no room for hatred and violence in a world where truth is recognized and love is practiced. Therefore, to bring about this kind of world, Gandhi ruled out all forms of violence, for violence only calls forth violence, further weakening the individual and society. Love, on the other hand, calls forth love, both within oneself and from others, strengthening oneself and others.

He was completely convinced that truthfastness and love expressed in

[5]*Gandhi Sūtras*, ed. D. S. Sarma (New York: Devin Adair, 1949), p. 24.

nonviolent resistance to injustice and wrongdoing would convince the wrongdoer of the hurtfulness of his or her wrongdoing, bringing about a change in heart to replace evil with good. Gandhi recognized that reason can sometimes change the head and that through the head the heart can be changed. But he knew that love goes straight from heart to heart and is therefore a much more effective means of social reform and human fulfillment than are rational arguments or political violence. But before love can rule the world, it must rule the hearts of the people.

Gandhi's emphasis on the need to purify one's own heart as a first condition of service to others reflected his personal efforts at self-discipline and self-purification, and his public efforts at political liberation and social reform. At the center of all his efforts at reform was the conviction that freedom, justice, and human dignity could be achieved only through the active forces of truthfastness and love and that these required personal purification, sacrifice, and faith on the part of every individual.

## Aurobindo

Aurobindo Ghose (1872–1950) was a yogin and visionary who turned from his early education in Western thought to a study of Indian thought and his own meditational experience and insight to find a vision of divine life on earth. This vision revealed that its realization required yogic practice and social reform.

He was sent to England as a young boy for a Western education that would minimize his "Indianness" and qualify him for service in the British government of India. But when Aurobindo returned to India in 1893, after distinguishing himself as a student at Cambridge, he rebelled against all his father's attempts to separate him from Indian contacts and, after a brief teaching career, joined the nationalist movement to get rid of British rule. His sense of the importance of political freedom showed itself most clearly in his resistance to British rule, a resistance that led him to join a revolutionary movement in the first decade of the twentieth century. His visionary experiences while in prison as an accused terrorist led him to see that real human freedom—which required a personal realization of the in-dwelling divine power through a radical transformation of existence—went far beyond its merely political forms. But he continued to see political freedoms, justice, and the general reform of society as necessary to the achievement of the radical transformation of human existence he envisioned and to the full expression of human life once this transformation was achieved.

The traditional Indian idea of spiritual progress, the Western notion of economic and material progress, and the idea of an evolutionary force at work in all existence combined to convince him that human life could be transformed into the "life divine." This transformation of human existence could be brought about through a series of stages in which social reform and yoga would combine to create the conditions requisite for the infusion of a deeper and greater power of life into the present human form, energizing and guiding the evolution of human life into a higher, spiritual form.

The fundamental premise of Aurobindo's vision is that to be human is to be more than merely a biological organism or a consumer of goods; the human being is essentially a striving-to-be-God. Our *svadharma*—the law of our being—is that we seek the attainment of the divine. In Aurobindo's words, ". . . all active being is a seeking for God, a seeking for some highest self and deepest Reality secret within, behind and above ourselves and things, a seeking for the hidden Divinity". But this divinity is not something separate from us. It is the ground and fullness of our own existence: "The seeking for God is also, subjectively, the seeking for our highest, truest, fullest, largest self."[6]

Because of his emphasis on spiritual life, it has sometimes mistakenly been thought that Aurobindo ignored social issues, such as freedom and justice. The fact is, however, that his impressive works on metaphysics and psychology (*The Life Divine* and *Synthesis of Yoga*, respectively) not only are supplemented by writings on social issues, but can themselves be seen as the foundation for his social thought. Society itself must be re-formed in such a way that all persons can transform their existence into a profoundly spiritual mode.

Preparing humanity for spiritual evolution requires that the entire fabric of social organization be designed to fulfill this function. Aurobindo insists that, although the institutions of society must provide for the satisfaction of the biological and economic needs of humanity, they must do so in a way that is conducive to higher, spiritual needs. As a first condition, both coercion and oppression must give way to freedom and justice. Ultimately, the individuals comprising society must become free from restraining laws and institutions external to themselves, replacing such coercion with self-imposed regulation.

Such an inner subjective standard, uniting persons in their freedom and serving as a means to the realization of the spiritual potential within them, must be reached through a progressive growth and awakening of society itself. Aurobindo does not see society as constituted by independent individuals who happen to be grouped together but as itself a unified whole consisting of the group's shared life. Owing its existence to the individuals who share their lives, society nevertheless gives to each individual life a new and greater dimension. Indeed, the primary function of society should be to foster the fulfillment of each person.

This view of the nature and function of society is supported by a comprehensive view of reality according to which all existence is ultimately spiritual but in which the different spiritual grades of existence each functions according to its own inner law or norm (dharma). The

[6]Sri Aurobindo, *The Human Cycle* (New York: E. P. Dutton & Co., 1953), p. 161.

gradations of spirit reach from the extreme of the inconscient or material level to the triune perfection of absolute being, awareness, and joy (*sat-cit-ananda*). Within this continuum of spirit the ascending gradations of life, psyche, mind, overmind, and supermind are marked off. The task of human becoming is essentially the task of transforming the lower grades of existence by the light and power of the higher, achieving what Aurobindo idealizes as "The Life Divine," a mode of life embodying a fullness of being, consciousness, and joy.

The transformation of all existence into the highest forms of spiritual reality is to be attained by the practice of integral yoga—an all-encompassing, integrative discipline—and the achievement of appropriate social conditions. According to Aurobindo, this transformation has three aspects: (1) a psychic change in which one's present existence becomes an instrument of the higher spiritual existence; (2) a spiritual change in which the higher forms of spirit descend into, and integratively transform, the lower; and (3) the complete spiritual transformation of human existence.[7]

Underlying Aurobindo's vision of human life transformed into divine life is his view of the nature of reality and human beings, a view deeply rooted in India's ancient wisdom. The salient features of this view can be expressed succinctly in a series of brief propositions. (1) The powers and forces that constitute the divine are within us. (2) We are, for the most part, ignorant of the deeper powers and forces within us. (3) To transform our existence into a higher mode of life we must search within ourselves to become aware of these deeper powers and forces. (4) The solution to the problem of our presently defective existence lies in achieving mastery over our deeper spiritual forces. (5) The power that constitutes the divine reality within human existence must be made to pervade and transform all dimensions of life; the material and biological aspects of spirit are not to be denied, but, rather, are to be seen as expressions of higher dimensions of spiritual existence. (6) Existential realization of our spiritual powers will mean living in the best possible way, following the highest direction of life. (7) Such a life, lived in the fullness of the highest powers of reality, in the awareness of what we truly are in the inner core of our existence, is what constitutes the spiritual or divine life.

Aurobindo's vision of the life of the person who has achieved his or her full spiritual potential rests on two basic assumptions. First, within human beings there exist as yet unrealized powers and forces that are ultimately identical with the basic forces and powers of the universe and that, when realized, will free human existence completely from the restraints of all other forces and powers.

Second, these ultimate powers manifest themselves according to certain rules, the ontological rules that guide and direct all activities in the universe. Only when humans come to direct their activities according to

[7]See Sri Aurobindo *The Life Divine* (New York: India Library Society, 1965), p. 173.

these rules will they realize a basic identity with the ultimate powers, thereby achieving complete freedom.

Aurobindo's model for the inner rules of existence is the Vedic concept of ṛta, the divine norm of reality, a concept that integrates the ontological and normative dimensions of reality. He viewed morality or dharma as essentially a matter of response to the inner regulation of existence according to its own spiritual base rather than as a human rule of reason imposed on the community. Through yogic discipline we can awaken ourselves to the inner spiritual norm of our existence, allowing it to guide our actions as a means to our spiritual evolution.

Although his emphasis on yoga as a necessary means to realizing the divine life is also traditional, what marks Aurobindo as a modern visionary and reformer is his integration of individual yogic means with the transformation of social conditions. This integration will enable each person to participate in this spiritual evolution with every fiber of being and every power of expression.

Aurobindo, like Gandhi, often spoke out against what was seen as excessive dependence on science and technology as the basis of social reform and the solution to society's problems. Neither was opposed to science or technology, but *both* saw that, by themselves, science and technology cannot provide an adequate social basis for human fulfillment and self-realization. In a similar way, both Gandhi and Aurobindo saw that merely changing the institutions of society does not go far enough. A transformation of human existence itself is required. Aurobindo put it this way:

> We do not believe that by changing the machinery so as to make our society the ape of Europe we shall effect social renovation. Widow remarriage, substitution of class for *caste*, adult marriage, inter-marriage, inter-dining and the other nostrums of the social reformer are mechanical changes which, whatever their merits or demerits, cannot by themselves save the soul of the nation or stay the course of degradation and decline. It is the spirit alone that saves, and only by becoming great and free in heart can we become socially and politically free and great.[8]

To become "great and free in heart" requires a spiritual evolution into a new kind of human being:

> What then shall be our ideal? Unity for the human race by an inner oneness and not only by an external association of interests; the resurgence of man out of the merely animal and economic life or the merely intellectual and aesthetic into the glories of the spiritual existence; the pouring of the power of the spirit into the physical mould and mental instrument so that man may develop his manhood into the true supermanhood which shall exceed our present state as much as this exceeds the animal state from which science tells us that we have issued. These three are one; for man's unity and man's self-transcendence can come only by living in the spirit.[9]

[8]Sri Aurobindo, *The Ideal of the Karmayogin*, 11th ed. (Calcutta: Arya Publishing House, 1937), p. 8.

[9]Sri Aurobindo, *Ideals and Progress* (Calcutta: Arya Publishing House, 1946), p. 56.

This ideal, which is developed in the large tomes on yoga and the life divine, should provide the guiding aim of society. As Aurobindo says,

> The object of all society should be, therefore, and must become, as Man grows conscious of his real being, nature and destiny and not as now only a part of it, first to provide the conditions of life and growth by which individual Man—not isolated men or a class or a privileged race, but all individual men according to their capacity—and the race through the growth of its individuals may travel towards this divine perfection. It must be [possible] secondly, as mankind generally more and more grows near to some figure of the Divine in life and more and more men arrive at it—for the cycles are many and each cycle has its own figure of the Divine in man—to express in the general life of mankind, the light, the power, the beauty, the harmony, the joy of the Self that has been attained and that pours itself out in a freer and nobler humanity.[10]

The vision is grand, the ideal noble. But is the vision true, the ideal realizable? Only time will tell, of course, but in the meantime there is no doubt that Aurobindo has inspired many thinkers worldwide. It is interesting that, although his influence has been primarily intellectual, his legacy includes the utopian community at Pondicherry called Auroville. At Auroville people from all over India and the world are trying to create the kind of ideal human community Aurobindo envisioned.

## Summary

The lives and thought of these four leaders reveal quite different concerns and attitudes. Yet all four embody key features of the modern world-view that came to India from the West along with British rule. The emphases on the individual; on social reform and human progress; on a secular, humanistic morality as a basis for reform and progress; on reason as the criterion and arbiter of truth; and on political independence—all are embodied in the thought of every one of these reformers, even Dayananda, who consciously rejected the ideas and values of the West. But all these thinkers also turned to India's own traditions for the ideals and values that could serve as a basis for a genuinely Indian form of modernity, thereby establishing the pattern for the renewal of the Indian way in the modern world.

## Suggestions for Further Reading

*The Brāhmo Samāj and the Shaping of the Modern Indian Mind*, by David Kopf (Princeton, N.J.: Princeton University Press, 1979), is an unusually perceptive analysis of the intellectual forces at work in the shaping of

[10]Sri Aurobindo, *The Human Cycle* (Pondicherry: Sri Aurobindo Ashram, 1962), pp. 83–84.

the modern Bengali perception of the world and society. The ideas and persons of Ram Mohan Roy, Keshub Chunder Sen, the Tagores, and other leaders of the Brahmo Society are brilliantly illuminated in this extraordinarily fine study. Because Bengal set the pattern for India's modernization, the book has significance for our understanding of all modern Indian thought.

*Dayānanda Sarasvatī: His Life and Ideas*, by J. T. F. Jordens (Delhi: Oxford University Press, 1978), is clearly the best available study of this great reformer. The final chapter is an excellent summary of Dayananda's most important ideas.

*Gandhi's Autobiography: The Story of My Experiments with Truth*, by Mohandas K. Gandhi, trans. Mahadev Desai, is available in various editions. There is no better place to begin one's study of Gandhi; the autobiography makes clear the interaction of personal life, actions, and ideas that richly deserved the title "Great-Souled One" (Mahatma) that Gandhi was, and still is, known by.

*The Philosophy of Mahatma Gandhi*, by Dhirendra Mohan Datta (Madison: University of Wisconsin Press, 1953), is a lucid description of his life and main ideas, in just 150 pages. One of the best studies of Gandhi's thought is *The Moral and Political Thought of Mahatma Gandhi*, by Ragharan N. Iyer (New York: Oxford University Press, 1973).

*The Mind of Light*, by Sri Aurobindo, with Introduction by Robert A. McDermott (New York: E. P. Dutton & Co., 1971), may be the best introduction to Aurobindo's thought and it has the advantage of being brief—about one hundred pages. *The Human Cycle*, *The Synthesis of Yoga*, and *The Life Divine* are Aurobindo's most significant philosophical writings. They are available in various editions easily obtainable almost anywhere in the world.

# 17

# Prospects for the Future

What are the prospects for the Indian way as we look ahead to the close of this century and the beginning of the next? Will India retain its traditional ideas and values? Or will it appropriate those of the West? If traditional and Western ideas are combined, what will be the basis for their synthesis and integration? To answer these questions, it is necessary to recall the fundamental ideas that have provided inspiration and guidance for Indian life for thousands of years and also to understand how modern India has responded to Western influence. In addition, we must examine the context and direction of contemporary Indian thought to understand what is at stake in this choice of ideas as a basis for the future Indian way.

Understanding the main ideas at work in contemporary Indian thought and their power to influence social and political events is extremely difficult. And the future, of course, is impossible to predict. Still, where wiser persons might not venture, we will take a few tentative steps toward suggesting some of the currents of contemporary thought and some possible directions for the future. To do this it will be necessary to identify and analyze the central challenges India faces and to look at patterns of recent efforts to meet these challenges.

## The Challenge of Development

In today's India it is quite impossible to divorce questions about the nature of reality and the self, or about liberation or self-fulfillment, from questions about socioeconomic development. Satisfying basic human needs for food, shelter, clothing, and health care is seen as a necessary condition of self-realization, not as a separate activity. Opportunities for a better life must be provided not only for a select few, but for everyone, according to contemporary Indian understanding of the nature of societal obligations. Two of the ideas that we examined in the last chapter, nationalism and social reform, are now embedded at the core of Indian consciousness. The idea of the Indian nation-state as a central unity that must be preserved and protected from both foreign and internal threats is now a sociopolitical reality of great importance. And the idea of social reform has been incorporated into the reality of the nation-state. India conceives of itself as a welfare state, dedicated to developing the resources and institutional means necessary to ensure the fullest possible development of each individual. The total well-being of each person is regarded as the proper business of the nation. To this end, the government has devised development policies and programs that, on paper at least, aim at producing and distributing the resources and creating the social conditions needed for personal and social development.

From the perspective of personal and social welfare, India's central challenge is the elimination of poverty, for the first condition of well-being is that the people have adequate food, clothing, shelter, health care, and education. But in India this condition remains unsatisfied for over half of her population of 700 million people. How serious is this problem? Estimates vary, but there is general agreement that, even if they spent their entire income on food, more than 300 million people would be unable to purchase even 2,000 calories per day. This stark reality must affect the thought and action of every Indian.

## DEVELOPMENT PLANS

The problem is not new, of course, nor is the government's recognition of it. More than twenty years before India achieved independence in 1947, the Congress Party had declared poverty and unemployment to be the most urgent problems facing the country. For the last thirty years, there has been a steady stream of development plans aimed at eliminating poverty and improving the general conditions of the people.

The guiding directives for all the five-year plans call for development along socialist lines to secure rapid economic growth, expansion of employment, reduction in disparities in income and wealth, prevention of concentration of economic power, and creation of the values and attitudes of a free and equal society. The strategy for this development has emphasized (1) rapid industrialization through emphasis on basic industries, such as steel, machines, electricity, cement, and coal; (2) land reform, including land-holding ceilings; and (3) education as a means for securing equality of opportunity, redistributing wealth, and creating the values of a free and equal society.

Until recently there has been no direct attack on poverty because it was believed that economic growth brought about by industrialization would automatically "percolate" down, thereby eliminating poverty at all levels of society. That the poorest 50 per cent of the people have, if anything, gotten poorer during the thirty years of planned development shows clearly that this assumption was unwarranted. It also suggests that there has been something basically wrong with the government's development policies and programs.

Not that India's planned industrialization has been a failure. Indeed, achievements have been remarkably successful when measured in terms of the government's indicators. Despite war with Pakistan, border skirmishes with China, a large refugee problem, escalating energy costs, and a steadily increasing population, science and industry have progressed rapidly. Today India is one of the top ten industrial nations in the world, only the United States and the Soviet Union have more trained science and engineering professionals, and real GNP has doubled in the last thirty years.

Despite these gains, poverty has worsened, making the development crisis more severe than ever. In 1975 a combination of political events and frustrated expectations led to such widespread protests, strikes, and riots that Prime Minister Indira Gandhi declared a State of Emergency, suspending many provisions of the constitution to give herself extremely broad powers to deal with the development crisis. Her lack of success, even with the emergency powers, led to her defeat at the polls when, after two years, she lifted the emergency and called for new elections.

For the first time since independence, the Congress Party was out of power. But the political coalition represented by the victorious Janata Party quickly fell apart. The people perceived the Janata Party as incapable of delivering the expected fruits of development, and at the next election, Mrs. Gandhi and the Congress Party were returned to office, giving them another chance. But recent events suggest that the Congress Party has still not learned how to deal with India's poverty; the poverty crisis appears no closer to resolution than ever. The poor continue to get poorer while the rich struggle desperately to maintain and improve their positions.

Why have India's development plans not worked? Defenders of these plans are quick to point out that the culprit is population increase, leading to increased unemployment. They point out that, if the current growth rate of 2.5 per cent per year is continued, India's population will be a billion by 1996. Even if the growth rate is cut to 2.2 per cent, a quite optimistic prediction, the population will reach a billion by the year 2000. And demographers expect that the population will probably reach 1.5 billion by the middle of the twenty-first century.

Granted the large projected increase in population and the recently experienced low rates of increase in employment opportunities, it appears that the number of people unemployed or underemployed, presently between 50 million and 100 million, will also increase. New job opportunities are not expected to keep pace with the number of new entries into the job market, thereby generating increased numbers of unemployed persons.

All can agree that population increase constitutes a tremendous challenge. But the claim that it is the primary cause of poverty is another matter. Indeed, poverty is as much a *cause* of population increase as it is an effect. The direct correlation between poverty and reproduction has been shown over and over again, lending credence to the argument that the most effective way in which to curb population growth is to reduce poverty.

I do not wish to argue here for or against particular demographic or economic analyses—much less to suggest specific solutions. I want only to establish the fact that India's central problems of poverty and unemployment are fully as severe today as they were at the beginning of the carefully planned development efforts to solve these problems thirty years ago. Government planners themselves recognize that the previous plans have failed to improve the conditions of the poorer 50 per cent of the people. But they tend not to recognize that the failure stems from a choice of inappropriate ideas and values as a basis for development.

## Westernization

The search for a development model based on ideas and values consistent with the traditional Indian way was begun by Gandhi sixty years ago. But when Nehru took over the leadership of the Congress Party and India became independent, the emphasis shifted to Western-style modernization. Gandhi's ideas seemed old fashioned and backward. His suggestions that development focus on the individual, working upward from the village level; that self-help and self-reliance were the keys to human and social development; that production and power should be decentralized; and that small-scale industries and appropriate technologies—symbolized by the spinning wheel—were the effective ways of eliminating poverty were either ignored or ridiculed by India's elite leadership.

With the achievement of independence in 1947, India was free of foreign rule for the first time in a thousand years. There was great hope that the country's leadership would now incorporate the ideas and values of the people. For a thousand years, during which the people seemed to grow increasingly poorer, the values of the leadership had been significantly different from those of the people. While the traditional Indian way survived among a people ruled first by the Muslims and then by the British, it did so despite the quite different ideas of their rulers.

But the hope that a united and independent India would bring an end to the wide gap between the values of the people and those of the rulers has not been fulfilled. When leadership passed from the British to Indians, the new elite leadership, who had been able to work with, as well as against, the British, inherited not only the legacy of British government and administration, but also most of the Western ideas and values that had formed the basis of British rule. Although during the last years of this rule it was fashionable to detest everything British, it seemed that as soon as they were gone many Indians tried to become even more British than the British had been! In any event, India's new leaders espoused a set of ideas that was significantly different from those of village India, the home of most of the people.

Mr. Nehru, for example, who in the 1940s inherited from Gandhi the leadership of the Congress Party—India's ruling party ever since independence, with the exception of the very brief Janata Party interlude—was much more of an Englishman than Gandhi. When Nehru "discovered" India he did so through the eyes of a foreigner, an outsider, and his vision was extremely Western.

The fundamental reason for the government's failure to eliminate poverty and secure the real development of the people is this gap between the mind of the ruling leadership and that of village India. Their own Westernization prevented Indian leaders from taking into account either the actual conditions of Indian society or the values of the people for whom, presumably, the development was intended.

Development plans cannot work unless they are appropriate to the actual conditions of the society for which they are intended. Development implies meeting real needs by improving the already existing base as well as supplying from new sources what is lacking in the existing base. Providing solar heat for people in a tropical climate is not development. Neither is wasting a country's resources by drilling for nonexistent oil or by building huge nuclear plants when there is an abundance of gas, oil, and solar energy. Providing electric refrigerators for hungry people who can afford neither food to put in them nor electricity to run them is not development, but a cruel absurdity.

Furthermore, since development plans can be implemented successfully only with the support and cooperation of those for whom they are intended, there must be some reasonable match between the values of the people and the values implicit in the plan. The values implicit in the proposed development must be seen by the people as valuable in terms of presently held values, for these values constitute the criteria for choosing among alternative ways of acting or among alternative goods. Present values also provide the motivation for acting to improve present conditions.

What were the relevant conditions when India began its planned development? In 1947, as today, India was a mostly rural society with a large population and relatively little capital. There were relatively few industrial resources, with relatively little industrial experience. Small-scale village industry and agriculture were the principal means of economic production. Granted these social conditions, a reasonable plan to eliminate poverty would have emphasized plans for rural development calling for development of the existing economic base of small-scale industry and agriculture in a labor-intensive way, capitalizing on the large population resource. This would have created jobs where they were needed and increased production that could immediately help the poor.

As we have noted, however, the primary strategy was to develop large-scale urban industry, a strategy that makes no sense for a country with India's social conditions. With tens of millions of unemployed and underemployed persons, it was absurd to emphasize *labor-saving* technology. With relatively little investment capital available, *capital-intensive* technology makes no sense. Why, in a country that was 80 per cent rural was development concentrated in urban centers? Why was *heavy industry* emphasized for a country whose experience and strength were in small-scale production?

The reason is that labor-saving, capital-intensive, urban-centered, large-scale industrialization was seen as *modern* development. The real aim was not development of India's existing resources and her people but *modernization*, where modernization was confused with Westernization.

The overriding objective of India's planned development was really not to improve the opportunities of the people to realize their human potential and to live full, satisfying lives but, rather, to become a "modern nation." Unfortunately, modernity was confused with becoming an industrial, urban society in which science, technology, and conspicuous consumption would gain recognition and esteem from the so-called developed world. India's natural temples were her villages, but planned development sought to replace them with "temples of modern industry," to use Nehru's phrase.

This explains why India's greatest resources, her people and her villages, have been consistently regarded as her greatest liability by most development planners. The great majority of India's people live in villages and towns, and the majority of them are poor. For these two reasons they are either explicitly or implicitly regarded as a burden rather than as a valuable resource. Because they are poor, they cannot contribute capital required for industrial development, and because they live in rural areas, they are not part of the urban industrial development that from Nehru's time has been identified with Indian development. Overemphasis on the "temples of industry" has desecrated the villages and robbed the people of their right to a decent life.

Nearly 80 per cent of India's 700 million people live in villages and small towns. These tend to be relatively autonomous, nearly self-sufficient social units, linked together loosely into regional networks. Each village is a whole society in miniature, providing its inhabitants with practically all the goods and opportunities needed in life. Since they are small, typically less than five hundred people, the inhabitants know each other well and personal relationships provide the basis for most transactions.

Because villages produce no heavy industry and no goods for foreign trade, generate little investment capital, and place little value on "progress," they were seen as obstacles to development. Instead of modernizing village technologies and improving village social conditions as means of developing a higher quality of life, the government plans, in effect, rejected the values of village economy and life.

## Dharmic Model

The confusion of Westernization with development that led India's planners astray during the first few decades after independence has come to be seen as a serious mistake by a number of Indian leaders in recent years. J. P. Narayan, Moraji Desai, and Deendayal Upadhyaya have been among the more famous and powerful of these leaders, all espousing Gandhian ideas as a basis for an alternative development model. They have rejected the Western atomistic view of society that emphasizes conflict and competition as the basis for human progress.

As noted in the previous chapter, Gandhi envisioned a world in which truth reigned supreme, in which social processes and human actions were rooted in truthfulness and energized by love. Reality is seen to be essentially harmonious at its core; all the different processes and manifestations of the deepest underlying truth are linked together in mutually supporting ways by their own inner laws. If human beings will but be true to their own inner laws, their dharma, and act out of love, then it will be possible, according to Gandhi, to provide the social and human conditions necessary for the achievement of the full development of every individual.

This vision calls for a model of development in accord with the fundamental dharma or truth of the individual and society and might, therefore, be called the *dharmic model*. From the perspective of this model, recent thinkers, including Gandhi, Narayan, Desai, and Upadhyaya, have leveled serious criticisms at conventional development models and strategies.

Focusing not on abstract theory, but on sociopolitical practices, they have criticized the capital-intensive, labor-saving, highly centralized production dominating both capitalist and socialist countries. Large-scale, centralized technology, they argue, is inherently labor saving, either throwing many people out of work or else assigning them to unrewarding and unfulfilling routine tasks. It is also capital intensive, giving capital and technology priority over the individual person. Those who control capital and technology have the power to exploit not only natural resources, but also people. In capitalist systems, rich capitalists justify their exploitation in the name of free enterprise, these critics claim, while in socialist systems, party bosses exploit the people in the name of the state.

Of course, neither socialist nor capitalist exploitation is an intended effect of these systems; it is an unintended side effect of a system that views society atomistically and takes economic aims to be fundamental. Both systems see human beings primarily as producers, consumers, or managers. All other aspects of human being are either ignored or seen as secondary, to be overridden by the primary concerns of production and consumption.

## UPADHYAYA

Upadhyaya, in a series of statements that were embraced by the Jana Sangh Party as its official philosophy, criticized both the capitalist and socialist systems severely. His criticisms are directed at these systems as they are practiced, not at the ideas underlying them. There is, for example, no analysis of Marxist thought, or of the philosophy of individualism or private enterprise. From his perspective, Upadhyaya sees both capitalist and socialist societies devaluing the individual. Regarding the capitalist devaluation of the individual person he said,

> Capitalist economy recognizes only "economic man," whose decisions are based entirely on calculations of gains and loss, in terms of material wealth. For this economic man, five rupees are always more than four rupees. He works solely to gain more wealth, and exerts to get the maximum gain. For him, just like other commodities, human labour is a commodity to be bought and sold in the market. This is free enterprise. It holds all other restrictions and regulations unjust, save the brake of competition. In the race no one is prepared to stop and give a helping hand to the weak who is left behind; nay, elimination of the weak is considered just and natural. He is uneconomic, a marginal unit, not fit to exist. This is what it advocates. By the elimination of such marginal units, the economic power accumulates in the hands of a few. This is considered normal and natural in a capitalist system. But when monopoly is established, even the check of competition ceases to operate. In such a situation the incentive resulting from competition is no longer available. Prices are arbitrarily fixed and quality of products deteriorates.[1]

His criticism of socialism is equally severe:

> Socialism arose as a reaction to capitalism. But even socialism failed to establish the importance of the human being. Socialists contented themselves by merely transferring the ownership of capital to the hands of the state. But the state is even more of an impersonal institution. . . . The capitalistic system thought merely of the economic man, but left him free in other fields where he could exercise his individuality. The socialist system went much further, and thought only of the abstract man [man as an idea]. After that, there was no scope for the development of the individual personality based on diverse tastes and abilities. The needs and preferences of individuals have as much importance in the socialist system as in a prison manual. There is no such thing as individual freedom in the socialist system.[2]

[1]Pt. Deendayal Upadhyaya, Shri Guruji, and Shri D. B. Thengdi, *The Integral Approach* (New Delhi: Deendayal Research Institute, 1979), p. 70.
[2]*Ibid.*, p. 71.

From the dharmic perspective, the most serious defect of the exploitive socialist or capitalist systems is their assumption that human greed, competition, and conflict constitute the driving forces of society. The heavy hand of the system must constantly intervene to stimulate competition, manage conflicts, and curb the excesses of greed. This results in a generally oppressive environment that inevitably exploits the individual and destroys personal freedoms. According to Upadhyaya the problem is that both these systems,

> capitalist as well as communist [socialist], have failed to take an account of the Integral Man, his true and complete personality and his aspirations. One considers him a mere selfish being hankering after money, having only one law, the law of fierce competition, in essence the law of the jungle; whereas the other has viewed him as a feeble lifeless cog in the whole scheme of things, regulated by rigid rules, and incapable of any good unless directed. The centralization of power is implied in both. Both, therefore, result in dehumanisation of man.[3]

Both the capitalist and socialist systems are said to be dehumanizing because they are based on wrong views of the nature of humanity and society and advocate inappropriate strategies for promoting human well-being. What is the alternative? What kind of system does the dharmic model offer?

## DHARMIC PRINCIPLES

The dharmic model, as the name suggests, draws upon the traditional conception of dharma as the ultimate norm of the individual and the universe. Our study of the Indian way has emphasized over and over again the traditional conviction that human beings share in the very powers that create and structure the universe itself. Reality is conceived holistically, with all the different manifestations and expressions of existence seen to be rooted in the same undivided wholeness that constitutes ultimate reality. Each manifestation—individual and species—has its own norm of being and action, but because of the underlying unity of existence, these different norms constitute a unified pattern of mutual support and cooperation, providing simultaneously for the well-being of the individual and the whole.

Within this integral vision, spiritual fulfillment or freedom (mokṣa) has generally been taken to be the highest aim in life. But as the fourfold conception of human aims (puruṣārthas) shows, righteousness (dharma), means of life (artha), and happiness (kāma) are also fundamental aims in life. Indeed, their fulfillment in society is typically seen as a condition of mokṣa. Even in Jaina thought, which sees all karmic embodiment as ultimately evil and which advocates, as a condition of liberation, complete cessation of all involvement in this world what-

[3]*Ibid.*, p. 73.

soever, this extreme liberation effort is understood to follow upon many lifetimes of righteous living in the world.

Furthermore, the traditional emphasis on dharma as the first aim and a necessary condition for the fulfillment of the other aims, requires that each person fulfill the various obligations that will ensure others of an opportunity to also fulfill these four aims of life. In other words, the individual person is seen as an integral unity of various needs and dimensions, all of which must be satisfied in such a way that one's own fulfillment and that of others are mutually enhanced. As the fundamental norm of life, dharma preserves harmony. It reconciles and overcomes differences, eliminating or minimizing competition and conflict.

The dharmic model also emphasizes the inseparability of means and ends. Since we shape our lives and social relations primarily through the means employed to achieve our ends, they must be given priority. No matter how lofty the end, the means used to achieve it must be appropriate to the inherent dignity of human beings and must not conflict with the requirements of dharma.

Although these principles of the dharmic model do not dictate a particular sociopolitical system or development strategy, they do point in certain directions. For example, they suggest that the development model should emphasize local units, where individuals and families are directly involved in securing their own well-being. Personal obligations to help others and social duties that contribute to the enhancement of opportunities for others are minimized in large-scale, highly centralized operations. There the system comes first, robbing the individual of dignity, freedom, and an opportunity for integral fulfillment.

Since decentralization is not really compatible with large-scale technological operations, the dharmic model also recommends small-scale industries. Gandhi used the symbol of the spinning wheel to emphasize the importance of self-help and self-reliance on every level. If individuals and communities produce what they need for themselves, their basic needs can be satisfied most effectively through personal cooperation and mutual sharing. The alternative is to produce specialized goods for foreign markets, generating revenues with which to buy the various necessities of life from other foreign markets. In the process, personal relationships are minimized as the dehumanizing demands of the large-scale system take over.

The same principles that underlie the move toward self-help and decentralization also imply that technologies should be appropriate to the actual needs of human beings, genuinely enhancing each person's opportunities for a better life. Only those technologies are acceptable that serve the lower, economic, needs in the most appropriate way, while simultaneously creating a society that provides the requisite conditions for the fulfillment of higher human needs.

Without going into specific development programs and implementation strategies, it is clear that, if the dharmic model emerges as a central feature of the continuing Indian way, it will have to meet a number of difficult challenges. Most obviously, it will have to overcome all the vested political and economic interests in the current system. The dharmic model is radically different, both economically and politically, and its adoption would almost certainly be perceived as a serious threat to the power of India's elite minority.

It appears that adoption of the dharmic model depends upon a powerful grass-roots movement. Yet such a movement would have not only to contend with the opposition of all the present vested interests, but would also have to be enthusiastically endorsed on the basis of presently held ideas and values among the ordinary people. Such endorsement is far from certain, for, although the dharmic model is clearly opposed to the Western model of development, its underlying ideas also differ from those of traditional village India. The challenge is twofold: not only will the Westernized leaders have to be convinced that the dharmic model incorporates modern ideas and will provide for modern development, but the ordinary people will also have to be convinced that these modern ideas are indeed supported by, and compatible with, Indian tradition.

## Modernity and Tradition

To see this twofold challenge more clearly, it will be helpful to compare the central ideas implicit in the Westernized development model with traditional ideas. Although there is no universally accepted concept of "modernity," the following ideas have shaped the Indian conception of Western modernity: (1) a society characterized by explicitly rational ways of action; (2) a rational legal system as a basis for social order; (3) government by a constitutional system emphasizing rights and freedoms of citizens and providing for elected representation; (4) the adoption and development of sophisticated, large-scale technology, along with the science that underwrites and accompanies it; (5) emphasis on continuously increasing production and consumption of material goods through the application of technology to production; (6) adoption of a progressive linear concept of time, according to which innovation and change become desirable in themselves; (7) an emphasis on individualism; (8) adoption of equality as a fundmental social norm; (9) growth through competition between individuals and maximum exploitation of natural resources; and (10) conspicuous acquisition and consumption as indicators of success.

Underlying these ideas is an atomistic view of reality and society. Nature is viewed as an organized collection of fundamentally different and separate particles. By analogy, society is seen as an organized collection of individuals, each of whom is regarded as complete and independent in his or her own being. Conceiving society as a collection of essentially separate and independent individuals raises the crucial question, "Why do they join together in social units?" The classic modern answer is Hobbesian: society provides protection against the destructive forces of nature and the nasty selfishness of other persons.

By contrasting the ideas constituting the Indian concept of Western modernity to their counterparts in traditional thought, one gets a sense of the opposition between tradition and modernity. That same contrast also gives one a feeling for the magnitude of social, cultural, and political revolution required to integrate these two different world-views. The following ideas are central to the traditional world-view: (1) authority, rather than reason, is the basic criterion for decision and truth; (2) traditionally, social order was secured, not by a rational legal system, but by morality (dharma reinforced by *daṇḍa*); (3) government by monarchy has been the basic pattern historically, functioning not on a basis of rights and freedoms of citizens, but on the basis of duties and loyalties to the ruling authority; (4) although technological invention and innovation were very much a part of the Indian scene historically, and although the Indian scientific genius is fairly well known, scientific and technological achievement were never really important personal or societal values; (5) consumption was traditionally regarded as standing in the way of highest spiritual attainments, and acquisition was regarded as a kind of *grasping*, which was a vice contrasted to the virtue of *giving*. (According to the āśrama system, one was expected to outgrow the quest for goods and enjoyment and, in renunciation of the material world, to seek ultimate spiritual fulfillment.); (6) traditionally, time is thought of as continuous rather than as discrete; innovation and change are viewed as threats to the order established through the continuity of time and are discouraged; (7) the authority of tradition and old persons provide canons of truth and value; change for its own sake is discouraged; (8) in contrast to the Western emphasis on the individual as the basic social unit, the tradition tended to see family, caste, and village as the basic social units. Because the individual's full existence can be realized and expressed only through these basic social units, emphasis was on the duties and responsibilities of the individual to these basic social units rather than on individual rights and freedom; (9) in contrast to the Western emphasis on equality, the Indian tradition views reality and society as constituted by a natural hierarchical order in which the lower is directed by the higher; and (10) harmony and cooperation are viewed as the basis for maintaining the well-being of the individual and society.

Underlying these ideas and values is a holistic view of reality and society. At its deepest level, reality is undivided; the experienced differences are simply the expressions and manifestations of an underlying unity. Family, village, and caste are also regarded as organic wholes in which each individual has an appropriate place and function, enabling him or her to contribute to the good of the whole while also satisfying basic personal needs. Society exists to preserve the natural harmony of the whole. Dharma is what maintains harmony among individuals, classes, and peoples.

Comparing these traditional ideas with the modern ideas listed earlier, we see that there is no fundamental inconsistency between traditional thought and the ideas of rationality, a rational legal system, or a constitutional government providing for elected representation and guaranteeing rights and freedoms to the people. The Western emphasis on the importance and dignity of the individual is also compatible with traditional values.

But there is a fundmental opposition between the Western atomistic view of reality and society and the traditional holistic view. From its atomistic perspective, the West has seen society as a somewhat arbitrary utilitarian system designed to protect essentially separate individuals from each other and from nature. Its chief function is to regulate conflict and competition between individuals and between groups of individuals. By and large, the Hobbesian view that people are mean and selfish, and that the various institutions of society exist to suppress and manage these inherently destructive tendencies, has dominated the conceptions of government and economic productivity.

The Indian view, on the other hand, has tended to see all of existence as one family, with individual persons and species drawing sustenance from, and making contributions to, the whole. Individuals are seen in terms of cooperation and harmony instead of conflict and competition. Gandhi's principles of truthfastness recognized that there is a truth for each being and that by living according to this inner truth the truth of all beings could be realized. His principle of love recognized the interdependent and cooperative nature of individuals. The whole emphasis on dharma traditionally has been to fulfill the duties and obligations necessary for the well-being of the whole.

Fortunately, the crucial question facing India is not that of whether these widely divergent metaphysical views can be reconciled but, rather, that of whether the traditional holistic view can become a basis for the positive modern values of equality, freedom, justice, and economic and social progress, values that appear to conflict with the traditional values. It will, therefore, be worth our while to look at some of the central teachings of the tradition with an eye toward seeing how they can become a basis for the new dharmic model of development.

## DHARMA AND PROGRESS

Consider the most basic teaching of the Upaniṣads, *tat tvam asi* ("The inner self is identical with the ultimate reality"), and its implication that the spiritual center of existence must be realized as the perfect mode of being. In this profound spiritual view, I submit, can be found a basis for a modern outlook. Uddalāka's teaching is that the reality of the self is to be found in the reality of all, not in isolation or estrangement. The world-view contained in this teaching is a holistic vision of unity in plurality. Here the self cannot be set over and against society or over and against the world. Society is ontologically rooted in the organic relations between selves, and each self is rooted in the deepest level of ultimate reality. Here is a basis for a way of life in which, as Gandhi saw, self-fulfillment is realized, not by denying society or the world but rather, *through* society and the world. By serving society and the world, one engages in an act of giving wherein self can be realized. To work for the well-being of society—so that persons might be fed, clothed, and educated—may be modern, but it is also traditional; it belongs no more to a work ethic than to traditional dharma.

If we carry this a step farther, we note that, according to the traditional view, a person is embedded in an all-connecting pattern of dynamic relationships. The individual is *not merely a part* of a larger process, but is unique in his or her own life. It is for this reason that no gift is greater than the very gift of life (to which nearly all the literature of India attests). Yet the uniqueness of the individual does not mean being separated from the rest of reality; the individual is not essentially alone but is embedded in the whole family of existence. On this basis, it is not hard to see humankind as a family and the earth as a living ecosystem, sustained by the fulfillment of one's *dharma*. This is traditional, but it is *not merely traditional*. It provides a basis for the recognized *equality of opportunity* because each person is part of the same family of existence and therefore entitled to share equally, with other members of the family, in the opportunities for growth and self-fulfillment, each according to his or her capacities.

In the recognized uniqueness of each living being, the traditional view also provides a basis for recognizing *freedom of the individual* (a freedom that traditionally has registered itself in an incredibly rich and diverse cultural pluralism). Because each individual is unique, she or he has a unique dharma. Since dharma sustains the individual, the group, society, and the whole universe, each person must be allowed to fulfill his or her unique dharma. Not only is it a basis for justice and freedom—two hallmarks of modernity—but it can also serve as a basis for adoption of science and technology. Insofar as science and technology constitute more effective means of fulfilling one's duties to other beings, their adoption is enjoined by dharma. Of course, to the extent that their adoption is harmful, dharma disallows their adoption.

Another point of comparison concerns the traditional view of change as something negative, an activity of declining and perishing, as opposed to the modern view of change as positive, a progressing and fulfilling of being. At first it appears that the values involved in this comparison are incompatible. But if it is noted, first, that the traditional negative attitude toward change holds only with respect to *māyā*, the realm of appearances and, second, that the very point of this negativity was to encourage *spiritual progress*, then we can see tradition as having a positive attitude toward change. If spiritual progress is linked to desirable social change, as Gandhi insisted it must, then the traditional values can also provide a basis for accommodating the modern value of progressive social change. The way of action that is emphasized in the Gītā and by Gandhi and the other reformers points the way to adoption of this idea of social progress. Furthermore, because of the traditional distinction between what a person *does* and what a person *is*, the Indian adoption of progress as a positive value does not identify one's success or failure in task performance with one's success or failure as a person—as, unfortunately, the West frequently does.

Although a basis for modernity is present in the Indian tradition, it must be admitted that the Hindu emphasis on dharma creates and reinforces modes of behavior appropriate to a "steady-state" society, not to a "growth" society. Dharma means duties and responsibilities, and the dharmic society emphasized fulfilling one's duties as determined by caste, work, family, and so on. Dharma implies not acquisition, but giving, as an appropriate mode of behavior. In a dharmic society one fulfills one's duties by giving of oneself rather than seeking satisfaction of desires and accumulation of goods. The whole basis of dharma is *giving*; the grasping and acquisitive mode is rejected as *adharmic* or evil.

The contrast between a mode of life emphasizing giving and a mode of life that emphasizes acquisition is fundamental. It is rooted ultimately in the difference between an atomistic and a holistic vision of society and reality. When individuals are seen as essentially separate from each other, competing for the same limited resources, it is natural to stress acquisition for oneself. Indeed, the primary motivation for acting comes from the perceived needs of self-protection.

On the other hand, when all individuals are seen as members of the same family of existence, sharing the same common resources, it is natural to consider the well-being of others. One's own self is not separate from others or from the whole. Seeing the mutuality of all beings, a person is motivated to act out of compassion for others rather than out of selfishness. Our study of the Indian way has shown that compassion, rather than self-interest, is the primary basis for action. Giving, not getting, is the fundamental human virtue. People are praised and honored not for what they have acquired but for what they have given. Because duties and obligations stress giving to others, dharma is a morality of duties and obligations rather than a morality of rights and freedoms. It is not a morality that fits a mode of life emphasizing acquisition of what serves one's self-interests.

## GIVING

Because giving is such a fundmental traditional value, we will pause to consider it further here. In Indian thought the basic cultural archetypes are of giving. The gods and spirits give; Brahman gives; the family gives; the oceans give; the earth gives (Mother Earth); the village gives; and the individual gives. Life—and the existence of the universe itself—is a gift of the divine creative force. This supreme gift requires giving in return, and this exchange of giving is what supports not only human and social processes, but cosmic processes as well. It is significant that, in the Vedic literature, ritual sacrifice (yajña) is regarded as supporting the universe itself, and even the gods are controlled by the power of this ritual exchange.

In Vedic thought the fundamental norm (ṛta), which supports the processes of the universe, is maintained by yajña. As the moral and social dimensions of ṛta come to be emphasized in post-Vedic thought, the concept of dharma—which subsumes both yajña and ṛta—becomes central. The entire cosmic exchange of giving that supports and maintains the universe is embodied in dharma. Accordingly, dharma is central, the fundamental norm of the universe and of human and social life. From a human and social point of view, it can be seen as a giving to others—family, community, caste, gods—in exchange for the gifts of life, membership in community, and caste that the individual has received.

Carrying this value of giving to its logical extreme, the Indian mind has recognized that ultimate value or perfect merit is realized by complete and perfect giving. Since the supreme form of giving is the returning of oneself to the spiritual source of all existence, this ultimate returning or giving is the highest value. This, of course, is seen clearly in the priority assigned to the value of mokṣa (liberation through spiritual return) relative to the other three fundamental human aims of dharma, artha, and kāma.

The manifestations and implications of giving as the ultimate value are many. Since the original gift—existence itself—is from the divine source, every subsequent gift has a divine source. Because life is a gift and taking life repudiates the gift, ahiṁsā (nonhurting of life) is a basic norm. The cow is "sacred" because it gives so many valuable gifts—ghee for yajña, calves, milk, curd, butter, urine, and dung—all important and valuable. The emphasis on giving shows up in the preoccupation with ritual purity, for the recipient of a gift is concerned to be worthy of the gift; when the gift is from the divine source of the universe, one must protect one's purity as a condition of worthiness. Gods and goddesses have more than two arms and hands, showing their increased capacity to give. Karma is so fundamentally important because it is the record of exchange. Sexual imagery is intrinsic to worship inasmuch as sexual giving and receiving is a basic kind of exchange, rooted in the biological basis of life.

If giving is the basic value, what does this imply for other values? To begin with, it means that increased opportunities for giving can be counted on to provide considerable motivation. Prestige in this society is often both directly and indirectly tied to the capacity to give. Superiority is established by increased capacity for giving. In the patron-client relationship characteristic of many communities, for example, it is quite obvious that the superior patron position is essentially a position determined by a capacity to give. Without the capacity to give something of value, patronage is impossible.

It should be noted, however, that it is not the *actual giving* as much as the *capacity to give* that creates superiority. There is, therefore, a built-in incentive to retain the capacity by not giving away the resources one controls, for once they are given away one loses the primary basis of superiority. At the same time there is a motivation for acquisition, for one must have in order to give. Those who have the greatest capacity to give the most valuable resources have the greatest superiority. If spiritual resources are regarded as most valuable, then the person who controls these will have the highest position in the society. Historically, these persons—priests, seers, yogins—were regarded as the superior persons in the society. To the extent that economic wealth is valuable, the rich, of course, will also be regarded as superior persons.

The brief sketch of traditional values and of the possibility of basing modernization and development plans on these values suggests the following: (1) Motivation for change and greater effort can be sought through emphasis on duties and loyalties and through increased opportunities for service and other kinds of giving. (2) Legitimacy for plans and approaches should be sought in the traditions of the people and in the authority of family, village, and caste leaders, for these are the traditional sources of authority for dharmic content. (3) The general hierarchical structure of the family, village, and society, which implicitly provides for patronage and support of the lower by the higher, can serve—at least in transitional phases of modernization—as a basis for social security. (4) Modernization schemes must be shown to provide for moral and spiritual development as well as for economic development. Even if social progress is not valued for its own sake, growth and development are necessary, of course, simply to maintain oneself, one's family, community, and society. Economic "development" schemes that threaten spiritual progress, which is highly valued, will, quite rightly, be rejected. (5) Organization and administration of development efforts must take into account traditional modes of organizing and administering social activities.

## ENVIRONMENT AND SCIENCE

Gandhi, Upadhyaya, and the other supporters of a dharmic model of development may well be instrumental in the shaping of the future Indian way. The traditional Indian way has shown tremendous resources and vitality in meeting a great variety of challenges over the past three thousand years. There is no reason to think it will fail future generations. Indeed, from two different fronts there are hints that the age-old wisdom of India may be also the wisdom of the future.

The first hint comes from a re-enforcement of the traditional emphasis on the undivided nature of reality found at the theoretical frontiers of contemporary science. Traditionally, all beings and processes are seen as sharing in the same ultimate reality; all are united in their ultimate source and energy. From science, in particular, high-energy physics, comes the revelation that the old world-view that takes the universe to be formed out of discrete, fundamental building blocks—the atomistic world-view—is theoretically unsatisfactory. Relativity and quantum theories have gone beyond the old model of the universe. A new world-view is emerging, a world-view that looks not to fundamental particles but rather to an undivided reality unfolding in patterns of energy. Within these unfolding patterns, various levels can be distinguished, accounting for the incredible manifested differences without negating the fundamental unity of existence enfolded therein. Here we see a modern movement of thought headed in the direction of the traditional conception of the ultimacy of Brahman.

The second hint comes from new perspectives on the interrelations of life and energy forms generated by the combined energy/pollution crisis. The idea of progress, combined with the power science and technology have given us to dominate nature, has led to the rape of nature in the name of economic progress. The grievous split between the rich and the poor nations of the world threatens not only economic progress, but life itself. Shortages of fossil fuels threatens the world with destruction if nations insist on going to war to protect their control of these resources. At the same time the careless consumption of scarce resources has resulted in a tremendous threat of contamination and possible pollution. Is the ozone layer threatened with destruction? Is all earth's life threatened with radiation contamination as we move into the nuclear age? Will modern methods of agriculture destroy not only weeds and insect pests, but all life in the process? Will salination and hardening of the soil destroy most of the agriculturally productive land in the world? Will careless "mining" of the ocean floor destroy the vital oxygen-producing capacities of the ocean? These questions are being discussed around the world today. Some predict doomsday. Others are optimistic, revealing great faith in our ability to solve these problems and create a better environment for human existence than has ever been seen before.

A personal prediction would be inappropriate here, but the very fact that these issues are perceived to have not merely local or national, but global, impact suggests that unlimited increases in consumption threaten the world. People around the world are being told that they need to sacrifice, that they must reduce their expectations. Conservation and sharing are now key words.

Indeed, the pendulum is swinging from growth-oriented thinking to steady-state thinking, which emphasizes growth for human well-being rather than growth for its own sake. We are being told that maintaining the relationships among all aspects of the environment, among minerals, plants, animals, and humans, is essential to our survival. All forms of existence and all processes of life are interconnected, say the environmentalists. A change in one place ripples through the entire system, sooner or later affecting every other part. All of us are responsible for maintaining the ecosystem in its optimal form. Change is now seen as a potential threat to disturb and destroy, not just to improve. A generally conserving attitude, which respects the rights of all life-forms, is being evoked. We cannot, as humans, simply impose our wishes on the world; we too are subject to the great laws of the universe and must respect the internal laws that regulate the processes constituting the entire system of life.

But this thinking is clearly similar to the traditional Indian concept of dharma, essentially the idea that there is a fundamental norm of existence in which all beings and processes participate, each according to its own nature. The relationships between the functions of these individual norms or dharmas hold together the entire world. The fundamental principle of action is to act in such a way as to follow the inner norm of one's own being, thereby maintaining that optimal pattern of interrelationships recognized by Vedic sages as ṛta and known by the succeeding tradition as dharma. The philosophy of dharma is not that of rights and privileges, but that of duties and obligations. We have an obligation to maintain the patterns of individual life, family life, village life, national life, and indeed, the entire ecosystem that imposes specific duties to be carried out by each person according to his or her place in the system. As the Ṛg Veda says, "All that is, is one; wise sages call it by many names."

## Suggestions for Further Reading

Most of Ghandi's writings are relevant, for he always thought about ideas and values in connection with programs of action. His *Sarvodaya* outlines his conception of the ideal society.

Deendayal Upadhyaya wrote very little, and these writings are not readily available. Perhaps the best insight into the man and his ideas is provided by a small paperback memorial volume entitled *Upadhyaya's Integral Humanism: Concept and Its Application*, ed. Mahesh J. Mehta (Edison, N.J.: Deendayal Upadhyaya Committee of America, 1980). Write to Dr. Mehta at 9 Koster Blvd., 4-A, Edison, N.J.

*Modern Trends in Hinduism*, by Philip H. Ashby (New York: Columbia University Press, 1974), focuses primarily on the religious trends, but of necessity relates this to philosophical ideas and to broader issues involved in social change.

*Village India*, ed. McKim Marriot (Chicago: University of Chicago Press, 1969), is a fine collection of material that provides insight into the processes of change and stability in village life. One gets a sense of the dynamics of the tradition as it operates on the local level.

*The Modernity of Tradition: Political Development in India*, by Lloyd I. and Susanne Hoeber Rudolph (Chicago: University of Chicago Press, 1967), is a classic study by two scholars with extraordinary insight into the Indian mind and social and political processes. Politics is treated in the broadest sense of the term.

*The Discovery of India*, by J. Nehru, is an autobiographical account of his discovery of his own traditions, providing considerable insight into this gifted Ango-Indian leader.

# Glossary

**Abhidharma** Buddhist scriptural texts interpreting the basic teachings. The "third basket" of the Buddhist cannon.

**Ādi Granth** Sikh scripture; also called Gurū Granth Sāhib.

**Advaita Vedānta** Nondualistic philosophy of reality interpreting the Vedas as teaching a wholeness that goes beyond monism and pluralism.

**Ahaṁkāra** Literally, "I-Maker," ground of ego.

**Ahiṁsā** "Nonhurting." A principle of compassionate action based on a vision of the wholeness of existence.

**Ājīvikas** Adherents of an ancient teaching (1000–600 B.C.) that both bondage and liberation are predetermined.

**Akṣara** Imperishable ultimate reality.

**Allah** Muslim term for God.

**Ānanda** Joy; the highest spiritual bliss.

**Anātman** Buddhist teaching of wholeness that denies the existence of a self separate from and independent of the interrelated processes constituting existence. "Non-self" doctrine.

**Aṅgas** Group of twelve scriptural texts of the Jainas.

**Anitya** Impermanence; Buddhist teaching of the conditioned and transitory nature of existence.

**Aparigraha** Nongrasping; Jaina vow of nonattachment.

**Āraṇyaka** Portion of the Veda dealing with meanings of rituals and symbols.

**Arhat** A person who has been enlightened in the Theravāda Buddhist and Jaina traditions.

**Arjuna** Pāṇḍu warrior to whom Krishna reveals Himself in the Bhagavad Gītā.

**Artha** One of the four basic aims in life, the aim of acquiring the necessary means of life.

**Āryan** Member of the Sanskrit-speaking group that came to dominate India from about 1500 B.C. on.

**Ārya Samāj** Society formed by Dayananda to regenerate the Vedic vision.

**Āsana** Yogic posture designed to facilitate control.

**Asat** Literally, "nonbeing." In the Ṛg Veda *asat* refers to unstructured potentiality for existence.

**Asatkāryavāda** Theory of causality maintaining that the effect is a genuinely new existence.

**Āśrama** Stage in life.

**Ātman** The ultimate Self.

**Avidyā** Ignorance of the true nature of self and reality.

**Auṁ** Sacred syllable containing the essential sound of all reality.

**Aurobindo Ghose** Hindu renaissance leader famous for his practice of and writings on yoga.

**Bhagavad Gītā** "Song of the Lord." Basic text of Hinduism containing Krishna's teaching to Arjuna.

**Bhakti** Devotional self-surrender to God.

**Bhavacakra** Wheel of becoming illustrating the interconnectedness of existence.

**Brahmā** Hindu God responsible for creation.

**Brahmacarya** The first of the four stages in life focusing on purity and the study of Brahman.

**Brahman** Ultimate reality; the ground of all existence.

**Brāhmaṇa** Member of the priestly class. Also the second portion of the Veda containing instructions for priests performing rituals.

**Brahma Sūtras** Aphorisms expressing the basic teachings of the Upaniṣads that have provided the basis for Vedānta.

**Brahmo Samāj** Society organized by Ram Mohan Roy to facilitate the modernization of Hinduism.

**Buddha** "The Enlightened One." Honorific title of Siddhārtha Gautama, the historical originator of Buddhism.

**Buddhi** Enlightenment. Also the faculty of illumination.

**Cārvāka** Materialist system of philosophy.

**Chāndogya Upaniṣad** One of the early Upaniṣads. Features the teaching of Uddalāka, *tat tvam asi* (you are Brahman).

**Citta** Mind-stuff. The faculty of attentive consciousness.

**Dānavas** Embodied forces of darkness and restriction. In the Vedic myth of Indra and Vṛtra, the enemies of the forces of light and freedom.

**Deva** Vedic word for God. Means "auspicious" and refers to the auspicious powers of existence.

**Devī** Feminine of Deva. In the Ṛg Veda used to refer to the Goddess of Speech-Consciousness (Vāc). In Hinduism a synonym for Durgā or Kālī.

**Dharma** Normative dimension of existence. What ought to be done, the first of the four basic aims in life. Also, in Buddhism, the truth of existence.

**Dharmakāya** Literally, "Dharma-body"; the true reality according to Buddhism.

**Dhāraṇā** Techniques for focusing consciousness; one-pointed consciousness.

**Dhyāna** Meditation in which consciousness is focused upon itself.

**Digambara** Sect of "sky-clad" or naked Jainas.

**Dravidic** Pre-Aryan culture of South India.

**Duḥkha** Suffering. The "out-of-jointness" that causes suffering.

**Gaṇapati** Elephant-headed God worshipped as Lord of Fortune or Success. Also known as Ganeṣa.

**Gandhi** Mohandas Gandhi, known as Mahatma. Leader of independence movement who identified with the poor and down-trodden to improve their condition.

**Guṇas** The three constituents or "threads"—*sattva*, *rājas*, and *tamas*—of all material and mental existence.

**Guru** Spiritual guide or teacher.

**Gurū Nānak** Originator of Sikhism.

**Haumai** Sikh concept of the self-centeredness that separates humans from God.

**Hinduism** Term applied by foreigners to the family of religions practiced in India that derived the Vedas and earlier religions sometime after 1000 B.C.

**Hiraṇyagarbha** The "golden seed" from which existence was born.

**Hukam** Sikh concept of the Divine Will as manifested in the orderliness of existence and the moral demands on humanity.

**Indo-Āryans** Those Āryanṣ who settled in India sometime between 1800 and 1500 B.C.

**Indra** A principal Indo-Āryan deity who freed existence from the grasp of Vṛtra, dragon of non-existence.

**Indus** Main river of northwestern India. Often used to refer to the early civilization of the Indus Valley.

**Islam** Religion of peace through submission to Allah. Established in India prior to A.D. 1000.

**Īśvara** The Lord; Brahman personified.

**Jaina** Adherent of a very ancient ascetic religion, probably prior to 1000 B.C., that emphasizes the sacredness of all life and nonhurting as the basic principle of action.

**Jāti** "Birth." One's social caste or group as determined by birth

**Jīva** In Jainism, the life principle or soul. In Hinduism, the embodied Ātman.

**Jñāna Marga** The path (to liberation) of knowledge.

**Kaivalya** Spiritual freedom.

**Kālī** God in Her feminine form, manifested as Goddess of Death and Destruction.

**Kāma** As the third basic aim in life, enjoyment in all its forms. Also desire, especially the desire of love.

**Karma** Action; the principle of the interconnectedness of all actions and their effects. In Jainism, the contaminating matter that binds the jīva to suffering.

**Karma Marga** The path (to liberation) of action that emphasizes acting without desire for the fruits of action.

**Karunā** Compassion.

**Krishna** A manifestation of Vishnu embodying joy, freedom, beauty, and love. Appears to Arjuna in the Gītā as the Supreme Lord and Godhead.

**Kṣatriya** Member of protector (warrior) class.

**Mādhyamika** Buddhist philosophy of the middle way emphasizing the wholeness or fullness of existence. Also, one subscribing to this philosophy.

**Mahābhārata** The great epic of India.

**Mahāvīra** The Jaina "Ford Builder" or spiritual hero of the present age who lived in the sixth century B.C.

**Mahāyāna** Buddhism of the "Great Vehicle" that spread to China, Korea, Japan, and so on. Emphasizes faith in the universal Buddha-nature and compassionate effort to free all beings from suffering.

**Manas** The mind as organizer of the senses.

**Mantra** Sacred sound carrying the deepest wisdom of reality.

**Manu** Ancient sage who spelled out the requirements of dharma for life in society.

**Mauryan** Great dynasty that united most of India under a single rule from 321 to 187 B.C. Chandragupta, Bindusara, and Ashoka were this dynasty's greatest rulers.

**Mīmāmsā** Philosophical system emphasizing scriptural knowledge and ritual performance as means of liberation.

**Muhammad** Apostle of God to whom the holy Qu'rān was revealed as the fulfillment of scripture.

**Nāgārjuna** Famous Buddhist Mādhyamika philosopher of the second century.

**Neti, Neti** The denial of characteristics attributed to Brahman. Literally, "Not this, not that."

**Nirguṇa Brahman** Brahman without qualities; the ultimate reality in its ultimateness.

**Nirvāṇa** Freedom from bondage and suffering.

**Niyama** Yogic observances of purity, contentment, ritual, study, and dedication.

**Prakṛti** According to Sāṁkhya-yoga, the ultimate nonspiritual reality.

**Prāṇāyāma** Yogic techniques for controlling breath and the vital life-forces.

**Pratītya Samutpāda** Principle of dependent origination according to which all arising and ceasing of existence is interdependent.

**Pratyāhāra** Yogic techniques for withdrawing the senses to focus on inner consciousness.

**Pudgala** In Jainism, "matter." In Buddhism, term for a subtle self that some thinkers postulated as a basis for the five skandhas.

**Puruṣa** The cosmic Person. In Sāṁkhya-yoga, the ultimate spiritual principle of existence with which the Self is identified.

**Puruṣārtha** Basic aim in life. Four basic aims, applicable to all, are recognized: *dharma*, *artha*, *kāma*, and *mokṣa*.

**Qu'rān** Holy scripture of Islam consisting of God's word as revealed to Muhammad.

**Rādhā** Krishna's divine lover.

**Rājas** The constituent (*guṇa*) of matter that energizes existence.

**Rāma** The hero of the Rāmāyana; an incarnation of Vishnu.

**Rāmānuja** Famous eleventh-century philosopher who emphasized the difference between God and Self despite the ultimate unity of reality.

**Ṛg Veda** A collection of some ten thousand "verses of wisdom" representing the oldest Indo-European literature and the basis of much subsequent Indian thought.

**Ṛṣi** A seer; one who sees into the heart of reality.

**Ṛta** Fundamental norm of existence, the ground of morality and cosmic order.

**Śabda** Sound or word. The ultimate reality manifested in sound.

**Saguṇa Brahman** Brahman with characteristics. The ultimate reality conceived as Being, Consciousness, and Bliss.

**Śaivism** The religion of Shiva's devotees.

**Śakti** Energy, usually personified as a Goddess, and associated with a God, especially Shiva, as the divine energy of His being.

**Śakyamuni** "Sage of the Śakyas." Term for the historical Buddha, who came from the Śakya clan.

**Samādhi** Absorption into the highest Self; union with the ultimate reality.

**Sāma Veda** "Songs of Wisdom." Hymns, mostly from the Ṛg Veda, set to music for singing in ritual performance.

**Saṁhīta** Collection, particularly of Vedic verses.

**Sāṁkhya** Dualistic system of philosophy stressing the absolute difference between matter and spirit.

**Saṁsāra** Cycle of repeated deaths and births that afflicts everyone who has not achieved liberation.

**Saṁskāras** In Hinduism, sacramental rites performed at important junctures in life. In Buddhism the impulses to action flowing from previous karmic residue.

**Samyak Darśana** In Jainism, true spiritual insight.

**Saṅgha** The Buddhist community.

**Śaṅkara** Famous Vedānta philosopher of the eighth century who emphasized the undivided nature of reality.

**Saṅnyāsin** The fourth stage in life, that of renunciation, where the Sȧnnyāsin abandons the cares and concerns of this world in favor a spiritual life.

**Sant** In Sikhism, a *sadhū* or holy person; a saint.

**Sat** Being or existence; what is fundamental.

**Satī** Literally, "virtue." Refers to the virtuous act by which a widow cremates herself to join her dead husband.

**Satkāryavāda** Theory of causality maintaining that the effect is not new, that it existed previously in a different form.

**Sattva** The constituent or thread of matter that is responsible for lightness and mental activity.

**Satya** Truth, truthfulness in the sense of "true to one's inner nature."

**Satyāgraha** "Truthfastness," in Gandhi's thought; the principle of holding fast to the truth in practical affairs.

**Sautrāntika** Buddhist school of philosophy midway between realism and idealism.

**Shī'ah** Sect of Islam insisting on the direct mediation of Muhammad's apostleship through the Īmāms.

**Śhiva** Major Hindu God seen as the great ascetic and the destroyer of the universe. Symbolized by the liṅga, Shiva is the unmanifest or completely transcendent reality in which all existence is grounded.

**Siddhārtha** Siddhārtha Gautama, the historical Buddha, born about 560 B.C.

**Sītā** Heroine of the Rāmāyana, Rāma's wife, and a paradigm of feminine virtue.

**Smṛti** The tradition, which is "remembered."

**Śruti** "That which is heard," namely, the sacred truth of reality heard in the hearts of the great seers and expressed in their teachings. Infallible truth.

**Śūdra** Social class consisting of workers.

**Sūfī** In Islam, a practicing mystic.

**Sunni** Major sect of Islam.

**Śūnyatā** Literally, "emptiness." Refers to the Buddhist teaching that the wholeness of existence is empty of independent and separate beings.

**Sūtra** Aphorism expressing the gist of a teaching. A collection of such aphorisms.

**Tamas** The guṇa responsible for inertia, dullness, and heaviness.

**Tantra** Spiritual practice based on the principle that a person is a microcosm of the universe and the principle that body and spirit are different manifestations of the same reality.

**Tapas** Heat-energy, especially as generated by ascetic practices and mental effort.

**Tat Tvam Asi** Literally, "you are that," meaning that each person, in the deepest level of the Self, is the ultimate reality.

**Theravāda** Literally, "way of the elders." An early orthodox form of religious Buddhism emphasizing attaining enlightenment through one's own efforts. Practiced today in Southeast Asia.

**Ṭṛṣnā** Craving, especially the craving for permanence that causes suffering.

**Upaniṣad** A secret teaching; collections of secret teachings about the nature of Self and ultimate reality constituting concluding portion of the Vedas.

**Vāc** Speech, also the consciousness behind speech. In the Vedas, personified as a Goddess.

**Vaibhāsika** Realistic school of Buddhist philosophy.

**Vaiśeṣika** Pluralistic and realistic system of philosophy.

**Vaiṣṇava** The religious system of the devotees of Vishnu.

**Vaiśya** Social class consisting of the ordinary people.

**Varṇa** Social classes, consisting of brāhmaṇas, kṣatriyas, vaiśyas, and śūdras.

**Vāsanās** Traces of previous actions embedded in the deeper levels of consciousness.

**Vedānta** System of philosophy based on the Upaniṣads.

**Vedas** Sacred writings of the Indo-Āryans, the scriptural basis of Hinduism.

**Vijñāna** The dsicriminating faculty of consciousness.

**Viṣhṇu** Major Hindu God, manifested in ten forms or avatars, including Krishna and Rāma.

**Vṛtra** The dragon embodying non-existence slain by Indra. Symbol of bondage.

**Vṛttis** The movements of consciousness obscuring the underlying Self.

**Yajña** The sacrificial celebration that, according to the Vedas, renews and sustains existence.

**Yajur Veda** Text of sacred wisdom containing formulas for ritual performance of yajña.

**Yoga** Techniques of discipline for overcoming bondage and suffering.

**Yogācāra** System of Buddhist philosophy emphasizing the ultimacy of consciousness ("mind-only").

# Index